SOVEREIGNTY AND AN
EMPTY PURSE

PRINCETON UNIVERSITY PRESS

PRINCETON, NEW JERSEY 1970

BY BRAY HAMMOND

Sovereignty
and an
Empty Purse

BANKS AND POLITICS

IN THE CIVIL WAR

PREFACE

IN AN ESSAY published in May 1861—in the period between Sumter and Bull Run—a British historian who was discussing the conflict broken out in America called it one "between centralization and self-government." Such a conflict, spoken not armed, goes on to-day, but it is voiced more insistently by those who denounce the hypertrophy of federal authority than by those who, in defense of centralization, complain that local authority is no longer adequate and competent.

The following study is concerned implicitly with this tension between federation and its parts, whether intra-national or inter-national. However, the study is not abstract but a narration explicitly confined to the difficulty of giving to the federal government of the United States— in 1861, '62, and '63—the means of withholding the South from secession. This difficulty lay in giving the federal government the power to restrain the Southern states without imparing the rights of the Northern states. For with respect to other matters than secession and slavery, the North was as jealous of states' rights as the South was; and it clutched them to the point of almost frustrating its decision to preserve the federal Union as it was.

Liberty is unquestionably precious; but what is the form of its bulwark to be, and how much is responsibility to be centralized—how much is sovereignty to be divided? The following account does not answer that question but narrates the struggle in the 37th Congress over it with respect to the Purse.

Responsibility for such merit as may be found in the following narrative must be shared by me with Melitta de Kern Hammond, Ellen M. Griswold, and the Dartmouth

332.1
H184P

College Library, whose former librarian, Richard Morin, his successor, Edward Lathem, and other officers and staff have been my patient hosts during the period of my research. I am under a further obligation to Princeton University Press.

Bray Hammond

Thetford, Vermont
March 1968

CONTENTS

vii

CONTENTS

ABBREVIATIONS

AHR American Historical Review

ASP American State Papers

HR House of Representatives

JPE Journal of Political Economy

LC Library of Congress

A STUNTED GOVERNMENT

I

In May 1861, the month following South Carolina's shelling of Fort Sumter and President Lincoln's order instituting the blockade of Southern ports, the young English historian, Sir John Acton—not yet Lord Acton—described the dissolution of the American Union as an accomplished fact. He found the South's secession "no accidental or hasty or violent proceeding but the normal and inevitable result of a long course of events." The period, just ended, "between the convention of 1787 and the election of Mr Davis," president of the new Southern republic, possessed "an almost epic unity. The question," he said, "on which the founders of the Constitution really differed and which has ever since divided and at last dissolved the Union was to determine how far the rights of the states were merged in the federal power and how far they retained their independence."

Acton found support for his assumption of an end to the American Union not in the dubious ability of the North to curb the South but in fallacious principles the Union rested upon. The Union was a democracy, and democracy was a form of organization wherein the most numerous and least responsible class of persons held the power and drove with it to anarchy. The Union was also a federation, wherein he found sovereignty to be divided confusedly and mischievously between the whole body and its components.

Though the main thread of his account was political, Acton offered a relevant defense of slavery. He thought it "essential to democracy" wherever the population comprised an inferior race and a superior one; he thought it good for both the blacks and the whites. As to the inferiority and superiority of races, he relied on the observations of contemporary anthropologists.

These judgments, May 1861, were presented in an essay which Acton entitled "Political Causes of the American

3

Revolution," the revolution he meant being not that of 1776, of course, but the current proceedings of the Southern states begun six months before in their attempt to withdraw from the Union. Acton, it should be repeated, was then a very young man. Five years later, after the end of the war, which had hardly begun when his earlier essay appeared, he discussed the subject very differently.*[1]

The premature judgments expressed in Acton's earlier essay were typical of much British opinion but not of all. In the same month that Acton's essay from which I have quoted came out, *The Economist*, London, could see "for the South . . . no possibility of a good issue for the war which its statesmen have provoked and commenced." Wealth and numbers favored the North overwhelmingly and must in the end make it win. For the Southern leaders "to rouse by gratuitous insult the mettle of a nation three times as numerous and far more than three times as powerful, to force them by aggressive steps into a struggle in which the sympathy of every free and civilized nation will be with the North, seems like the madness of men whose eyes are blinded and hearts hardened by the evil cause they defend." The greater the Southerners' initial success, *The Economist* said, "the greater must be their ultimate humiliation." Back in December, when the South took its first steps in departure from the Union, *The Economist* thought the action anomalous. "It seems an infatuation," it said, "that the slave states should speak of secession. That the free states should do so would be intelligible." In January it still thought so. Why, it asked, in its issue of 12 January 1861, should the North feel outraged by the South's threat of secession? Why shouldn't it welcome the South's depar-

---

* In 1863 Professor Edward A. Freeman of Oxford published the first volume of his projected *History of Federal Government, from the Foundation of the Achaian League to the Disruption of the United States*. This history was never completed, but a second edition under an altered title and including an account of federalism in Italy was published in 1893. The 1863 title, however, reflects the same opinion of American affairs as Acton's held by a more mature scholar than Acton then was.

ture? Northerners, it said, "must have felt that the semi-barbarism of the South was infecting and degrading their manners, that the terrible social blot of the South was their ceaseless opprobrium in the eyes of the civilized world, and that the violence and cupidity of the South was forever marring their policy and disturbing their peace. We should naturally have fancied that they would . . . have been anxious to shake off such an incubus and to purify themselves from such a stain; and have looked forward with sanguine enthusiasm to the noble and splendid career of progress which lay before them when relieved from such a moral weight and social fetter." Again, late in January, it was inexplicable to *The Economist* that the North should object to separation from the South, four-fifths of whose white population, it said, comprised "perhaps the most degraded, ignorant, brutal, drunken, and violent class that ever swarmed in a civilized country. . . . Probably large bodies of the 'mean whites' will be organized into irregular troops, half soldiers, half police, in order to control and suppress the negro population; and the condition of restless fear, barbarism, and intestine hostility, already bad enough, will grow yearly worse, more shocking, and more intolerable." In the circumstances, *The Economist* thought the North should let the South go—gladly. Victory for the North would be an "objectless and unprofitable folly." These, one may suppose, were all the convictions of Walter Bagehot, who became *The Economist*'s editor January 1861 and had been already a contributor to it. Certainly, five months later, October 1861, Bagehot had an essay in the *National Review* entitled "The American Constitution at the Present Crisis" and in it blamed the crisis, as Acton had done, on the Constitution itself, which, he said, "is now failing from the necessary consequence of an ineradicable defect"—its equivocal division of sovereignty between the states and the federal government.[2]

The determination which led South Carolina, after Lincoln's election, to decide upon secession immediately and her closer neighbors to take very little more time was not matched in the North. There disbelief that secession was more than a conspiracy of hot-heads vied with uncertainty what to do about it and with some inclination to do the very thing *The Economist* expected. Among those Northerners who abominated slavery there was a disposition to let the South leave the Union and to consider it good riddance. For those who condoned slavery, coercion of the South was outrageous, and a few went so far as to leave the country for good rather than stay either as defeated champions of civil liberty or copperheads.*

The same revulsion against extreme action had manifested itself among loyalists in the Revolution, among New Englanders in the War of 1812, and in the North generally in the forties against the war with Mexico. In like circumstances, such revulsion has manifested itself repeatedly since then.

Dissidence was minor, however, and Northerners were moved more by British hostility than by British sympathy. In June 1861 a private letter of admonition was addressed to Baring Brothers, merchants and bankers, London, by an American correspondent of theirs in New York. The letter concerned reports reaching the States by mail and by word of mouth that "men of eminent commercial standing" in Great Britain appeared "to favour the idea of forcing their supplies of cotton from this country, without delay, at any hazard or cost." For the British textile industry was accustomed to a constant supply of cotton from America

---

* One such was Thomas L. Nichols, a New York journalist, born in Orford, New Hampshire, who went to England and remained there. In his *Forty Years of American Life*, he wrote (page vi):
"When Mr Seward ordered that no citizen should leave the country without a passport, I came to England. America was a prison, with Mr Seward for jailor. And so one day in a small sailing ship, avoiding the large packets and steamers which were watched by the police, we glided down the bay, past Fort Lafayette, the federal Bastille—past the watch-dog war steamer in the Narrows, and saw the spires of New York, the beautiful hills of Staten Island, and the blue Highlands of Neversink disappear below the horizon. And our curious little company of refugees all breathed, I think, more freely when we saw only the bright heavens above and the blue waters around us."

of such quality as could be obtained in ample volume from no other source, and the prospect of finding its supply cut off by blockade was alarming to it and to its ancillaries. The Barings' correspondent was John Austin Stevens, president of the Bank of Commerce, New York, the largest bank in the States. The Barings had been among the bank's original shareholders and Stevens himself had been known to them long and intimately. Stevens sent the Secretary of the Treasury, Salmon P. Chase, to whom he was an unofficial adviser, a copy of what he wrote the Barings. His letter, dated 15 June 1861, was written immediately after his return from a visit to Washington, where he had been a house guest of Secretary Chase. The circumstances indicate that the letter's substance had been discussed in advance with members of the Lincoln Administration and that it was a diplomatic message sent informally through responsible private channels. It read as follows:

City of Washington Steamer

New York 15 June 1861
Bank of Commerce

Dear Sirs,
The ordinary bank letters have supplied all needful information since my absence in Washington.

Permit me to say that some uneasiness existed there and I find the same here amongst well informed men, arising from the tenor of recent advices and the reports of passengers by the late arrivals, to the purport that men of eminent commercial standing in G. Britain appear to favour the idea of forcing their supplies of cotton from this country, without delay, at any hazard or cost. If I can express any opinion with confidence it is that any such attempt will lead to an immediate and obstinate War—more, to a popular War.

Persons abroad can not well conceive of the intensity and universality of the feeling at the North—the whole United North—to put down this revolt in the most sum-

7

mary manner—once and forever—cost what it may of men, of treasure, or of suffering. They will brook no interference from abroad in this domestic quarrel. It will not shake this determination if every city on the sea board is threatened to be laid in ashes. The attempt to get cotton by force this season might fail or might succeed perchance, but it would be the last supply ever raised by slave labour, or perhaps even by white labour, for years, for the whole institution of slavery in any thing like its present form, or perhaps in any form would, before the war was over, disappear from this Union.

I repeat the conviction that the adjustment of our present difficulties will be final and thorough, and this is the opinion of every well informed statesman, and all that the most moderate can do is to endeavour to soften the tone of negotiations with foreign powers. The continental diplomats in this country aim at the same object but notwithstanding all that can be done in this direction, if the opinion shall get to be general here that men of distinction—outside of political combinations and the necessities of the moment—on your side look to a war as the best solution, rely upon it, it can very easily be had—at the hazard of all that men of our race hold most dear and most important to the well being and progress of mankind.

I write in haste

and am very truly yrs

Jno A Stevens

Pres.*

Messrs Baring Brothers & Co
London

* The original letter, in Stevens' hand, is in the *Baring Papers*, the Canadian National Archives, Ottawa; a copy, not in his hand, which was sent to Chase in Washington, is in the *Chase Papers*, the Historical Society of Pennsylvania, Philadelphia; the Barings' reply to Stevens, 6 July 1861, and a letter of Chase's to Stevens, 15 June 1861, are in the *John A. Stevens Papers*, the New-York Historical Society, New York.

The original in Stevens' hand is less legible than the copy in another hand, which was sent to Chase, and it is punctuated with more

The Barings promptly and politely acknowledged Mr Stevens' admonition, to which they said "deserved attention" would be paid. But, they went on, "we do not think the European powers"—including Great Britain—"will interfere with the blockade of the southern ports should it be kept up rigourously." And they politely reminded their correspondent that since Great Britain's blockade of American and French ports in the War of 1812 had been evaded now and then by swift vessels of the Americans, the same thing might now be done successfully by others.[3]

The letter of John Stevens to the Barings had been written a month after the arrival of Charles Francis Adams in London as American minister and about a fortnight after receipt in Washington of his first report to Secretary Seward. Though studiously private and within the scope of long-established relations between John A. Stevens and the Barings, the letter dealt directly with a prime question at issue just then between their respective governments, and might well have been instigated in Washington in order to strengthen Minister Adam's position *vis-à-vis* Downing Street in his efforts to avoid foreign recognition of the Southern Confederacy and foreign attempts to force the blockade of Southern ports.[4]

Months later another friend and adviser of Secretary Chase's made a statement about the current conflict that goes along with what John Stevens had written the Barings. This was Samuel Hooper, a Boston merchant-banker, capitalist, and representative from Massachusetts in Congress. Hooper, pleading in the House for vigorous monetary action, 3 February 1862, said: "This is a war, on the part of the South, inspired by slavery against the free labor of the North; and hence the sympathy it receives from those who favor aristocratic institutions. The prosperity of the North, like that of England and France, is mainly to be attributed to the skill that it has developed in manu-

dashes, either long or short, than commas. I have verified the less legible words of the original with those more legible in the copy and have used more commas, fewer dashes, and fewer capitals.

factures, the enterprise that it has displayed in commerce, and the constant investment of its accumulated wealth in industrial pursuits of every kind; while the South, from policy, has preferred that its labor should be unskilled and ignorant, suited only to the employments of a peculiar agriculture, keeping itself dependent upon foreign trade for many of the conveniences and luxuries which it has not the ingenuity to produce. It is important in this great struggle to show the superiority of the principles of freedom, of education, of the elevation of mankind, upon which society at the North is based, over those of slavery, which doom men to hopeless ignorance in order to insure abject obedience."[5]

The two Americans just quoted, John A. Stevens of New York and Samuel Hooper of Boston, both responsible and practical men of affairs, were resolute. And most Americans in the North came to the same decision. As Anthony Trollope observed, to let the seceding states go was not "the way of men's minds." A minority would willingly or gladly have let the South depart in peace; another minority would have wooed it back in peace with compromise. But no; for those who prevailed neither alternative would do; preservation of the Union was a duty; the South was to be held by force.

Where, however, was the power, the means, to hold it? The answer is that it was decentralized, disorganized, diffuse. The federal government was as little ready to accomplish main purposes as a man for years bed-ridden; and it was in this condition not merely by inadvertence but, as Acton said, by deliberate policy, long and religiously pursued. In London, *The Economist*, which saw the political facts much as Acton did but held other opinions, expected that this weakness would end. "The war," it thought, "will draw together the Northern states as they have never been drawn together yet . . . and finally will impress them with the absolute necessity of a closer union, a stronger central power . . . in one word, with the duty of turning the federal government into a really supreme power." The war would teach the Americans that there can be "no genuine freedom without a strong central government and the surrender of those atomic political privileges which minister to local jealousies and general anarchy."[6]

II

The foregoing observations from England might be taken as a prompting followed at once by the 37th Congress at its first sitting a few weeks later. For what the 37th began and what with recurrent anxiety and occasional reverses has continued in the hundred years and more that have since elapsed, is the strengthening of "central power" which *The Economist* expected. With the popular will behind it and a complete absence of *coups* and violent seizures of office by cliques, the federal government has been rebuilt "into a really supreme power." And at all times the extensions of its power have been such as, in popular opinion, there can be "no genuine freedom" without.

It was in 1861, in the face of Southern secession, that Andrew Jackson's universally popular notion of a federal government passive in domestic affairs began to be abandoned. In the face of opinion adverse "to governmental activity and especially to federal operations," wrote the late Professor Leonard White, the central government was doing "very little in 1860 that it had not undertaken before 1830. Its only large public service was the post office." The government, however, did not "stand motionless." It had "established some lifesaving stations on the Atlantic coast, developed the collection of commercial statistics and in a very small way agricultural statistics, and allowed the distribution of free seeds . . . Jeffersonian doctrines of strict construction of national power and of freedom of the individual from government control to the widest extent were so congenial to Americans before the Civil War that the federal government made few advances in its services or activities." Democrats and Whigs alike "left businessmen, merchants, farmers, and craftsmen to follow their for-

11

tunes free from government supervision. At some points the government conferred benefits and subsidies, ostensibly for public and national reasons—the tariff, mail subsidies to steamship lines, land grants to railroads, and a long-established bonus to the codfisheries. At two or three points the government imposed slight regulations on private enterprise—notably in the inspection of boilers and hulls of steamboats, the requirement of minimum facilities for comfort and health on trans-Atlantic passenger vessels, and the inspection of imported drugs."[7]

The most obvious contrariety in the relative state and federal powers was that there was no real national army and no provision for one. Even the military act produced by the special session of Congress—after Sumter and after Bull Run—maintained such a mixture of states' prestige with federal that it was apparently the individual Northern states as much as the federal government that were preparing to prevent the Southern states from seceding. Recruiting was a local responsibility. Regiments bore state identification. Good state governors were those who showed the most energy and jealousy in guarding the local and regional affiliations of army units. For a time, enlisted men chose their junior officers, the junior officers chose their regimental majors and colonels, and all were commissioned by the governor of the state; the President commissioned generals. There was prejudice against officers trained at West Point—a federal institution—and a preference for "gifted amateurs," as Mr Allan Nevins calls them. "Naturally," Mr Nevins says, "privates thought of themselves as Vermont men, Wisconsin men, and Pennsylvania men, not as national troops"; and their officers looked to their governors "for control and support, not to Washington." The few efforts made to mingle forces according to military need were sacrificed to state pride and regional prejudices. "To the end of the war the Western forces remained largely of Western origin, the Eastern forces of Eastern antecedents. . . . And, as a second consideration, the War Department was totally unequipped to raise a national

12

army." The individual states retained "the task of preparing forces." In a letter to Joshua Bates of Baring Brothers in London, 9 February 1863, John A. Stevens, of the Bank of Commerce, New York, alludes to the purchase of arms abroad by the state of New York for the government at Washington—presumably because the state's credit was good and the federal government's was not.[8]

"It is well known," President Jackson had said in his farewell address to his fellow Americans in 1837, "that there have always been those amongst us who wish to enlarge the powers of the general government, and experience would seem to indicate that there is a tendency on the part of this government to overstep the boundaries marked out for it by the Constitution. Its legitimate authority is abundantly sufficient for all the purposes for which it was created, and, its powers being expressly enumerated, there can be no justification for claiming anything beyond them. Every attempt to exercise power beyond these limits should be promptly and firmly opposed, for one evil example will lead to other measures still more mischievous; and if the principle of constructive powers or supposed advantages or temporary circumstances shall ever be permitted to justify the assumption of a power not given by the Constitution, the general government will before long absorb all the powers of legislation, and you will have in effect but one consolidated government. From the extent of our country, its diversified interests, different pursuits, and different habits, it is too obvious for argument that a single consolidated government would be wholly inadequate to watch over and protect its interests; and every friend of our free institutions should be always prepared to maintain unimpaired and in full vigor the rights and sovereignty of the states and to confine the action of the general government strictly to the sphere of its appropriate duties."[9]

Jackson's un-Hamiltonian words expressed nothing novel but were a restatement of popular ideas that had been vigorously expressed in the convention of 1787, in debates on ratifying the Constitution, in the first ten amendments, in

13

the Kentucky and Virginia Resolutions of 1798, in Jefferson's first inaugural address; and they had been repeatedly reaffirmed officially and unofficially ever since. They rounded off pronouncements decisive in Jackson's Maysville and Bank vetoes and in his transfer of federal monies to state banks. Jackson by act and by word gave the principle they expressed greater force than Jefferson had, though Jefferson had formulated the principle. With the force Jackson gave it, the principle dominated governmental practice and theory until the Civil War.

Jackson's influence, while retaining hold of the agrarian population, extended also over the new and more aggressive part of the business world, which, inspired by the industrial revolution, was drawing its energy and its numbers from the farm and from immigration. The 18th-century Federalists had taken to the industrial revolution, but their inclinations were authoritarian and monopolistic, and they presently found the new business world passing them by. The democracy was taking it over. The revolution was altogether too sweeping and comprehensive for a fraction of the population to control, the merchant being but one man in ten. Hence, the industrial revolution, though it gained capital from the merchants at first, gained more personnel from the farm than from the countinghouse. It was manned by the country-born, both native and immigrant, who constituted the country's great reservoir of entrepreneurial energy and resourcefulness simply because they comprised the most people. The business world became democratic. The abundance of America's resources, given new uses and values by machinery, and the country's growth as a market, made room for multitudes; and the old commercial interests which, dominant in 1787, had fostered the federal Union's formation, had shrunk in relative importance. With it had shrunk the Federalist party, for Jeffersonian democracy was more agreeable to the new business world than the conservative aristocratic spirit of the Federalist merchants could be. The new business generation, fired by the industrial revolution, found the political clichés

14

and agrarian vocabulary of its background quite adequate to express its need of economic freedom and opportunity for its enterprise. After 1800, in respect to practical domestic affairs, the Federalist habit of thought waned rather than waxed; it held fast only in the federal judiciary.

In 1799 an epitome of what modification the economy underwent was presented by Aaron Burr's obtaining the Manhattan Company's charter from the New York legislature. The ruse by which he did it broke the monopoly maintained by the Federalist merchants in New York City, opened the local field to energetic newcomers, and destined it to development as the country's business center. His ruse also broke the hold of the Federalist party and let the city and state become Democratic, as they continued to be till the Civil War.* The change was a blow to urban Federalism generally and a boon to enterprising men everywhere who had energy and inventiveness but needed a foothold and access to capital. Thereafter, the world of business enterprise, served by waterpower, steam, and credit, became one of multitude as well as diversity. Its inventors, investors, and managers were Americans who looked enthusiastically in new directions and to whom the doctrine of *laisser faire* was the same as that of the Declaration of Independence and the Bill of Rights. It is a natural consequence that most of Jackson's party leaders and personal advisers were business men—who knew how to flatter him—and that his proud victory over the second Bank of the United States served directly the calculated purposes of Wall Street.

By 1861, the sluggish current of the federal government's growth lagged in astonishing contrast to the rushing energy and widening extent of the country's economic growth,

* For example, from 1825, when the last term of Rufus King ended, till 1849, when William H. Seward's first term began, every New York senator was a Democrat. In the 29th Congress, 1845-1847, about the time members of the new Republican party began to be elected, New York's representatives in Congress were 21 Democrats, 7 Whigs, and 6 others, some of whom might be Democrats. (*Biographical Directory of the American Congress.*)

15

which had turned the economy of 1800 into one whose most striking characteristics were no longer agrarian but industrial and financial. The American interest in governmental science, which had produced political independence and the federal Union itself, had given way to preoccupation with natural resources, business enterprise, and the techniques of the industrial revolution—toward preoccupation, that is, with getting rich, which is what America seemed to have been made for. Along with this shift of interest came an enthusiastic cultivation of the spirit of *laisser faire*; it gave substance to what had begun as an abstract preference for state authority rather than federal. The states were deemed responsive to popular and local interests; their powers seemed not to clash with *laisser faire*; those of the federal government seemed obviously to do so, being remote from local control and too much like the Old World absolutism from which the Americans had freed themselves.

It is paradoxical, of course, that the prestige of the national government should have continued to grow at the same time that its powers were being restricted. But popular pride in it flourished because, as was explicitly declared, it was a government that allowed a free people to do what they wanted. This was something the peoples of the Old World were prevented by their paternalistic governments from doing. The American nation was the most prosperous and happy on earth and its benign but circumscribed government the best. The only form of domestic activity in which the federal government engaged irrepressibly—that of territorial expansion—was one for which the Americans were as grateful as for their economic freedom. The territory acquired insured the freedom; everyone knew that. The inhabitants of the entire area west of the Mississippi in 1860, which already contained eight states of the thirty-four, owed their homes to the federal government's pursuit of the country's Manifest Destiny, to its diligence—diplomatic and military—in their behalf, and to its generosity. Nothing the government did in Washington can be reckoned more important and fruitful than what it let be done.

Yet, as in a parent's overindulgence of his children, the partition of authority was steadily to the disadvantage of the federal government. Jackson left the Union enshrined in sentiment but with its powers sheared close. Its position was like that which rugged men were glad to give Woman, putting her aloft on a pedestal, idealizing her, protecting her, letting her bless the Home, but not for a moment allowing her purity to be tarnished by her leaving what was called her "sphere"—making indeed her weakness her glory. Jackson sought first to keep the federal government "pure" and modestly within its constitutional limits—its virtue to be not that it did great things but that it left its people free to do them. He succeeded too well.

His toast in 1832, "Our Federal Union—It must be preserved," and the vigorous action he took against the South Carolina nullifiers, belonged to a very different crisis from that of 1861 and, as an editorial in the *New York Times* of 26 February 1861 observed, was of very different moment. The threat in 1832 had been that of a minority, within one state, incensed over a tariff on imports; whereas the threat of 1861, with a bitterness intensified by thirty years of emotional conflict over slavery, was that of a whole region and a majority of its people. It had involved no general defection—particularly none of federal personnel—and no such strain on federal powers as there was in 1861. Jackson in 1832 could chastise John C. Calhoun and the impudence of South Carolina in full consistency with his modest conception of federal powers. These powers were not aggrandized by his action but merely maintained in their limited though sacred scope. Lincoln in 1861 faced very different conditions. He could not restrain the South without exercising federal powers in a fashion and to a degree that conflicted with tradition and that, even though it might be reconciled with the Constitution, was not less revolutionary than secession was. The mainly negative influence of Jacksonian policy on federal powers, paired with the

17

sentimentality in which the Union was enshrined by it, left the federal government a pretty hollow sort of sovereignty, cloudy and rhetorical. Lincoln inherited the Jacksonian anomaly of a relationship—actual, whether or not constitutional—in which the domestic powers of the states were positive, North as well as South, and those of the federal government were neutral and submissive. This anomaly is apparent in the resolution introduced by John J. Crittenden of Kentucky in the special session of Congress, Friday, 19 July 1861, just before the battle of Bull Run, and, just after it, adopted almost unanimously with unessential changes of wording. According to this resolution, war was not being waged against the Southern states with the "purpose of overthrowing or interfering with the rights or established institutions of those states, but to defend and maintain the *supremacy* of the Constitution and to preserve the Union with all the dignity, equality, and rights of the several states unimpaired." There was a mysticism in joining the supremacy of the Union with the unimpaired rights of the states which apparently presented few difficulties to a generation still accustomed to theological subtleties. But as conquest of the South was impeded far beyond expectations, a nationalistic impatience to cut Gordian knots and elevate federal powers began to prevail, accomplishing one departure after another from the dear past and a trampling on states' rights that could not be accomplished temperately but only with fanatical commitment.[10]

III

The Jacksonian measure of most direct relevance to the Union's desperate weakness in 1861 was the independent Treasury act of 1846, which had been adopted nine years after the close of Jackson's presidency and a year after his death. It may be considered a memorial such as he would have cherished, having had his support for years and being consonant with his deepest political convictions. He had said himself that he distrusted not only the Bank of the United States but all banks; and the independent Treasury act accomplished what was still to be done after he detached the Bank from the federal government. According to a statement of Senator Thomas Hart Benton's, he had proposed early in Jackson's first term that this be done and Jackson had taken to the proposal "at once." The government was dissociated from all banks—from the federal one first and then from the others—and thereafter the Treasury kept all its money in its own vaults, or tried to. The state banks, Benton said, would have to be temporized with and their help accepted until the federal Bank was disposed of, and then their turn at the block would come.*[11]

In a letter written at the Hermitage, 6 August 1837, to James K. Polk, Jackson had reported news just come from the city of Washington. "I have recd. lately," he wrote, "some very pleasant information from the city. all is harmony and the object of the Executive Government is, and will be, to seperate [sic] the Government from all Banks, Collect and disburse the revenues by its own agents; receipts of all public dues in gold and silver coin, leaving the Banks and the commercial community to manage their transactions in their own way; reduce the tariff to the real wants of the Government. no credit on duties, or public dues, and all disbursements in gold and silver coin. this and this only is the basis of real prosperity, and the perpetuity of our republican Government. . . ." The arrangement had been proposed three years earlier by Senator William F. Gordon of Virginia, who, "in support of the old-fashioned, constitutional notion of a hard-money government," sought "to disconnect the government entirely from the system of banks, whether state or federal" and to "re-

* This aversion to banks rose mostly from their corporate nature, believed to be inherently monopolistic and corrupt; it was not felt in the same degree, if at all, toward unincorporated partnerships or individuals engaged in banking without the invidious privileges and distinctions which corporate charters, then bestowed by legislative act, were supposed to convey.

19

store the public deposits to the authority of the Treasurer of the United States."[12]

A statute to this effect, authorizing an independent Treasury, was not enacted till 1840, and it was repealed in 1841 by the Whigs. A like statute was again enacted by the Democrats in 1846 and was still in force when the war began in 1861. It required that "all duties, taxes, sales of public lands, debts, and sums of money accruing or becoming due to the United States, and also all sums due for postages or otherwise . . . be paid in gold and silver coin only, or in treasury notes. . . ."; and that "every officer or agent engaged in making disbursements on account of the United States . . . shall make all payments in gold and silver coin, or in treasury notes if the creditor agree to receive said notes in payment. . . ."[13]

The Treasury notes mentioned here were interest-bearing obligations of the government receivable in payments to the government, but not being a legal tender they could not be forced upon the government's creditors. They were not, in the customary sense, a part of the money in circulation. The use of Treasury drafts between depositories was authorized and so even was their restricted sale for private transactions, but the Secretary of the Treasury was told "to guard as far as may be against those drafts being used or thrown into circulation as a paper currency or medium of exchange."[14]

Sub-Treasuries were maintained in various cities and depositories of lower rank in others, to the general end that the government keep all its money in its own possession. The officers in charge of it were forbidden to deposit it in banks and were declared by the statute to be felons and embezzlers if they did. But though required to keep the government's money safe they were seldom provided with the means to do so. Descriptions of depositories in an official report of 1854 by a veteran Jacksonian, W. M. Gouge, to the Secretary of the Treasury, read like directions for the stage settings of a farce. Some officials deposited the public funds not *in* banks, which was a felony, but *with* bank

20

officers, or with merchants or brokers who had safes and who might, if they had the nerve, make use of the money to their own profit and that of the Treasury officials responsible for it. For since gold might be legally required in private transactions as well as in payments to the customs houses and other offices of the federal government, the business of trading in it or letting it for hire was profitable.[15]

Such conditions were known and deprecated, but Congress had done nothing to correct them. The independent Treasury was considered on the whole a magnificent institution; it gratified the emotional conviction that the less government had to do with corporations the better. It also gave effect to the principle of states' rights. In his 1854 report to the Secretary, Gouge had described the federal government's freedom from responsibility for banks and banking as follows: "Having separated itself entirely from paper money banks, the United States government is no longer responsible for the evils they produce. For the correction of those evils the people must look to the state governments by which these institutions have been created and by which they are sustained. The action of the United States government is necessarily negative in its nature and consists in having nothing to do with the fabricators of paper money. 'The less government has to do with banks and the less banks have to do with government the better for both.'" Banks were the responsibility of the states, and as a corollary they were not to be touched by the federal government. Such principles were affirmed by the Democratic party in all six presidential campaigns from 1840 to 1860 in the following words: "The separation of the moneys of the government from banking institutions is indispensable for the safety of the funds of the government and the rights of the people."[16]

The Whigs had controverted the Democrats' "independent" or "constitutional" Treasury but on grounds that lacked the evangelical simplicity of the Democrats' convictions. The Whigs themselves held the precious metals, coined, to be the only real money, but they accepted interchangeable substitutes for it in the form of bank notes, they would have the federal government use banks, and they condemned its not regulating the monetary system. They sought what since has been long established—mainly by later generations of Democrats—except that they never dreamed of outlawing gold for domestic use, as has since been done.[17]

The "independent Treasury," long abandoned, seems now a quite extraordinary affair. It was the product of various fetiches, antipathies, and notions, including Andrew Jackson's obsession with "purity," the agrarian's aversion to the business community, the latter's wish: *"laisser-nous faire,"* the popular cant about governmental matters being somehow holier than private ones, an emotional reverence for gold, the uneasy longing for something immovable in a society where growth in numbers, in complexity, and in specialization was accelerating, and other contradictory things. It had the double effect of stunting federal powers and of turning loose those of the economy, though to some inconsiderable degree the enclosure of the government within a wall of precious metals cast a restrictive influence on economic expansion by confining a substantial part of the country's gold to idleness. It rested on the fallacies that government lay outside the economy, that banking was not a monetary function, and that the federal sovereignty had no constitutional responsibility for it. These were solecisms in actual practice and in fundamental law. Banking, though older by centuries, was as characteristic of the developing nation as were steam-engines and the telegraph; but a naive, agrarian will to prohibit what it disliked, combined with the aversion of business enterprise to official control, kept the major source of money out of the federal government's lady-like sphere.

The government remained, meanwhile, not only within the economy but its largest single transactor, though hobbled. It was less a beneficiary of the independent Treasury arrangement than a victim of it. Had the Union Pacific Railroad Company, incorporated by Congress in 1862, been forbidden to deposit its money in banks, to accept checks or bank notes or any means of payment but coin, to pay its employees and suppliers in anything but coin, and to borrow anything but coin, the prohibitions would have seemed irrational. But, though the federal government had far greater monetary transactions than the railway, far greater receipts, far greater payments to make, far more employees, and far greater debts, still in the way most men then had of looking at it, the government's being prohibited the convenience of banking services and its being restricted to gold, which it had to keep in its own premises, seemed a fine thing, good for every one. It was not required to haul its property by ox-team only, not required to authorize official travel by horseback only, and not required to light the government offices by candle only, though it might as reasonably have been. For while the economy in general had the use of convenient means of payment congruous with the new mechanical devices whose invention and adoption were characteristic of the age, the federal government was constrained to accept payments and to make them in an antiquated medium from which the commercial world had been, long and gradually, freeing itself. To keep relations between the government and the economy "pure" and wholesome, tons of gold had to be hauled to and fro in dray-loads, with horses and heavers doing by the hour what bookkeepers could do in a moment. This, moreover, was not the procedure of a backward people who knew nothing better; it was an obvious anachronism to which, in keeping it tied around the federal government's neck, a mystical virtue was imputed. Actually its only beneficiaries were handlers of gold and speculators in it.

The banks that had joined Jackson in ending the federal Bank's existence and had themselves obtained the federal deposits, might be supposed to have disliked the loss of the latter and to have opposed the change. They did, but they were too few to have influence; ninety-one in 1836 seems to have been their largest number, and usually they were less than half that and never so many as ten per cent of the total number. Moreover being a government depository bank had often meant being too much under the thumb of the Treasury to be pleasant. Banking and commercial interest, originally Federalist, had become largely Democratic, thanks to Aaron Burr, Thomas Jefferson, and Andrew Jackson, to each of whom it had owed freedom from the interference of government. The party loyalty of the Gallatins and of the *Journal of Commerce* was not exceptional.[18]

Suddenly in 1861, however, the anachronism and impracticality of the independent Treasury became obviously dangerous when Southern secession forced the government to enter the market for funds, goods, and services in immense volume. Tents for the soldiers, shoes and uniforms for them, weapons and ammunition, food and transport could all be furnished quickly and efficiently by machines powered by steam and by water, and military operations could be keyed to the performance of which machined weapons and engineering were capable. But all this was to be impeded by the government's limitation to means of payment suitable for the Wars of the Roses but not for the first of modern conflicts four hundred years later.

In the 'thirties Abraham Lincoln had opposed Andrew Jackson's monetary schemes; in the 'sixties he became their victim. In 1839, speaking at Springfield, Illinois, against President Van Buren's early effort to get an independent Treasury bill enacted, Lincoln had defended the Bank of the United States, whose charter Jackson had vetoed seven years before. Between the time, Lincoln said, that the Bank "got into successful operation and that at which the government commenced war upon it," there had been "no such contractions or expansions" of the currency as the Jacksonians alleged. "The Bank could not be expected to regulate the currency, either *before* it got into successful operation, or *after* it was crippled and thrown into death convulsions by the removal of the deposits from it and other hostile measures of the government against it. We do not

24

pretend," he said, "that a national Bank can establish and maintain a sound and uniform state of currency in the country in *spite* of the national government; but we do say that it has established and maintained such a currency, and can do so again, by the *aid* of that government; and we further say that no duty is more imperative on that government than the duty it owes the people of furnishing them a sound and uniform currency." The Bank was never more justly and understandingly defended than in these few words. Of Jackson himself, Lincoln remarked in the Illinois legislature in 1841 that he was proud of the victory of New Orleans and of General Jackson's military fame, "though he could never find it in his heart to support him as a politician."[19]

Meanwhile, another important limitation obstructed the federal government's power to tax. Here the Constitution was at fault, its authorization being confused and impractical. No attempt to raise an internal revenue had been made for years, mainly because duties on imports provided the federal government all the money it needed, but also because abstention from direct taxes had fostered a feeling that the federal government had come under a positive obligation to abstain from them, having surrendered the field to the states. This feeling made the government hold back from taxing property and income lest the states' sovereignty be violated; yet the war it sought to finance was itself a violation of states' sovereignty.

Such limitations on legislative and administrative powers had kept the federal government in a stunted condition which for years had been acclaimed a blessing by most Americans. But now, suddenly, a choice had to be made between disunion and loss of the blessing. For to avoid disunion dear traditions had to be abandoned and measures taken from which all but the most radical of the Union's defenders shrank—military government, impairment of civil rights, suspension of *habeas corpus*, meddling with the independent Treasury act, recourse to legal tender notes, the end of a "tax-free paradise." It might be affirmed "without extravagance," said President Lincoln in July 1861, "that the free institutions we enjoy have developed the powers and improved the condition of our whole people beyond any example in the world." But could so liberal a government defend itself? For many if not most Northerners the dilemma was resolved into a fanatic nationalism which accepted any sacrifice for the Union and brought the federal government out of the war a far ampler sovereignty than it earlier had been, more powerful, more ambitious, and more besought. It was the 37th Congress that began this revolution.[20]

IV

In the four months between Lincoln's election in November 1860 and his becoming President in March 1861, the North had not yet had to face the difficulties still to arise from the underlying conditions I have described. But it had been beset by two others. One was the intrepid movement of the South toward independence. The other was the sloth of the Buchanan Administration in the face of that movement.

During the summer of 1860 confidence in the economic position of the country had been buoyant. Recovery from the panic of 1857 was general, and production, both agricultural and industrial, had thriven. The South, after five years of increasing yields, was bringing on the largest crop of cotton it had ever made and was doing well with other products too. The West also looked forward to larger exports than ever before. In the North, manufacturing, transport, and trade were active, and there was a strong public demand for investment securities. But late in the summer these pleasant developments began to be darkened by the growing probability that Lincoln would be elected and by the growing fear of trouble from the South if he were. In New York, borrowings at the banks contracted, the stock market became dull, and withdrawals of gold to the South tightened the money market.[21]

There was in 1860 so little of the economic diversification characteristic of the States a century later that the South, the West, and the North were then in relationships of fairly primitive interdependence. The South produced cotton, the export of which produced sterling, which paid for the bulk of the country's imports. The West produced meat and grain, which it sold abroad, to the South, and to the North. The North produced manufactured goods and provided the financial services by which payments to and from the outside world and among the regions of the country itself were made. Because the South was so much absorbed in the production of cotton and procured from the North and West most of what its people needed, including credit, the Southern banks were regularly in seasonal debt to the North and the West for the South's purchases. Apprehension now spread among wholesale merchants and bankers in the North and West lest political trouble with the South interfere with the remittances due from it. Actually this apprehension was less than fully borne out, for some Southern banks, and notably those of New Orleans, which were prominent among the strongest in the country, continued remittances to the North and West in defiance of Southern politicians and warriors and to a degree that by the brutal standards of the 20th century would seem either treasonable or simple-minded.[22]

But apprehension is itself a form of reality and often tends to produce what it fears. As autumn progressed into winter, many Northern and Western merchants who were awaiting remittances from the South found themselves sucked into bankruptcy. "Payment of a large part of their debts must be delayed, if not finally lost; and in the modern use of credit, delay is fatal." Consequently, "all paper resting in any degree upon Southern trade had upon it the taint of a rapidly increasing suspicion." Within a fortnight after Lincoln's election, business in New York was at a stand. In the West, it was worse, for panic struck in the midst of grain shipments to the seaboard for export, and shippers who had parted with their stuff faced the too lively possibility that they would not be paid for it. In New York relief was afforded by the clearing house banks' pooling of their reserves, which had shrunk by then, for some, to less than a quarter of their liabilities—the minimum they had mutually agreed to maintain. Their action, however, and their receipts of specie from abroad eased the tension in the money market. But confidence was not restored. Stagnancy and gloom persisted, save for a strong demand for foodstuffs from across the Atlantic, where crops had failed.[23]

Four days after the presidential election, the South Carolina legislature, by unanimous vote, had called for the popular choice of delegates to convene 17 December and consider the withdrawal of the state from the federal Union. At Charleston, 20 December, the convention adopted, also by unanimous vote, "an ordinance to dissolve the Union between the state of South Carolina and other states united with her under the compact entitled 'The Constitution of the United States of America.'" By this measure, South Carolina resumed, or purposed to resume, the absolute sovereignty she had qualified by accepting the federal Constitution seventy-two years before and the Articles of Confederation a decade before that. In Washington four days later, 24 December 1860, members of the House of Representatives from South Carolina informed the Speaker that "the people of the state of South Carolina, in their sovereign capacity, have resumed the powers heretofore delegated by them to the federal government of the United States" and had thereby ended their delegation's membership in Congress.* Within ten days South Carolina had taken over the customs house and other federal offices and property at Charleston and in the harbor, except Fort Sumter.[24]

By 1 February 1861 seven other states had followed South Carolina in withdrawal from the Union. Forts, arsenals,

* The senators, elected by the legislature and therefore deemed representative of the state and not of her people, had already resigned before the session.

arms, ships, customs houses, and customs receipts had been seized, and an unarmed vessel with provisions and reinforcements for the federal troops in Charleston harbor had been warned off by hostile fire. With their departure from the Union the seceding states were taking over the federal property situated within their boundaries. They did this at first with studied attention to legality and equity. South Carolina in December had sent three commissioners to Washington to negotiate for the formal transfer of such property, payment of her share of the federal debt, etc., deeming it "but fair and proper" that she not withdraw from her partnership with the other states of the federal Union without settlement for her share of the common assets and liabilities. Jefferson Davis, later the president of the Confederacy of seceding states, believed all of them desired such settlement. But the North contemptuously refused to recognize any element of legality in secession or its attendant conditions, and the South ceased its offers. This firmness of the North in some matters was offset by its dismay and confusion in others. It was much quicker in committing itself than in preparing to effect its commitments.[25]

One finds it obvious now, a century later—as it was then to *The Economist* in London—that the South's effort to leave the Union was utterly futile once the North got its powers pulled together. The South's only chance lay in persuading or discouraging the North before things had gone too far. There were times when that possibility, on either ground, seemed reasonable. Besides the initial advantages of resolute action, the South had reasonable grounds for the legality of secession. And while it was acting on the right claimed by it to withdraw voluntarily from a compact into which it had entered voluntarily, Northern leaders were not agreed that they would be worse off if they let it go. Many preferred to be freed from the stigma of association with a thing so vile as slavery and could believe that the South would in time grow sick of its "peculiar institution" and want to come back into the Union.

President Buchanan, whose judgments in a general way

were temperate and correct, was irresolute in crisis and inhibited particularly by the nearing end of his tenure. His cabinet was fiercely divided, its division gradually lessening as the Southerners in it one by one resigned. These included Howell Cobb, of Georgia, Secretary of the Treasury, who left in December from "a sense of duty to the state of Georgia" and returning there became active in promoting secession. Cobb's uneasy and incompetent successor, Philip F. Thomas of Maryland, held office some three weeks and then also resigned. His place was taken by John A. Dix, a highly respected New York lawyer who had the confidence of the business community. Under authority of an act of 17 December, he sold ten million dollars of Treasury notes, nearly all bearing interest at rates running from ten to twelve per cent; the rates asked by bidders ranged up to thirty-six per cent. All the funds raised in this period were absorbed in quite ordinary payments, the government's mere living expenses, and not in military preparations. At the end of December, Dix obtained a million and a half in gold from the Bank of Commerce, New York, for the express purpose of paying the interest due 1 January 1861 on the public debt. A further amount of three and a half million was then obtained from the same source to pay members of Congress, officers of the army and navy, departmental clerks, and others.[26]

Secretary Dix had found the Treasury demoralized. It seemed to have become its practice "to pay nobody," according to the *New York Herald*. "Soldiers, sailors, employees in every department of the government had been coolly informed by Mr Dix's predecessors that there was no money for them and no remedy. Nor was this concealed from Mr Dix when he first took office, and the books and accounts of the Treasury Department were in such confusion that it was impossible to discover the true state of affairs without much labor." This took weeks apparently, for it was not till the middle of February, the *Herald* said, that the Secretary ascertained the amount of overdue claims. He needed from eight to ten millions, an amount smaller than some of the government's borrowings but within the range of most. "As it was feared that a government loan would not sell above eighty-five," an understanding was had with Massachusetts, New York, Pennsylvania, and Ohio that they would guarantee the loan. But a request for the approval of Congress came up on the day reserved for the two Houses to count the electoral votes for President and Vice President, and the "scheme was defeated by the objection of Mr Garnett of Virginia," a Southern state which had not yet seceded. Garnett sarcastically explained first that he did not wish to see the federal government "placed before the world in the aspect of a mendicant" and later, more bluntly, that "after the recent declaration of war by the President elect" he deemed it his duty "to interpose every obstacle to the tyrannical and military despotism now about to be inaugurated." His statement, according to the *New York Times,* provoked "shouts of derisive laughter" in the House and "suppressed hisses." But opposition was not disloyal only; two important members of the Ways and Means Committee, Elbridge Spaulding of New York and Justin Morrill of Vermont, both Republicans and ardent champions of the Union, opposed the guarantee. With time being counted by hours and Secretary Dix finding it necessary to act "today," 13 February, he arranged to borrow immediately eight millions without the four states' guarantee and at a discount which he feared would amount to ten per cent or eight hundred thousand dollars. "Such was the humiliating condition of the government of the United States," wrote John Sherman—a sovereignty that had far less credit in the market than most of the states it comprised.[27]

These pitiful borrowings would have been unnecessary had not customs receipts shrunk to almost nothing with the decline of imports. Ever since its foundation, the government had regularly obtained the bulk of its income from import duties, and now, suddenly, in the last quarter of the year 1860 those receipts had fallen to half what had been "reasonably and confidently expected" a few months before.

31

In the decade ending with 1860, customs had yielded ninety per cent of federal income. Moreover, so much of customs payments as were now received by the Treasury included all that the payers could muster of Treasury notes, whose receipt cancelled existing obligations of the government but provided no specie with which the government could pay its bills. With respect to the Southern ports, Secretary Dix reported, 21 February 1861, his belief that the duties on imports were being collected at the customs houses in South Carolina, Georgia, Alabama, Louisiana, and Florida and that vessels were being entered and cleared there in the usual manner. But so far as he knew, he said, "the collectors assume to perform their duties under the authority of the states in which they reside and hold the moneys they receive subject to the same authority." The federal Treasury got nothing.[28]

The low state of things is also indicated by Secretary Dix's pathetic reminder that the Treasury had some twenty-eight millions of dollars in the hands of individual states and might consider the possibility of recovering it. This "resource" was the federal surplus distributed to the states in 1837; one would think it lay as near the Treasury's reach —especially that due from the states in secession—as it would have been lying somewhere on the moon, but as things stood, an able administrator considered it worth mentioning. At the Treasury, the *New York Times* reported two days before Abraham Lincoln became President, there had been "a constant run upon government funds" and several bureaus had "exhausted to-day their last dollar." Such statements may have been inaccurate but they nevertheless were evidence of trouble and may well have understated the government's penury as often as they exaggerated it.[29]

In the circumstances, Secretary Dix had no opportunity to exercise the ability he possessed. He did, however, display vigor and loyalty. For as head of the Treasury he was in command of the Revenue Cutter Service (now the Coast Guard), whose basic duty was protection of customs; and when Captain Breshwood, stationed at New Orleans, in command of the federal cutter *Robert McClelland*, was about to deliver his ship to the state of Louisiana, Secretary Dix, 20 January 1861, sent the Treasury's agent at New Orleans the following telegram, which was made public and lifted somewhat the spirits of the North: "Tell Lieutenant Caldwell to arrest Captain Breshwood, assume command of the cutter, and obey the order I gave through you. If Captain Breshwood, after arrest, undertakes to interfere with the command of the cutter, tell Lieutenant Caldwell to consider him as a mutineer and treat him accordingly. If any one attempts to haul down the American flag, shoot him on the spot." This, of course, was a manly gesture with the sword, but it put nothing in the North's empty purse. Nor did it save the cutter, for the message was intercepted by the authorities of Louisiana.[30]

Upon Lincoln's becoming President, Secretary Dix was succeeded as head of the Treasury by Salmon P. Chase, a lawyer and former Democrat, with administrative experience as governor of Ohio but with no experience in business or finance. He was politically important for reasons less impressive now than then, and had been a rival of Lincoln's for the Republican presidential candidacy. He was proud, correct, and without magnanimity, but "a very fine, powerful-looking man," with such impressive confidence in his own abilities, which were great but less than he thought, that he filled people with awe. He was kept aloft in his self-esteem by his brilliant, ambitious, and adoring daughter, Kate. He was asked to be Secretary of the Treasury because President Lincoln needed prestige for his Cabinet and to this end sought prominent and politically influential men rather than proved administrators. The President could do this with little misgiving because for many years the growth of the country—unmatched by any such growth of the federal government—and the abundant duties paid on imports had made it appear easy to run the Treasury and because the military and fiscal difficulties that lay ahead were not as yet conceived. Chase sought to decline the appointment, as he had reason to do, and accepted it with reluctance. In the Senate he could have exercised his powers for good; in the Cabinet he was a troubler with but legal skill in finance.[31]

2

SUMTER, BULL RUN,
AND THE SPECIAL SESSION
APRIL TO AUGUST 1861

I

Fort Sumter fell before the fire of the South Carolinians and their friends 13 April 1861. On the 15th President Lincoln called up the militia to the number of seventy-five thousand men and summoned Congress to meet in special session 4 July. In South Carolina, Georgia, Alabama, Florida, Mississippi, Louisiana, and Texas, the President said, forces had arisen that were obstructing execution of the laws of the United States and that were "too powerful to be suppressed by the ordinary course of judicial proceedings or by the powers vested in the marshals." He said the militia's first task would "probably be to repossess the forts, places, and property which have been seized from the Union." Four days later he proclaimed a blockade of Southern ports. Later in the month he issued the first of several executive orders authorizing the commanding general of the army to suspend the issue of *habeas corpus* writs, "or in other words, to arrest and detain, without resort of the ordinary processes and forms of law, such individuals as he might deem dangerous to the public safety." Early in May he ordered an increase of some eighty-three thousand men in the army and navy. These were acts of sovereignty, but behind them lay doubt of their success.[1]

When the special session convened 4 July, with Republicans holding ample majorities in both Houses, the President reported what he had done. And, in order that the war be made "a short and a decisive one," he asked for "at least four hundred thousand men and four hundred millions of dollars." Answering his own question—"Must a government, of necessity, be too *strong* for the liberties of its own people, or too *weak* to maintain its own existence?"— he saw "no choice was left but to call out the war power of the government; and so to resist force, employed for its destruction, by force for its preservation."[2]

The ancient questions of the sword and the purse were considered more particularly in the reports of the Secretaries

37

of War, the Navy, and the Treasury. The Secretary of War, Simon Cameron, said the generosity of responses to the calls already made for men was such that it was difficult "to keep down the proportions of the army and to prevent it from swelling beyond the actual force required." The Secretary of the Navy, Gideon Welles, reported recruitment of "a sufficient number of seamen to man the vessels added to the service with almost as much rapidity as they could be prepared, armed, and equipped." Never had the American navy had "so great and rapid an increase." Secretary Chase asked for only four-fifths of the money President Lincoln had mentioned; he reckoned that three hundred and twenty million dollars were needed, and of this sum, he proposed that eighty millions for ordinary needs be drawn from revenues and two hundred and forty millions for military needs be borrowed.[3]

The Secretary's plan of borrowing three times what he sought from taxes was presented by him as having the warrant of both principle and tradition. But of more practical significance at the moment was the extraordinary ease of the metropolitan money market. "Industrially," *The Economist*, London, had observed, "the country has never been so prosperous." Its prosperity was abnormal, though, being the product of unusual domestic factors on the one hand and foreign on the other. The first was the frightened halt given enterprise by the threat of disunion; it was a time for the business man to lie low, to reduce his imports of foreign goods, and to keep out of debt. The other factor, a quite fortuitous one, was a demand for foodstuffs from across the Atlantic caused by severe, extensive, and prolonged crop failures. Thus to the domestic bank reserves already made idle by the indisposition of the business community to borrow and to buy abroad were added greater and greater amounts of gold coming from Britain and western Europe in payment for purchases of American farm products. Outward shipments of gold fell off, and receipts of gold to pay for foodstuffs mounted. To the latter was added the steady inflow of gold from the gravels of California.

Month after month business commentators in the press noted with astonishment the continued and unprecedented shipments of gold inward and additions to the banks' gold reserves in New York, Boston, and Philadelphia. But the result of these trends, coincident with the restiveness of general business, was the prospect, strange in the American economy, of the bankers sitting on idle reserves of gold, starving to death. They were hungering and thirsting for loans and eager to deal with the Secretary of the Treasury, besides feeling the patriotic impulse to help save the Union, and being more aware than the general population was that it could not be done without money. They had no idea, however, of becoming the permanent holders of all the government's obligations. It was their function and their expectation to be distributors thereof, making large and instant advances to the Treasury, receiving the government's obligations in return, and selling these to permanent investors. The great risk in the banks' undertaking was lest private investors be too few and too timid. Most Americans were either farmers or entrepreneurs, that is, proprietors of small productive properties, and unaccustomed to the ownership of investment securities. So borrowing proved to be hard, partly because of the enormous sum asked for. Taxing might have proved easier, because the typical American, though averse to taxes, was at least accustomed to them, whereas when first urged to purchase bonds, he merely stared, amazed to be thought a millionaire. But the federal government had no adequate legislative authorization to collect revenue and no administrative means of collecting it. Borrowing was easier, if only the lender would lend.[4]

Aside from the disadvantages the government was under, whatever its course, Chase was neither experienced nor facile. As a finance minister he knew too little and as a lawyer he knew too much. He believed on good grounds that the existing currency of bank notes issued under authority of the states as sovereignties was unconstitutional; but the belief was an obstacle to proper action, not a help.

What would have helped was a practical understanding of the money market. Instead, when Chase outlined his program to the July session he talked in terms of precedent, principle, and tradition. He did not describe the propitious state of the money market at the moment, nor the fortunate irony of an international trade balance which, though it diminished receipts from what hitherto had been the prime source of federal revenue, was now piling up reserves in the city banks and augmenting their power to lend. Instead, whether or not he was impressed by these conditions, he put forward a plan based, without acknowledgment, upon the ideas of his distinguished predecessor, Albert Gallatin, Secretary of the Treasury a half century earlier, when the States, battered from both sides during the later Napoleonic wars and uncertain whether Great Britain or France offered the greater danger, had had to expect attack by either combatant, or even both.

Gallatin had had magnanimity, skill in finance, and a clear intellectual grasp of the problem confronting the country. But of the extraordinary future he knew no more than anyone else. Though war had hung dangerously close at the time, he had believed the Americans would seldom be drawn into it; for they themselves would never be aggressors, and they were protected by the Atlantic from the powers from which aggression might be expected. In these circumstances, viewed rationally, he had advised resort to borrowing in order to cover the *extraordinary* expense which war would impose and reliance upon revenue to cover the *normal* expense of government that continued in war as in peace. Losses and privations caused by war "should not be aggravated by taxes" beyond what was necessary to replace revenues diminished by war-time interruption of imports. Instead, the capital already accumulated by the people should be borrowed; it was a fund already at hand for use in the overriding need of defense. In a letter to the Senate, 5 November 1807, Gallatin had said that "experience having now shown with what rapid progress the revenue of the Union increases in time of peace," and "with what facility the debt formerly contracted has in a few years been reduced, a hope may confidently be entertained that all the evils of the war will be temporary and easily repaired, and that the return of peace will, without any effort, afford ample resources for reimbursing whatever may have been borrowed during the war."

In 1808, Gallatin had reaffirmed this judgment. "The geographical situation of the United States," in his opinion, "their history since the Revolution, and, above all, present events remove every apprehension of frequent wars. It may therefore be confidently expected that a revenue derived solely from duties on importations, though necessarily impaired by war, will always be amply sufficient, during long intervals of peace, not only to defray current expenses but also to reimburse the debt contracted during the few periods of war." In 1809 he had again maintained this position. If war occurred, then "loans reimbursable by instalments and at fixed periods after the return of peace must constitute the principal resource for defraying the extraordinary expenses of the war." In 1811, the policy had again been confidently affirmed.[5]

Gallatin's reasoning was based on war as he knew it, in a world he knew; the nation had not yet been revolutionized industrially, the economy had not yet become ominously complex, armed conflict had not yet become reliant on the mechanized industry of the combatants, and it still took weeks to cross the Atlantic. Warfare had not yet become what we call "modern." Gallatin knew it as still waged by relatively small professional armies seeking victory in decisive battles, such as Austerlitz and Waterloo. But in the forty-six years between Waterloo and Bull Run, the industrial revolution had altered the implements and the nature of warfare beyond understanding and made any precedent of war finance of doubtful worth.

Unlike Gallatin, who had knowingly appraised the conditions confronting him, Chase seems to have thought the country was merely bigger than before and otherwise unchanged. He showed a determination to remain unruffled

41

and orthodox. "In every sound system of finance," he said in his recommendations, it was "indispensable" that taxes be looked to "for the prompt discharge of all ordinary demands, for the punctual payment of the interest on loans," and for the "redemption of the principal." He noted the preference that had "always been evinced by the people of the United States," by Congress and by the Executive, "for duties on imports as the chief source of national revenue," the advantages of which lay, "above all, in the avoidance of federal interference with the finances of the states." He proposed no departure from this established policy except such as would compensate for the certain shrinkage of revenue from the usual sources; this shrinkage, he believed, would not be prolonged; the current restiveness of business would be redressed. It was "hardly to be doubted" that the great body of Southerners would soon sicken of "the calamities of insurrection" and force their leaders to turn from "the criminal folly" of disunion to "order and peace and security for all rights of property and for all personal and political rights in the Union and under the Constitution." And then, the Secretary expected, "with restored Union" there would come "not merely renewed prosperity but prosperity renewed in a degree and measure without parallel in the past experience of our country."[6]

To make up the eighty millions of revenue Chase asked the special session for, he counted on fifty-seven millions from duties on imports and three millions from sales of public lands. This left twenty millions which could be obtained either from direct taxes on land and buildings or from excise taxes on luxuries and consumable goods. The Secretary preferred that Congress decide on which or both, insisting, however, on "the absolute necessity" of assuring such revenue as would "manifest to the world a fixed purpose to maintain inviolate the public faith by the strictest fidelity to all public engagements." This was the limited purpose of taxes in time of war.[7]

With respect to the two hundred and forty millions to be

borrowed—and with which, according to Gallatin's principle, war was to be waged—Chase first recalled the investment market's cold responses to the Treasury in the twelve-
month just ended. In October 1860, Secretary Cobb had
asked for ten millions and got seven; in February 1861, Secretary Dix had asked for eight millions and got seven; in
April 1861, Secretary Chase himself had asked for eight and
got somewhat less; in May, asking for nine, he had got eight;
and having just asked for bids on fourteen, he had got
none. Chase took this sobering experience into account in
asking now for eight times as much as had been obtained
in the preceding efforts. He suggested that the forthcom-
ing appeal for funds be made as popular as possible and
not confined to the investment market; one hundred millions or more should be sought from the sale of Treasury
notes in denominations running as low as fifty dollars each
and to be paid for by the taker in ten instalments over a
period of five months. This would put the notes within reach
of almost every family. The interest would be seven and
three-tenths per cent per year, which meant a penny a day
accruing on each fifty dollar note.[8]

"It is beneficial to the whole people," the Secretary wrote,
"that a loan distributed among themselves should be made
so advantageous to the takers as to inspire satisfaction and
hopes of profit rather than annoyance and fear of loss; and
if the rate of interest proposed be somewhat higher than
that allowed in ordinary times, it will not be grudged to
the subscribers when it is remembered that the interest
on the loan will go into the channels of home circulation
and is to reward those who come forward in the hour of
peril to place their means at the disposal of their
country."[9]

Besides this "national loan of not less than one hundred
millions of dollars," which was intended for wide-spread
subscriptions by small investors, the Secretary proposed the
issue of another hundred millions in "bonds or certificates
of debt" intended for large investors both at home and
abroad. These would be in denominations as high as five

thousand dollars, payable in dollars or sterling, and bearing seven per cent interest. And "as an auxiliary measure" to the two foregoing, the Secretary recommended fifty more millions of Treasury notes in small denominations suitable for circulation and either bearing a low rate of interest or redeemable on demand. It was these that he presently attempted to put in circulation as a "national currency" which should replace the universal but unsatisfactory currency of bank notes. He had in mind another possibility which impelled him to say that the "greatest care" would have to be taken "to prevent the degradation of such issues into an irredeemable paper currency, than which no more certainly fatal expedient for impoverishing the masses and discrediting the government of any country can well be devised."[10]

Chase's recommendations as to borrowing procedure accorded fairly well with the advice he had from Wall Street that he seek his money in the domestic market, not the foreign, that he make the purchase of government bonds popular, that he look to the bankers not as permanent holders of the bonds but as distributors, and that the interest be at an attractive rate secured by the pledge of specified revenues and payable in gold. Feeling as they did about the domestic crisis and knowing what they did of British feelings, the bankers thought it impractical to seek money for defense of the Union in the foreign money markets. To this end, the manager of the New York Clearing House, George D. Lyman, had written a long letter to the Secretary, 20 June 1861, just before the special session opened, urging that the government "borrow from *its own people*." This it might do if it made its securities "popular, safe, and desirable." He had recommended one hundred dollar bonds bearing seven per cent interest, maturing in twenty-five years. As an investment this would be "the best government loan in existence." The people of the loyal states were "patriotic, united, and rich," Lyman had said, "and ready to support their government; let then the government debt be distributed among them in small amounts . . . they will show the world that a government dependent upon the people may be as strong and as rich in resources as it is free." But certain things Lyman had warned against: A currency should not be made of the public debt, as he saw many newspaper writers were urging; the "government must not expect to borrow upon better terms than its people are able to do"; nor should the banks "be expected to absorb the government debt." For the banks' debts were payable to the people on demand, and their assets must be such as would enable them to meet that demand. The banks could meet current needs, but the permanent holders of the government's obligations should be the people themselves. Chase had not followed the foregoing advice slavishly, but neither had he recommended anything in conflict with it.[11]

The press, reporting the Secretary's recommendations, breathed confidence. The *New York Times* said that his words had been "received by Wall Street with eminent satisfaction." The *Herald*, in cooler tones, said that public opinion on the report "appears to be in the main favorable." The *Tribune* praised the Secretary's plans heartily but vaguely, thinking it "admirable," pleased with his attention to the need of economy, convinced that the war should be over by Christmas, but insistent that the success of financing was dependent on "an immediate and resolute advance from all points upon the rebel forces." The *Independent*, influential religious weekly, noted the "satisfaction" with which the Administration's financial recommendations to Congress had been received and their "ready acceptance in Wall Street."[12]

The money market's response to the Secretary's report justified the hopes of the press. Prices in the government bond market rose. On 9 July, in response to a telegram received at noon from Washington, an advance of five millions sought by the Treasury was pledged by 3 o'clock, three millions in bullion being furnished that afternoon and the remaining two the next day. The sub-Treasury was overwhelmed with offers. Nothing "could have come more acceptably to the banks," then full of idle funds, than a real borrower such as the Treasury was showing itself to be. The *Times* reported a buoyant confidence that the government had "already established its power, both moral and material, to suppress the Southern rebellion." Bonds had risen "three per cent in the open market since last week, in the face of the acknowledged future wants of the Treasury."[13]

II

Meanwhile, on the 10th, the national loan bill recommended by Chase had been brought up in the House by Thaddeus Stevens, chairman of the Ways and Means Committee, and passed after almost no debate by a vote of 150 to 5. Wall Street felt the "utmost satisfaction." The terms of the loan, said the *Times*, "are understood to reflect the advice of a number of distinguished business millionaires of this city who were called to Washington in consultation with Mr. Chase." The *Times* was happy every way. "There is practically only one party in Congress," it said editorially. "Whatever measures are reported by the committees proceed to a vote without discussion and are accepted by a majority which is almost tantamount to unanimity. Measures which involve millions of men and money, which inaugurate or abolish systems of revenue and administration, which create armies and navies, and give to the Executive the plenary powers requisite in such grand national emergencies, are hastened from the committee room to the engrossing clerk with a rapidity which in ordinary times would suggest the idea of the legislature having surrendered all but the formal exercise of its constitutional functions."[14]

In the Senate, the loan bill demonstrated what the *Times* said; it passed, 15 July, with some amendments to the House version and almost no discussion. President Lincoln approved it the 17th. Meanwhile on the 13th the buoyant *Times* reported expectations that there would be but a short war now that the federal government had established its ability to win a long one; and remarking on the "stagnation of business" produced by the war, its editor advised people to buy bonds. That would end both war and business stagnation.[15]

The loan act so promptly adopted authorized the Secretary to borrow, in various ways, an aggregate of two hundred and fifty millions, the full amount he had asked for. The most important provisions were the following three: for the sale of Treasury notes bearing seven and three-tenths per cent interest and maturing in three years; for the sale of bonds bearing interest at a rate not exceeding seven per cent and maturing in twenty years; and for the issue of two classes of Treasury notes, one bearing no interest but payable on demand, and the other bearing interest at a rate half that of the bonds, into which they were convertible after three years. All this was within the terms of the Secretary's recommendations, with the important exception that a provision of the original bill allocating certain revenue to payment of interest was omitted.[16]

The omission left the press less satisfied with the statute than it had been with the bill. The *Times* in an editorial deplored the absence of such a pledge and the supposition that "the United States, amid all the tremendous pressure of the pending war, can borrow money to any amount, on its naked credit, on terms equally favorable with the governments that carefully provide and pledge specific revenues to meet their engagements." The *Herald,* less temperate, daily condemned the ignorance and effrontery of Congress in fixing the rates the government would pay and in trying to borrow on its own terms; the government was no better than any other borrower, and efforts to force favors from lenders must work to its own hurt. For Congress had limited the interest to seven and three-tenths per cent and had forbidden the sale of bonds or notes at less than par. This seemed a bit too much like indifference to the distinction between borrowing and taxing. The loud complaints in the press were evidence that Chase was right when he insisted that in a war which was

47

to be financed with borrowed money the explicit pledges investors were accustomed to were indispensable. Congress was wrong in omitting them.[17]

At the moment, meanwhile, North and South presented a curious contrast: the North, possessed of every potential advantage in wealth, industry, and population, but slowly and painfully organizing the powers that were to give it, within three years, irresistible force; and the South, without comparable resources but with ardency making the most of what it had, which, however, its economic limitations and its greater loyalty to the divisive principle of states' rights prevented it from ever augmenting. The tide of Northern power that was to submerge the stubborn rock of Southern resistance had barely begun to rise.

III

While the terms of borrowing were being decided, taxes to provide revenue were being devised in committee, where the disposition was to get more from them than Chase had proposed. That disposition indeed was general. Men more sophisticated than Chase doubted if the principles he accepted from Gallatin were still sound. The doubt was expressed publicly, as in the press, and privately. But it was no easy matter, in the absence of experience with federal taxation, to determine how much could be got from what sources and how to get it. So long as men could remember, import duties, which were now sadly shrunk and inadequate, had provided the bulk of federal income. Aside from the excise on alcoholic beverages, tobacco, and a few odds and ends, no internal taxes had been levied by the federal government since 1816—fifty-five years in the past. The individual states had levied their various taxes, of course, but each in its own way, and they gave Congress a variety of examples, none readily agreed upon. The first legislative result achieved by Congress was the act of 5 August 1861 (largely superseded at the next session by that of 1 July 1862), which increased the duties on certain

48

imports and levied a "direct" tax on property and another, not then deemed "direct," on income.[18]

At the time, as at others, there was no definite and uniform understanding of the term "direct tax." The Constitution was laconic about it. In Article I, section 2, it said: "Representatives and direct taxes shall be apportioned among the several states . . . according to their respective numbers. . . ." In Article I, section 9, it said: "No capitation or other direct tax shall be laid unless in proportion to the census" to be made every decade. James Madison had reported in his record of the 1787 convention that on 20 August "Mr King asked what was the precise meaning of *direct* taxation," and "No one answered." Why no one answered is not apparent, for at least one or two other members of the convention might have done so. Gouverneur Morris had proposed on 12 July that taxation be proportioned to representation, as was done; and he had implied, though not explained, a distinction between direct taxes and "indirect taxes on exports and imports and on consumption." Other members who had joined the colloquy, and James Wilson in particular, seemed familiar with the distinction. As Professor Charles Dunbar wrote in 1889, it had been attributed by Alexander Hamilton in 1796 to the Physiocrats, who made land the basis of all wealth and logically, therefore, the ultimate source of all taxes. For the Physiocrats taxes on the land itself were accordingly "direct," though it was not clearly agreed or affirmed that all others were indirect. Personal taxes were also sometimes classed as direct. In the American colonies, however, there had been head taxes and "faculty" taxes, neither levied on land but obviously direct in any but a Physiocratic sense, and this experience seems to have led the convention of 1787 to speak of capitation *or other direct* taxes. In the same way, following the argument of Alexander Hamilton, the Supreme Court in the Carriage Case, 1796, had called both land and capitation taxes "direct," but no other. Consequently, by the time of the Civil War it was generally understood that an income tax was

49

not a direct tax; instead it was called a "duty." This understanding held till 1895 when the Supreme Court, being now removed more than a century from the Physiocrats and attentive to a literal logic, not to history nor to change in usage, unexpectedly concluded that an income tax was also "direct" and that such a tax, if federal and not apportioned according to the census, was unconstitutional. The Court's judgment invalidated the federal income tax law of 1894 because it was not so apportioned, and this brought about the 16th amendment to the Constitution, which exempts federal income taxes from the need of apportionment on the basis of population and permits them as now levied. It looks as if a little more historical scholarship on the Court's part might have made its 1895 decision the opposite of what it was and the 16th amendment superfluous.*[19]

In his report to the special session, 4 July 1861, Secretary Chase had estimated, as already said, that in the fiscal year just beginning the government would have to expend three hundred and twenty millions, of which two hundred and forty millions should be borrowed and eighty obtained from revenues. Of the latter amount, twenty millions from existing duties, thirty-seven millions from new or increased duties which he thought could be imposed—mostly on sugar, tea, and coffee—and three millions from sales of public land and other, miscellaneous sources would provide sixty millions. The twenty millions still needed could be obtained, he had said, by resort either to "direct taxes or to internal duties, or to both." He had left the choice "to the superior wisdom of Congress," along with some observations on the constitutional and practical problems inseparable from the levying of direct and excise taxes. These ob-

---

* Professor Dunbar, in an essay entitled "The Direct Tax of 1861," and published in the *Quarterly Journal of Economics*, July 1889, made the following statement: "The judicial interpretation of the phrase, 'direct taxes,' is well settled therefore and in close accordance with the usage found in the writings of the French economists of the last century." In the same journal, July 1895, Professor Dunbar had to regret the Supreme Court's historical error in the 1894 decision and also its inauspicious denial therein of a major federal power. (Dunbar, 98, 133.)

servations, offered in his verbose and opaque prose, were certainly of little value to the Ways and Means Committee, not one of whose members knew less about the matter than he did. This may help to explain why in his next report, submitted when Congress convened in December, he barely mentioned taxes. Yet I think his treatment of taxes at no time arose from political fear; instead it arose from conventional misjudgment, in which he displayed the same unshakable powers that he displayed when he was right.[20]

It is regrettable, but what the special session did about federal income has to be told either in detail too tedious for most readers or with a severe brevity that blurs and confuses the facts. I have chosen to be tedious. The reader who is impatient with details, therefore, is invited to skip the following six paragraphs.

The Ways and Means Committee started by preparing two revenue measures. The first, HR 54, was called a tariff bill, being directed at import duties, and was brought up in the House 17 July, the day the loan bill was approved. It was based on a draft submitted by the Secretary with his report. It proposed duties substantially higher than those of the Morrill tariff act, which had been prepared and adopted by the House in 1860 with no thought of war influencing it, had passed the Senate unchanged late in February 1861, and had received President Buchanan's approval 2 March 1861, two days before his presidency ended. The increased duties levied by this act had met vigorous condemnation, partly because they fell on tea, coffee, and sugar, not previously dutiable and consumed mostly by the poor, and partly because higher rates, it was contended, would discourage imports and produce less revenue rather than more. Justin Morrill, of Vermont, author of the existing tariff law, thought some of the duties in the new bill too high but defended it nevertheless because there must be revenue to "pay the interest on the public debt, meet the ordinary current expenses of the government, and provide a sinking fund" for the final extinction of the principal. Thaddeus Stevens, chairman of Ways and Means, forced the bill through the next day, 18 July 1861. He wanted, he said, "to try the naked question" without further talk and see if the House would sustain his committee or not; because, he said, "it depends altogether on that whether we will deem it worthwhile to proceed any further in attempting to raise revenue." His challenge succeeded, talk stopped, and the bill (HR 54) passed, 82 to 48. So much for import duties.[21]

Six days later, the 24th, the House took up the domestic tax bill (HR 71), drawn at the Treasury, which would authorize levies of two sorts: first, direct taxes upon real estate, apportioned among the individual states—those in secession included—according to their population, as the Constitution prescribed; and second, excise taxes on distilled spirits, watches, carriages, horses, bank notes, *et cetera*. This bill, called at the time a bill for "additional revenue," was described by Chairman Stevens, with some hyperbole, as "an exact copy" of legislation prepared by Albert Gallatin and enacted in 1813, 1815, and 1816. The direct tax provisions of the bill reproduced the scope and principles of acts of 9 and 14 July 1798, of 22 July and 2 August 1813, and 9 January 1815, the latter of which was merely modified and continued by the act of 5 March 1816. Much of the language of 1798 had been retained in later legislation, with additions, substitutions, and modifications, and was continued in that of 1861. But the antiquity of the measure's provisions and the respectability of their authorship helped little if at all. Protests beset the measure from all sides. Despite its precedents, it was called rashly experimental. Because its levies were mainly on real estate, it was said to put an outrageous burden on the farmer, leaving the banker, the merchant, and the capitalist—who had been few in 1798—scarcely touched. For the same reason it was said to fall lightly on the East and heavily on the West. It would send a hateful army of federal tax-gatherers upon the people. Incidentally, nothing could be got from states in rebellion until they were reconquered.[22]

These protests were not unreasonable. The Constitution's requirement that direct taxes (meaning land taxes) be proportioned to the population had been defensible for a people mostly agrarian and without the immense differences in wealth and economic engagements which, since 1787, had come to pass. But in the three-quarters of a century subsequently elapsed, as a consequence of the industrial revolution, the growth of population, and the diversification of economic interest, land had shrunk in relative importance. Wealth was now represented as much by trade, the professions, factories, banks, and railways. A tax on land did indeed leave these other forms of wealth untouched, save indirectly, and left the East, where they were mainly held, less burdened than the West, which was still mainly agrarian. Thaddeus Stevens' scarcely adequate defense was that "all taxes were odious," that the need was desperate, and that the time was short. Schuyler Colfax, Republican of Indiana, proposed that the direct tax of thirty millions be stricken out and in its place there be "a tax on stocks, bonds, and mortgages, money at interest, and income tax in addition to the other personal taxes" already in the bill. The proposal was not accepted, being untraditional if not even unconstitutional. But on the motion of Roscoe Conkling, Republican of New York, the bill (HR 71) was recommitted to Ways and Means with instructions to arrange, if possible, that the tax on real and personal property provided therein "be levied, assessed, and collected" by the several states themselves. This preference for Conkling's proposal over Colfax's may be taken as evidence of greater distaste for the invasion of the states by federal tax collectors than for the inequity of concentrating taxes on land; but it seems also to have reflected the imperious distaste of Thaddeus Stevens for the opinions of Schuyler Colfax, who made the mistake of implying that the government's need was less great and less pressing than Stevens said it was. And Conkling's proposal that the tax be collected by the states for the federal government fared little better; for the next day, 25 July, Thaddeus Stevens reported that his committee was unable to devise anything that would "be constitutional and carry into effect the instructions of the House."[23]

The wrangle was resumed, with an incidental conflict among abolitionist members over a tax on slaves. Thaddeus Stevens and John Bingham, of Ohio, both Republicans, defended the tax because it threatened the slaveholders and because it had precedent in statute and jurisprudence. Owen Lovejoy, of Illinois, also Republican, thought it outrageous because it accepted the grouping of human beings with horses and cattle as forms of personal property. On the 27th it was proposed that the bill (HR 71) be returned to the Ways and Means Committee for reconsideration and be brought up at the next session with changes including imposition of a tax on such property as stocks and mortgages. Instead the House followed the plea of John A. McClernand, Democrat of Illinois, that the bill not be postponed to the next session but returned to Ways and Means with instructions to report a substitute that would reduce the direct tax and tax other personal property correspondingly. Two days later the bill came back to the House with the changes demanded. As reported by Valentine Horton, of Ohio, Republican and committee member, the sum to be obtained by direct taxes had been reduced from thirty millions to twenty, and the option, earlier rejected, had been given the states of collecting their shares of the tax for the federal government. They could not, under the Constitution, be *required* to collect it. At the same time, the committee, Horton explained, had "enlarged the sphere of internal duties" and reduced the tax on "the landed interests of the country." It was putting a tax on watches and carriages, which was later deleted, and a tax on personal and corporate incomes in excess of six hundred dollars a year. This last was the most notable part of the measure; an income tax had been mentioned already as possible, though none had ever been enacted in Congress before. Yet in spite of its being a radical novelty in federal legislation, it was entertained quietly and approvingly, whereas other parts of the bill had been warmly controverted. This,

54

perhaps, was because the income tax was a novelty only in federal taxation; otherwise it was known from British experience and that of individual states. Justin Morrill, in his turn, explained that the committee had taken it to be "the sense of the House that a much larger amount of personal property and personal wealth should be subjected to taxation; and this bill," he explained, "accomplishes that object." For, "in the course of the discussion," he said, "it leaked out from all sides that money, bonds, and mortgages, stocks, and various incomes from such sources should be included in the tax list." The committee's changes were accepted, and after an abortive attempt to get the bill returned to Ways and Means a third time, with instructions to replace the tax apportioned to the states by a demand for repayment to the Treasury of the federal surplus distributed to them in 1837, the bill (HR 71) passed the House, 29 July, 77 to 60, and followed the tariff bill (HR 54) to the Senate.[24]

Meanwhile the Senate had been discussing the latter bill (HR 54), which it had received from the House and referred to its Finance Committee 19 July. The committee had prepared a substitute and reported it out 25 July— which must seem soon rather than late if it be recalled that the first battle of Bull Run had meanwhile been fought and lost. The substitute, which was presented by Senator Simmons of Rhode Island, increased the duties on imports and also established an income tax, drawn, Simmons said, on the pattern of Great Britain's. This addition, in the Senate's Finance Committee, of an income tax to the "tariff bill" (HR 54) preceded by several days the like action of the House on the "revenue bill" (HR 71). The tariff provisions were accepted by the Senate with relatively little discussion and the income tax provisions with even less; the bill passed the Senate, 30 July, 22 to 18, and went back to the House, which the same day declined to accept the Senate's changes and asked for a conference on the matter.[25]

The conference committee formed to deal with the differences between the two Houses took up not only the bill for increased revenue from imports, *et cetera* (HR 54), but also the direct tax bill (HR 71), which had not yet come before the Senate. It transferred the substance of the latter, with changes, to the former, which itself was considerably changed. This made a new and different version of the bill for increased revenue (still HR 54), the other (HR 71) as a separate measure being abandoned. The merged bill retained the schedules of import duties; a direct tax levied state by state, which the states might collect for the federal government, withholding fifteen per cent for their pains; and a tax, mostly of three per cent, on income in excess of eight hundred dollars a year.[26]

The rates on imports were to go into effect at once. The income tax was to become due upon assessment after 1 January 1862; and the direct tax was to become due on the completion and posting of property assessments in the individual states as of 1 April 1862. The measure (HR 54 amended) as drawn by the conference committee was brought up in both Houses 2 August and passed in each after brief discussion, the vote for it being 34 to 8 in the Senate and 89 to 39 in the House. It was approved by President Lincoln the 5th.[27]

The special session closed the next day. Its performance, shaken by Bull Run, was distinguished enough to be accepted with a shrug, when one considers the exasperating nature of the legislative process at best. The Executive got all it had asked and more. The minority had had its way. Clement Vallandigham of Ohio had been vigilant and resourceful in obstruction and bold in decrying President Lincoln's "forked tongue and crooked counsel," his "wicked and most desperate cunning," his Administration's "enormous and persistent infractions of the Constitution, its high-handed usurpations of power"; and Lazarus Powell of Kentucky had told the Senate that "having opposed the war, having voted against the loan, having voted against the army supplies," he would vote against the taxes needed to continue the war—which he did. The program of much borrowing and little taxing, the latter long deferred, had been accepted by a few with misgivings but by the most with hope. The borrowing was to begin at once and so were the excises and increased duties on imports. Since taxes on property and incomes were to begin the next year, their imposition did no more than support the government's credit with promises, hearten the bankers who were to lend the Treasury millions of dollars, more than ever before, and perhaps make it easier for the bonds they took to be sold to the public. Senator Fessenden, in bringing up the conference bill in the Senate, where revenue had been much less discussed than in the House, had made it ancillary to the borrowing program—a move tardily righting omission from the loan bill of the customary pledge of revenue to discharge principal and interest. For it would determine, he said, whether the money authorized to be borrowed could be borrowed. He had it "from the most reliable sources," he told the Senate, that unless the bill were passed and payment of interest on the proposed hundred and fifty millions loan were assured, the attempt to borrow so much would fail. In other words, internal revenue was being levied less with the expectation of collecting it than of inducing investors to lend.[28]

Yet the tax bill's inadequacy can scarcely be taken as evidence of pusillanimity on the part of Congress nor blamed on Chase in particular, as it often has been. It resulted from a collision of harsh reality with a callow addiction to stunted federal powers. The government was in a state of impotence produced by conceptions of its duties which had become firmly established in Andrew Jackson's day, which had come to be taken for granted, and which now could not be dismissed instantly from most men's minds, as it could from Thaddeus Stevens'. In the intervening years, the Union had deferred to its component states time after time; and members of Congress, though legislators for the Union, seldom put second their sentimental and practical loyalties to the sovereign states of which some were ambassadors and to the local interests of which some were representatives. They remembered who elected them. They shrank from sending armies of federal tax-gatherers to violate state sovereignties; and while they cursed the rebels, swore to punish them, and voted for taxes, they chose measures that put off the dreaded break with the dear and happy past. They were not ready to do what was necessary to enlarge federal powers and reduce those of the states, except those states that sought to preserve slavery and leave the Union. They had grown up taught and believing that the federal government was the best in the world because it interfered with them so little. The Union had accepted faithfully and modestly the Jacksonian dictum, "the world is governed too much." And now it had to gird itself to restrain the intransigence of South Carolina and her sisters, without offending Kentucky, Ohio, New York, and others loyal to the Union. In the teeth of custom, tradition, and the existing polity, it had to maneuver its way into power; and this, no less then President Lincoln's search for competent generals to lead its armies, was to impede its sovereign purposes. In respect to fiscal powers, the lead in this maneuvering was to be taken not so much by the Secretary of the Treasury as by the Committee of Ways and Means.

There was also the mischievous hope, shared by too many with Secretary Chase, that the war would soon end. Bull Run did not cure it, and Thaddeus Stevens chided the expression of it barely a day after the event with his Rhadamanthine judgment that the war would be long and bitter. "Some gentlemen have an idea," said Stevens, 24 July, "that our enemies, being rebels, will surrender—will succumb in the course of a few months and with little expense and that they will not fight the battle they have undertaken. I flatter myself with no such hope. I believe that the battles which are to be fought are to be desperate and bloody battles; and that they are to be numerous. I believe that many thousand valuable lives will be lost and that millions of money will be expended. The only question is whether this government is prepared to meet all these perils and to overcome them. If they are [sic], they must submit to taxes which are burdensome—which the people, I know, at any other time would not submit to for a moment but which I believe they will now submit to."[29]

On the whole, members of Congress being used to what the Union was—a federation of "sovereign" states which fully illustrated the evils that had moved Alexander Hamilton, seventy-five years before, to recommend their political extinction—the accomplishments of the special session were no worse than might have been expected. Had President Lincoln or Secretary Chase understood what the industrial revolution had done to the country in their lifetime —and to the policy of Albert Gallatin—they would have sought taxes at the very outset; but they had not that understanding. Nor had Congress. And had they had it, they would still have lacked the assessors and tax-gatherers and the other necessary organizations and powers far more than they lacked soldiers. Federal inexperience with internal taxes and the absence of any organization to collect them made the North no better prepared with its purse than it was with its sword.

IV

The defeat and rout of the Union forces at Bull Run, Sunday, 21 July 1861, occurred in the middle of the special session. First reports of the engagement, as of Monday, 22 July, were exhilarating and moved the *New York Times* to rejoice over a victory that avenged Sumter and "must thrill every loyal heart." But what had to be reported later of soldiers throwing away their rifles and running from the field was "in the intensest degree disastrous." The stock market was in a panic and for days "continually agitated" by reflections on the defeat and the general management of the war. Yet exports were immense thanks to the crop failures abroad; gold kept arriving from Europe and California, bank reserves kept mounting, idle funds lay unlent, and the Treasury got another advance of six millions.[30]

For fifteen years of dizzy national growth, to which the federal government's response was the building of more lighthouses and post offices, the Treasury had got on comfortably with a handsome surplus of revenue most of the time and with the small occasional loans it sought obtained readily in gold delivered to it by the lending banks. But now instead of six millions the government needed two hundred and fifty. The banks could deliver no such sum, which was four times the combined reserves of the banks in New York, Philadelphia, and Boston and possibly more than all the gold there was in the country. The initial borrowing was to be one hundred and fifty millions, but it was obvious that the specie requirement of the independent Treasury act threatened to prevent the government's obtaining even that much. Though the metropolitan banks held double the amount of gold they had ever held before, they had less than half the amount the hundred and fifty million dollar loan would call for. Not every one was blind to this fact.

Secretary Chase had sent his friend, Judge Simeon Nash, of Gallipolis, Ohio, a copy of his report to the special session, and the judge had thanked him for it in a letter written 18 July, the day following passage of the loan act and three days before Bull Run. The judge was not a devotee of the independent Treasury act and saw clearly the difficulty that lay ahead. So long as the specie clause of the act remained in force, he told Chase, the loan that had been authorized was "an *impossibility*." It would be different if the loan were a small one, like those of the past, but for such loans as would be sought now, "coin can not be had without a sacrifice no government should submit to." Nor was coin needed. The Treasury should use the banks, as the people did. "It is war supplies that the government wants and whatever will secure them is all it should require." That meant bank paper, checks and notes. Otherwise Nash apprehended suspension of specie payments and resort to irredeemable paper money, to which governments were commonly driven by war. "Now by getting rid of the foolish

60

provision as to coin for government, you may ward off the suspension of specie payments. . . . Unless this is done, you will fail in raising one half of your two hundred and fifty millions while yet the materials to carry on the war are abundant in the country. If you can not get these materials of war until you have first raised the coin, a failure to raise the coin will prevent you from obtaining these materials; while if you would receive bank paper you could get that, and that would bring the materials needed."[31]

The specie requirement, Judge Nash continued, "while the country was at peace and daily paying out what it received . . . could do no great mischief; but in a time like the present when the government wants millions, those millions can not be raised in coin except at an enormous sacrifice. . . . I know just now these notions are not popular; the men holding coin do not like them, since they would emancipate the government from their clutches, and politicians who have advocated such notions are unwilling to face about and hence will probably hold on until the crash should come. . . ." Late in August Nash repeated that "the specie clause must be got rid of." This was more than advice; it was a forecast of what happened within six months. Other Western correspondents gave Chase the same urgent advice.[32]

But Chase was unmoved. Within a week of his friend's first warning, he had written Senator Fessenden, chairman of the Finance Committee, that much was being said "about suspending the operations of the sub-Treasury act so as to allow the receipt of specie-paying bank notes for loans and of course the disbursement of them for expenditures. I confess," he had said, that "this proposition does not strike me favorably, but I submit it to the better judgment of the committee." Why the proposal failed to strike him favorably Chase did not explain.[33]

His note to Fessenden, presumably, was his response not only to what he had heard from Ohio but to what he heard from Wall Street; and the congressional committeemen, it seems, were themselves already considering the problem—novel to them—of borrowing more money than existed. One of the House committee's most active members, Elbridge G. Spaulding, a banker from Buffalo, later reported his having expressed to the committee "the opinion that the loan of two hundred and fifty million dollars . . . could not be made and the gold actually paid over into the sub-Treasury without so weakening the banks that they would be obliged to suspend specie payments." Two of his colleagues, he said, William Appleton and Erastus Corning, who were Boston and Albany bankers respectively, the first a Republican, the second a Democrat, had agreed with him. So, evidently, had most of the committee members, including Thaddeus Stevens, for Spaulding and Appleton were made a sub-committee to prepare an amendatory act and to confer with Senator Fessenden about it. Other business men were also consulted and the conclusion had been reached, apparently, that the Treasury, if it were to borrow the amounts authorized, must be freed, more or less, from the requirement that what it borrowed be delivered to it on the spot in dray-loads of gold. The magnitudes imposed by the war made it clear, to those who could see at all, that the specie requirement of the sub-Treasury act was not a protection to the government but a burden from which its citizens and the business world were free, except in their transactions with the government. The individual states, of course, did not deny themselves the use of bank credit. And to the banks it was a threat; for the law in many states, including Massachusetts and Pennsylvania, mutual agreement in New York, and experience everywhere, required that banks maintain gold reserves in proportion to their liabilities. Deliveries of gold to the Treasury on the scale now in prospect seemed bound to push the banks into violation of these requirements.*34

* The independent Treasury act applied to both silver and gold coin, but the mention of silver was idle because the coin in circulation was practically all gold, except for subsidiary pieces. Silver was impracticable for large payments, sixteen tons of it being needed to equal a ton of gold. Besides that, the silver dollar contained more than a dollar's worth of silver, was therefore worth more as metal than as

This apprehension, of course, seems to conflict with the current volume and continuing growth of bank reserves —both volume and growth being without precedent—but the condition could not be considered lasting by any but the naive and irresponsible; it was wholly fortuitous— dependent on the weather in Europe. On the basis of these customary considerations, Spaulding drafted an amend- ment, according to a later statement of his, "which in gen- eral terms suspended the sub-Treasury law" in respect to what the banks lent the Treasury, allowing the gold to remain on deposit with the lending banks and "authoriz- ing the Treasurer to check, from time to time, directly on the banks" in payment of the government's creditors. "In this way," Spaulding said, "the great bulk of the supplies and material of war for the army and navy could be paid for by the usual bank expedients and by offset through the Clearing House of New York and other cities without ma- terially disturbing the gold reserves of the banks, except in the payment of balances." Spaulding's explanation, in general, was the same as that already made by Judge Nash to Chase.[35]

It seems strange that this important proposal was not brought up till two weeks after the loan bill became law. Perhaps it was because not everything could be done at the same time; perhaps it was because any tinkering with the holy independent Treasury act was sure to run into trouble—being an offense against the memory of Andrew Jackson—and friends of the amendment had to approach the text circumspectly, the more so because Chase had al- ready disclosed to Fessenden his dislike of the change. At any rate, the matter came into the hands of a conference committee on a bill, supplementary to the loan act, which had passed both Houses but with differences that had to

---

money, was rarely coined, and when coined was exported because it could buy more abroad than at home. Senator John Sherman, later Secretary of the Treasury, doubted if there were as many as one thousand silver dollars in the country in 1861. Gold comprised bullion and foreign coin as well as domestic. (Sherman, I, 254.)

be reconciled. In the conference committee's report reconciling the differences was included an amendment affecting the specie requirement of the independent Treasury act. Fessenden, Stevens, and Spaulding were members of this committee.

When the conference report was brought up in the House 1 August, Thaddeus Stevens explained that among other things it effected a "partial modification" of the sub-Treasury act so drawn that the Secretary need "not instantly" take possession of the gold lent by the banks but instead might at his discretion allow it to remain in the banks till actually needed by the Treasury. This was not what Judge Nash had urged, but it tallied exactly with what Chase later did. Stevens also said that according to "competent men," the loans which had been authorized could not possibly be made, "if, on the instant, the whole coin of a loan" had to be delivered to the Treasury by the lenders. Two congressmen, Vallandigham of Ohio, Democrat, and F. A. Conkling of New York, Republican, at once denounced the wicked proposal, but it was adopted, 83 to 34.[36]

The same day Fessenden brought up the amendment in the Senate, where it was adopted by a voice vote without discussion. The day following, however, 2 August, Senator Lyman Trumbull, Illinois Republican, asked for reconsideration on the ground that the amendment had not been understood. He protested "repeal" of the requirement that the government's money be held wholly in its own vaults and return to the "old system" of keeping it in banks. Senator Jesse D. Bright of Indiana supported him. Bright was sometimes a Democrat, sometimes a Republican, but he was always for the independent Treasury, which he called "one of the fundamental principles on which this government rests"; he opposed anything, war or no war, "that looked to the repeal of any feature of the sub-Treasury act." Thereupon Senator Fessenden demanded a vote "at once" rejecting reconsideration. He first explained the importance of the amendment but did so in terms very different from those of Thaddeus Stevens in the House the day before. The banks, he said, were required by their states' laws to maintain reserves of coin in their vaults, and without violating those laws they could not furnish the Treasury the funds it needed in the coin required by federal law. The solution was to suspend the restrictions of the federal law and let the Secretary of the Treasury take credit on the books of the lending banks. "If we insist upon retaining the law in its present condition," Fessenden said, "the banks, which must have by the laws of the states a certain quantity of specie in their vaults to do their business and accommodate their customers, can not do what they are disposed to do, and that is to take largely . . . of the government loan . . . ; because if the law stands as it is at present, they are obliged to take the specie out of their vaults in order to do it." So, he said in substance, if the banks were allowed "to become depositories," the Treasury could leave the money on deposit with them and disburse it as other borrowers did, and the banks could lend to the Treasury without violating the state laws governing their reserves. "It is thought to be exceedingly necessary and wise to have this provision," Fessenden said, "and every businessman acquainted with banks and their operations will see its necessity under the laws of the states. . . . That is the opinion of the Secretary of the Treasury and the opinion of the committees of both Houses." With respect to the states' laws, Senator Fessenden was right, except that not all states had such requirements; and in any case the law was of less general importance than the practical necessity of reserves.* With respect to the opinion of the Secretary, as soon became obvious, the senator was wrong. Senator James A. McDougall of California, Democrat,

---

* As it happened, there was no such statute in New York, where the most important banks were and where the Treasury was to get most of the money it needed; but the New York banks were governed none the less by the natural law, written or not, that banks must have reserves with which to meet their obligations; and in New York City they were governed by mutual contract.

warmly supported Fessenden, to whose demand the Senate acceded by rejecting the motion to reconsider.[37]

As enacted 2 August and approved by President Lincoln 5 August the amendment read that the provisions of the independent Treasury act were "suspended, so far as to allow the Secretary of the Treasury to deposit any of the monies obtained on any of the loans now authorized by law to the credit of the Treasurer of the United States in such solvent specie-paying banks as he may select; and the said monies so deposited may be withdrawn from such deposit for deposit with the regular authorized depositaries, or for the payment of public dues, or paid in redemption of the notes" payable on demand that Congress had just authorized. In effect, the amendment permitted the sums lent to be left on deposit till transferred to the Treasury's depositories for disbursement therefrom; it said nothing about their being disbursed by check or by bank note. Practically speaking the amendment said nothing at all; it was otiose; the specie requirement remained what it had been. Time was allowed by implication, but not how much time and only for transfer of the coin lent from lending bank to Treasury. Disbursement was still from the Treasury only. Chase thereafter, and others too, stated the substance of the requirement as unchanged in any respect whatever.[38]

V

The press, meanwhile, had mostly been extolling the amendment, but with varying degrees of inaccuracy. The *New York Times*, 2 August, said the change would make "peremptory deposit of gold" in the sub-Treasury by lending banks unnecessary. (But nothing beyond custom had ever made it "peremptory.") "The proceeds of such loans may remain with the banks to the credit of the Treasurer of the United States until drawn out in the regular course of disbursement." The amendment would save "a vast amount of trouble and annoyance"; though, the *Times* complained, "the importance and influence of the measure can not yet be determined," because no official copy had been received. Nevertheless, "we rejoice," the *Times* said in its monetary column the next day; it was fair to the banks and generally desirable that there be "as little disturbance to the money market and as light movement of bullion as practicable." Transfers of gold were "nothing" to the credit of the government; they endangered the "steadiness of the money market" and were to the government's detriment as a borrower. The same day, 3 August, in its legislative report, the *Times* celebrated the amendment as "a virtual repeal of sub-Treasury law, . . . a fundamental change, . . . without beat of drum or notice to the country, by which the sub-Treasury policy . . . was virtually thrown to the winds." It was "a skillful *coup d'état*, totally revolutionizing the long-settled policy of the country." Again, on the 4th, the *Times* quoted the amendment and said: "This leaves the Secretary free to negotiate through the banks and to leave on deposit with them the proceeds of any part of the two hundred and fifty million dollar loan authorized by the present Congress or of the unexpended loans of the last Congress. . . ." On 5 August it said: "The late practice of the government was arbitrarily to force upon the public creditor as well as to exact at both the customs house and land office nothing but gold and silver. It also demanded of all lenders to the government the immediate transfer in gold of the entire amount subscribed for, to the sub-Treasury, irrespective of the immediate wants of the government and without consulting the state or convenience of the money market, thereby locking up and rendering useless to business for the time being sums of five or ten millions every few weeks, as well as unnecessarily taxing the ability of the market to pay a liberal rate for the public securities." The practice, "so far vexatious, would have been ruinous in face of impending needs."[39]

Any but the most suspicious reader, seeing it reported, 3 August, that the independent Treasury act had been "virtually thrown to the winds" by a fundamental change "totally revolutionizing the long-settled policy of the country" and letting the banks enter their loans to the Treasury on their books as deposit credit, would suppose that the Treasury intended to pay its bills by bank check. And it would be a surprise to read in the *Times* two days later, 5 August, that "the specie principle of the sub-Treasury law" would be "in no sense departed from." Surprise would give way to bafflement when in the same sentence the *Times* said that payment by the Treasury would be, "at the option of the public creditor," in "bank or Treasury notes redeemable on demand in specie." The *Times*'s reports, positive and approving in tone but wavering in substance, echoed the strangely unlike explanations that Stevens and Fessenden had offered in Congress—Fessenden explaining the amendment as needed and as intended by its friends, and Stevens explaining it as signifying little or nothing and as administered by Chase.[40]

James Gordon Bennett's *Herald* meanwhile was happy to report that the amendment, "abolishing the sub-Treasury act for the time being," would make federal depositories of every bank that lent to the government, that creditors of the government would henceforth be paid by the government "in drafts on our banks," and that "instead of regarding the sub-Treasury as their natural enemy, whose vaults become filled at their expense, the banks will now consider that institution in the light of an ally." The "heavy transactions of the Treasury" would create "less disturbance in money markets." The *Herald* also said editorially, 8 August, that one of the best things in the recent legislation was "the virtual abolition" of the independent Treasury system. "It is fitting in a commercial country that there should be a more perfect equalization of interests between mercantile and national finance." If the New York banks were to help finance the war, it was "preposterous to expect them to carry on simultaneously a war with the government for specie."[41]

The New York *Journal of Commerce* reported passage of the amendment with sharp disapproval, calling it "a most extraordinary measure" that effected "nothing less than the virtual abandonment of the sub-Treasury system." The *Journal* was "opposed to the present unholy war" and also to abandonment, even temporary, of the independent Treasury act; it said the action had practically suspended specie payments. It foresaw paper money and "absolute ruin."[42]

The *Independent*, sternly correcting the *Journal*, told a very different story. "It has been urged by the rebel press of this city," the *Independent* said, "that the government have abrogated the sub-Treasury system, but this is altogether false. There is no change at all, but permission is given to such banks as will subscribe to the new loan to hold the sums so subscribed on deposit subject to the demand at any moment of the Secretary of the Treasury and then payable *in coin*. This is instead of their paying at once into the sub-Treasury the whole amount of their portion of the loan." Accordingly, the *Independent* said, the objection of the *Journal of Commerce* "has no weight—no foundation in fact." Yet the *Journal of Commerce* a week later again said that the sums lent to government were not "to be paid by the banks into the sub-Treasury" in specie; instead the government would "make its disbursements directly from these institutions." Reports on the amendment more contradictory and confusing could scarcely be imagined.[43]

Since the editor of the *Boston Daily Advertiser* at this time was Charles F. Dunbar, who later became professor of political economy at Harvard and one of the ablest of American authorities on money and banking, it might be expected that the *Advertiser* would be especially informative about the amendment. But it seems to have been less concerned to explain exactly what the amendment authorized than to assure the public patriotically that it was necessary, and, tangentially, that the loan should be generously supported. Unlike the New York press, the *Advertiser* was not dogmatic and rhetorical. It recorded briefly Thaddeus Stevens' explanation to Congress that the purpose was to permit periodic rather than continuous deliveries of gold to the Treasury and was silent about Fessenden's very different explanation, merely recording his sponsorship of the measure in the Senate. And later it briefly but repeatedly mentioned the importance of the amendment to success of the loan, but in terms of Stevens' explanation, not of Fessenden's or the bankers'. Beyond that, the *Advertiser's* language was ambiguous—perhaps from some covert uncertainty of its own. Thus it said one time that in Wall Street there was a "good deal of discussion" of the amendment, which had come as "something of a shock to the sticklers for hard money and a rigid sub-Treasury system." Another time it was editorially cognizant of objections to the amendment but no more specific about its effect than to commend the periodic rather than instant delivery of gold for sums lent to the Treasury. "The liberal system of deposits now adopted will enable the government to secure assistance which, it is safe to say, *could not* have been given it otherwise." But no shred of supposition was expressed that the Secretary might leave the banks in possession of their reserves and make his disbursements by checks drawn on them—or that there had ever been grounds for thinking so. The *Advertiser* explained the amendment exactly as it had been explained by Thaddeus Stevens and exactly as it came to be administered by Chase.[44]

But at the moment, presumably under pressure of adjournment, the complete contradictions were left unresolved.

SECRETARY CHASE AND
THE BANKERS

I

SECRETARY Chase centered his negotiations for a loan upon the banks of New York, Boston, and Philadelphia. He had concluded, he said in his annual report the following December, that to get the money he had been authorized to borrow, the "safest, surest, and most beneficial plan would be to engage the banking institutions of the three chief commercial cities of the seaboard to advance the amounts needed. . . ." They would receive in return three-year Treasury notes bearing seven and three-tenths per cent interest to be resold to permanent investors. The banks' advances, that is, would supply the Treasury with funds at once and bridge over the longer period required to get the "national loan" in the hands of the public. Meanwhile, he would also, "to a limited extent" and "in aid" of the banks' advances, "issue notes of smaller denominations than fifty dollars, payable on demand."* These demand notes were the modest start of what became a national currency, which since Andrew Jackson's presidency the country had had only as a constitutional pretense.[1]

The Secretary began the loan negotiations as soon as he could after the special session adjourned, Tuesday, 6 August 1861. He arrived in New York Friday, the 9th, having made his way roundabout through Annapolis and the Eastern Shore in order to evade capture by General Beauregard, whose men were raiding from north and west of Washington. The evening of the Secretary's arrival in New York, he met the bankers at the home of John J. Cisco, the Assistant Treasurer. Thereafter meetings were held in the parlors of Wall Street banks, mostly in those of the Com-

---

* For the confusion of posterity, Chase's initial program comprised "notes" of two kinds. One was investment securities bearing interest at the rate of seven and three-tenths per cent (a penny a day on each $50 note). These "notes" were short-term obligations maturing in three years. The other kind of note constituted a national currency, substituting for coin, and professedly redeemable on demand in coin, which in fact it seldom was.

73

merce and the American Exchange, the two largest. The meetings also were attended by representative bankers from Boston and Philadelphia.[2]

The condition of the money market appeared ideal for a finance minister needing to fill an empty purse. The war had made business sluggish in all but the export trade, and few bank customers were borrowing. Imports had fallen off drastically, but heavy exports of foodstuffs continued because Europe's crop failures prolonged from 1860 to 1861. Consequently, the balance of payments being greatly in the Americans' favor, the banks' reserves were augmented by incoming shipments of gold from Europe and San Francisco. As never before the city banks were able to lend, eager to lend, and under pressure to lend lest they fail to make their dividends. Individual states were already borrowing to equip regiments which they jealously considered their own though furnished to preserve the Union, but their borrowings were from their local banks and did not take up the slack in the metropolitan money markets.[3]

The current receipts of gold were almost twice the largest amount in any earlier year. For a country falling in two this was remarkable. New York in 1861 received thirty-three millions in gold from California and thirty-seven millions from Europe—amounts small beside what the twentieth century has become used to but for the nineteenth century enormous. In August, when Chase was in New York negotiating for his loan, current receipts reached a total of fifty-seven millions for the first eight months of the year; and the reserves of the city's banks were twice what they had been when the year began. The reserves held by New York banks, 10 August, at the outset of the meetings was close to fifty millions; with thirteen millions shared about equally by Boston and Philadelphia, the banks of the three principal money markets held about sixty-three millions. They had never before held so much.[4]

Yet reckoning the government's probable needs, which were as far from precedent as the gold supplies were, and sensing the ignorance and inexperience in Washington, Wall

Street and the New York press had become uneasy about the loan negotiations. For the Secretary arrived with the particulars of his program tucked far up his sleeve. The *Times,* despite its loyalty to the Administration, could not learn why so little information about the loan was reaching New York; no copy of the act authorizing it had been received. And when the *Times* announced Chase's arrival, it greeted him with the hope that he and the bankers would meet "in a liberal spirit of mutual confidence and accommodation." Press comment during the negotiations was lengthy and full of conjecture and apprehension, as if dependent on scraps of information and misinformation. The *Herald* was disgusted because Congress, it was told, had set unreasonable terms for the loan; the government's bonds and notes were not worth par and bore inadequate interest. The bankers, according to the *Herald's* picture of market rates, were being invited to lose twelve dollars on every hundred they lent. The *Herald* lacked words to describe the "ignorance and obstinacy which induced Congress in the teeth of the most solemn warnings" to hamper the Treasury with impracticable conditions. "As it is, the government has no money; Mr Chase does not know where to get any; the banks see no chance of profit and some prospect of loss in loading themselves with Treasury notes; and the public, disgusted at their money being demanded of them at a rate fixed by the borrower alone, hang back and evince no anxiety to operate in government securities." The *Independent* also scolded Congress for the conditions it had set. For investors to buy bonds at par which were going down to ninety-five or ninety "is never a pleasant operation," the *Independent's* guess at the market's discount being more moderate than the *Herald's.* The government's penny-wise policy was going to keep the Treasury empty. The press also continued to find fault with the omission by Congress of the original bill's usual assignment of certain revenues to the payment of interest on the government's borrowing and to the repayment of principal, for such departures from the customary impaired the confidence of investors. The *Herald* felt especially put out at "Mr Fessenden's abominably stupid loan act," called his because the bill was adopted, with revisions, from the original made by him as chairman of the Senate Finance Committee. And yet, the *Herald* said, should Wall Street accede and "take the loan at the terms fixed by Congress, the storm may be averted." The press seems to have been unaware that the assignment of revenues, which had been omitted from the loan act, had been put later, at Senator Fessenden's insistence, in the revenue act.[5]

The banks were in a very unfamiliar and uneasy situation. The abundance and idleness of their reserves put them under pressure to lend, but they faced a revolutionary change in their business, with a different kind of borrower. Personally Secretary Chase was a stranger to them except as a Westerner of political prominence, and the amounts he needed to borrow were prodigious. Loans to the government had always been small and never the overshadowing venture they were about to become. Banking in principle and practice had been till then characteristically commercial in that banks lent almost exclusively to merchants engaged in the buying and selling of commodities at wholesale. There were loans by city banks on corporate shares and bonds, but they were not orthodox nor was their volume great. Good bankers filled their portfolios with notes and drafts which financed specific transactions in commodities and which, when acquired, were within two or three months of maturity. They could do this because business, in the absence of twentieth-century manufacturing, transportation, and the service of what are called utilities, was itself mainly commercial, that is, a matter of trade in commodities and the source of the most active and immediate demand for credit. They thought it obligatory to do so because their deposit and note liabilities, being payable on demand, logically required that they hold liquid assets and cash which would keep them in readiness to meet that demand. And since the Americans were not yet a nation of investors, there was no great market for securities, such as there is to-day, in which large holdings of bonds could be sold readily. Consequently the bankers faced alarming uncertainties, intensified by the *mélange* of information and misinformation in the press, when the Secretary of the Treasury came up from Washington to sell them government notes in an amount greater by many times than they had ever bought before or than experience assured them they could manage.[6]

A number of other things bothered the bankers. One was their fresh memory of the panic of 1857, which but four years earlier had made most of them insolvent temporarily and had permanently destroyed some of their former competitors. They knew what trouble was. Still other difficulties lay in their mutual jealousies and fears. There were nearly sixty banks in Manhattan, and the numerous small banks regarded the power of the strong ones with restless misgivings. The few large and powerful ones regarded the irresponsibility of the small ones with uneasiness and contempt. All were afraid of their creditors as well as their competitors. The necessity and advantage of co-operation was beginning to be recognized, but the tradition of cutthroat rivalry and rugged individualism persisted. Clearly as they saw the government's need, many of the best of them doubted their moral and legal right to jeopardize their solvency and the claims of their creditors in favor of the United States Treasury. Some of the bankers were Republicans, some were Democrats, and political disagreement sometimes influenced business judgment, sometimes not. The bankers varied in their differences with one another about as much as in their common differences with the Secretary. But they were as one in realizing that they should not hold permanently the government obligations they were to take and in fearing lest they have to do so and end up holding slow assets and threatened with quick liabilities.

In contrast to the divided and distracted bankers, the Secretary of the Treasury had only himself to satisfy, and he possessed a cast-iron confidence in his own judgment which enabled him to shed any protests or pleas not to his liking. To the bankers he was the most important man in Washington, as he was to a vast number of others who for other than financial reasons thought he should be in the office Lincoln occupied. He was big, handsome, ceremonious, imperturbable; and the bankers seemed less like lenders negotiating with him than bees thrown into a dither by a disturber of their hive.

Negotiations began, according to George S. Coe, president of the American Exchange Bank, with his proposal that the banks which were to participate in the loan to the Treasury unite as the New York city banks had done when they had associated themselves with one another nine months earlier, a fortnight after Lincoln's election, for the purpose of making advances to the Treasury. The new and larger association would include banks in general throughout the North. The proposal, Coe reported later, "met the hearty approbation" of the bankers "and arrested the earnest attention of the Secretary," who later, however, in his December report to Congress, let it appear that the proposal was his. The representatives of the Boston and Philadelphia banks acquiesced at once; "it was greatly desired to include also the banks of the West," but it could not be done. The only banking organizations out there "under a compacted system," according to Coe, were those of Ohio, Indiana, and Missouri; to get the first two proved impracticable, and Missouri in August 1861—its banks "surrounded by combatants"—was in a state of political and military chaos amidst the contentions of Governor Claiborne Jackson, Congressman Frank Blair, General Nathaniel Lyon, and General John C. Frémont. So the procedure was limited to the banks of the three cities. Put in general terms, the plan was that the banks advance fifty millions to start with and then a second and a third fifty, through three periods of about sixty days each. The banks would be reimbursed as soon as possible from sales of the obligations to the public. They were to depend on conditions over which they had no control except by prayer.

For the public upon whose purchases they were dependent was either sophisticatedly doubtful of the federal government's credit or unsophisticatedly mistrustful of investment in anything less tangible than real estate.[7]

II

Plans for the advances having been agreed to in principle, Chase and the bankers at once collided over the form in which the advances were to be made. The bankers knowing what should be done, and having heard and read that an amendment to the sub-Treasury act had authorized it, supposed the procedure to be followed was a simple matter of the Treasury's accepting the means of payment which other borrowers accepted and which "the experience of all civilized nations had found most efficient." That is, the sums lent to the Treasury would be credited to it on the banks' books and the Treasury would make its payments to the government's creditors by check. The banks would retain their needed gold reserves. Everyone in Wall Street said so. It was as late as 15 August that the *Journal of Commerce*, denouncing the amendment, reported that "no specie" was to be delivered by the banks to the sub-Treasury; instead the government was "to make its disbursements" by drawing on them. Other papers, praising the change, said the same. Copperheads denounced the procedure; patriots praised it. Well the latter might. This was the nineteenth century, a great crisis was faced, and it was time for the Treasury to adopt a monetary practice appropriate to an age of steam, credit, and artillery.[8]

Instead, to the consternation of the bankers, Chase refused to do what everyone, whether for or against, understood was the purpose of Congress when it authorized him to suspend the specie requirements of the independent Treasury act. According to Coe, the Secretary "declared upon his authority as finance minister, and from his personal knowledge of its purpose" that the amendment "had no such meaning or intent" as the bankers supposed.

He would still require what he borrowed to be delivered to him in gold—"not instantly," as Thaddeus Stevens had explained to the House and as the *Boston Daily Advertiser* told its readers—but at something like weekly intervals. Disbursements would be made directly to the government's creditors by Treasury warrant, not by bank check.[9]

So it was. Chase did have the banks deliver gold to him in the amounts they advanced, and he did make disbursements to the government's creditors in gold and Treasury notes only, as the sub-Treasury act had long stipulated. He merely modified the former procedure by calling for the gold at convenient intervals, as if to kill the banks by inches and not at one blow. And what he said when his friend Judge Nash wrote him from Gallipolis a few weeks later, repeating that he should make his disbursements through the banks, was that "until Congress shall decide otherwise, I must execute the law as it exists and receive and pay out only coin and government notes." The next year in his annual report to Congress he remarked, as a matter of course, and despite the amendment, that "the law confines national payments and receipts to coin and notes of the United States" and that all federal officials "must observe and enforce this law." That is, the independent Treasury act had not been altered in its essential purpose, if at all, for the Treasury's withdrawals "on the instant" of the money lent it in the small amounts typical of the past had been a custom rather than a literal requirement of the statute. Besides the Secretary, Hooper and Sherman, in the House and in the Senate, said the same thing.[10]

Not everyone, by any means, was surprised as the bankers were by Chase's action under the amendment. The *Independent* certainly had not been, nor Thaddeus Stevens, though Senator Fessenden probably was. Up in Boston, the same day, 15 August, that the *Journal of Commerce* in New York said "no specie" was to be delivered to the Treasury by the banks, the editor of the *Daily Advertiser*, who had already explained the force of the amendment in Chase's terms and thought them satisfactory, told his read-

80

ers that the difficulties in the way of the advances "would have been vastly greater but for the judicious legislation of Congress," which, he implied, allowed time for transfers to be made. For, he said, Boston's share of the advance "will very likely exceed the total amount of specie in bank in this city," and "a heavy draft would be made even upon the immense reserves of New York, but for the suspension of the rule forbidding government deposits in private institutions." New York would, indeed, have delivered more than half its reserves in a single transaction and done it three times between August and February—by which time specie payments had stopped. Though the *Daily Advertiser* correctly saw in the amendment no more than authorization of periodic in lieu of "instant" deliveries of back-breaking sums to the sub-Treasuries, it was evidently aware of the bankers' alarm and offered the assurance that "Mr Chase will use his powers with moderation." The amendment seems to have been read carefully in Boston and in New York not. It is odd that, though the *Daily Advertiser* explained the amendment as administered, it did not mention the common misinterpretation of it repeated by the bankers.[11]

Sometime after the first conference on the advances, instead of saying merely that what the bankers wanted was forbidden by law, Chase also argued that what they wanted would have been essentially bad. He wrote John E. Williams, president of the Metropolitan Bank of New York, that "however harmless or beneficial" the Treasury's use of bank funds for disbursement might be "if confined to the New York banks"—whose strength he indirectly conceded —it would result in a general use of bank notes in Treasury disbursements, in consequent over-expansion of the note issues, and lastly in "vast injuries to the sound banks."[12]

This was fanciful. What the bankers expected would have resulted in greater bank deposit entries, in the Treasury's use of checks for large payments and bank notes for small, and in no injuries to sound banks—in all a nor-

81

mal, reasonable, and safe procedure for the Secretary no less than everyone else.

Sometime later Chase also wrote John T. Trowbridge of Boston that the bankers "had constantly urged" him to "draw directly upon them for the sums . . . placed on their books to the credit of the government." He had asked them, he said, in what funds his drafts would be paid, and, when they answered, he had then put their answer in his own words: "That is to say, in coin if the holder insists on coin and the bank is able and willing to pay; but in bank notes if he will consent to receive bank notes." This is not what their answer would have been; it was merely an easier one for him to rebut. For, he told Trowbridge, he had said: "I can not consent to this, gentlemen. You ask me to borrow the credit of local banks in the form of circulation. I prefer to put the credit of the people into notes and use them as money." His resolution, he wrote, was "seen to be unalterable." But again, as always, he was thinking of bank notes, as the banks were not.[13]

In this letter to Trowbridge, Chase also reports that the bankers talked of the limit to the amount of bonds they could hold and thought him insufficiently considerate about other things, the rate of interest especially. So, he told his correspondent, he was "obliged to be very firm and to say: 'Gentlemen, I am sure you wish to do all you can. I hope you will find that you can take the loans required on terms which can be admitted. If not, I must go back to Washington and issue notes for circulation; for, gentlemen, the war must go on until this rebellion is put down, if we have to put out paper until it takes a thousand dollars to buy a breakfast.' "[14]

This was a *non sequitur* of remarkable proportions. It was also a threat of the very evil he professed to be avoiding—"vast injuries to the sound banks." The bankers had not suggested that the effort to put down the rebellion be stopped. Nor, being banks with a deposit business and very little circulation, had they expected the Treasury to pay its bills with bank notes. But the Secretary implied that they had and that disobedience to his wishes obstructed the cause of the Union. The contrary was true. His statement is the worse because his words as quoted were written down in cold blood some time after he spoke and whether precisely as uttered or not they were in a form that must have satisfied him. Williams, in a letter to Chase a few weeks later, confirmed what Chase told Trowbridge he had said. Chase's false logic and lofty manner must have cowed and confused the bankers so much that they could contrive no proper response. Any of them, however, who had been reading sonnets recently might have thought of Shakespeare's words about "folly, doctor-like, controlling skill."[15]

To the bankers the gravamen of Chase's refusal lay in its threat to their existence. But unlike Br'er Rabbit, whose argument against his being eaten by Br'er Wolf was that it would violate the law, the bankers seem to have neglected the consideration, which should have embarrassed Chase, that his demands would force them to disobey the state laws to which they were subject. As Fessenden a week before had told the Senate, the states commonly required banks to maintain reserves in proportion to their deposit and note liabilities. Everywhere banks were required to pay their creditors in specie; a failure to do so exposed them to insolvency proceedings and forfeiture of their corporate charters. In the past legislatures had validated general suspensions, but it was uncertain what they would do in the future, except in New York, where the constitution of 1845 forbade any such indulgence. Though New York banks were not under a statutory reserve requirement, those in the city of New York were under a voluntary agreement to maintain reserves of not less than twenty-five per cent of their liabilities. Yet these laws and contracts, in the judgment of any good banker, would be secondary to his basic obligation, moral and practical, to maintain his solvency, which the Secretary of the Treasury was going to make it difficult to do, if not impossible.

Their resistance was useless. Chase seems to have hypnotized them, and still more the press. At the time, the autumn of 1861 and a year before emancipation, the Lincoln Administration was out of favor with the abolitionist and radical Republicans. This was not merely because it was waging war without obvious success but even more because while stressing preservation of the Union and courting the border states, it was keeping as quiet as it could about slavery and punishment of the detested Southern leaders. Its policy did not sit well with that of the New York *Independent* and the *Tribune*, though Horace Greeley himself remained friendly to Chase. But it was agreeable to James Gordon Bennett of the *Herald*, who was tender toward slavery. In these circumstances, incongruously, Chase had the personal support of the *Tribune, Times,* and *Herald* all at the same time. The *Times*, within a week of having joyously approved the scuttling of the independent Treasury act, had turned around after Chase's arrival in New York and argued confusedly that the banks should accept his terms. They should assure him, the *Times* said in an editorial, that they would take his bonds and pay him for them "the same as they would pay an ordinary creditor or depositor." This was exactly what the bankers wanted and what Chase did not. By yielding to him the *Times* said, "they could if they chose retain the larger portion of their specie." Of course they chose to retain their specie —it constituted their reserves—but by yielding to Chase they would lose it. The *Herald* was equally irrational. In a wandering, prolix defense of the Secretary later, 23 September, it said that so long as the government had to pay a million a day to troops, sailors, contractors, commissaries, builders, and merchants, the coin disbursed by it could go nowhere but back into the banks. This was untrue: the coin could go into hoards and into the strong-boxes of speculators. It could leave the country. But there are times when the truth seems deadly, and the loyal press was driven to utter nonsense in support of morale and the Administration. It was attempting to convince the bankers that they should not rock the boat, but it gave no assurance that the Secretary would not do so; for if they did not meet Chase's terms he would issue Treasury notes till it took a thousand dollars to buy a breakfast.[16]

III

The loan negotiations continued for a week, the Secretary standing still like Gibraltar, the bankers tearing their hair, and the press nagging them daily. The *Herald* reminded them that their reserves had mounted to "double the highest" ever held before and were still growing. "Does not this warrant some liberality to the government?" it asked. The Boston banks, the *Herald* reported, had formally authorized a committee of theirs to inform those in New York and Philadelphia that "the banks and bankers of Boston and of the state of Massachusetts and its people are prepared, ready, and willing and determined to do all in their power in view of their duty to themselves, their trusts, and their country to aid it in suppressing the present rebellion by furnishing men and money to the utmost extent of their ability now, henceforth, and forever." A little later, however, when the Boston banks realized that what they lent the Treasury must actually be delivered in gold and that what they would have to deliver might exceed what they had, they declined to lend as much as they had said. To compensate for this, the New York banks increased their own part correspondingly.[17]

Though there was some regret later that Boston's courage in backing up had not been emulated by New York and Philadelphia, the impulse to intransigence was not strong enough to resist Chase. Arrangements were completed 16 August after a week of negotiations, and the bankers signed their suicide pact. Badgered by the forced optimism of the press, embarrassed by the abundance of their idle funds, by their own lack of unity, and by knowledge that they must do something, they agreed to do what they did not believe that they could do. They adopted a resolution thanking Secretary Chase for his "patient, clear, and forcible manner" of presentation and affirming their "confidence in the wisdom, integrity, and efficiency" with which the Treasury was managed; but they also adopted one in which they betrayed their veiled misgivings by begging "leave respectfully to express to the President of the United States" their confident expectation, "in assuming the grave responsibility of furnishing means to sustain the government," that federal affairs would be so conducted "as to insure vigor, integrity, economy, and efficiency" in every department. The *Times* gave them its generous approval and kindly urged investors to hurry with their subscriptions lest they find the government's obligations all taken. It noted that the advances were being promised by the capitalists "without a qualification"—but it also recorded their nervous expectation of fair treatment. Bank reserves were high and gold was still flowing steadily in. The loan, the *Times* said, was opportune, "since dullness of general trade" would make banking unprofitable. Business would be quickened by it, for the funds were "to be expended in provisions, clothing, payment of soldiers and officers, and the like."[18]

According to the plan agreed upon between Chase and the bankers, advances by the latter to the Treasury, aggregating fifty million dollars in gold delivered to the sub-Treasuries, began the latter part of August. The first fifty millions was completed the latter part of October. The banks were given receipts for the amounts delivered, the negotiable notes themselves not being ready. The Treasury was also to issue more demand notes of small denominations in payments to its creditors. The banks had the privilege of making a second series of advances aggregating another fifty millions, and this they undertook 15 October, about a week before completing deliveries of the first fifty. They also had the privilege of undertaking delivery of a third fifty, to which they agreed 15 November. The program was sometimes called "the hundred and fifty millions loan" and sometimes, toward the beginning, "the fifty millions loan."[19]

The bankers, forced to do nothing or to take government

obligations of doubtful value and part with gold needed for the reserves which their business obligations and the laws of certain of their states required, had no choice but to go along with the Secretary. For their success, conditions the most favorable—military, economic, and political—had to persist. No good banker could expect such fortune. In brighter circumstances ten months later, 12 June 1862, a report of the New York loan committee, of which the City Bank's president, Moses Taylor, was chairman, described the gloom of the situation when the agreement was made. "The credit of the government had become impaired to such a degree that a large loan could not be obtained in any ordinary way, nor even a small temporary loan except for a very short period at a high rate of interest. Men's hearts failed them; the rebellion was upon so large a scale and had so unexpectedly broken out and raged with such fury that to subdue it seemed to most persons to be impossible. Then it was, after careful deliberation and consultation with the Secretary of the United States Treasury, that the banks decided it to be wise for them to depart from their usual and legitimate business and sustain the government credit and stand or fall with it."[20]

IV

Fear aroused by Chase's demand that what he borrowed be delivered in gold became aggravated by his efforts to replace coin with the fifty millions of demand notes that Congress had authorized. These notes were an inchoate sort of national currency, which eventually it was his important but imperfect achievement to provide. His purpose in this matter was practical and statesmanlike. He wanted the federal government to resume its constitutional responsibility over money, which President Jackson had abandoned thirty years before when he vetoed the charter of the United States Bank. This purpose was one that, in vague terms probably, Chase long had held. In his inaugural address as governor of Ohio in 1856 he had said: "A sound and suf-

ficient currency is indispensable to the welfare of every
civilized community. . . . Such a currency, however, is only
attainable through the legislation of Congress and the
action of the general government." Now in October 1861,
two months after the amendment was enacted, he wrote
Joseph Medill, editor of the *Chicago Tribune*: "For myself,
I never have entertained a doubt that it was the duty of
the general government to furnish a national currency.
Its neglect of this duty has cost the people as much as
this war will cost them. It must now be performed, not
merely as a duty but as a matter of necessary policy." In
his December report to Congress, he wrote: "It is too clear
to be reasonably disputed" that the federal government was
authorized by the Constitution "to control the credit
circulation."[21]

But just how that duty was to be performed was probably not yet resolved by him. There were two possible
courses. One was the use of Treasury notes, not merely as
evidence of occasional public debt but as a circulating
medium under federal control. This course had been mentioned casually by Alexander Hamilton, it had been considered by Thomas Jefferson as a means of replacing state
bank notes, which he deemed a nuisance and unconstitutional besides, and it had been advocated energetically,
but not publicly, by a Tennessee friend of Andrew Jackson's, John Catron, whose advice Jackson spurned but
whom he appointed to the Supreme Court in 1837 and
who was still a member of the Court in 1861. Chase, as a
constitutional lawyer, would be aware of this possible arrangement, for it was no secret, though so far little more
than theoretical. The alternative, which he adopted eventually, was the continued use of bank notes but on the
security of federal bonds, not state, issued by banks incorporated under federal law, not state.[22]

Chase seems to have attempted the first of these alternatives before choosing the second and to have initiated it
with the recommendation to the special session that the
issue of fifty millions of Treasury notes be authorized—

which was done. He asked for no legislation differentiating these notes from Treasury notes previously authorized, except that they bore no interest, but tried simply by administrative action to prevent their being mere "paper money." They were nowise a legal tender but simply obligations of the federal government which professed to be redeemable in specie on demand. Though he did not say that he was trying to initiate a new national currency, his silence cannot be taken as evidence that he saw in the notes no such significance. On the contrary, in his letter to Medill he had avowed his commitment to a national currency, and in his December report, when he first proposed such a currency explicitly and officially, though not in precise terms, he alluded to his scheme as already having been "partially adopted." Only fifty million dollars had been recommended and authorized, but since the amount of state bank notes in circulation was reckoned to be about two hundred millions, the contemplated shift to federal control, if successful, was expected to provide a market of that sizable amount for federal bonds.[23]

Now, as soon as Chase had found it was being said that the specie requirement of the sub-Treasury act should be suspended lest the banks be unable to lend him the money he had been authorized to borrow, he could not have failed to see that the currency reform he conceived faced a fatal threat; for his notes would require a gold reserve in the Treasury for their redemption and unless he got the gold from the banks he would have no such reserve. Having already in mind a recovery from the states of the federal government's constitutional monetary authority usurped by them, he could not have welcomed a change in the law which would permit—but in effect probably require—that he accept monetary services which he held to be unconstitutional. This acceptance would strengthen the position of the state banks, confirm their independence of federal control, and make the achievement of a national currency hopelessly difficult. So, if he accepted the amendment, any plan for a national currency of Treasury notes redeemable on demand would have to be foregone, and the Treasury would be sealed fast to the state banks and to a currency the Constitution forbade. On the other hand, if he opposed the amendment, he would have to explain why; he would have to divulge his purposed reform—which was no less constitutional than the war he had to finance—and raise a storm not only with the banks but with the states whose bonds were held by the banks. He very evidently decided at once, for time was short, upon a course he very evidently followed. He had told Fessenden, and probably others, that he disliked the idea but also that he submitted to the judgment of Congress. Then, when given the committee's draft in accordance with protocol, he obligingly adapted it to his own quite different purpose, omitting the authorization he did not want and leaving the requirement that what the banks lent the Treasury be delivered in gold but in periodic instalments instead of all at once. What he returned to Fessenden and Stevens was a version which sounded purposeful but was so wordy and dense that it deceived both its friends and its enemies—its friends hurriedly supposing that it still meant what they intended and its enemies hurriedly supposing that it still meant what they feared. Despite the changes in language, the requirement of the mighty independent Treasury act was left in substance unchanged, as Chase asserted soon afterwards. The anfractuosities of his mind did not always achieve such success. But by first pompously allowing the specie requirement of the act to be "suspended," his language wandered off into an obscure jargon which sounded impressive but meant little. And that little was far from what the amendment's sponsors intended. It is certainly not believable that the amendment's friends, who understood their purpose perfectly and explained clearly what must be done if the government were to get the money it required, would themselves make the amendment say the opposite of what they intended. In the stress and stir of adjournment it was accepted by both committees and both chambers.

The next day, however, as recounted in the previous chapter, a few statesmen, too few and too late, rose to rescue the independent Treasury act from emasculation. Thereupon Fessenden, in the Senate, explained and defended the amendment, but not at all as Thaddeus Stevens had explained it in the House the day before. Both men testified to Chase's approval of it as adopted, but they offered very different explanations—Fessenden's identical with that of the bankers, Stevens' with that of Chase. No mention was made of conflict between the two.

The text of the amendment, so differently interpreted, reads as follows:

> Sec. 6: *And be it further enacted,* That the provisions of the act entitled "An act to provide for the better organization of the Treasury and for the collection, safe-keeping, transfer, and disbursements of the public revenue"; passed August sixth, eighteen hundred and forty-six, be and the same are hereby suspended, so far as to allow the Secretary of the Treasury to deposit any of the moneys obtained on any of the loans now authorized by law, to the credit of the Treasurer of the United States, in such solvent specie-paying banks as he may select; and the said moneys, so deposited, may be withdrawn from such deposit for deposit with the regular authorized depositaries or for the payment of public dues, or paid in redemption of the notes authorized to be issued under this act, or the act to which this is supplementary, payable on demand, as may seem expedient to, or be directed by, the Secretary of the Treasury.
>
> (The foregoing was Section 6 of an Act supplementary to an Act entitled "An Act to Authorize a National Loan and for other purposes," approved 5 August 1861. 12 US Statutes 313, Ch. xlvi.)

To put it pointedly, the circumstances embrace a clear concatenation of facts respecting the amendment: that Fessenden clearly explained the amendment to the Senate as making the lending banks government depositories, that

91

Chase had already expressed disapproval of such arrangement, that a draft of the amendment was submitted to Chase for revision, and that what was returned by him with his approval did not at all suspend the specie requirement but maintained it, as he and others repeatedly said. In the absence of any more direct evidence than the foregoing, one has the choice of concluding either that the drafted amendment reached Chase authorizing what its sponsors intended and was wordily altered by him to authorize what *he* intended, or that it reached him authorizing what he intended and the opposite of what they intended, in which case there was nothing he need do but supply wordy evidence that the draft had received his careful attention. I do not see how the second alternative can be preferred to the first.

If my conclusion be accepted, the episode may be taken to show how much better it is to do things quietly and obscurely than with a lot of noise and illumination. For as the amendment read, it enabled the Secretary to meet the bankers in New York with a simple and truthful declaration that the law did not permit him to do what they wanted. It spared him the need of bringing into premature discussion his plan for a national currency. And it avoided having his reform bastardized by the lack of a reserve in the Treasury for redemption of his Treasury notes. The success of Secretary Chase in this episode contrasts favorably with the failure of Secretary Seward a few weeks before to make himself President Lincoln's Prime Minister and of Chase's own effort in December of the following year to achieve changes, with the radical Republican senators' help, which would put the Administration under a guidance— his own—much more competent, he doubtless thought, than President Lincoln's.*

To what the banks really wanted, of course—the Treasury's use of deposit credit disbursed by check—Chase seems not to have given a thought. He never mentioned it. One

---

* On the respective efforts of Seward and Chase to which I refer, see E. D. Adams, Chapter IV, and Nevins II, page 352ff.

might suppose he had never been told that bank checks existed and that they effected a greater volume of payments than bank notes did—that they were indeed a more important part of the country's means of payment than bank notes were. It is doubtful if Chase ever understood the substantial identity between credit represented by a bank note in the hands of the public and credit entered on the banks' books in favor of depositors. In this his understanding was that of nearly every one of his contemporaries. Bank notes were a kind of money, but to him, probably, deposit credit was merely something of record—a detail of accounting and a check no more monetary than a lease, a deed, a conveyance, a mortgage, or other document dealing with monetary payments. Consequently he would think (or feel) that acceptance by him of the banks' notes was more seriously compromising than acceptance for a few days, as a mere matter of material convenience, of a book credit about to be discharged in gold. Being so compromising, it would strengthen the opposition to his projected national currency. Furthermore, had he considered it seriously, he or members of his staff would probably have condemned the arrangement as obviously complex and burdensome. Was the Treasury to have a thousand checking accounts, more or less, and if so how would it manage them? It would borrow from any bank that would lend, but could it leave the money in any and every bank? Some means of concentrating accounts might be devised, but how? The Treasury of 1861 was not used to that sort of thing, being at its best when doing least.

V

Before going to New York for his first conference with the bankers about the loan he sought, Chase had begun his effort to get acceptance of the demand notes by taking them himself in payment of his salary and getting other officials to do the same. But the notes were given in general a suspicious and hostile greeting. The Secretary himself in July had denounced paper money, and now, a month later, he was trying to get it accepted. At least one of his colleagues in the Cabinet, the bristly Gideon Welles, called him, in the silence of his diary, a reckless inflationist. Chase intended to get the banks' gold and evidently hoped that his possession of it and a professed readiness to redeem the first notes presented for redemption would assure the public that the notes were "good"; when that assurance was established, the demand for redemption would cease. He would do as Secretary of the Treasury what honest and successful bankers had been doing for years. But that was something he could not do without winning first the confidence and help of such bankers themselves, most of whom thought him, as a financier, ignorant and untrustworthy. He had therefore no protection for his scheme from the great majority of the Americans, who had long been taught by Jefferson and Jackson and daily experience to shun paper money—if possible—as they would the devil himself. Their fear of paper money ran back to the South Sea Bubble and had been confirmed by the continental currency and the *assignats* of the American and French Revolutions. No bit of folklore was more plausible, excusable, and stubbornly cherished. The prevailing reverence for hard money, so soon to be abandoned in favor of the greenbacks toward which Chase was pushing affairs with no conscious intent, is apparent in the holy horror displayed by statesmen when the independent Treasury act was threatened with abandonment. It was true that governments often tried to get something for nothing, and that they could not in all circumstances be trusted. And now, after having been warned for years to beware of paper not redeemable in coin, people found themselves being offered just such paper and offered it by a debtor known to be in trouble.

In one quarter, the laborers on government works pushed back the notes offered them in payment of their wages and demanded to be paid in "money"—unimpressed by the sub-Treasury's "explanation" that the notes *were* money.

In another quarter, bankers, more learned than laborers in such matters but no better satisfied, protested to Chase with even more vehemence and pertinacity. One of the most prominent of them, James Gallatin, was said to be ordering the notes to be "thrown out"—refused, that is—by his tellers. Bankers obstructed their use partly because they resented the government's interference with their own privilege of note issue but more importantly because the deposit liability which they incurred by acceptance of the notes was one which they were obliged to discharge in legal tender, which meant gold. If a banker were asked to cash a government note, he could refuse; but if he accepted one of Chase's demand notes on deposit, and entered it on his ledger as such, he could not refuse to cash, with gold, a check drawn against the deposit. This put him under a liability that the government evaded. In brief, the Secretary's plans would force the banks into a situation where they would have to take at par notes which were of uncertain value, which bore no interest, which almost certainly would not be paid on demand, which could not be thrust off readily onto another taker, and which threatened to deplete, dollar for dollar, their necessary reserves.* This was not true of all banks, however. Those with few or no notes of their own were disposed to hope with the Treasury that its new demand notes would be accepted generally; because if they were the demand for coin would be

---

* Modern governments have taken over possession of all domestic gold, but they have been able to make their credit and authority a substitute that now, legally and in practice, is of equal value and greater convenience. In the remote past, the sovereign—at his best— used his power to provide coins whose weight and fineness made them, for his own people and for others, an acceptable means of payment and measure of value. To-day, domestically, the sovereign power uses its authority to provide an acceptable currency that is defined in terms of gold and, though without intrinsic value, has become universally exchangeable within the nation for goods and services at conventional or market rates. It can also, of course, use its authority to its own advantage much as monarchs used to do by clipping coins and debasing their content. In contrasting past practice with present, I do not imply that the present is perfect. It is, however, accepted and workable in the existing economy.

abated. Singleton A. Mercer, president of Philadelphia's largest bank, the Farmers and Merchants, reported a belief that "the judicious and restrained use" of the notes would "not be prejudicial but beneficial to the designs of the Treasury and the associated banks" and that their emission should not be suspended or discontinued. The Bank of Commerce, New York, which had practically no notes circulating and whose president, John A. Stevens, was a close adviser to the Secretary, sought the notes to take the place of coin.[24]

The metropolitan press, as if in response to pleas from Washington, benevolently urged acceptance of the notes. The *Herald* was already praising them when Chase arrived in New York.* "No sane person," it said, 9 August, "can question the soundness and intrinsic value of Treasury notes. As a currency they are superior to anything we have in the country, and it can not be doubted but they will eventually supersede all other currencies." Three days later, the *Herald* declared that "it would be the greatest boon imaginable if the government could distribute a hundred millions of these Treasury notes throughout the country and so drive out of circulation the uncertain and various bank notes which are now used in trade." Several weeks later, 5 October, the *Herald* called the notes "a new national currency," but said the public still asked for gold and had to have it explained that the notes "are money." But there was "no hoarding of gold anywhere," it said optimistically 16 October; "on the contrary the people of all sections have evinced a ready willingness to receive and circulate the new paper money issued by government in the shape of United States notes, and even the drafts of

* James Gordon Bennett and his *Herald*, being Democratic, had attacked the Lincoln Administration at first. But being disciplined by the Administration's refusal to give it news, the *Herald* grew soft discriminatingly: it continued to blaze out at the Republican Congress for being ignorant, stupid, stubborn, and fatuous, but it grew considerate of Chase and fawning about Mrs Lincoln, her parties, her frocks, and her charms. No *spretae injuria formae* was to block Mr Bennett's access to news. (*New York Herald*, 7, 13, 14 August 1861.)

the disbursing officers are retained many days and weeks in the West as currency."[25]

The *Times* also was drumming for the notes as for the loan. It reported, 19 August, that the Treasury would immediately begin the gradual issue and employment of United States notes of the convenient denominations of fives, tens, and twenties, payable on demand in specie at the sub-Treasuries. The notes would take the place of small gold coin. But their use would not be forced. The last of September it reported with satisfaction Mr Chase's confidence that the new currency "of United States notes payable on demand" would soon be fairly established and that in consequence the second and succeeding loan negotiations would work out "even more kindly than the first."[26]

Though the following passage from an editorial in Horace Greeley's *New York Tribune* is vague about the nature of "true paper money," its long-winded statement of contemporary opinion and practice is informative, being a mixture of understanding and misunderstanding, and typical of the way most people thought. "The convenience, the utility, the beneficence of true paper money are too palpable to need elucidation. As coined money effected an enormous saving of time and trouble in estimating values and making payments, so paper money effects a still further saving in the same direction. . . . When, instead of bowing and sweating under a heavy bag of coin, . . . the buyer simply hands out billets inscribed with thousands, hundreds, and tens of dollars, paying the fractions only in coin—or (better still) gives a check on his banker for the precise amount of each purchase, . . . the perfection of economy in time, labor, and expense would seem to have been attained in a currency worthy of and honorable to Christian civilization, wherein, although . . . ," and so on. But Mr Greeley doubted the wisdom of making such money a legal tender.[27]

It is true that in the ante-bellum period note issue was of importance to most banks—to some of greater importance than deposits. The wild-cats, typically, had no deposits at all, but though numerous, they were small and had much the same relative importance in the business world that swindlers have. That is, they were pernicious but not a dominant economic factor. The deposits of the New York, Boston, and Philadelphia banks in August 1861 were one hundred and sixty millions; their circulating notes were about a tenth of that—sixteen millions.[28]

VI

Long-lived confusion among historians over the amendment was insured later by Congressman E. G. Spaulding's account of what occurred. The second edition of his account, published in 1875, reviews action taken on the amendment and in an appendix quotes correspondence thereon. Both in his introduction and in the quoted correspondence Spaulding appears credibly as the amendment's original author, which his position on the Ways and Means Committee would warrant. In one of these letters, dated 29 March 1870 (five years before publication of the book in which it is quoted), and addressed to James S. Gibbons, a New York City banker, Spaulding says that he had expressed during the special session of 1861 "the opinion that the loan of two hundred and fifty million dollars . . . could not be made and the gold actually paid over into the sub-Treasury without so weakening the banks that they would be obliged to suspend specie payments." Accordingly, he says in his book, he had drafted an amendment permitting the funds borrowed to be left on deposit with the lending banks so that the United States Treasurer might "draw his checks directly" against those deposits "in payment of war expenses." These checks would be paid by the banks in their notes, "then redeemable on demand in gold, or in the ordinary course of business . . . they would pass through the New York Clearing House and the clearing houses of other cities and be settled and cancelled by offset without drawing large amounts of specie."* But

* An incidental oddity of Spaulding's account is that it omits what

Secretary Chase, Spaulding says in his letter to Gibbons, had opposed the amendment as "at first drafted by me" and got it "considerably modified and limited."[29]

This statement that Spaulding made in 1870 accords with Chase's expressed dislike of the idea before the amendment embodying it was brought up. In saying that Chase "modified and limited" the amendment, the statement also accords with Chase's later denial, "from his personal knowledge" of the amendment's purpose, that it authorized what the bankers said it did. But it differs radically from what Spaulding himself says five years later in his book, published in 1875. There he says nothing of changes having been made by Chase. Instead he quotes the amendment *as enacted*, presenting it as if, in that form, it were wholly his own product, and a perfect one, on authority of which Chase refused to act. Yet in his appendix he includes his letter of 1870 in which he says the amendment as at first drafted by him was "considerably modified and limited" by Chase. Thus in 1870 he blames Chase for having *garbled* the amendment; and in 1875 he blames Chase for having *disregarded* it. In 1870 he says the language of the amendment, as adopted, was the Secretary's; in 1875 he says it was his own. And he puts both stories in his book—one in his introduction and one in the appendix—but takes no notice of the direct conflict between the two. Although most contemporaries mistook what the amendment authorized as enacted, explaining it in the terms which the bankers used at the time and which Spaulding used later in his book, it is significant that two respectable journals—the *Inde-*

Fessenden stressed, namely, the requirement by state laws that banks maintain reserves of specie in proportion to their liabilities, and says nothing about the conflict involved between these laws and the specie requirement of the independent Treasury act, so far as loans to the government were concerned. The explanation of Spaulding's silence may be that in his state, New York, there was as yet no such law; it might also be that as a banker himself he considered such laws superfluous, as bankers commonly did, because the maintenance of reserves was a necessity that dominated banking, statute or no statute. Another explanation might be that though he was a successful banker and politician, he was a careless author.

pendent and the *Boston Daily Advertiser*—understood it from the first and explained it correctly as Thaddeus Stevens did at the outset, as Chase did a little later in New York "upon his authority as finance minister and from his personal knowledge of its purpose," and as John Sherman and Samuel Hooper did months later. This evidence supports Spaulding's early account of Chase's interference in the drafting of the amendment and confutes his later allegation that Chase refused to do what it authorized him to do.[30]

His letter of 1870, which gives the earlier and unquestionably the correct account of what happened, gives also the account more creditable to him (as banker, not historian) and the one more consistent with probability. For being a banker and having two banker colleagues to consult, he certainly could have said what he meant in 1861 as well as he could say it in 1870. So it is credible that his amendment as originally drawn in 1861 expressed plainly what he and other bankers wanted, that Chase garbled it to his own ends, and that this garbled version was hastily accepted and enacted without recognition of the change it had undergone. Then, too late, Spaulding recognized what Chase had done, and in his letter of 1870 he told Gibbons of it. But in 1875, instead of sticking to his statement of Chase's having "modified and limited" the sense of the amendment before its adoption, he shifted back to an assertion of Chase's disregard of its meaning. In doing this, he implied that the language of the amendment as enacted was his own. If it were, then he had been unable to say what he meant—and was still so.

It is conceivable that one phrase in the amendment might be taken to authorize disbursement of the borrowed funds by check: it is one permitting withdrawal of the funds for transfer to the regular authorized depositories *"or for the payment of public dues."* Spaulding in quoting the amendment italicizes these words, as if to imply that they did authorize the Secretary "to draw his checks directly" on the lending banks; and that, had the Secretary desired to make his payments by check, he could have interpreted the stressed words as authorizing him to do so. But the words are not those of a man who desired and earnestly intended such an interpretation—which is to say that they do not clearly convey the purpose Spaulding claims clearly enough that he meant to convey. They are more likely the words of a man who did not want to make disbursements by check, who nevertheless saw some possible occasional advantage in withdrawing specie from the banks for direct payments to government creditors instead of moving it first to the regular depositories and thence to the creditors, and who wished to use language that would combine obscurity with convenience. Spaulding himself attributes no specific meaning to the phrase and merely implies its importance by his use of italics. Given Chase's word and subsequent action, however, one discerns in the amendment the purpose Chase himself attributes to it; the purpose which Spaulding and the other bankers attributed to it is not discernible in it at all. The only effect of the amendment—and undoubtedly the only purpose of whoever put it in final form—was to avoid the requirement of daily and perhaps hourly or "instant" deliveries of gold to the Treasury as fast as loans were made. In the past, instant and complete deliveries had been a matter of course because they were small. Now, in a matter of many millions, the process was a continuing one, and it was a convenience—practically a necessity—that the money being lent currently be allowed to accumulate for occasional and periodic transfers, which in fact were made, under the terms of the amendment, every six days or so.[31]

It is hard to refrain from speculating about the curious fact that Thaddeus Stevens, chairman of the House Ways and Means Committee, explained the amendment briefly but exactly as it was later administered by Chase, and that, at the same time, Fessenden, chairman of the Senate Finance Committee, explained it at some length as its original sponsors intended it to be administered—in terms which Chase repudiated from his personal knowledge of its purpose. But I venture no more than to suppose that Stevens,

101

with his growing nationalism, was less impressed by observance of the laws and rights of the states than Fesssenden was. As to Spaulding's saying in 1870 that Chase garbled the amendment and in 1875 that Chase simply refused to comply with it, my guess is that pride as well as haste changed Spaulding's story, consciously or unconsciously—as if he hated to acknowledge that Chase had taken him in and preferred to join the bankers in their conviction that Chase was arrogantly refusing to do what the amendment authorized. Had he at once, in August 1861, detected and denounced Chase's redrafting of the amendment, he would have had solid ground under his feet; but having failed to do so, he was embarrassed. In March 1870 he still mentioned, though rather quietly, Chase's having "modified and limited" the terms of the amendment; but my guess is that by 1875—when Chase had become Chief Justice and had incurred much condemnation in the legal tender cases—Spaulding, shifting with the sands, joined in the belief of his banker friends that Chase's fault was arrogance not deviousness.

As might be supposed, the subsequent history of the amendment became one of contradictions and misunderstanding. To start with, the press reported one thing one day and another the next. For years thereafter, the bankers continued to denounce the Secretary's refusal to comply with the amendment but never criticized or acknowledged its obscurity. The historians also, one after another, slighted the amendment's language and what the legislators concerned with it had said but perpetuated the bankers' tale of Chase's refusal to carry out the amendment's purpose. Yet Chase repeatedly and openly spoke of the specie requirement of the independent Treasury act as unamended —and this without notice or contradiction by any contemporary, so far as I have discovered—except the bankers who continued like so many parrots to talk of Chase's flouting of a law that he was in fact strictly obeying. Nor were statements of the facts and allusions to them by Samuel Hooper and John Sherman given any heed. In the House,

20 February 1862, Hooper alluded to the "existing laws," which, he said, "require all government receipts and payments to be made in coin." In January, a year later, Sherman mentioned in the Senate the past proposition "that the specie clause, as it is called, of the sub-Treasury law should be repealed," plainly indicating that it had not been; and in February he said: "We were then in the peculiar condition of a nation involved in war without any currency whatever which by law could be used in the ordinary transactions of the public business." Again, years later, he repeated in his *Recollections* that at the time of which he was speaking, 1862, the Secretary of the Treasury was still "forbidden by the sub-Treasury act of 1846 to receive notes of state banks and was required to receive into and pay from the Treasury only the coin of the United States." The Treasury, Sherman repeated, had had "no authority to receive from individuals or banks any money but coin." His statement took no cognizance of any amendment whatever.[32]

Yet Albert S. Bolles, in his *Financial History*, 1886, said only that the bankers had been right; and he questioned the wisdom of their giving in to Chase, since "they saw so clearly the need of adopting the policy recognized by Congress when authorizing the Secretary to suspend the operations of the sub-Treasury law." Bolles thought Chase "unquestionably wrong." He said nothing of any vagueness or obscurity in the amendment but seemed to take it for granted that it said what the bankers said it did.[33]

In 1895, Horace White described the amendment as "suspending the operation of the sub-Treasury act so as to allow the Secretary to deposit public money in 'solvent specie-paying banks' and to withdraw it at his own convenience and pleasure for the payment of public dues," and that, "in short, he was permitted to handle the proceeds of the three loans in whatsoever way he pleased." This meant, White said, that the Secretary could "draw checks on the banks, as an ordinary customer would do, for his various disbursements" and "allow these checks to be settled at the clearing house." The bankers, White

103

continued, very much as Bolles had done, should have made it a condition of their loan that the Secretary do so; for the latter's insistence on "carrying away the gold and scattering it through the country"—with the incidental result that "it cost a good deal to cart it around"—was a "fatal act." Had Chase done what the amendment authorized him to do, White said, suspension would have been avoided. Later, upon reading an account by Wesley Clair Mitchell, White concluded that the gold removals were not so important; but he still seemed to think that the amendment made them unnecessary.[34]

It was also in 1895 that John Sherman in his *Recollections* said the amendment of 5 August 1861 permitted the Secretary of the Treasury to have borrowed funds on deposit in banks till transferred to government depositories but did not permit him "to receive from individuals or banks any money but coin."[35]

In 1896, Professor William Graham Sumner, in his *History of Banking in the United States*, wrote that though Chase was "apparently authorized to draw" on the banks in payment of what the government owed, he "did not use this permission."[36]

In 1900, John Jay Knox, in his *History of Banking in the United States*, seems to have thought the amendment authorized to some extent what the bankers wanted; all he said was that Chase would "not, however, permit" it.[37]

In 1902, Professor Davis R. Dewey, in his *Financial History of the United States*, quoted a statement of James Gallatin that the amendment "was particularly intended to authorize drafts for disbursements against the deposits created by the taking of loans" to the government by the banks; he also mentioned the Secretary's having "strictly construed the sub-Treasury bill and insisted that the banks should make their settlements in specie." Then, more attentive to the record than his predecessors, Dewey thought that "possibly" the amendment may have intended what the bankers wanted, though its intent was "not clearly expressed." He said, however, "without attempting to locate the blame, that the first material mistake in the management of the war finances occurred when the government declined to use the bank check and the clearing house."[38]

In 1903, Professor Wesley Clair Mitchell, without offering any definite interpretation of the amendment, implied in his *History of the Greenbacks* that it authorized the Secretary to make disbursements by check, for he said Chase "declined" to do so and "permitted no modification of the sub-Treasury system." Mitchell did not mention Chase's statements that the amendment gave him no permission to do what the bankers wanted but only the Secretary's disapproval of what they wanted.[39]

In 1915, A. Barton Hepburn in his *History of Currency* restated as in an earlier edition entitled *History of Coinage and Currency*, 1903, that the banks, under the terms of the amendment, had "rightfully expected" the funds they lent Chase "to remain on deposit and be checked out to meet the government's needs as they arose."[40]

In 1947, Dr. Fritz Redlich, taking up the question afresh after it had long been left untouched, called the amendment a "half-hearted measure" for which Congress, not Chase, was responsible. He said it authorized no more than Chase said it did and doubted if bankers who thought it meant more had ever read it. Dr. Redlich, so far as I know, is the only historian of the amendment whose account of it accords with what Chase, Sherman, and Hooper said about its effect on the independent Treasury act. I differ from him only in thinking it was Chase himself who made the amendment what it was. All the other historians have accepted—or at least have not questioned—the account given by Spaulding in 1875, when after quoting the amendment—of which he claimed authorship—he very clearly explained its original purpose without explaining why, if that were its purpose, he had not made it say so.[41]

105

AUGUST TO DECEMBER 1861

I

UNDER THE arrangement with Chase, concluded 15 August 1861, the banks of New York, Boston, and Philadelphia began making the Treasury a series of advances in coin as called for by him at intervals of six days or so. These advances became less regular by winter, for the gold the Secretary took from the banks did not return to them as he supposed it would, and whether he liked it or not his calls had to be tempered to the ability of the banks to meet them. Still less regularly the banks received the three-year Treasury notes of the "national loan," which they were to sell, if they could. In order to help them, the Secretary had agreed to appeal to the people for subscriptions, and from the proceeds of these subscriptions as well as from the sale of the notes they got from him, the banks were to be reimbursed for what they had advanced.[1]

So he later told Congress. But in the appeal itself, published 3 September, the professed purpose was that "the advantages as well as the patriotic satisfaction" of lending to the government be offered "not to the capitalists of the great cities only but to the people of the whole country." The appeal had but passing effect. In cities where there was no sub-Treasury, Chase appointed agents to take subscriptions to the "national loan," and there was a brief spell of sales. Then, the agents' efforts—with some exceptions—proving insufficiently successful, the Treasury stopped them. Reasons for the failure were not recondite—the first being that the public knew little or nothing of investment securities. In an editorial effort to get the loan to the government "popularized," the *Boston Daily Advertiser* said warningly, 11 September, that "a United States loan has never hitherto been heard of far outside of the larger cities." The Treasury itself, having customarily negotiated with bankers for the relatively small loans needed in the past, had no procedure for dealing directly with the general pub-

109

lic. It was known as a borrower only in the financial centers. Then there was so far no ready supply of investment notes to deliver to purchasers. Later the same month the *Daily Advertiser* printed a report from New York that arrangements were "in progress" for supplying subscribers "at once" with notes in exchange for their money to end the "cumbrous" and "annoying" routine followed so far. But it was long before the process became prompt and comprehensive.[2]

Another difficulty was that "the people" Chase appealed to had to pay gold for the three-year notes that he was trying to sell, and they did not possess gold nor could they, by reasonable means, obtain it. Aside from the bankers who had contracted to deliver gold to him, those who had it were speculators, professional or not, who held it for sale at a premium. Some of these speculators were banks, either chartered or unchartered, outside the group of metropolitan banks in Boston, New York, and Philadelphia with which Chase had his agreement.

Chase's friend in Gallipolis, Ohio, Judge Simeon Nash, who had warned Chase back in July that his national loan would fail if he demanded gold, continued to give the Secretary sound advice, unheeded. The judge wrote again 17 September: "I wish you could receive bank paper for the popular loan and then the *people* could take a part of it; now it is limited to monied men living in towns and cities. The coin is not in the country." Nash feared "that a monetary crash [would] come" unless bank credit were accepted in place of coin. Incidentally, he told Chase, "your officers [meaning the officers in charge of the Treasury's local depositories] have sold gold" and used local bank notes to pay "for labor and produce." This, of course, was in violation of the sub-Treasury act, though the requirements of the act itself were what invited the violation. In November Judge Nash wrote Chase again that the loan was going slowly and that "the people have not the coin" demanded for the government's securities.[3]

A correspondent wrote Chase from Cincinnati: "If the

law would permit and your instructions to the United States depository had allowed him to receive bankable funds for subscriptions to the loan, the amount of them here would have been greatly enlarged. Many persons have small sums of money they would gladly invest but know nothing about exchange, have no correspondents in the eastern cities, and do not know how or where to buy gold." Another correspondent reported from Cincinnati that the loan was "not going off in this city as it should," and one reason was the requirement that notes be paid for in gold. Still another, in Pittsburgh, wrote Chase that "the loan goes slowly," in part because subscribers found it hard to get gold and had to pay a premium for it.[4]

There is also the possibility that Chase made his appeal for the national loan over-hastily, with the press unprepared and uncultivated. This is suggested by a letter of 9 September from James Gordon Bennett, publisher and editor of the *New York Herald*. Bennett acknowledged receipt of Chase's "kind note" and continued: "I wish I could do more for your department, but the iron should have been struck when it was hot. All the newspapers here and in Boston and Philadelphia should have prepared for this loan weeks ago and the movement would have been more successful."[5]

The associated city banks meanwhile had been stumbling forward with their periodic deliveries of gold to the sub-Treasury, and when Chase was in New York the last of September to arrange for the second advance of fifty millions, the program was badly behind. The *Herald* reported 30 September that the last instalment of the first fifty millions would not "be payable" till 15 October and that the Secretary wanted it sooner. The *Herald* said he wanted the remaining seventeen millions still due on the first fifty and about as much more on the second. "It might embarrass the banks very seriously to pay thirty-four or -five millions into the sub-Treasury in the course of a fortnight, especially as the Secretary's drafts are so slow in coming to hand for payment and the gold remains so long locked

111

up in the sub-Treasury." Since the New York banks had but thirty-eight millions, the demand expected of the Secretary would well-nigh strip them. But the *impasse* was got through somehow, and the *Independent* reported 3 October that the banks had "voted unanimously" to continue their advances with the second fifty millions on the same terms as before.[6]

At this second conference with the Secretary the bankers had renewed their effort to have him use book credit and let them keep their reserves. But he again refused. The *Herald* reported the matter in subdued fashion: "A slight difference of opinion," it said, "has arisen in regard to the intent of the recent act of Congress relating to the sub-Treasury. When that act was passed it was believed here that it amounted in fact to the abolition of the sub-Treasury for the time being and that henceforth or during the war the government would keep its account with such solvent banks as lent it money. . . . In effect, however, there has been no change in the system . . . Mr Chase draws as heretofore upon the sub-treasurer and not on the banks. His drafts do not constitute, as was expected, a part of the banking currency of the North but actually operate antagonistically to the banks. It is argued by many bankers who are heart and soul devoted to the government and the Union that Mr Chase would serve his own purpose better if he administered the act of last session in the sense in which it was understood here when it was passed and really used our banks as banks of deposit for the government and [here went the *Herald*'s syntax but not its grasp of the facts] by strengthening them would strengthen public confidence, without which the money now required by the government can not be borrowed."[7]

The feelings of the bankers were expressed in a vigorous letter written to Chase by John E. Williams, president of the Metropolitan Bank, New York, after this second conference. Since Chase had expressed confidence in the metropolitan banks, Williams said, he should have used their services. He said that what Chase seemed to regard as dangerous, the bankers considered essential and that what he thought would guard against suspension of specie payments in their opinion would bring it on. Recurring to the power he said had been given the Secretary to suspend the independent Treasury act's requirements he reproached Chase for declining to use it and restated the bankers' conviction of his unreasonableness and disregard of what Congress intended. Sharing the general confusion over the amendment to the sub-Treasury act, he insisted that "Congress *meant something* . . . when they passed the act of August 5th, 1861, suspending so far the sub-Treasury act as to *allow* you to do what we ask, namely, draw on the loan banks." He said that he hoped he could make Chase "understand our surprise that you should not take our judgment in this matter but rather argue on the supposition that we do not understand the legitimate operations of our own business so well as you do." And this, he said, despite the fact that "but for the banks, the Government could not pay at all. It would have been bankrupt six weeks ago."[8]

The Secretary was again in New York the middle of November to arrange a third loan of fifty millions. The sale of the three-year Treasury notes bearing seven and three-tenths per cent interest having broken down, the third loan was made on different terms from the two preceding. It was secured by bonds having twenty years to run, bearing six per cent interest, and intended for sale in Europe as well as the United States. The bonds were to go to the banks at a discount of about ten per cent, which made them yield seven per cent—a fairly marketable rate. This concession by Chase—which bound the government to pay fifty millions for forty-six—was offset by his making no promise to reimburse the banks as he had agreed to do but had not done with respect to the two preceding loans. As before, the banks engaged to deliver instalments of gold, which they began in December and completed in February. By the middle of December all their capital was in Treasury notes and bonds—except that only a portion of the notes and bonds had been delivered to them. None had been ready for delivery in August when the advances began and none were received till January; there were simply not the means of printing and engraving them in ample amounts. The banks received no securities until four months after they had been paid for, their loan committee later reported, and then the securities' value in the market was less than the price at which they had been purchased. The banks, the committee continued, "having invested their entire capitals in them, were naturally very desirous to receive their property" in order that they might sell the securities "at the earliest moment possible and before they become further depreciated." Eventually the securities recovered, thanks to the energetic salesmanship of Jay Cooke, but meanwhile the banks were surrendering their assets for receipts from the local sub-Treasury which were not negotiable and to a government to which they were loyal but in whose Administration they had little confidence.[9]

The banks could not surrender their reserves without violating the recognized basic principle of banking and the legal obligations they bore as chartered institutions. They knew that the federal statute impeding their loan to the government was to have been suspended and they had met Chase on that understanding in order to arrange with him the details of the loan he was to obtain. He had dumbfounded them by denying that any such suspension had been authorized and by demanding that what they lent him be delivered to him in gold. Angry but bewildered, they had capitulated. Then instead of disbursing the gold to the government's creditors and allowing it to be redeposited in the banks by its recipients, he had begun to accumulate it in the Treasury as a reserve for the national currency of Treasury notes which he disbursed instead. These notes, not being a legal tender as gold was, could not be counted by the banks as reserves nor were they generally acceptable to the banks' creditors—that is, their depositors—as the equivalent of the gold to which the creditors were legally entitled.[10]

II

The whole program of advances dictated by the Secretary depended for success on an uninterrupted continuance of unfailingly favorable conditions—and this, in the circumstances, was something certain not to be realized. The picture he seems to have had in mind was that of some fifty millions of dollars in gold flowing in a circuit around and around, rapidly and steadily, like a running stream turning one mill-wheel after another. The flow would begin with the banks in Boston, New York, and Philadelphia, which together held a little more than sixty millions of specie. It would start with less than a tenth of that, but be repeated every week or so for about ten weeks. The stream starting from the banks in Wall Street would be more than twice as large as those starting in State Street and Chestnut Street. The three would pour into the sub-Treasury in each of the three cities and thence would be apportioned in the amounts due each creditor of the government for materials and services furnished it. These thousands of persons, receiving the gold due them, would hasten to the sub-Treasury or agency nearest them where they would buy the government's three-year fifty dollar notes, each bearing interest at a rate of a penny a day. With this gold received from the purchasers of notes, Mr. Secretary Chase would repay the banks for their latest advance; whereupon the banks, their gold restored, would make another delivery of it to the sub-Treasury. This naive view of the way things worked—logical, theoretical, unrealistic—was simplicity itself, and may well have made the Secretary wonder why other men considered finance a difficult matter or expected a suspension of specie payments to occur. "Never, so long as I am Secretary of the Treasury," he is reported to have said of suspension, though making it as certain as anything could be.[11]

An important complication in the Secretary's scheme was his own effort to get his demand notes accepted in payment of government expenditures and simultaneously to accumulate gold in the Treasury as a reserve needed to make the notes acceptable. This engaged the Secretary in the same hoarding operation that was going on outside. The effort to pay his bills in demand notes and retain his gold increased the demand for gold and the objection to his notes. The banks were triply the victims of the procedure, as explained in the preceding chapter, being required to maintain reserves of gold in proportion to their liabilities, to pay their depositors in gold, and to deliver in gold what they lent the Secretary of the Treasury. Several times in the past they had broken down under pressure of the first two requirements. So long as Chase was Secretary of the Treasury and imposed the third requirement, they were certain to break. Not famine in Europe, nor *el dorado* in California, nor a cessation of imports—nor the actual combination of the three—could prevent the suspension of specie payments.

The Secretary's procedure began at once to provoke the suspension. The *New York Herald* reported 30 September that in the six weeks since transfers of gold to the Treasury began the specie reserves of the local banks had declined from forty-eight millions to thirty-seven, or by about one-quarter. The gold accumulated in the local sub-Treasury—some thirteen millions—about equalled what the New York banks had lost. Chase was drawing more gold from the banks than he was disbursing to the government's creditors.[12]

The banks in New York City were agreed, with minor exceptions, to maintain specie reserves equal at the least to one-quarter of their deposits and notes; and their specie, 17 August, about the time deliveries of specie to Chase began, had been twice that, inter-bank balances excepted.* Though the reserve requirements in New York were not statutory, they were in practice of more importance than those in Boston and Philadelphia that were statutory; they

* Whether balances "due to other banks" and "due from other banks" were then taken into account in published figures I do not know. But I doubt if they were.

116

were higher and concerned with a greater volume of transactions. Pennsylvania banks were required by law to maintain specie reserves equal at the least to eight per cent of their notes only. This was no requirement at all, practically speaking; but in fact the specie of the Philadelphia banks was more than three times the amount of their notes—that is, three hundred per cent as against the statutory eight per cent. It was forty per cent of their deposit and note liabilities combined. Massachusetts banks were required by law to keep specie reserves equal at the least to fifteen per cent of their deposits and notes; and the Boston banks, 17 August, reported twenty-seven per cent. Yet a few weeks later one bank was fined by the state's bank commissioners for letting its reserves fall below the fifteen per cent required by Massachusetts law. Collectively the reserve position of the banks was still strong in all three cities, especially in New York and Philadelphia—strong, that is, for the moment—and the bankers were unready to rebel. Instead they anxiously let their condition grow worse in compliance with Chase's demands.[13]

They had not long to wait. In New York, 2 September 1861, the procedure having been in effect but a fortnight, "the payments which had been made on account of the government loan had reduced the specie of some of the banks below the proportion of twenty-five per cent to net liability, which each of the associates had agreed to carry." This did not signify that the banks maintained uniform ratios, of course; the loan committee pooled the reserves of all, the excess of some offsetting the deficiencies of others. The arrangement was scarcely a happy one. The Chemical Bank (notably conservative and known as Old Bullion) held reserves, 21 September 1861, which amounted to sixty per cent of its deposit and note liabilities; the Commerce (twice as large) held reserves of thirty per cent; the two might seriously disagree about what was fair and proper, even though both held reserves above the agreed twenty-five per cent. Banks with deficient reserves were a burden to all the rest. The banks taken as a whole—in spite

117

of abundant receipts from abroad and from California—were surrendering to the Treasury more gold than was returning to them, with the result that the aggregate was slipping fatally downward. The situation, as between bank and bank and for the banks as a whole, was full of menace. In one week, 7 to 14 September, the New York City banks lost a tenth of their reserves. If that fall continued, reserves by the end of October would be down to the minimum of twenty-five per cent or below it. Though the gross amount of the metropolitan banks' reserves was still extraordinarily large, it was shrinking when it should have been increasing, and its distribution among the banks was alarmingly uneven. Chase's withdrawing their specie weekly instead of hour by hour merely gave them temporary reprieves, and the protracted inflow of gold kept lessening the loss of reserves and obscuring the mischief the Secretary was doing.[14]

III

The unprecedented inflow of gold at the moment of greatest need was the irony of good fortune running on paradoxically in the midst of bad. It put a delusive aspect on a sinister situation. In the fiscal year from July 1860 through June 1861—that is, through the presidential campaign, the heightened bitterness, Lincoln's election, the secession of one state after another, the departure from Congress of one state delegation after another, the demoralization of President Buchanan's administration in its closing months, the appropriation by the seceding states and their delegations of federal funds and federal property—including books from the Library of Congress—the loss of Fort Sumter, the growing military threat to Washington, and the collapse of the federal forces at Bull Run—through all this, the exports of foodstuffs had continued in miraculous abundance. During the same period, gold imports had been greater than ever before and nearly double those of the greatest year preceding. They continued at the same high rate beyond the end of the fiscal year, through July, August, September, and October of 1861. But they fell off so much by December that their total for the fiscal year ending 30 June 1862 was barely a third of that for the fiscal year which had ended 30 June 1861.[15]

As of that date, on the eve of the special session, the *New York Herald* had remarked that "the failure of the European food crops last year causes our export of produce to continue heavy. . . ." and in return, "specie continues to arrive by each steamer from Europe." Nearly three millions a month besides was arriving from California. In the six preceding fiscal years, 1855 to 1860 inclusive, the value of breadstuffs and provisions exported had averaged fifty-four million a year; but in the year ending 30 June 1861 it was ninety-five millions, and the year following it was a hundred and nineteen millions. These shipments and the accumulation of gold produced by them compensated a little for the want of victories in the field and for the harsh fact that Secretary Chase's bonds and penny-a-day notes were not moving into the hands of "the people" but were stuck fast in the banks, where no one—least of all the bankers—wanted them to be.[16]

Yet the *Herald*, for a time, still boasted that the banks were recovering much if not all of the gold they delivered to the Treasury. In its issue of 10 September—midway in their advances to the first fifty millions—it said that *at least half* the gold taken out of the New York banks and delivered to the sub-Treasury the previous week had returned to them "very nearly" as fast as the sub-Treasury disbursed it. Since the banks and the sub-Treasury together still had as much as they had had 17 August, "the specie is all here still and has not been hoarded or dispersed as alarmists predicted it would be." This was pushing the truth pretty far; it was as much as to say that Secretary Chase had been right in persisting with his demand for specie. A week later, 17 September, the *Herald* exclaimed that a million dollars a day had been disbursed and "will not leave the country." Learnedly but not very helpfully it added words

119

to words: "The decline in the deposits and in the loans is about what was expected. The deposits fall off as the sub-Treasury balance increases and the public withdraw their funds from banks to invest them in Treasury notes. The thirty-five million dollars lent to the government on the 19th of August appears in the discount column but not in the deposits. Had a like sum been lent to private individuals, the increase in the one would have been balanced by a corresponding increase in the other." On the 23rd, in innocent abandon, the *Herald* returned to its happy theme. "So long as the government has to pay a million a day to troops, sailors, contractors, commissaries, builders, and merchants, the coin . . . can go nowhere but into bank." Six weeks had now elapsed, the *Herald* said, 30 September, "since the banks placed their specie resources at the disposal of the government"; they had then held forty-eight millions and the sub-Treasury four; "now they hold over thirty-seven and the sub-Treasury about thirteen"; the coin was in the city still—as if it made no difference *where* in the city. Three days later, 3 October, the *Herald* mentioned gold receipts of forty millions from Europe already that year (1861). The 15th it said the country was buying but half what it was selling.[17]

In August bank reserves had been double what they had ever been before; at the end of December they were but little more than half what they had been in August. The decline had at first been barely perceptible, but at the end it became precipitate. Till then, had the gold not gone into hiding a little faster than it was received from abroad and California, the banks and the Treasury should have been bulging with it.

The *Journal of Commerce*, which had much the same kind of political axe to grind for Secretary Chase as had the *Herald*, carried on in the same fashion. It dwelt on the buoyancy in financial affairs that had been reported for weeks and mentioned the Secretary's return to New York for arrangement of the banks' second fifty millions of advances under "cheerful" conditions. It also mentioned the

120

amendment concerning suspension of the independent Treasury act's specie requirement and said, somewhat cryptically, with respect to the form of the banks' advances—"whether in specie" as theretofore or in deposit credit disbursable by the Treasury's checks to its payees—that there would be no change. It said the banks had found the advances of specie easier to maintain than had been expected, though there was some doubt about a third fifty millions. In all this the *Journal of Commerce*, like the *Herald*, expressed satisfaction because the gold stocks were remaining high, never dissatisfaction or surprise because they were not higher. And when the *Journal*, 18 September, after a month of advances by the banks to the Treasury, reported the New York banks' delivery of three and a half million more and added that "the stock of specie in New York has decreased only three million during the last month and is now more than twice as large as at the corresponding period in either of the past two years," why did it say "only"? Why, with the receipts from Europe and California, had the stock of specie decreased at all?[18]

The *Times*, 8 October, noted that western Europe's current demand for foodstuffs "relates not to the old but the acknowledged deficit of the new crop of wheat in England and France and the reported short supplies in Spain, Belgium, and Holland." A heavy demand was certain to continue "without intermission." This had been affirmed by the *Boston Daily Advertiser*, which had reported, 5 October, that the traffic of the New York Central and the Erie railways in farm products was "so enormous that the supply of cars is entirely insufficient for the freight moving toward the seaboard." The Pennsylvania had notified "its western connections that it does not desire any more western freight for New York, Boston, or Baltimore." In the same issue the *Advertiser* expected still further "heavy imports of specie from Europe" in payment "for our heavy shipments of produce" thither. "The increasing exports of foodstuffs will require the return of gold." Among other like statements in the *Advertiser* from day to day was one, 24 October, of elation over the specie movement, which promised for 1862 a balance of a hundred and fifty millions in gold; and another, 4 November, that the large receipts of specie and bullion from California and the imports of coin from Europe were together affording a larger stock of gold, in all probability, than there had ever before been in the country.[19]

The fact of these magnitudes was the more deceptive to observers because there was no demand in the money market, aside from the Treasury's. Money was easy, the *Boston Daily Advertiser* kept saying. Money was never more abundant, the accumulation of gold from Europe and California was surpassing anything so far known. The total receipts for the fiscal year, instead of reaching the *Advertiser's* estimate of one hundred and fifty millions, turned out to be less than half of that. The idleness of funds, the lifeless demand for them, sharpened attention to the abundance of bank reserves but dulled it to realization that they were less abundant than they should be.[20]

The specie reserves of the New York city banks did not recover the high levels at which they stood when the banks' advances to the Treasury began. In late October they were twenty to twenty-five per cent lower than in August and September. If no reference be made to the amounts of gold received from Europe and California, the amounts held through the weeks of autumn look like stability and put a persuasive gloss on the journalists' optimism. But with the indicated amounts *held* by the banks and the Treasury, with the indicated amounts *received* by the banks and the Treasury, with the indicated advances and disbursements, the bank reserves should not have merely held steady—they should have become larger and larger. Since they did not, but scarcely held their own till the moment in December when they fell over the brink, it is evident that private hoarding roughly equal to current receipts had been going on since late October at least.[21]

IV

And now, instead of a spectacular turn for the better, there came a spectacular turn for the worse. It had begun, 21 October, in the rout of Union forces at Ball's Bluff, twenty miles up the Potomac from Washington. The engagement had been smaller than at Bull Run three months earlier but ravaging to morale nevertheless. Then, less than three weeks later, Captain Charles Wilkes, in command of the U.S.S. *San Jacinto*, had stopped the British R.M.S. *Trent* on its homeward course between Cuba and the Bahamas, 8 November, and had had his officers forcibly remove from it four passengers. These were James M. Mason and John Slidell, Confederate commissioners to Britain and France respectively, and their two secretaries. When the news reached the public some ten days later, there was juvenile elation among the vast number of anglophobes in the North. They made a hero of Captain Wilkes at once and professed a jingo readiness to fight everybody —Great Britain, for the third time, if she wished, as well as the South. Even the *Boston Daily Advertiser*, swept off its feet, reported the exploit of Captain Wilkes sympathetically. "A thrill of delight ran through the land," it said; and though the *Advertiser* acknowledged that the legality of the action was in doubt, it showed no sign of alarm.[22]

But in the stock market realism prevailed, and prices fell sharply under what the *Herald* called "a concerted bear attack." There was also an advance in exchange with London which excited Wall Street, shocked the *Herald*, and brought down charges of treason on brokers and bankers. The *Times*, 14 December, reported that exchange was almost up to the gold points. The market had repeated sinking spells. "There is an uneasy feeling," the *Journal of Commerce* reported, 21 November, "in certain quarters of the financial circle and a great deal of unnecessary alarm, as it appears to us, growing out of anticipated trouble in our foreign relations." Foreign exchange continued heavy. The

23rd the *Journal* reported the market "less buoyant," but found difficulty in telling why, except that some people had fears about what Britain would do. The 24th the market broke again. The 25th it was still excited; francs and sterling were in demand; there was a report that London expected the American banks to suspend shortly. The uneasiness continued on into December, the market waiting for news from Europe and then becoming disturbed by rumors about the report due from Chase when Congress met again in December. The *Independent*, 21 November, speaking of the "cheering effect" of Chase's third accord with the banks and of "the other exhilarating incidents of the last ten days at sea and on land," was piously whistling to keep up its courage. The *Boston Daily Advertiser* praised the banks, praised Chase, and rejoiced at the abundance of specie as if nothing more wonderful had happened since Danaë's visitor came to her in a shower of gold.[23]

There was obvious confusion, rapidly merging into dismay but cloaking itself in mock confidence. Perplexity had already been expressed at the low price of bank shares, though the banks were tottering; the *Herald*, 4 November, had found it inexplicable that the American Exchange Bank's shares in particular should be down twenty per cent from par. The impression given was that with bank reserves standing at twice what they had been in any prior year, everything should be fine. Little concern was evinced over the fortuitousness of the inflow of gold, for which hunger abroad, prolonged but not to continue forever, was to be thanked. That the inflow had so far outrun a weakness which was now overtaking it was, in the news, ignored. But however grand the resources and the future of the North might be, the federal government's notes were not being bought, its soldiers and suppliers were not being paid, its armies were not whipping the rebels. The banks had advanced all their capital to Chase, and the securities still due them from him in return and intended to be sold to the public when received were "hanging over the market in prospective competition" with those still to be sold by him. Presumably those who might have understood the situation shrank from speaking out lest the truth do more harm than good. In this state of confused dismay, money went into private hoards or fled abroad. The heavy exports of farm products, despite the blockade of cotton, did not fall off, but the gold receipts paying for them did; brokers left their funds abroad instead of fetching them home. And California gold was diverted to London after the *Trent* seizure, lest complications arise from its being captured by the British on its usual course from San Francisco to New York. In other words, money was considered safer with the prospective enemy than it was at home or homeward bound. Though basic factors favored the North ineluctably, the stunted condition of federal powers, the Jacksonian tradition that they should be so, and the dogged, contrary procedure imposed by Secretary Chase were all insuring an imminent breakdown.[24]

V

From late September a contrary accompaniment of the effort to make the government's demand notes an acceptable "national currency" had been the rising complaint of the Treasury's tardy payment of its soldiers, contractors, and suppliers. On 26 September Chase had written his friend, Judge Nash, as if on the edge of trouble. "Whether we shall be forced to a depreciated currency or not," he said, "can not now be foreseen. . . . So long as the government is able to confine its transactions to coin and its own notes redeemable in coin, we shall be comparatively safe. At any rate until Congress shall decide otherwise, I must execute the law as it exists and receive and pay out only coin and government notes." Less than a week later, 2 October, he wrote another correspondent: "The expenditures everywhere are frightful. . . . The average daily drafts on the Treasury for two weeks past have been a million and three-quarters at least. . . ." The first loan was gone and the second largely anticipated. "The banks do not expect to be called on at the rate of more than a million a day. . . . The drafts on the Treasury are largely in excess of its means, which mortifies and distresses me beyond measure." A minor element in the mounting federal costs was that the Confederate army was arming and supplying itself substantially at the expense of the North. It was doing so by successful raids and captures. According to the observations of Lord Wolseley a year later, the Confederate forces were using equipment, wearing clothes, sleeping in tents, hauling in wagons, and driving horses seized from the enemy.[25]

The *New York Herald*, after pushing the demand notes for weeks, regretted at the end of October that the Treasury was slow in paying its bills. "Great complaint is made of the tardiness of the Treasury Department in settling the bills due to the creditors of the government." Accounts approved a month ago were still unpaid. Two failures of unpaid creditors of the government had occurred in Boston recently, and suppliers were raising their prices to compensate for the interest and other charges the delay in payment entailed.[26]

In this situation, Secretary Chase had also the pressure of powerful states and politicians upon him. "I am sure," Governor Morgan of New York wrote him 28 October, "that your prompt and favorable consideration of the application for monies on behalf of the United States disbursing officers in this state will be fully appreciated by the large number of persons whose official and individual embarrassments will be at once relieved thereby. Every effort has hitherto been made by this state to respond to the call of the government, and with this pleasing evidence of the appreciation of its labors, renewed energy will be given to the work of aiding in putting down the wicked rebellion."[27]

The *Journal of Commerce*, 19 November, said the Treasury was "anxious to settle with contractors" and relieve the many who were waiting for their money; on the 22nd it said things could be "more comfortable if the government would make its promised disbursements a little more rapidly." Claims were being discounted five per cent. Secretary Chase had expressed "his earnest desire that the government creditors and especially those engaged in clothing and feeding the soldiers" have their money at once. Editorially, the *Journal* remarked on the decline in specie since 19 August, the date of the first advance of fifty millions, and ventured to blame the Treasury's own slowness for the trouble. "Let the government, which is doing nine-tenths of the business, pay its debts as rapidly as possible; everybody else can then pay theirs, and money will be abundant." In a letter of 21 December to Chase, the president of the Corn Exchange Bank, New York, wrote: "The Army and Navy Departments are both proverbially *slow* in paying bills audited and which ought to be paid promptly. The spirit of the people who serve the government is wearied and broken by waiting from day to day and week after week for their money. I hear the most piteous complaints from all quarters on this head." Even when there was money on hand, the Secretary was told, disbursing officers were slow and indifferent; and of course the credit of the government was "materially injured" by these delays. But one would scarcely expect a lively performance by bureaus belonging to a government which had been at its best when doing the least, confronted with greatly augmented tasks, and required to compete with the economy and the armed services for competent personnel.[28]

At no time since Bull Run had there been much more than false confidence, and after late October there was scarcely that. The Union rout at Ball's Bluff and delayed dismay following arrest of the *Trent* had produced confidence neither in the government nor its notes. The Administration had done well during the autumn in establishing the blockade of Southern ports, the export of cotton was being effectively obstructed, General Grant had achieved modest success in the West, and extraordinary problems, political and personal, were being got out of the way; but none of this satisfied the demand for spectacular successes, and in December radical Republicans in Congress formed a Joint Committee on Conduct of the War to put pressure on the Administration for more action.

Up to this point, December 1861, the situation in the North was politically much the same as that in the South. In both, a so-called sovereignty without power commensurate with its pretensions was obtaining from its men of property the means of realizing its pretensions; and it was promising them in return IOU's of very doubtful value, mostly delivered very late. In the South that procedure did not cease till the resources of its people were exhausted and both the so-called sovereignty and the economy it was presumed to head were bankrupt. In the North, where resources were far greater, men of property rebelled and initiated a fiscal policy which in time gave substance to sovereignty, established its credit, and so far from letting either the sovereignty or the economy go bankrupt, enriched both. To this new policy Chase adjusted himself grudgingly, yet won from immediate posterity considerable reputation as a financier. What he himself contributed was constitutional and official; beyond that it was either not original or not efficient.

5

THE DECEMBER COLLAPSE

I

DECEMBER WAS dominated by three things: the threat of war over the *Trent's* seizure, the uneasiness intensified by Secretary Chase's report to Congress, and the prospective suspension of specie payments.

Till the middle of the month, Britain's response to the *Trent's* seizure was awaited—with bravado in public and with apprehension beneath the surface. The shock when it came was violent, but it was short. For British anger and American glee yielded fortunately to common sense and to a constraining awareness by each government that the stand it was tempted to take was contrary to what it had fought for in the past. It would also be costly, especially for the Americans. When the news of Britain's wrath arrived in mid-December, the *Boston Daily Advertiser* exclaimed that "no more important crisis has ever befallen any Administration in the history of our country." Early measures, it said, should be taken to prevent the export of specie. For if the crisis impelled the great holdings of American securities abroad to be returned home for liquidation, the resultant loss of gold could not be borne.[1]

Four weeks earlier, about the time that news of the *Trent's* arrest first reached New York, the *Herald* had noted the "remarkable fact" that after eight months of war the reserves of coin in the New York banks were still double what had been customary in prior years. The country's balance of trade was highly favorable: exports were up, imports were down, and receipts of gold continued. "The position of our banks," the *Herald* had said, "is very solid and their profits, under the arrangements with the government, must be very large."[2]

Less than three weeks later the *Herald* reported, 7 December, that bankers were considering suspension of specie payments. On 10 December an account of Secretary Chase's report to Congress was received in New York; it confirmed apprehension about federal finances and produced contradictory interpretations of the Secretary's proposal of a national currency. Two days later came news of Great Britain's fury over the *Trent*. The *Herald* said the next day that on the Street the report was "overshadowed" by the news from Great Britain.[3]

The 17th the *Boston Daily Advertiser* returned to the news from London with alarm. "The specie basis on which our financial system now rests is ample beyond precedent," the editor observed; but its preservation "is a matter of public duty and ordinary self-protection." Continuing with its thesis the following day, the *Advertiser* was aware that "the balance of foreign trade continues in favor of the United States. . . . The produce exports continue on a large scale, and the receipts of grain and flour at the various shipping points are heavy; so that in all probability the exports will continue in excess of the imports for some months to come." It was also still true that exports of specie were "merely nominal." But that was not all. The *Advertiser's* comment the day following was still full of restrained alarm lest the country's precarious good fortune end suddenly. "Foreign exchange in New York," it said, "under the recent excitement is more irregular and has advanced to 110½. Any further advance will cause the export of specie, which can not but seriously embarrass the financial operations of the Treasury. The banks would be forced to contract their loans to the government, which are so necessary to the successful prosecution of the war." Editorially the *Advertiser* hoped that the threatened loss of specie would have "the immediate attention" of the government. The excitement prevailing in Europe at last accounts must speedily send home American securities, "held abroad in vast amounts . . . and must prompt the early reduction of all balances due from this country." Some had already been received. "No one doubts that this will result in an early flow of specie to Europe." American exports of foodstuff, great as they were, would be insufficient to halt the loss. "Warlike preparations continue in England."[4]

In a pacific message to Whitehall, Secretary Seward dealt formally with law, but behind his words lay recognition such as the foregoing of the Union's precarious situation —financial as well as military—and its need of an amicable settlement. This was achieved by the end of the month through surrender to the British of the *Trent*'s four captive passengers and the official snubbing of them by the British when they reached London. American recognition of the facts was indicated by the *Boston Daily Advertiser*'s report so early as 23 December that "the recent excitement is quietly subsiding and business matters are progressing slowly." Money was in a quiet state. Specie shipments were "very little." Gold in the Boston banks, though it should have been of greater amount, was still nearly thrice what it had been a year before. It is evident that though ardor over the *Trent*'s arrest had not cooled universally, it had yielded to common sense, fact, and precedent in Wall Street, State, Chestnut, and on Pennsylvania Avenue, where the question had soon ceased to be whether to back down but how to do so. By the time the affair had ended with the surrender of the Confederate quartet to the British in Provincetown harbor late in December, the implications of Chase's report and the pressure on the banks had brought on suspension. The *Trent* incident had helped develop a state of nerves conducive to that humiliation.[5]

II

In his report to Congress Secretary Chase had unsuccessfully cloaked gloomy facts in a fog of calm and confidence. He told Congress that he had obtained one hundred and forty-six millions by arrangement with the associated banks of New York, Boston, and Philadelphia for three successive advances and that he had also issued fifty-one millions of Treasury notes, a little less than half of which were payable on demand, bore no interest, and circulated as money. Fifty millions more, he hoped, might be obtained from the

133

associated banks on the terms of the August negotiations. The borrowing had gone well, he said, as if it really had.[6]

Of his inability to pay the government's bills, of the inadequacy of what he had got, and of the unappeased resentment of the bankers, on whom he still had to rely, he said nothing. In other respects also there were no grounds for his seeming satisfaction. Revenue from direct and income taxes was not yet due, of course, and he thought Congress prudent in having put off their imposition. What had been looked for from imports had failed. The "circumstances of the country," he explained, had "proved, even beyond anticipations, unfavorable to foreign commerce." In reality, they were unfavorable only to imports; exports of foodstuffs continued to bring the country gold but yielded the government diminished revenue, aside from which there was the loss of what was collected, or might have been, at Southern ports. Instead of fifty-seven millions from import duties, the Secretary said, little more than thirty-two millions could now be counted on; and receipts from land sales and miscellaneous sources, minor at best, were falling short of what had been expected.[7]

At the same time that income was shrinking, expenses were mounting. In April, according to Secretary Cameron of the War Department, "the entire military force" had been "16,006 Regulars, principally employed in the West to hold in check marauding Indians." By December it was "an army of 600,000 men." For these numbers, prodigious amounts of arms, ammunition, food, clothing, equipment, and pay had been needed, were still needed, and would be needed. Not only more men but increased pay and rations for each man had been authorized. Increases for the navy also were still to come. To give these authorizations effect, enlarged appropriations had been made but more must follow, and the Treasury's task must grow, not abate.[8]

"One of the greatest perplexities of the government," President Lincoln had said in July, "is to avoid receiving troops faster than it can provide for them." This had not been wholly a matter of money, of course, for time was required to obtain supplies and distribute them. But by December it had become *mainly* a matter of money; supplies were growing short because suppliers were not being paid, and they were not being paid because the Treasury had not the means. Gold had been removed from the banks, where as monetary reserves it had its only use, and allowed to fall into the possession of hoarders and speculators, whence some day it might be enticed but not now when it was desperately needed. President Lincoln had suggested the Treasury's getting four hundred millions, Chase himself had proposed getting three hundred and twenty, Congress had authorized the borrowing of two hundred and fifty, and the Secretary had obtained so far one hundred and ninety-seven. Revenue, as estimated for the year, might provide another thirty-five millions or so. Ever since Bull Run, expenses had grown and provision for them had shrunk.[9]

The Secretary, taking up proposals for ways and means of getting the needed funds, began with an exhortation to rigid economy and with advice that the property of rebels be confiscated. This was his characteristically legal and moralistic confrontation of his fiscal problems. But unfortunately the nature of war made rigid economy delusive; and confiscation could produce nothing until possession of the property to be confiscated had been obtained. With respect to taxes, the Secretary restated his conviction—which more reasonably had been Secretary Gallatin's fifty years before—that taxes should be relied on "for ordinary expenditures, for prompt payment of interest on the public debt, existing and authorized, and for the gradual extinction of the principal." This was "indispensable to a sound system of finance." But Chase's sense of the importance of taxes did not extend to the need of them for *extraordinary* expenditures nor to recognition of their usefulness in confining the war-time advance in prices. Taxes remained "indispensable" in his system, but secondary. The most he could expect from them, even with increases, was ninety

135

millions, including ten millions from the income tax, which, however, he thought so uncertain a source that he doubted if the effort to collect it were warranted. All in all, taxes promised little. For most of what was needed, he said, "reliance must be placed on loans." This led to his bold but unpromising proposal that Congress authorize a national currency of bank notes secured by the pledge of federal bonds, a proposal which did not overcome the resistance it aroused till the war was half over; and even then it produced little money. The amount he hoped to find sufficient was two hundred million dollars, which was about the amount of state bank notes then in circulation. He thought it reasonable to expect that the Southern people would come to their senses within six months and ask that the war be stopped.[10]

The Secretary's basic conviction that the circulating medium should be under the federal government's control was correct for both practical and constitutional reasons, but it was scarcely relevant to his immediate task. He was mistaken in thinking, as he seems to have done, that an improved currency, however much improved, was the main requisite of an immediately adequate finance program, that note circulation was the principal and essential banking function, that bank notes were a more important means of payment than bank checks, and that the opposition to his proposed reform and the difficulties of organizing a new monetary system could be overcome in time to do the Treasury any good. This last error was the more egregious in one who thought that the war would be ended in six months. But perhaps Chase thought that announcement of so important a purpose would of itself help decisively in bringing the South to its knees; or that his constitutional reform could be accomplished only as a war measure and must be undertaken at once or never.

It is true that the country would be better served by a currency of uniform style, "bearing a common impression and authenticated by a common authority." As much had already been proved by experience with the hodgepodge of notes, good, bad, and indifferent, then issued under the various laws and varying economic conditions of the individual states. It is also true that the country would have been better served with more efficient railways, but no one, so far as I know, recommended that the levelling and straightening of roadbeds, the consolidation of short lines, and the standardization of gauge be undertaken regardless of the delay that would ensue in the movement of troops, equipment, and supplies. Yet the existing system of banks, if allowed to retain its powers and whether constitutional or not, was fully as competent to serve the Treasury as the existing railways were to serve the armed forces —and probably more so. For banking, though it had been disgracefully abused in a new country seething with acquisitive enterprise, was a skilful art, centuries old, whereas railways were little older than most men.[11]

Again, it is true that the weight of professional opinion was against the constitutionality of the existing currency, which had in its favor, besides vested interest, the weak decision of a Jacksonian court under Chief Justice Roger Taney in the *Briscoe* case fourteen years past. But the constitutionality of many things was at the moment moot, including secession on the one hand and federal sovereignty on the other. The constitutionality of the currency was not of paramount importance in financing the war. The banks could and would be no less useful to the Treasury as they were than as Chase would have them, and they and the state legislatures and bureaucracies that chartered, regulated, and borrowed from them would fight tenaciously against what they considered his offensive, unnecessary, and unconstitutional interference with their rights. Since Chase deferred attention to revenue and put reliance upon loans, it was of first importance that the source of loans be the readiest and most fruitful. By simply allowing the requirements of the independent Treasury act to be suspended, he could have borrowed far more than he did. Instead he rejected the readiest means of borrowing— from the existing banks but on realistic terms—and hinged

137

it on a constitutional reform bound to produce dissension and no money for a long time.

His program, moreover, besides being unproductive of money, worked in direct conflict with Lincoln's policy toward the states in general and the border states in particular. The President's first purpose being to preserve the Union, he refrained as long as possible from statements and acts which would affront the border states, where there was slavery, and weaken their loyalty to the Union. Slavery was a peculiarly important matter of states' rights; but so was banking. It had been one of the most persistently controverted issues of intra-state politics since the Revolution and of national politics from the Constitution to the triumph of Jacksonian polity, which, by the Bank veto of 1832, the *Briscoe* decision of 1837, and the independent or "constitutional Treasury" act of 1846, had minimized the federal government's monetary responsibilities and sanctified the states' usurpation of them. Save with respect to fugitives, slavery impinged on the states' rights only in the South and along the border, but banking, though it had less moral importance, impinged on them as a practical matter in every state; and Chase's national bank scheme offended not only states that encouraged banking but also those that restricted it and those that prohibited it.

This produced no conflict between the Secretary and President Lincoln, however, for the President, a former Whig, had held, no less consistently than Chase, the views of national monetary authority now urged by Chase. On this ground it was to be expected that he would support Chase, as he did. But he had also more sensitive political faculties than Chase, and these might well have impelled him to restrain an attack on the states' political interest in banking as they impelled him to restrain attacks on slavery in the border states. For some reason they did not; and he must share blame for an untimely insistence upon an untimely monetary reform. But Chase was a rival of formidable resources and the President had to be circumspect with him. Later he could spare Chase gladly and let him go; but in

138

December 1861 he could not.* Moreover the danger that Chase's proposal would arouse conflict with the states in general over banking jurisdiction may well have seemed less serious than conflict with some over slavery. Thus, though Kentucky might leave the Union over slavery, New York would not leave the Union over banking.

Incidentally, the approach of Chase to public problems— as of most of his contemporaries and their immediate predecessors—contrasts notably with that of the Revolutionary and Federalist generations on the one hand and of their twentieth-century successors on the other. By the late eighteenth century, men had looked in the records and observations of the past for help, but their conclusions were based on reason and common sense—not on tradition or credulity. To-day their descendants rely on surveys and the findings of "panels," "task forces," "ad hoc committees," et cetera. In 1861, despite the novelties of the conflict which had arisen, most of its participants hurried like ants into what they knew of the past and looked there for the formulas that would remove their difficulties. Like wizards, they hurled lethal precedents at one another. The appeal to permanent and oracular principles and to the immutable lessons of history was habitual. Chase himself always spoke as if he had just looked up from poring over the Sibylline leaves and finding in them the answers he needed. His public strength seems to have rested on a pontifical recourse to "eternal verities" by which a vast number of contemporary Americans were hypnotized. He was notably proficient in the traditional and credulous approach to current problems; no one was less so than the President, whom he thought he should replace.

In a way, however, Chase's course had a logical or, better, a psychological influence. He was like Tom Sawyer, who, Huckleberry Finn observed, had read all the books,

* When the break came in June 1864, it was over a stand in which Chase was right: he insisted that the important position of Assistant Treasurer in New York be held by a man of exceptional standing and financial experience and not by a politician.

and insisted on things being done the right way no matter how unnecessary it was. He sought to discharge his fiscal duties on a plane compatible with the great purposes of the war; and that impelled him to make his decisions on the impressive grounds of constitutionality rather than expedience. He insisted less on what was merely necessary than on a sweeping correction of the states' unlawful pretensions. He was not alone in this. It was a time when most men committed to uncompromising defense of the Union—whether in Congress or not—began committing themselves to a militant elevation of all federal powers, long neglected, and to a curtailment of states' powers. This was conspicuously true of Thaddeus Stevens. A less passionate man, Senator John Sherman, was certainly so committed when a year later in an effective appeal for Chase's monetary reform, he cited the existing banks as typical of the states' usurpations and an abatement of constitutional authority like that over which the war was being fought. Similarly, Chase in his commitment to defense of the Union, was moved to sweep into its train the unconstitutional monetary system, with which it was part of his task to deal. It was "too clear to be reasonably disputed," he declared, that the federal government was authorized by the Constitution "to control the credit circulation" and that "the time has arrived" for the exercise of that authority.[12]

Chase's national currency first took form as the demand notes authorized by the special session on his recommendation in July 1861, being thereby "partially adopted," as he said. In order to make the notes redeemable, the Secretary had tried, during the autumn just passed, to build up a fund in the Treasury with gold exacted from the metropolitan banks' reserves. Now, however, though he thought the plan had merit, he forbore recommending it. "Possible disasters" too far outweighed "probable benefits." He now recommended, in his report of December 1861, a "national currency" of bank notes secured by federal bonds instead of state. This was the second stage of his effort. "Through the voluntary action of the existing institutions," he said,

140

"the great transition from a currency heterogeneous, unequal, and unsafe, to one uniform, equal, and safe may be speedily and almost imperceptibly accomplished." The banks' large holdings of federal bonds might, he hoped, "impart such value and stability to government securities" that it would not be difficult for the Treasury to borrow what it needed during "the current and the succeeding year at fair and reasonable rates." The Secretary did not then say explicitly whether the banks whose notes were to constitute this national currency would have national charters, though this, a year later, was said to have been "expressed." A third stage was reached, December 1862, when he did say explicitly that the banks issuing the national currency secured by federal bonds might be either new banks "organized under a general act of Congress" or old banks organized thereunder by surrendering their state charters for federal and transferring "the capital of the old to the use of the new." A fourth stage was reached in 1865, after Chase had left the Treasury, when a ten per cent tax was levied on state bank notes with the intent of driving banks with state charters entirely out of existence. The swing from state to federal loyalties in respect to a national currency went fast and far. Nor was this the end. The national currency proposal, being of general concern, fomented commitment to the policy of enlarged federal powers, which became familiar and popular, even with those who disliked the particular form Chase and his advisers gave it.[13]

III

The Secretary's report of December 1861, presenting the first stage of his proposal that constitutional control of the monetary system be resumed by the federal government, confirmed much that had been rumored for months, but no bill had been drafted embodying his ideas, which were doubtless clear as to law but not as to practice, and his recommendation was cast in very general terms. What he first proposed in so many words was no more than transfer of authority over bank-note issue from the states to the federal government, his object being the two-fold one of achieving a national currency and a market for federal bonds by requiring that bank notes, which constituted the bulk of the country's currency, be secured by the pledge of such bonds instead of state bonds. Just how this was to be done and just what the new procedure would mean to the existing banks was not indicated.[14]

In June a plan for a national currency had been proposed in the press by John Thompson of New York, a friend and supporter of Chase, who had also proposed the demand notes recommended by Chase and authorized in the July loan act.* The undefined idea of a national currency was generally welcomed. But as the proposal was subjected to analysis and definition, differences of opinion and of understanding had arisen. Within a very few months the country had become full of people with varying ideas on the subject. In Chase's correspondence there is a letter from a fellow Ohioan, John W. Caldwell, 22 October, that went beyond the Secretary's vague proposal. "Let the evidence of the national debt," Caldwell said, "be all of such character that it may circulate as money." He would supplant the states' authority over bank circulation, and have "the government of the United States furnish to the banker, for his money, what is necessary for circulation." The government he believed could "*now* do what it never before could have done."[15]

In the *Tribune*, the *Herald*, and the *Times* the new demand notes had repeatedly been spoken of with approval in terms of their potential virtues as a national currency. In August the *Herald* had said in its financial column that they were superior to anything of the sort the country had;

* Thompson later organized the First National Bank of New York and subsequently the Chase National, also in New York; he was successively president of each. The first of these banks survives in the First National City Bank, the second in the Chase Manhattan National Bank Association. Why "association" is explained in my *Banks and Politics*, 580ff.

142

"they will eventually supersede all other currencies"; for "with a sufficient reserve of coin here to redeem them as they are presented for payment, they will answer every purpose of a safe, uniform, and convenient circulating medium." Editorially the *Herald* had expected in the same issue that the whole currency of the country would be superseded by the new notes of the government and that the specie in the city banks would be used only "to pay the balances between this country and Europe."[16]

In this early period, what became in time the national bank system was spoken of as a national currency, the means and the end being confused in men's minds—a national currency being the end, national banks being a means to that end. But a national currency might be either government notes, as Chase had already put in use, or bank notes secured by federal bonds, which he recommended in December. Out of contention as to which was the better there developed eventually the long-lived greenback agitation that dominated politics for three decades after the war, kept on rumbling for three more, and still survived in fugitive fashion into the 'thirties of the present century, when the American monetary system took on its present form. Meanwhile, opinion in the banking field itself was varied. The great majority of bankers wanted to be left as they were, in the states' hands. But a minority especially in the cities, urged the shift to federal control. The *Bankers' Magazine*, in its issue of December 1861, the month of the Secretary's proposal, presented a spirited argument for a national currency. "An unfortunate construction of the Constitution," it said, "has fostered the policy of independent action by the state governments in reference to the currency. The spurious doctrine of 'state rights' has wormed itself among the people, and one of the true functions of the general government, viz., the sole control of the currency for the people, has been wrested from it and placed with the authorities of thirty or more states—each one aiming, at the instigation of its own capitalists, to create as large a volume of bank paper as can possibly be sustained."

Thus there was left to "the promptings of cupidity or individual profit that which should be established and maintained only on the broad grounds of national and public welfare." Such observations exemplified readiness for currency reform in the new spirit of nationalism being fostered by the war.[17]

Well before the Secretary's report came out, rumor had reached the press in wildly varying terms. The *Journal of Commerce* had heard back in mid-November, when Chase was in New York, of official consideration being given to "some change in the banking system" which would make federal bonds "part of the basis of circulation." It this were done, it said generously (for a copperhead), "and a certain percentage of specie to liabilities provided for, the American banking system would be the best in the world." The *Times*, considering 2 December whether the Secretary would recommend a third United States Bank or free banking, preferred the former. The *Herald*, the same day, also understood that a third federal Bank would be recommended. On the 5th the *Herald* reported that the Street was full of rumors about the Chase report, with everyone discussing the "relative merits of a national bank, a large issue of irredeemable government paper, and further issues of Treasury notes bearing interest." On the 6th, the *Herald* said: "Mr John A. Stevens, President of the Bank of Commerce, is in Washington in consultation with the Secretary of the Treasury. Mr Stevens is popularly supposed to be in favor of a national bank of issue, whose notes shall be a legal tender." The *Tribune*, on the 7th, also reported that Stevens was in Washington with Secretary Chase and that he was said to favor the "scheme . . . for a national bank," which other bankers opposed. But the same day the *Herald* commented on serious consideration by some of New York's bankers of the desirability "of a general bank suspension in the event of a large issue of paper money." In the *Herald's* opinion, if the government were to issue paper money "and make it a legal tender, our banks will have to suspend. . . ." After the text of the report reached Wall

144

Street, 10 December, the *Herald* said the New York bankers disliked Chase's national bank currency, not so much on their own account as on that of their country correspondent banks, for which circulation was important; Wall Street did not want its country correspondents "molested"—their accounts were too important. Yet the *Herald* itself was inclined to favor making Treasury notes a legal tender, which, it seemed to imply—and if so, quite mistakenly—was what Chase wanted done. In the absence of "a brilliant victory in the field," the government's bonds would not rise in price and the banks could do no more than they were already doing. But the *Herald* reported 16 December that the national bank plan was approved by all but country banks; which however, were the more numerous and politically the more influential. About the same time *The Economist*, in London, was also informed that the opposition of country banks to the Secretary's recommendation was very strong.[18]

As to the merits of Chase's recommendation, the *Boston Daily Advertiser* came closer to the heart of the matter than the New York press. Its reception of the report was not wholly consistent, however, probably because it had to speak before it made up its mind. It generally supported the Administration with warmth, and its first comment on Chase's report, 11 December, was commendatory both editorially and in its news columns. "The Treasury," it found occasion to say, "has been beyond all comparison the most important department of the government from the moment the war began to threaten." On the 12th it discussed Chase's program with wavering approval. On the 13th it recurred to his report on the government's finances, which was viewed, it said, with general favor but "with some distrust" in respect to his suggestions for a change in the currency. For, it said, "there is nothing with which the wise statesman is more chary of meddling than the currency of the country at such a period of commercial disorder and public difficulty as the present."

"If the question were now altogether an open one and if

145

we were now establishing our currency under the Constitution for the first time," the *Advertiser* thought the Secretary's plan might be superior to any other. But it was "certainly foreign to the subject as it now presents itself. The advantages of the scheme in the way of a uniform currency are entirely incidental and aside from the main purpose. No statesman would propose to change our currency at this moment above all others for the sake of securing a better one." Considering the principal object of the Secretary's proposal to be the creation of a market for federal bonds, the *Advertiser* found it "wholly insufficient to justify the risk incurred by a revolution in the currency at this time." For the proposal raised constitutional questions about the "respective rights of the general and state governments" such as had been agitated in Andrew Jackson's day; "and few persons then alive can have forgotten the fury with which the controversy raged or can desire to see anything like a renewal of it in the fearful embarrassments in which the country is now placed."

Turning from the constitutional issue with the uneasy remark that "the topic is one on which it is not advisable perhaps to enlarge," the *Advertiser's* editorial took up two fiscal weaknesses in Chase's scheme. "The Secretary," it said, "relies upon issuing a hundred and fifty millions of government bonds to the banks above what they might otherwise have taken. It is palpable that to take these the banks must either throw upon the market a vast amount of state, county, or town securities or must diminish the loans they now make to the public. . . . Whatever loans were obtained from the banks in this shape could be so much subtracted from their ability . . . to lend in some other shape. . . ." This was something stressed in subsequent opposition to Chase's recommendation in congressional debates, but in reality the anticipated embarrassment never arose—not because the Secretary's "well approved sagacity," was applied to the problem, as the *Advertiser* hoped it would be, but because prolonged delay in enactment of his measure and failure to get enough national banks organized to carry weight in the market gave time for the government's securities to advance in value and to become widely distributed.

The *Advertiser* concluded this most searching and intelligent of criticisms aroused by Chase's proposal with allusion to his inconsistency in approving the traditionary American aversion to a permanent public debt, in suggesting procedure for its retirement, and at the same time in recommending such debt as the permanent basis of a reformed currency. His plan, the *Advertiser*'s editorial said, "contemplates a permanent supply of United States bonds and a permanent public debt; although elsewhere in his report the Secretary advises some provision for the final liquidation of our whole war debt, on the ground that 'the idea of a perpetual debt is not of American nativity and should not be naturalized.' "[19]

IV

What the states thought of Chase's national currency proposal is fairly well represented by New York's Superintendent of Banks, H. H. Van Dyck, in his annual report, 26 December 1861, little more than a fortnight after Secretary Chase's proposal became public. The Secretary, observed Van Dyck, proposed that the federal government enact banking legislation adapted from that of New York, "extending it under authority of Congress to the banking institutions of all the states and basing the issue of currency solely upon its own stock, to be primarily purchased and deposited with it by the banks."[20]

Van Dyck's first objection was a practical one. Federal bonds had a lower market price than the eastern states' bonds; they were poor security, like the bonds of western states, and Chase's national currency would suffer as that of the western banks had. At the same time, Van Dyck supposed the eastern banks, and particularly those of his own state, would have to sell their state bonds in order to buy the federal government's, and in doing so they would suffer a loss from the break in prices that would follow their throwing present holdings on a depressed market. Van Dyck, turning constitutional, then remarked that Chase's "proposition involves the establishment of a class of banking institutions subordinate to congressional authority and wholly independent of the state legislatures." Would this be lawful? he asked. "Would the subordination of existing state institutions to the jurisdiction of Congress and the creation of an unlimited number of corporations within the states by that body be an exercise of constitutional power?"[21]

His question harks back to the complaints of Maryland and Ohio which the Supreme Court had rejected forty years before in affirming the constitutionality of the Bank of the United States and its so-called "invasion" of the sovereign states. It harks back also to the veto in which Andrew Jackson denied what the Supreme Court affirmed and refused to let the federal government exercise the "unconstitutional" power which Secretary Chase still declared constitutional and wanted exercised. Van Dyck quoted from the message of his old political leader, President Martin Van Buren, to the special session of 1837: "'The federal government will find its agency most conducive to the security and happiness of the people when limited to the exercise of its conceded powers. In never assuming, even for a well-meant object, such powers as were not designed to be conferred upon it, we shall in reality do most for the general welfare.'" Van Dyck went on to quote also Van Buren's refusal to have the federal government do anything to relieve the disasters of the panic of 1837, Van Buren's conviction being that the appropriate powers were "not within the constitutional province of the general government and that their adoption would not promote the real and permanent welfare of those they might be designed to aid."[22]

Van Dyck recognized in Secretary Chase's unwelcome proposal evidence of a contemporary trend. "At this peculiar juncture in public affairs," he said, "parties and individ-

148

uals feel a willingness to strengthen the hands of the national Administration. Measures that would arouse the most determined resistance in times of peace are now acquiesced in, if not applauded. But there must be a limit to encroachments upon constitutional rights if we would preserve the constituent elements of our present form of government." In fact, of course, Secretary Chase was seeking to "preserve the constituent elements" of the American form of government, but not in a fashion agreeable to New York's banking superintendent. "Instead of departing more widely from constitutional principles," the New Yorker argued, "it becomes us rather to lay to heart and practice the beneficent counsel of the patriot Jackson, who says: 'Nor is our government to be maintained or our Union preserved by invasions of the rights and powers of the several states. . . . Its true strength consists in leaving individuals and states as much as possible to themselves; in making itself felt, not in its power, but in its beneficence; . . . not in binding the states more closely to the centre but leaving each to move, unobstructed, in its proper orbit.' "

No state, wrote the superintendent in closing his report, had a deeper interest in the question raised by Secretary Chase's proposal than had New York; and in his opinion, "the CONSENT OF THE LEGISLATURE seems imperatively demanded before congressional interference with the institutions of the state can be for a moment tolerated."[23]

These quotations disclose not only a difference of opinion as to what the relative powers of the federal government and the states should be but also a difference of opinion as to what the Constitution intended them to be. The Constitution was specific up to the point of authorizing the federal government to coin money and determine its value; and also to the point of forbidding the states to coin money or issue bills of credit or impair contracts. But it nowhere mentioned banks, or gave the federal government power to incorporate them, nor did it take that power from the states. This had given Jackson, Van Buren, and the states' rights people generally occasion to deny their opponents' Hamiltonian claim, on behalf of the federal government, to powers not literally delegated to it but reserved by the tenth amendment to the states. To get around the Constitution's silence, Chase and other Hamiltonian interpreters had to deduce powers implied in those delegated. A document prepared for a small, simple 18th-century economy, mostly agrarian and partly mercantile, had to be made practicable for a vastly greater one complicated by growth and the industrial revolution; and this required a Hamiltonian interpretation. Such an interpretation a great number of persons were incapable of following, and a great number of those quite able to follow it nevertheless rejected it because they disliked the consequences—as the New York Superintendent of Banks did. Subsequently, however, that official himself followed the drift and served the federal government as one of its assistant treasurers.[24]

It is obvious, of course, that the arguments used in the North against Chase's proposed national currency paralleled those used in the South in defense of secession.

V

The *Journal of Commerce* had reported 26 November that London expected banks in the United States to suspend in December. This meant that there was already the same expectation in New York—in some quarters, that is. True to this expectation, the money market had begun to sink. In general, the press nervously asserted confidence and strove to neutralize alarming news. But it could be heard said repeatedly that wars always had induced suspension, the implication being that the same thing was to be expected again. Uneasiness was aggravated by distrust of Chase, of the Administration, of the military leadership. Exports of foodstuffs, already above all previous volume and still mounting, should have been fetching back specie in payment and making foreign exchange cheap. Instead, the money due from Europe for the shipments of grain and meat was being left there. And exports of specie from New York were growing from less than four thousand dollars in August to nine hundred thousand in December. Drafts on London were advancing to a premium of ten per cent or more—double what it had been. These unnatural conditions nourished fear and uncertainty. Like Laurence Sterne's caged starling, the "wise money" wanted to get out; and a man would give ten dollars in New York for nine or less in London. The New York banks' receipts of gold from California, amounting to something less than three millions a month, were still keeping the banks' heads above water but could only postpone suspension, not prevent it. Depositors with large bank balances who had considered converting them into gold now began to do so.[25]

The Economist, London, had had a report from Philadelphia, dated 25 November, saying that though the banks and the public had supplied, so far, only eighty millions of the six hundred millions "which the annual government expenditure now probably amounts to," the banks "are already trembling for their specie." (They had "supplied" only eighty millions but by February were to deliver the remaining seventy-six they had promised.) Those in New York, Boston, and Philadelphia were "so far committed that they must go on and sink or swim with the government." In its issue of 28 December, when its latest news was of Secretary Chase's December report, The Economist found the apparent cost of the war appalling—far more than twice that of Britain's conflict with Napoleon*—and discrepancies between the Secretary's July and December estimates prodigious. The American government was borrowing too much and taxing too little. The Economist's correspondent foresaw great opposition to the Secretary's "currency scheme."[26]

Doubly frightened by coincidence of Chase's report with prospects of war with Great Britain, the market was seized anew with panic. The New York Times reported Sat-

* In 1861 the battle of Waterloo was not so far in the past as the end of World War I at this writing, 1967.

urday, 14 December, that foreign funds were being ordered home and that exchange was nearly up to the gold points. On Monday the 16th it said that stoppage of payments was being discussed on the Street as a "temporary and precautionary" step; on Tuesday the 17th, that the gold reserves of the city banks were down, foreign exchange was up, and the condition presupposed an immediate suspension of gold payments by the banks. In other words, the question for the banks was whether they should stop cashing checks and close their vaults at once or do it later. On Wednesday the 18th the *New York Tribune* reported discussion of the question "both in and out of bank parlors" as a result of gold withdrawals "combined" with the Secretary's national currency proposal, which the banks considered "inimical to their interests." The *Tribune* said that "the necessity of ultimate suspension was generally conceded, and the question was whether it should take place with full or empty vaults." At a meeting the night before, in a resolution offered by Moses Taylor, president of the City Bank, it was decided to continue payments as usual.[27]

Mr Taylor's resolution said that the public mind had become "unduly agitated" and that this had led to a premature discussion of the question; that the bullion in the country was eighty million dollars more than it had been the year before and "a fair proportion" of it was in the banks; that shipments of cereals had replaced shipments of cotton, and that current exports too far exceeded imports to warrant outward movements of coin; that the "pending difference with Great Britain" would "probably" yield to diplomatic solution and fears on this score were "premature and groundless"; that what the banks of the city had to advance to the Treasury (they were already in arrears) "do not exceed thirty-one million five hundred thousand dollars, provided the Secretary in his drafts therefor" would consult their wishes, which might be expected of him "from motives of interest and policy as well as from his promises"; and, finally, that "independently of all these considerations it is not only unbecoming but bad faith" for banks "to refuse the just demands of depositors, . . . and nothing but an entire want of public confidence or great national considerations rendering it impossible to comply with all engagements can ever justify such refusal." The New York banks, therefore, being assured of co-operation from Boston and Philadelphia and relying "confidently on the harmonious action of the government, on the continued confidence of their depositors, and on the patriotism of the people," resolved to maintain specie payments.[28]

This admirable language showed habit and illusion triumphant over common sense, but it had little influence. The *New York Times* said as of the 18th that "the business day in Wall Street had been a very excited one. Financially, the action of the associated banks last night did us no good. It was rather productive of mischief than otherwise." The *Times* thought the resolution weak and wordy, the action a "game of mutual self-deception," which would not reduce the premium on foreign exchange, stop "the quiet transfer of gold in bank to special account," or steady the price of money in the Street. The *Herald*, also as of the 18th, had nothing much better to say. "The resolutions passed at the bank meeting yesterday, though excellent in spirit and generally judicious, failed to improve matters to-day. . . . Stocks fell off heavily this morning, partly on the foreign news and partly on the bank resolutions. . . . At one time a perfect stampede prevailed." New York Central fell 1-1/4; Erie preferred, 3; Michigan Central, 4; and so on. But the market improved, the *Herald* reported, after Secretary Chase, who was in New York, "expressed the opinion that the trouble with Great Britain was susceptible of a pacific solution and that his negotiations with the banks were progressing satisfactorily." The Secretary's words, however, did not deter bank depositors, who kept on presenting their checks, and the banks kept on paying out their gold. Though some bankers thought it sensible to stop payments before their gold reserves were all gone, more shrank from refusing to pay their obligations while they still were able to do so.[29]

CHAPTER 5

The Secretary was in New York at the time trying to arrange the fourth loan of fifty millions which he had mentioned in his report as a possibility, the banks having an option to take it 1 January. But their experience with him and the crisis they were in precluded further advances. The *Times*, however, reported that Chase had had an "amicable meeting" with the bankers. The *Tribune* said he told them he was hopeful of "stirring events" soon and an end to the war by summer. The *Journal of Commerce* reported that the meetings produced no decision, that the bankers complained of not being reimbursed for their advances of specie, and that they insisted on reimbursement or the Treasury's use of deposit credit, but got nothing, seeming to be cowed by Chase's eloquence. In a letter from New York dated the 21st, however, the president of the Corn Exchange Bank, E. W. Dunham, assured the Secretary that the banks "ought not, can not, and will not take another fifty millions. . . . It would be suicidal."[30]

In three weeks of uninterrupted losses preceding suspension (from 7 to 28 December), the New York banks' gold reserves had shrunk almost one-third. It is not evident how much of their cash was paid out to depositors who took it away and how much was converted into "special deposits," that is, specie held in the banks' vaults but earmarked as the customers' property. The press reported that special deposits were being refused by the banks, but one can not even guess how frequent and important the refusals were. For the banks' customers, hauling away large amounts of gold and secreting them was embarrassing and difficult. In the panic of 1857, according to James Gallatin, when depositors in alarm "drew out coin and carried it home, they found themselves in a much worse position than they were before." He said "some people had to sit up in their houses all night to watch the treasure; and the fear of losing it was found to be increased rather than diminished by drawing it from the banks." It was much better to leave the gold in the bank as a deposit for safe keeping; and large depositors were usually too influential

154

to be denied. If small depositors were denied they could withdraw what they had. The gold most readily hoarded, however, was that disbursed by the government and either secreted by its recipients in countless hiding places or locked in the safes of brokers.[31]

Meanwhile tension over the *Trent* was being treated officially with generalities such as Secretary Chase's opinion that the trouble was "susceptible of a pacific solution" and the feckless observation of others that what the British objected to was what they themselves had done for years. Putting it that way sounded as if the Americans were acknowledged by the British to have been right and the matter could be called quits without having a war about it. Though Washington was moving, as much comment indicated, toward a "pacific solution," much of the original anglophobic noise continued and news that was bellicose vied with news that was apprehensive and with news that was peaceful. The *New York Herald*, 20 December and again the 23rd, denounced "silly rumors" that Mason and Slidell would be released, saying there was "not the slightest word of truth in the report." On the contrary the report was quite true and the rumor not silly; yet as late as the 26th the Street was "kept in a fever all day" by contradictory rumors. That day Secretary Seward ordered the Confederate commissioners released to the British; settlement of the affair was announced the 29th.[32]

The night before, Saturday, 28 December, the bankers threw over their resolutions of the 17th "after a long and rather stormy session of some seven hours" and voted to let go of no more coin. Most of them had wished to do this before but had been "over-ruled" by the managers of "two or three prominent" banks. If they then knew that Washington had acknowledged error in the seizure of Mason and Slidell and ordered the two of them and their secretaries returned to the British, the news did not relieve their anxieties enough to deter them from stopping gold payments. War with Britain had been but one of the things to scare the money market. There was still the fact that the rebellion was not being overcome. The army seemed active mostly on parade and in retreat. General McClellan was dangerously ill. Distrust of President Lincoln and the government was common. The radical Republicans in Congress had got together their Joint Committee on Prosecution of the War, whose function, according to one's point of view, was to help the Administration or to hound it. The public was not supporting the government by buying bonds, and the government was not supporting its suppliers and its soldiers by paying them. All this was too much. And at the heart of the market's anxiety was Secretary Chase, who to ignorance of monetary practice joined a stubborn, dogmatic wrong-headedness. He talked down to the bankers as if they knew nothing of their own business. He had refused their advice, abused their obligations, and steered arbitrarily for trouble. Lastly, to top all this, he had proposed transfer of their business from state to federal jurisdiction.[33]

The amendment of 5 August had sought to avoid suspension. Chase had made avoidance impossible. He was aware by 28 December that gold was being withdrawn from the banks at a rate which would leave them empty in a short time, but in conference with the bankers he had refused to yield. They proposed that the remaining reserves of the banks of New York, Philadelphia, and Boston, and the federal bonds they owned be segregated "as a special security for two hundred millions of notes, which could then be immediately issued by the associated banks from their own plates and be verified and made national by the stamp and signature of a government officer." This was a direct and simplified version of the national currency proposed by the Secretary himself in his annual report earlier in the same month. It would make the existing banks government depositories, as banks later formed under a national bank act became; it would employ bank credit transferable by government checks as it was employed in the business world; and it would avoid a radical protracted reorganization of the banking system such as the Secretary's

156

scheme eventually required. The scattering of gold through government disbursements would have ceased and thanks to California's streams and Europe's need of food, gold reserves would presently have had a providential opportunity to resist dissipation and support a means of payment that reduced rather than magnified the difficulties of war. It would also effect in substance the federal government's constitutional control of the monetary system. But to initiate this simple course, either the language of the amendment of 5 August or the Secretary's interpretation of it would have had to be changed, and to that, as to the whole suggestion, the Secretary refused his assent, "preferring," as one of the bankers said, "the system of national banks which he had already conceived" and which differed from their proposal in being merely more formal, legalistic, complicated, immediately unattainable, and gratuitously objectionable.[34]

So the following Monday, 30 December, the bankers opened their doors as usual but shook their heads when asked for gold. New York was joined by Philadelphia and Boston and by banks throughout the North. The public could still make payments by check, certified if that were desired, or by Treasury notes or bank notes; but gold, which was sought almost wholly for hoarding, was paid only in rare cases, as when required under a contract. The action of the bankers was, of course, unlawful. But there was no alternative except to postpone the inevitable a few days. Bank reserves, which three weeks before had been forty-two millions, were now but twenty-five. The *Herald* thought the bankers stupid in having put off suspension as long as they did. The final rapid decline had begun with the resolution a fortnight earlier, which by announcing that the banks would not suspend, worked, in the circumstances, as a warning to depositors to get their money out as soon as possible, since none would be left for latecomers.[35]

Though most of the banks and most of Wall Street distrusted Chase, his helpers included a number of important

monied men—particularly John A. Stevens of the Bank of
Commerce; John Thompson, broker and later banker; Jay
Cooke, Philadelphia banker; and Samuel Hooper, Boston
merchant and banker, now a member of Congress and of
its Ways and Means Committee. Some of these were perhaps less disposed to trust Chase than to influence him, if
they could. The metropolitan press usually supported the
Secretary, sometimes to the point of stultification. The
Bankers' Magazine, for example, in January 1862, said that
he had "completely succeeded in the negotiation of the public loan," and demonstrated his "financial skill." Events, it
said, "have fully proved the wisdom and foresight of Mr
Chase. . . . And all will admit that the integrity as also the
energy with which the affairs of the Treasury department
have been administered, notwithstanding the overwhelming duties devolved upon it, have justly inspired that confidence in its management which has elicited the generous
and patriotic responses of the whole people, when appealed to by the Secretary for financial support."[36]

Possibly this was the language of make-believe, spoken
to command quiet and confidence, for nothing of the sort
had happened. An account closer to the facts, dated 28 December, appeared on a later page of the same issue of the
Bankers' Magazine: "The month has been a highly excited
one in commercial and financial circles. There were no disturbing causes early in the month beyond the present rebellion and the fear that the recent seizure of Messrs Mason
and Slidell might interrupt the friendly relations between
the United States and England. On the 16th of this month,
however, intelligence from London reached this city to
the effect that the British government and people were
highly excited by the violation, as they charge, of international law by this government through the act of Commo-
dore Wilkes. On Monday the 16th the New York stock market sustained a heavy fall in values. . . . The Street was filled
with rumors as to an agreement among the banks to suspend
specie payments. On the 17th the banks adopted resolutions
giving assurance of their ability to maintain specie pay-

ments. The market since has been continually excited and depressed, and capitalists were more cautious than before in their movements. To-day the banks in convention agreed to suspend specie payments."[37]

After four months the banks had not even received the notes they had purchased in August, "the appeal" to the public to buy the penny-a-day bonds had failed and been given up, both the banks and the Treasury had had to suspend specie payments, soldiers were going unpaid, government suppliers were living on the edge of insolvency, army supplies were failing to keep up with needs, and the initiative in formation of policy had passed from the Treasury to Congress.

VI

When Secretary Chase's December report was submitted, the Ways and Means Committee of the 37th Congress comprised the following members:

Thaddeus Stevens, chairman, Pennsylvania Republican, lawyer, iron manufacturer.

Erastus Corning, New York Democrat, banker, manufacturer, president of the New York Central Railroad.

Samuel Hooper, Massachusetts Republican, China merchant, banker, manufacturer, successor in Congress and in Ways and Means to his business partner, William Appleton, deceased since the special session.

Valentine B. Horton, Ohio Whig, lawyer, mine owner.

Horace Maynard, Tennessee Whig, lawyer, mathematician.

Justin Morrill, Vermont Republican, country merchant, bank shareholder, self-taught scholar.

John S. Phelps, Missouri Democrat, lawyer.

Eldridge G. Spaulding, New York Republican, lawyer, banker.

J.L.N. Stratton, New Jersey Republican, lawyer.

Ways and Means had two sub-committees, of which Morrill and Spaulding respectively were chairmen. Morrill's sub-committee was charged with preparing a tax bill; Spaulding's with implementing the Secretary's recommendation for a national currency as a means of borrowing. Thaddeus Stevens, chairman of the main committee, kept charge of appropriation bills besides oversight of the two sub-committees.[38]

The two other members of Spaulding's sub-committee were Samuel Hooper and Erastus Corning, but the latter being a Democrat, a banker in Albany, unsympathetic to the Secretary's recommendation, and away from Washington considerably, the task fell wholly on Spaulding and Hooper. Spaulding, when he asked Chase to furnish a draft of the bank bill he presumably had in mind "for a national currency based on a pledge of public stocks," was informed that none had been prepared. Spaulding then wrote Corning, 24 December, for a copy of New York's free banking statute, which was the model for the proposed national system. Corning complied in a letter of the 26th from Albany—perhaps from the bank in Albany of which he was president—with the laconic statement that in his judgment the scheme would not "meet the approval" of New York. That same day the report of the New York Superintendent of Banks confirmed Corning's words, as Corning probably had advised that it should and known that it would. Spaulding and Hooper went ahead, however, drawing on the free banking statutes of both New York and Massachusetts—the latter of which Hooper had got through the Massachusetts assembly when he was a member of that body—and prepared a bill which was printed for the use of the committee.[39]

This task seems to have been accomplished between 18 and 28 December, while the monetary crisis was swiftly worsening. By the 28th, when the banks decided to stop specie payments, Spaulding said he had concluded that the "national currency bank bill . . . could not be passed and made available quick enough to meet the crisis then pressing upon the government for money to sustain the army and navy." Accordingly, he "drafted a legal tender Treas-

160

ury note section to be added to the bank bill," which would enable the government to pay its expenses during the months it would take to organize the system from which the Treasury was to borrow; and the text of this section he gave the *New York Tribune*, which published it Tuesday, 31 December. But then, "upon more mature consideration," Spaulding concluded "that the bank bill, containing sixty sections, could not, with the state banks opposed to it, be passed through both Houses of Congress for several months and that so long a delay would be fatal to the Union cause. . . . Hesitancy and delay, with the expenses of the war running on at an average of two million dollars per day, would have been fatal." Spaulding therefore detached the legal tender section he had just prepared, changed it into "a separate bill with alterations and additions," and introduced it as such in the House 30 December. It was referred to Ways and Means, as HR 182, "to authorize the issue of Treasury notes payable on demand." The heart of this measure lay in the words, momentous as an expression of sovereignty and long thereafter the occasion of intense political controversy, which made the notes "receivable for all debts and demands due to the United States, and for all salaries, dues, debts, and demands owing by the United States," and "a legal tender in payment of all debts, public and private. . . ."[40]

Spaulding had not thought of all this by himself. A conviction that something would have to be designated as a legal tender in lieu of gold was common, except among farmers and politicians. The *New York Herald*, already quoted, had reported early in December that John A. Stevens, president of the country's largest bank, was understood to favor the issue of legal tender notes. The *Tribune*, 24 December, reported that several bank officers were in correspondence with Mr Chase and that most of his advisers "fall back upon an irredeemable government currency, to be made a legal tender, the constitutional question being waived for the present." The *Tribune*, 25 December, quoted a bank president who thought it very

161

clear that the government's demand notes, which were in fact irredeemable but not a legal tender, could "not be received by banks under their present legal obligations to treat all credits on their books" as payable in coin. For whatever a bank accepted on deposit, it was required to pay in gold, when gold was demanded. The *Herald*, also the 25th, reported that the president of a leading bank had got out a pamphlet saying the banks could not bear the drain of nine millions of their cash reserves in a fortnight and that the "expense of the war must be defrayed by the issue of inconvertible paper money." Unless the banks were to lose all their gold, they must have a legal substitute for it. Secretary Chase refused to admit the predicament, but to many if not most bankers and others familiar with the laws to which banking was subject, it had appeared unavoidable and, for the want of anything better, desirable that the paper money be made a legal tender. For without a lawful substitute for coin, which was the only legal tender, the banks, unable otherwise to maintain their reserves and pay their debts, would find themselves in the courts. So would other debtors. The New York banks, the most important group of all, were shut off from legal relief by a clause of the state's constitution which forbade the legislature to validate, as had been done in the past, the suspension of specie payments; though they had the possible comfort of a court decision in 1857, *Livingston* v. *Bank of New York*, condoning the refusal of a bank to pay its obligations in coin during a general suspension. The result of suspension for the Treasury was going to be that instead of having the assistance of the banks in its financing it would become a victim of their predicament and without legal means to pay its various creditors—civilian and military personnel, suppliers, and others. Spaulding, as a banker, would be aware of the need, and, as chairman of the appropriate sub-committee, the one upon whom responsibility for action officially devolved. The banks needed the legal tender notes as much as the government did—or more, since banks cannot make laws. Sovereignties can.[41]

162

In these circumstances, Mr Chase's national currency proposal was deferred, and a bill to make Treasury notes legal tender, which the Secretary opposed, was given first place. The bankers, by advocating recourse to these notes, instigated an exercise of federal sovereignty far more revolutionary than that which Chase had recommended, but also, in the circumstances, far more practical. A trend, or force, quite beyond any party's choice or foresight had set in. Incidentally to it, the initiative in policy had passed from the Treasury to Congress, where men more experienced and practical than Chase, devised—not without dissidence—a program which he at first resisted but—not without faltering—administered. His loss of the initiative he acknowledged in his annual report a year later, when he explained that it was not necessary for him to recommend the legal tender notes. "The enlightened senators and representatives who composed the financial committees of the respective houses" had required no prompting from him. "They saw clearly the necessities created by the suspension and at once adopted the measure demanded by them. The Secretary, concurring entirely in their judgment, had no duty to perform except that of giving such information and such aid as they called for and he could supply." This approval he later repudiated in fact by concluding, when Chief Justice, that the legal tender act was unconstitutional.[42]

MAKING PAPER A LEGAL
TENDER

I

THE BILL TO make the government's paper a means of payment which creditors could not refuse lay in the lap of a committee about equally divided for and against it. Spaulding and Hooper supported it, and so did Chairman Thaddeus Stevens, after overcoming some qualms about its constitutionality which his nationalism had not yet become radical enough to dismiss instantly. Maynard, a Whig, also supported it. Morrill, Horton, and Corning—Republican, Whig, and Democrat respectively—steadfastly opposed it from first to last. Phelps, Democrat, was absent in Missouri. Stratton, Republican, was on the fence. Since the traditional opinion that the Constitution barred paper money was the favorite ground of objection, Spaulding turned to Attorney General Bates, who, after coming up to the question circumspectly, replied, quite to the point, that the Constitution said "no state" should make anything but gold and silver coin a legal tender or emit bills of credit; but that the restriction applied "to a state only and not to the nation." Moreover, he continued, "the prohibition to emit bills of credit is quite as strong as the prohibition to make anything but gold and silver a legal tender; yet nobody doubts —Congress does not doubt its power to issue bills of credit." However, the Attorney General, hurriedly answering in the evening an important question asked in the afternoon, made no mention of the tenth amendment nor of the historical evidence that most members of the 1789 convention had meant that Congress should have no legal tender powers.[1]

The Attorney General's opinion at first changed no minds in the Ways and Means Committee. On a vote three Republicans and one Whig—Stevens, Spaulding, Hooper, and Maynard—were for the bill and two Republicans, one Whig, and one Democrat—Morrill, Stratton, Horton, and Corning—were against it. Then, moved perhaps by unwillingness to kill in committee a measure earnestly favored by three of his four Republican colleagues, Stratton changed his vote. The bill was reported to the House the next day, Tuesday, 7 January, and referred to the Committee of the Whole. It was in substance the same as that introduced by Spaulding 30 December but altered in details and described as a bill "to authorize the issue of demand Treasury notes."[2]

Whether purposed or not, the omission from the bill's title of any reference to "legal tender" did not deter the enemies of paper money. They showed a prompt and formidable opposition. Between them and the bill's advocates, Chase was in an awkward position; though he disliked the bill as much as anyone, its advocates were party leaders with whom he could not break. However, within four days, Saturday, 11 January, he was host to a delegation comprising, in their own words, "representatives from boards of trade, chambers of commerce, and banking institutions" who came to Washington to oppose paper money and whom members of the monetary committee of the House and Senate were invited to meet. The delegation seems to have been made up principally of bankers, and James Gallatin was their spokesman. The procedure recommended was that taxes be levied to raise a hundred and twenty-five millions over and above revenue from imports; that the issue of demand notes not be increased but that one hundred millions of two-year notes be sold instead; that the sub-Treasury act be suspended and the Treasury be authorized to use banks as depositories, accepting book credit like other borrowers and making payments by check; that the government sell its obligations at the market; and that in borrowing of the banks its obligations be pledged and sold at the market, if necessary. There was nothing here that Chase liked; the program was merely a little less evil than the alternative.[3]

Nor did it promise much. It would have been sensible six months earlier, and then it would have lightened or possibly have avoided the present difficulties. But it was now impracticable. It was like shouting to a drowning man to

168

get out of the water. There had been too many mistakes, too many disasters, for so normal a procedure to avail now. The state of the Union was parlous, and the monetary disorder produced by Chase was but a part of the trouble. Military supplies were everywhere inadequate, leadership distracted with incompetence and jealousy, strategy confused, and tactics unskilful. Without money for prompt payments, suppliers broke down, and with neither unity nor victories to sustain confidence, money was not readily obtainable. The Joint Committee on the Conduct of the War was standing evidence of legislative dissatisfaction with the Executive; distrust of Simon Cameron as Secretary of War had led to his replacement by Edwin M. Stanton; the country was growing breathless with impatience over General McClellan's procrastinated advance on Richmond. The President's War Order of 27 January for an early general offensive was in the making. In the existing situation, what the government's obligations would fetch in the market could only be guessed, but it would certainly be well below the value at which banks and other investors carried what securities they already had. It was generally expected that the fall in value of federal obligations would destroy the aggregate capital of the banks and make them not only delinquent but insolvent. On these grounds principally, the delegation's program repelled the legislative committee to which Gallatin presented it. Spaulding vehemently denounced "the knocking down of government stocks to seventy-five or sixty cents on the dollar" but did so in a flag-waving style, as if it were merely a matter of patriotism. Hooper also objected decidedly and urged again the advantage of making government notes a legal tender.[4]

Though Secretary Chase had stood against everything the delegation proposed, and could not be pleased by disregard of the "national currency bank" plan, to which he had given so much attention in his annual report, he and the delegation were close together in abominating an issue of legal tender paper. So although both legislative committees from then on snubbed the Gallatin delegation, Chase con-

169

tinued to confer with its members. And as before, in his negotiations with the banks, he bent the delegation to his wishes. The result was a statement to the Associated Press, published 15 January, of an arrangement or understanding to the effect that "the general views of the Secretary" were assented to; that the banks would receive and pay out the Treasury's demand notes already authorized "and sustain in all proper ways the credit of the government"; that the Secretary would, within the next two weeks, continue the current daily payments of a million and a half dollars in United States demand notes (which were not legal tender) and would also pay the further sum of at least twenty millions in three-year notes "to such public creditors as desire to receive them"; that the issue of demand notes would not be increased beyond the fifty millions already authorized but that other forms of obligation should be made more attractive; and that enactment of the "national currency bank bill" recommended by the Secretary was "thought desirable." It was expected, according to the statement, "that this action and legislation will render the making of the United States demand notes a legal tender or their increase beyond the fifty million dollars authorized in July last unnecessary." Mention of increased taxes was omitted. So was suspension of the independent Treasury act.[5]

The statement shows Chase's tenacity and the force of his will. All the concessions were made by Gallatin and his associates, who, in assenting to the Secretary's "general views," in keeping silent about taxes, in agreeing to use Treasury notes, in subscribing to the national currency proposal, in abandoning their advice that the Treasury accept their banks as depositories, were getting down in the dust. The report of the *New York Tribune* was that Mr Chase listened politely to the delegation but acted on his own judgment. Outside their conference room, however, it made little difference what the Secretary and the delegation did, for the Ways and Means Committee ignored their statement. The day it was published, 15 January, with the

170

legal tender bill soon to come up, a joint resolution (HR 32) was introduced from the committee affirming the intent to raise taxes in excess of the amount mentioned by the delegation and in despite of Chase's having the latter's mention of it omitted. The resolution was adopted the same day, after brief discussion, by a vote of 134 to 5; and in the Senate two days later, after still briefer discussion, it was adopted 39 to 1.[6]

The resolution did no more than state that "in order to pay the ordinary expenses of the government, the interest on the national loans, and have an ample sinking fund for the ultimate liquidation of all public debts, a tax shall be imposed which shall, with the tariff on imports, secure an annual revenue of not less than one hundred and fifty million dollars." It was introduced by Erastus Corning, of the Ways and Means Committee, which was unanimous for it. Corning, New York Democrat, was opposed to both the legal tender and national bank measures. The resolution probably reflected in part the suppressed wish of the Gallatin group to head off the legal tender measure by a reassurance as to taxes that would bolster the government's credit and make its securities attractive enough that legal tender notes would be unnecessary. But the legal tender advocates wanted the taxes as much as anyone and said so. At this stage every advocate of making Treasury notes a legal tender seems to have meant the measure to be temporary and the notes to be redeemed as soon as possible. The result was practical unanimity for the tax resolution but for opposing reasons: one side, mainly Democratic, hoping the resolution would stop the legal tender proposal, and the other, Republican, believing legal tender paper was needed but only to bridge the gap till taxes could be collected.

Justin Morrill, who was preparing a revenue bill and like Corning wanted taxes but no legal tender notes, asked for the resolution as an assurance to "the country, which has an impatience that is becoming chronic, that whatever the army may be said to be doing, the committee of Ways

171

and Means have not *hutted* nor gone into winter quarters." The preparation of an adequate tax bill was excessively difficult and the committee had "for the entire session been diligently prosecuting the subject," Morrill said. "Our public archives, as is well known, are extremely meager in statistical information in all that relates to the industry and resources of the country." In scale and scope and terms of need the task of the committee was dismaying; the unreadiness of Congress to bring in an adequate tax measure was comparable to the unreadiness of the army to strike conclusively.[7]

Meanwhile, the legal tender advocates had been busy in other efforts to undercut their opponents. It was of first importance to win Chase to their side, for so long as he opposed them he divided the Republican majority in both Houses. If the Republican vote were split, the legal tender bill might be lost, for the Democrats were solidly against it, and the coolness or opposition of Chase would encourage that result. Accordingly some parts of the bill were rephrased and a second section was added authorizing the issue of twenty-year bonds in the amount of five hundred million dollars, bearing six per cent interest, and designed to be acceptable to creditors of the government as means of payment, whether they were contractors or employees. This was to be done in part by authorizing bonds in amounts as low as one hundred dollars each to be offered "to officers, employees, and individuals in payment for services rendered, for supplies, subsistence, and materials furnished to the United States." When the bill was discussed with Chase, details respecting the proposed legal tender notes were also discussed. Then, Spaulding says, "the original bill and additional section were finally left with the Secretary to put into such form as he desired, incorporating the amendments which he had proposed in order to enable him to execute the provisions of the bill with facility as soon as it should become a law."[8]

The changes Chase made were of minor administrative importance. The bill underwent numerous amendments on

172

its course back and forth between the two Houses and their committees; but in its final form as enacted the essential clause declaring the Treasury notes to be "lawful money and a legal tender in payment of all debts public and private within the United States" remained and still remains unaltered from the original version introduced by Spaulding 30 December 1861. Whatever Chase may have done the previous summer to make nugatory the amendment of 5 August "authorizing" suspension of the specie requirement of the independent Treasury act, he now did nothing that impaired the main purpose of the legal tender act.[9]

Yet the effort to get the Secretary to endorse the measure had little success. For when he returned the bill, 22 January, he merely explained some changes in practical details and then expressed himself as "regretting exceedingly that it is found necessary to resort to the measure of making fundable notes of the United States a legal tender but heartily desiring to cooperate with the committee in all measures to meet existing necessities in the mode most useful and least hurtful." In this verbose fashion, liberal with modifiers but sparing of verbs in the indicative, Chase contrived a dense ambiguity that revealed nothing and concealed much. The committee nevertheless adopted the amended bill and that same day, 22 January, Spaulding reported it to the House as a substitute, (HR 240), for the one reported on the 7th, (HR 187). It was made the special order for the following Tuesday, 28 January.[10]

By then, actually but not formally, the measure had first been advocated in the House, Thursday, 23 January, by John B. Alley of Massachusetts, addressing the House in Committee of the Whole. This was the day after Spaulding reported it but five days before he opened the debate. Alley was not a member of Ways and Means, and he was neither a House veteran nor a prominent speaker. He had entered Congress in 1859. He was a business man who manufactured shoes in Lowell and dealt in hides and leather in Boston. He became a director of the Union Pacific Railroad Company, which Congress incorporated five months later. He was a close friend of Samuel Hooper, with whom, when both were members of the Massachusetts legislature, he had had a responsible part in enactment of that state's free banking law. Although Spaulding was officially responsible for the legal tender measure, my conjecture, as already mentioned, is that Hooper's responsibility for it was actually the greater; Hooper was abler and more influential, he was closer to Chase, and he supported all three of the measures being put forward to fill the Union's empty purse, viz., legal tender notes, taxation, and a system of national bank currency secured by federal bonds. Chase records in his diary that Spaulding, Hooper, and Horton of the Ways and Means Committee called on him after the conference with the Gallatin delegation, 15 January, and that "Mr Hooper expressed his decided opinion that the U.S. notes must necessarily be made legal tender. Messrs Spaulding and Horton expressed no opinion. . . ." Spaulding's account may exaggerate his responsibility for the legal tender act, but his silence, on this occasion, if Chase's statement is correct, may have arisen from some apprehension lest his words carry less weight with the Secretary than Hooper's.[11]

My conjecture is that Hooper and probably Thaddeus Stevens, without whose assent little of parliamentary importance was done, preferred to have the ice broken on the floor of the House by a member of greater conservatism, modesty, and judiciousness than Spaulding. The latter made no mention of Alley's presentation either in his opening of formal debate or in his book, in which addresses *following* his own, including another of Alley's, were quoted lengthily. Mention was perhaps omitted merely because Alley's speech was not indexed in the *Globe*, which Spaulding would probably have used in writing his book. Spaulding could not have rejoiced in having Alley take priority but neither could he yield to resentment. He knew, as he wrote Chase, 24 January, that it was important to have the "full co-operation" of the press, the Cabinet, "and all our friends on the financial measure pending in Congress to overcome the opposition already developed...."[12]

In his preliminary, Alley did not speak in advocacy of legal tender notes alone but of a three-fold program of which they were but one element—the immediate and temporary one—the other two being taxation and a "national currency." No members of the Ways and Means Committee but Hooper and Stevens could advocate the three-fold program, for no others fully and explicitly accepted it. Spaulding later opposed the national bank measure, but not finally. Stevens had his hands full and though Hooper might have made the program's presentation, it was possibly advantageous to have it made by one outside the committee but familiar with its problems. It was on Stevens' motion, 23 January, that the House resolved itself into the Committee of the Whole, whereupon Alley at once got the floor. And when Alley concluded, it was Stevens who moved at once that the committee rise. It seems obvious that Stevens was participating in an arrangement for Alley to introduce the program.[13]

What Alley urged was comprehensive. It was a fiscal program such as the Union so far had lacked. He began by chiding his colleagues. "Here in mid-winter," he said, "with a stagnant trade and all the industrial energies of a great people palsied by the nightmare that is upon us, we whom the people have sent here to provide ways and means of relief have done nothing; and so far as our monetary affairs are concerned, if we except perhaps the Committee of Ways and Means, are apparently as unmoved as though all was well. With our Treasury upon the eve of bankruptcy and those who have been supplying the wants of the government knocking at the doors of the Treasury for the payment of their honest dues until hundreds are already ruined and unless something is speedily done you may soon count them by thousands—yet hour after hour, day after day, and week after week, we have done but little except waste our valuable time in continual talking about comparatively unimportant matters."

175

There were three great financial measures before Congress, he said, whose adoption would revive industry, improve the currency of the country, establish confidence, and place the public credit on a firm foundation: "First, authorizing the issue of a hundred million dollars of Treasury demand notes . . . to be made a legal tender. . . . The second—simultaneous with this—the levying of a tax of a hundred and fifty millions. Thirdly, to provide a uniform currency by adopting the recommendation in the able report of the Secretary of the Treasury" for the issue by banks of notes secured by federal securities. "I should not be in favor of either of these three measures standing alone; but in combination, each with the other, they will be found to confer the triple benefit of relief to our immediate necessities, establishing confidence on a firm foundation, and giving the people a safe currency which shall be uniform in every section of the country and ample for all the requirements of trade."

As to the authorization of legal tender notes, Alley said, "it furnishes a currency which supplies fully, without interest, the wants of the government at a time when the government is unable to meet its liabilities for any great length of time without making a forced loan." It "will save thousands from bankruptcy and afford immediate relief to the creditors of the government and through them the entire community. . . ." Alley was deliberately trying to make Congress see that money was organically important, in a sense not generally understood by people who, though intensely interested in "making money," still thought that monetary policy was merely a matter of confining the Treasury's transactions to gold. He held this from his personal experience as a business man and from the study of history; and he sought "to show how intimately connected the system of currency is with the prosperity of government and people in every age." He perceived "that increasing or decreasing the volume of the currency, in all countries and every age, produces the same effect: Its undue expansion stimulating unhealthy business, causing high

176

prices and apparent but deceptive prosperity; while, on the other hand, contraction, causing stagnation in trade, distress and ruin are sure to follow in its wake." The proposed note issue would indeed enlarge the volume of the currency and raise prices. This, Alley said, was in the minds of many the greatest objection to it; but in his opinion it was, "at the present juncture, a great merit." Though he had always been "an advocate of a restricted currency" and "would always fetter paper issues with stringent provisions," nevertheless he did not think restriction was everything. "There are times in the histories of nations as well as individuals," he said, "when contraction is detrimental to their interests and expansion the salvation of all." The general belief was that contraction, like purging, was *always* best. This he thought fallacious.[14]

Alley's emphasis on the three-fold nature of the program and the necessary inter-relation between the three parts of it was characteristic of him and of Hooper. Thaddeus Stevens threw himself into the support of all three measures with his egregious energy and parliamentary skill. Hooper tried also to keep Chase and the Administration associated with the program as a whole in spite of Chase's obtuseness. Hooper did this casually as if to keep the pressure gentle and prejudices and obsessions quiet. His speeches, like Alley's but more frequent, were cool and reasonable in tone—and probably duller to listen to—while Stevens and Spaulding struck hard and made the sparks fly. Two years later, 6 April 1864, speaking for the second or rewritten national bank act, Hooper had occasion to defend Chase from the extra-mural attacks of James Gallatin, echoed in the House by James Brooks of New York; and he then said in soothing retrospect that "the loan bill, including the issue of legal tender notes, the national bank act, and the tax law were recommended by the Secretary of the Treasury as the three means to be relied upon to carry the nation through its financial difficulties." This was glossing things over to the brink of absurdity, but it was also an example of Hooper's repeated stress upon the co-

177

herence of the policy which Alley and he had first advocated and which, when he now spoke, had come into effect. Chase had thought only of loans and a national currency of bank notes; he had been sluggish about taxes, and the greenbacks he had had to have crammed down his throat. It was Hooper and Alley who thought in terms of a coherent program. The others concerned with the majority's fiscal policy, except Thaddeus Stevens, had mostly been either sitting on the fence or kicking over the traces.[15]

In this first speech on the legal tender notes, 23 January 1862, Alley said nothing about their usefulness to the bankers. No one well informed about the need of the measure could have been ignorant of the banks' predicament nor unaware that the measure might be obstructed, not prospered, by mention of the bankers' interest. Those not already informed were probably hostile anyway. So the less said about the technicalities of banking and the interest of the bankers the better. The interests of the Union were the controlling ones and sufficient. Nor was more emphasis put upon legal tender note issue than upon taxes and the national bank currency, except to the extent that it was the measure antecedent to the others and the one for which the need was the most immediate.*

Meanwhile Ways and Means committeemen were in disagreement about Secretary Chase's position. Most of them and many members of Congress believed that he had not committed himself and that if pressed to a decision he would declare the proposed legal tender notes unconsti-

---

* So far as I know, my account of Alley's address of 23 January, in which he explained the need of making Treasury notes a legal tender, is the first mention of it by any historian. Spaulding, Bolles, Dewey, and Mitchell say nothing of it. The address presumably escaped earlier notice for several reasons: it preceded the calendared discussion opened by Spaulding the 28th, it dealt with a fiscal program of which the legal tenders were but a part, and it is not indexed in the *Congressional Globe*. In the debate which followed, however, it was mentioned by several speakers whom it impressed. During that debate, Alley spoke again. B. Hammond, *AHR* LXVII (October 1961), pp. 8-9; *Congressional Globe*, 37th Congress, 2nd Session, 5 February 1862, pp. 659-61.)

tutional. His letter of the 22nd to Spaulding had barely and inconclusively mentioned the heart of the matter. Only a week before he had joined the Gallatin delegation in a proposal "expected" to make legal tender notes "unnecessary." Then in his letter of the 22nd he had really done no more than wordily express himself as "regretting exceedingly" their being found necessary; and using a tone of acceptance, he had avoided a statement of acceptance. So the committee resolved to send the bill (HR 240) back to him and ask "his opinion as to the propriety and necessity of its immediate passage by Congress." This was not a mere repetition of what had been done but formal action by the committee to obtain something from the Secretary more definite than the bland opacity of his reply to Spaulding's personal and informal inquiry.[16]

II

On the afternoon of Tuesday, 28 January, Spaulding opened debate upon the legal tender bill. His presentation of it, unlike Alley's five days before, was slashing and peremptory. He asserted the constitutionality of the measure and its necessity. Alley's earlier statement had wooed the opposition by its balance and reasonable tone; Spaulding swung a club. "We were never," he said, "in greater peril than at this moment. . . . The bill before us is a war measure, a measure of *necessity* and not of choice, presented by the Committee of Ways and Means to meet the most pressing demands upon the Treasury, to sustain the army and navy until they can make a vigorous advance upon the traitors and crush out the rebellion. These are extraordinary times, and extraordinary measures must be resorted to in order to save our government and preserve our nationality." The Treasury had funds for "only a few days longer." Notes, amounting in all to a hundred and fifty million dollars, would have to be authorized and "declared lawful money and a legal tender in payment of all debts public and private, within the United States. . . ."[17]

"The bill," he said, "is simple and perspicuous in its terms and easy of execution." The need was immediate. "This measure is brought forward as the best that can be devised, in the present exigency, to relieve the necessities of the Treasury." The government's bonds, if put on the market and offered to the highest bidders, could not in present circumstances be disposed of "except at ruinous rates of discount." Doing so "would depreciate the bonds already taken by the banks and the people." Spaulding feared they would fall to seventy-five, seventy, sixty, or even fifty cents on the dollar and ruin their owners. The committee, he said, had had a bill prepared embodying the Secretary's plan for the purchase by banks of federal bonds to be pledged as security for a national currency, but it could not, even if adopted, meet the needs of the Treasury soon enough. And import duties and taxes would also "be wholly inadequate to meet the requirements of the Treasury in the present emergency during the next six months."[18]

Accordingly, Spaulding asked, "If you can not borrow . . . except at ruinous rates of discount and can not make the new banking system available in time and can not realize the amount required from your tariff and tax bills, in what mode can the means be obtained and the government be carried on?" He believed it could be done only "by issuing Treasury notes payable on demand and making them a legal tender in payment of all debts public and private and by adequate taxation" to be imposed by new measures. This would "bring into full exercise all the higher powers of government under the Constitution." Instead of hopelessly seeking funds from the conventional sources, Spaulding would "assert the power and dignity of the government by the issue of its own notes, pledging the faith, the honor, and property of the whole loyal people. . . ." This was no less a constitutional argument than a monetary one.[19]

Anticipating the argument that the Constitution did not permit anything but silver and gold to be made a legal tender, Spaulding recurred to interpretations by Hamilton, Marshall, and others which emphasized the authority of Congress to make all laws necessary and proper for exercise of its enumerated powers. He stressed in particular its power to maintain the army and navy. "In carrying on this existing war and putting down the rebellion, it is necessary to bring into exercise all the sovereign power of the government to sustain itself." This, Spaulding said, would comprehend the raising of a hundred and fifty million dollars by taxation, the issue of the proposed hundred and fifty millions of legal tender notes, and the borrowing of about five hundred millions on long-term bonds—making eight hundred million dollars in all. The legal tender notes were for immediate needs. They "would meet the present exigencies of the government," by enabling it to pay what it owed its soldiers and sailors and the contractors who were furnishing it supplies, materials, and munitions. The notes, circulating "in the hands of the people, would enable them to pay the taxes imposed and would facilitate all business operations between farmers, mechanics, commercial business men, and banks."[20]

The following day, 29 January, George H. Pendleton, of Ohio, a lawyer and Democrat, later a railway president and greenbacker, made a learned argument against the constitutionality of paper made a legal tender. He said the pending bill differed from all previous authorizations of Treasury notes in several essential particulars: the proposed notes bore no interest, had no date of maturity, being payable only at the pleasure of the debtor, and were "to be made lawful money and a legal tender in discharge of all pecuniary obligations," private or public. "Not only, sir, was such a law never passed, but such a law was never voted on, never proposed, never introduced, never recommended. . . ." The measure meant "a departure from the settled financial policy of the government" and a launching forth "upon an ocean of experiment upon which the wise men who administered the government before we came into power, warned by example of other nations, would not

181

permit it even to enter." The proposal, he said, brought the government to a crisis which it might not survive. It might, he said, "overcome the evils of secession"; it might successfully "defend itself against those in arms against it; but I firmly believe," he said, "that it can not maintain itself against the shock of the accumulated and manifold dangers which follow inevitably, closely in the wake of an illegal, unsound, and depreciated government paper currency."[21]

Every monetary obligation, Pendleton said, "is in legal contemplation a contract for the payment of gold and silver coin," and under the Constitution always had been. "Every promissory note, every bill of exchange, every lease reserving rent, every loan of money reserving interest, every bond issued by this government, is a contract to which the faith of the obligor is pledged that the amount, whether rent, interest, or principal, shall be paid in the gold and silver coin of the country." In the courts "every verdict which has been rendered, every judgment which has been entered up, every decree for the payment of money, has been made upon that hypothesis." Yet now a bill was being considered with provisions which would impair every contract of a monetary kind, provisions which would release the debtor from his obligation and divest the creditor of his rights. "I need only state the proposition," he said, "to shock the mind of the legal profession of the country," long and thoroughly imbued with a sense of the sanctity of contractual obligations.[22]

"In all its external relations," Pendleton declared, the federal government was sovereign, but domestically it was not. "In its relations to its own citizens, in its relations to the states, in its relations to its own constituents," it had only those powers granted it specifically. "Its powers are all delegated, and delegated by the terms of the Constitution itself." He said that not having been granted to the federal government, the power to issue legal tender currency was not possessed by it. And he offered positive evidence that the power was withheld deliberately and intentionally: it was recorded that members of the convention of 1787 had in mind specifically the disorder arising from the issues of legal tender currency by both the Continental Congress and individual states and mentioned it in arguments against granting the power to emit bills on the credit of the United States.* On this point, Pendleton concluded that "if the language of the Constitution and the weight of authority can settle any proposition, it is that Congress has not the power" to issue the legal tender currency which it was now proposed that it exercise.[23]

Turning last from the constitutional to the practical, Pendleton foretold depreciation and disorder from the purposed action. "The wit of man," he said, "has never discovered a means by which paper currency can be kept at par value, except by its speedy, cheap, certain convertibility into gold and silver." The consequences to be foreseen were obvious. "The currency will be expanded; prices will be inflated; fixed values will depreciate; incomes will be diminished; the savings of the poor will vanish; the hoardings of the widow will melt away; bonds, mortgages, and notes—everything of fixed value—will lose their value; everything of changeable value will be appreciated; the necessaries of life will rise in value; the government will pay twofold—certainly largely more than it ought—for everything that it goes into the market to buy; gold and silver will be driven out of the country."[24]

Pendleton's speech presented the gist of the succeeding arguments against the legal tender proposal. But it is no more interesting for its comprehensive statement of the conventional objections to the notes which later came to be called greenbacks than for the change of mind which transformed Pendleton eventually into a prominent greenbacker. Nothing in what he said foreshadowed that future apostasy.

Meanwhile, Secretary Chase's attitude continued to be embarrassing to the legal tender advocates. When Spaul-

* This question of the Constitution's intent is considered at length in Chapter 4 of my *Banks and Politics.*

183

ding had opened debate on the bill, 28 January, no reply had been received to the committee's formal request (following the Secretary's evasive note of the 22nd) for his "opinion as to the propriety and necessity of its immediate passage." The next day, interposing in Pendleton's address, Roscoe Conkling, Republican of New York, had asked about Chase's opinion of the constitutionality and expediency "of making paper a legal tender in payment of debts"; and Spaulding had replied that the Secretary's opinion had been requested, had not been received, but was expected "every hour." When discussion of the measure was resumed after the week end, Monday, 3 February, Thaddeus Stevens stated on the basis of a lukewarm letter from Chase dated 29 January, that the Treasury was "urgent" for passage of the bill, and Spaulding at last could announce that he too had "just received" a letter from the Secretary to that effect. He asked the clerk of the House to read "an extract" from the letter. "Immediate action is of great importance," the clerk read. "The Treasury is nearly empty. I have been obliged to draw for the last instalment of the November loan. So soon as it is paid, I fear the banks generally will refuse to receive the United States notes unless made a legal tender. You will see the necessity of urging the bill through without more delay."[25]

Spaulding himself, urged by Maynard of Tennessee, a like-minded colleague on the Ways and Means Committee, read another passage from Chase's letter, as follows: "I came with reluctance to the conclusion that the legal tender clause is a necessity; but I came to it decidedly and I support it earnestly. I do not hesitate when I have made up my mind. . . . The conclusion I have arrived at has convinced me that it is important to the success of the measure."

Now, both this passage which Spaulding read himself and the "extract" he had the clerk read vary from what Chase wrote. This is plain from comparison of what was read with the full text of Chase's letter as recorded in the *Globe*, in Schuckers's biography of Chase, and by Spaulding himself in his book. Spaulding seems to have edited while on his feet the passages which were read to the House and to have done so with no great respect for Chase's diction. To Chase's statement—"I fear the banks generally will refuse to receive the United States notes"—he gave greater force by adding, "unless made a legal tender"; but in quoting Chase as having written—"The conclusion I have arrived at has convinced me that it is important to the success of the measure"—he made mere gabble of what the Secretary had expressed pointedly.[26]

For all his reluctance, however, Chase had given his formal assent, and Spaulding merely exaggerated the cheerfulness with which it had been given. The Secretary was at the end of his rope, and alone there. In his own department, both Assistant Secretary Harrington in Washington and John J. Cisco, the Assistant Treasurer in New York, insisted that the legal tender clause was necessary. Chase's closest financial adviser in Congress, Samuel Hooper, who was one of the few members ready to support his national bank scheme, also insisted that the legal tender clause was necessary. So did Thaddeus Stevens, so did Chase's New York adviser, John Stevens, and so did the larger part of the influential city bankers, whose aid to the Treasury was as indispensable as that of the manufacturers to the War Department.[27]

The Secretary hated the crime about to be committed, but he could not afford to refuse acceptance of its benefits—perhaps chastened by the consequences of his having refused five months before to be released from the statutory requirement that he deprive the banks of their reserves. That refusal had made refusal of the legal tender notes impossible. The banks could not be deprived of their reserves of gold unless afforded a substitute for it. Chase's discomfort is expressed in a plaintive letter to Spaulding, 30 January (not put in the *Globe*), about shortcomings in Spaulding's address of 28 January. Chase is sorry that his banking plan is being neglected as a measure of relief and that in respect to the Treasury's borrowings in the previous

185

months he is merely let off without censure when he thought himself entitled to some credit. His two first loans had been negotiated considerably above the market rate, he said, and the last at a rate nearly equal, after which, "almost immediately," the market fell. He had, indeed, far more than that to complain of in the long run. For exaggeration by Spaulding of the cheerfulness with which he had assented to the legal tender notes helped to establish the myth of his responsibility for them and sharpen the criticism of his later contention as Chief Justice that they were unconstitutional. Instead of having thought them up and urged their authorization, which for years was unjustifiably held against him, he had merely yielded to what he had himself made unavoidable—that is, a formal act of bankruptcy, which the legal tender measure was. It is not of much help to Chase's reputation to change the indictment from inconstancy to stubbornness, but accuracy requires it.[28]

It is likely, of course, that Roscoe Conkling, the prominent New York Republican who had asked the embarrassing question about Chase's opinion of the legal tender proposal, was already quite aware of Chase's views and pressed for disclosure of them in the House, not for his own information but to make things awkward for the legal tender advocates, who, with the Democrats solidly opposed, must husband Republican votes. The day after, 4 February, chairman Stevens had to acknowledge that though the bill, when reported, had had the concurrence of most members of the Ways and Means Committee, since then some members had "changed their views." This meant, for one, John L. N. Stratton, Republican of New Jersey, who had gone over to the minority in support of the substitute offered by Justin Morrill, Republican of Vermont. The situation of the Republican sponsorship was uncomfortable.[29]

The day Chase's letters were considered, 3 February, Clement L. Vallandigham, Ohio copperhead, in his fiery fashion declaimed the stock objection to making paper a legal tender, though his colleague, George Pendleton, he said, had already "disposed of that question forever." He was followed by Samuel Hooper, who reverted to the pattern of Alley's original presentation eleven days before. Three measures had been considered in committee, Hooper said, which "form a comprehensive system by which it is believed the government will be enabled to procure the sums necessary to the successful prosecution of the war." The first was the bill before the House, which would authorize issue of one hundred and fifty million dollars of legal tender notes; the second was the tax bill still in committee, which with import tariffs, would "insure an annual revenue of at least" an equal amount; the third was "a national banking law," which would require the deposit of federal bonds as security for bank notes constituting a national currency. The two latter were "designed to be more permanent" elements of the proposed finance program. Hooper described the tax bill and the bank bill briefly. This was factual but not appealing. In respect to taxes it went well enough, perhaps, but in respect to the national bank proposal it was merely inflammatory; for it denied a right exercised by the states ever since the Revolution, threatened all the existing banks, and promised an undoing of Andrew Jackson's greatest achievement. Roscoe Conkling, in particular, was contemptuous of the national bank proposal and found the legal tender bill the less acceptable because Hooper united it with the bank plan. Hooper also sought to identify his and Alley's three-fold program with Chase's December recommendation; for he said that the plan he was sketching "in its several branches fills up the outlines of the policy submitted by the Secretary of the Treasury in his very able report." This was attempting a shotgun marriage of Chase's proposals and those of Alley and Hooper himself. For the latter started with legal tender notes, which Chase abominated; it stressed taxes, which he shunned; and it put last what he put first—his national bank scheme. To be sure, he had swallowed, squeamishly, the legal tender bill, but the Hooper-Alley program was far from being what he had himself recommended.[30]

187

In this part of the House debate, which, as mercifully as I can, I am presenting only in fragments, Samuel Hooper adverted to the unrealistic habit the legal tender opponents had of denouncing legal tender paper as inimical to coin —unrealistic because there was no currency of coin. Currency of coin was a legal fiction. "Every intelligent man," Hooper said, "knows that coined money is not the currency of the country." Irredeemable and depreciated state bank notes were; and the real question was whether these notes of state banks or notes of the federal government should serve not only as an actual medium of payment but as a legal one. This was an indirect but substantial argument for making the federal government's domestic sovereignty a reality.[31]

Hooper's thoughtful, comprehensive, and analytic advocacy of the legal tender bill on Monday, 3 February, was matched on Tuesday by the address of Justin Morrill, Republican of Vermont, who with comparable ability and greater forensic skill denounced the measure. Morrill stressed its "impolicy," for he thought the war would not last much beyond the coming spring, which in Washington and where the armies were was but six weeks or so away. He was probably thinking of spring in Vermont. But he was reasonable in his opposition, unlike Vallandigham and Conkling. He declined to expect ruin from making paper a legal tender but expected little short of it, fearing it would be "the precursor . . . of a prolific brood of promises, no one of which is to be redeemed in the constitutional standard of the country." He feared the adoption of legal tender notes would make the enemy "grin with delight"; he had as soon provide the army with "Chinese wooden guns" as the Treasury with paper money. He deplored making circulating notes worth more than bonds. The legal tender bill was "a measure not blessed by one sound precedent and damned by all," despite its authors' "thorough knowledge of the subject and large acquaintance with the monetary circles of the country." The legal tender notes would "infinitely damage the national credit, . . . increase many fold

the cost of the war, . . . slide into the place of proper taxation, . . . and tend to a premature peace." They would be
of doubtful constitutionality, "immoral, and a breach of the
public faith." They would at once banish all specie from
circulation, dampen the ardor of men, degrade America in
the estimation of other nations, cripple American labor, and
make the wealthy wealthier. Mr. Morrill made it plain that
he did "not object to the issue of United States notes to a
limited extent to circulate as currency" but thought it "both
convenient and proper." He did "protest against making
anything a legal tender but gold and silver." He offered a
substitute bill which would authorize more notes but not
make them a legal tender and which would avoid "all the
material and, we might say, fatal objections to the original
bill." It was "entirely practical and feasible in its character"
and would "not only relieve the Treasury from its present
necessities but do something towards making provision
for future wants."[32]

Following Morrill's attack on the legal tender bill and
another, more rhetorical, by Roscoe Conkling, a fervid defense of it was made by John A. Bingham, Republican of
Ohio. Bingham was a radical and fire-eating spellbinder
whose talents as a grand-stand bully were later displayed
in the prosecution of alleged parties to Booth's murder of
President Lincoln and again in the impeachment proceedings against President Johnson. Bingham's course, which
was quite without the conservatism, experience, and practical judgment which marked Hooper's and Alley's, was
perhaps more effective than theirs and close to that of the
later greenbackers. It was one of nationalism, flag-waving,
and ascription to the federal government of any and all
power. Spaulding, and more notably Alley and Hooper, had
advocated the exercise of federal authority to provide a
temporary, irregular, but desperately needed means of
payment. Bingham, however, seemed less interested in getting the government's bills paid than in having Treasury
notes made a legal tender as a manifestation of federal
sovereignty and an end in itself. With Bingham, as with

189

Thaddeus Stevens, the Constitution was liable to any interpretation necessary for a Northern victory and a vindictive treatment of the South. His speech appealed strenuously to the emotions and scarcely at all to judgment. If it were necessary—or even merely convenient, one suspects —for the federal government to issue legal tender notes, then there was nothing to hinder its doing so. He repelled constitutional objections to them with the cry that he could not be silent when efforts were being made to curb "the power of the American people to control their currency, a power essential to their interests. . . ." He asserted "the rightful authority of the American people as a nationality, a sovereignty, and by virtue of their Constitution." That is money, he declared, which sovereignty declares to be money.[33]

In practice nothing could be further than this from the orthodox conviction that only gold and silver were money and that God had made it so. And nothing could be closer to it in mysticism. Implicitly one absolute authority was to be replaced by another—the first divine, the second earthly.

Two days later, 6 February, William Kellogg of Illinois, took an even more enthusiastic course than Bingham. He loved the idea of the federal government asserting itself "in this our extremity, while we are struggling to perpetuate our government." In the circumstances, he said, he was "willing to go to the very verge of the Constitution." He pleaded for devotion to the federal government. "Whether my home is on fire to-day or not I care but little if I have no confidence in the government under which I live." And "before this Republic shall go down," he cried, "or one star be lost, I would take every cent from the treasury of the states, from the treasury of capitalists, from the treasury of individuals, and press it into the use of the government." Yet even though he stressed the current peril of the Republic and said he might possibly doubt the constitutionality of legal tender paper in peace time, his argument was substantially that of the Populists later. For he expressed

190

the familiar agrarian disaffection with the "huckstering capitalists," the bankers and brokers, and saw in the government's issue of paper money a means not only of waging war but of countering "the harpies" who sought to "make merchandise of the hopes and fears of the Republic." The country had suffered enough from the current bank note currency. In particular, he said, "there is a necessity, a pressing necessity, for some relief to the producers of the West, if nowhere else, in the way of a currency to represent our productions. . . . Our barns, our granaries, our storehouses are filled. . . . We have property; we have agricultural and mineral wealth in abundance. Give us a reliable currency, as this will be, to represent this wealth. Save us," he begged, from the bankers and speculators. Without the proposed paper, he told Congress, "your tax laws will remain unexecuted," for there was no money with which to pay taxes. "Pass this bill, and business and commerce will revive; confidence will be restored; and the wealth and productions of the West will be known and represented in the national Treasury." When politics was bristling with such arguments by Western Populists ten years later, Kellogg was far away, a consul in Japan. But his words in 1862 indicate the ripeness of Western minds for the greenbacks and the substitution of federal monetary authority for the intrinsic value of certain metals.[34]

The same day Thomas M. Edwards, Republican of New Hampshire, lawyer and business man, spoke for the legal tender bill in the tone of Alley and Hooper. He particularly distinguished the committee bill from the substitute presented by Justin Morrill, fellow New Englander and Republican, which would authorize the issue of more notes but not make them legal tender. This, Edwards argued, would leave the Treasury dependent on taxes and borrowings. With Albert Gallatin, he thought taxes in the unprecedented amounts required were impracticable; they could be counted on only for the civil expenses of the government and for interest on the public debt. Borrowings would break down. "Does anyone believe," he asked, "that two or three hundred millions of bonds of the United States could be negotiated without a ruinous discount, if they should be taken by our capitalists at all; or that, if we should rely on them for the larger amounts needed, we could realize more than one dollar in hand for two to be paid hereafter?" Edwards thought the Morrill substitute had all the disadvantages of the legal tender measure and none of its advantages. He regretted the need of either but chose the legal tender measure as the more practical and prompt. Six years later, in a personal letter, Edwards wrote of the question as having been "of immeasurable interest and importance at the time"; and, without change in his opinion, he said that the legal tender bill had offered (the italics being his) "the *best* mode of *using our national credit, in the absence of all other resources,* to enable the government to maintain the terrible conflict in which we were then engaged."[35]

General debate on the bill, which Spaulding had opened 28 January, came to an end 6 February with a brief restatement by him of the measure's necessity and of the need of taxes to support it, and with a more comprehensive argument for it by Thaddeus Stevens. The latter said that the daily expenses of the government were about two million dollars and, that before the next session could act, the Treasury would need about seven hundred millions. Taxes could not provide it soon enough. Nor could loans. The Secretary of the Treasury "has used his best efforts to negotiate a loan of but fifty millions and has failed." If the attempt to borrow seven hundred millions were made and bonds "were forced into the market" as wanted, he had "no doubt they would sell as low as sixty per cent, . . ." as in the last war with Britain, "and even then it would be impossible to find payment in coin." The depreciated notes of state banks would have to be accepted. The Secretary's project for the chartering of national banks would take too long; and besides the government, whose credit he maintained on moral grounds was better than that of the banks, should have the profit of circulation. The question of constitutionality now gave Stevens no difficulty whatsoever, for it was his growing conviction that Congress had any power needed to maintain the Union. "The first duty of every nation is self-preservation," he had already declared in a most notable address 22 January. "This government is empowered to suppress insurrection; its Executive is enjoined 'to see all the laws faithfully executed'; Congress is granted power to pass all laws necessary to that end. If no other means were left to save the Republic from destruction, I believe we have power, *under the Constitution and according to its express provision,* to declare a dictator, without confining the choice to any officer of the government." He could not doubt the power of Congress to make the paper of the government lawful money. For, he contended, like Alexander Hamilton, "whenever any law is *necessary* and proper to carry into execution any delegated power, such law is valid. That necessity need not be absolute, inevitable, and overwhelming—if it be useful, expedient, profitable, the necessity is within the constitutional meaning. Whether such necessity exists is solely for the decision of Congress." Nor would he consider any other course. The Ways and Means Committee, he said, had done the best it could, and unless the bill were "to pass with the legal tender clause in it," then it was "not desirable to its friends or the Administration that it should pass at all." He and other advocates of it would vote against it, and if it failed to pass he himself would "be modest enough not to attempt any other scheme." It had been given "most anxious consideration," with the help of "the best qualified" advisers. The Ways and Means Committee's majority, Stevens said, "believe that the credit of the country will be sustained by it, that under it all classes will be paid in money which all classes can use, and that it will confer no advantage on the capitalist over the poor laboring man. If this bill shall pass, I shall hail it as the most auspicious measure of this Congress; if it should fail, the result will be more deplorable than any disaster which could befall us."[36]

On the other hand, Owen Lovejoy of Illinois, a Republi-

can too, but also a minister of the gospel and an abolitionist, countered Stevens' praise of the measure with
vehement denunciation of it. "Sir," he cried, "there is no
precipice, there is no chasm, there is no possible, yawning,
bottomless gulf before this nation so terrible, so appalling,
so ruinous, as this same bill that is before us and that it is
proposed to pass under the pressure of these influences
brought to bear upon it." Roscoe Conkling, New York Republican, followed with the warning that "no possible result to which the committee or the House can arrive will
be so bad, so lastingly detrimental, will lay the founda-
tions of regret so enduring, as the adoption of any plan by
which paper is to be made a legal tender for the payment
of debts, past, present, and future. . . ."[37]

Despite these Republican outcries, Thaddeus Stevens
dominated the vote. A pending amendment to remove the
legal tender clause was defeated and the bill intact was
adopted by 93 votes to 59. On the vote to pass the bill,
the Democrats were almost wholly negative, only five or
so voting for it; being the opposition and the party of Jacksonian hard money, none should have voted aye. The Republicans were in four groups: those versed in monetary
matters and in favor of the bill on sensible grounds, who included Hooper and Alley of Massachusetts, Spaulding of
New York, and Edwards of New Hampshire; those zeal-
ously for it on nationalistic grounds, including Bingham of
Ohio and Kellogg of Illinois; those divided in their own
minds and reluctantly for it as a party measure, including
Riddle of Ohio, who called it dangerous and unconstitutional, but voted aye; and those firm as adamant against
it, including Morrill of Vermont, Lovejoy of Illinois, and the
Conklings of New York.[38]

In the foregoing debate nothing was made of the circumstance that the bill had its origin in the predicament
of the bankers, who needed a legal tender to replace specie,
maintain reserves, and comply with state laws. Morrill
merely alluded to that fact in derogation, saying on doubtful authority there were "more sharks and brokers, . . . by

one half at least," working for the legal tenders than against them. Most persons supposed that bankers would automatically oppose the legal tenders, as indeed many did; but H. G. Blake, Republican of Ohio, was more badly mistaken than Morrill when in a speech advocating them he asserted that the bankers had used "all the influence within their power to defeat this bill with the legal tender provision." The leadership undoubtedly realized that this belief would help the bill and took care not to correct it.[39]

Of the twenty-four principal participants in discussion of the measure in the House, only three were Democrats. These were Pendleton and Vallandigham of Ohio, and H. B. Wright of Pennsylvania; the rest simply voted. Of the twenty-one Republicans (including one Whig and one Unionist), thirteen advocated the measure and eight opposed it. The arguments on both sides were uniform and conventional and involved two considerations, one of which was constitutional and the other practical. Opponents of the measure declared it unconstitutional because the federal government had been delegated no power to enact such a law and therefore did not possess it. They also said that paper money was dangerous and would bring on disaster. Proponents of the measure declared it constitutional by implication in the power given the federal government to coin money, in the power to do what was necessary in exercise of the powers specifically given it, and in the obligation the government had to defend itself. So strong and widely held were hard money convictions and strict constitutional interpretations that obedience to them was to have been expected. It is the abandonment of them that is remarkable. It is also remarkable how little common interest, economic or regional, the innovators had; for they included, especially in their leadership, both Easterners with important business interests—Alley, Hooper, Spaulding, Stevens—and Western extremists—Bingham and Kellogg—whose constituents were mostly agrarian.

The situation illustrated a political weakness of the Republicans, a party united on slavery and secession but in whose formation monetary and fiscal principles had had no influence. For a decade or so nothing in politics had been deader than the subject of the currency—an issue that seemingly burnt itself out with the achievement of the Jacksonians in killing the federal Bank, thirty years earlier, in turning the currency over to the states, and in making the federal Treasury "independent." Now, when faced with recourse to an "unconstitutional" issue of paper money, most Republicans had nothing to fall back on but their former principles, either Democratic or Whig. With both, hard-money convictions prevailed, the difference being that the Democratic background was the more doctrinaire and the Whig the more practical. This difference was enough to divide the Republicans but not enough to defeat the bill.

III

Secretary Chase had been aware for weeks that influential bankers wanted Treasury notes made legal tender —and in particular that two of his most important advisers, John Stevens and Samuel Hooper, were among them—but the collapse of the Gallatin group's proposals in mid-January must still have been instructive to him. Immediately after the delegation dispersed, John B. Austin, president of the Southwark Bank, Philadelphia, wrote the Secretary, 18 January, that he had been urged to join it but had declined to do so because he did not agree with its members "in their financial theories." Austin said that besides levying taxes sufficient to satisfy the holders of government obligations that interest and principal would be paid them promptly, it was necessary that the government issue "at least a hundred million dollars of United States Treasury notes, receivable for all dues and being a *Legal Tender* for all obligations." Such notes, he said, could be safely taken by the banks to any amount because in all circumstances they could be used to "pay the obligations of the banks; whereas, unless they be a legal tender, banks would fear that whilst they may receive any amount of them to-day, to-morrow their creditors may not receive them, leaving the banks to suffer whatever loss or inconvenience may arise." But if made a legal tender, the notes would always be kept on hand in amounts sufficient to meet the banks' daily demands. They would supplant bank notes and provide the government funds without bearing interest. Austin also approved, he said, the plan by which banks might obtain their charters "directly from the United States government" and hoped it might "be matured in such manner as will make it the interest of banks and bankers to change their allegiance from states to the federal government."[40]

The foregoing letter from a Philadelphia banker who had refused to join the Gallatin delegation was followed closely by word from a Boston banker who had joined it. According to one of Chase's biographers, the banker, on his return home, 20 January, telegraphed Chase that the Boston banks would not assent to the arrangement agreed upon in Washington and advised making United States notes a legal tender. This was from Samuel H. Walley, president of the Revere Bank. On top of it came a letter from John A. Stevens, of the Bank of Commerce, dated 21 January, apparently written in answer to a request from Chase for his advice, and stating the courses open in "the unhappy state of financial affairs." Stevens, perhaps unaware that Erastus Corning's tax resolution had passed both Houses already, said: "First" that Congress, "at once by resolution and soon by well-digested legislation, must make manifest to the nation its determination to pass a large and efficient tax bill." Then "Second," he wrote, "Exchequer bills should be used in payments to contractors, but not in excessive amounts," bearing interest and convertible into twenty year bonds. These proposals could not have pleased Chase, who clung to Albert Gallatin's outgrown preference for borrowing to meet the cost of war and to an idea of his own that short-term borrowing was better than long. John Stevens' "Third" prescription was prefaced by the admonition that "much is required and that quickly." It called for a choice between two alternatives: Either "the government must at once flood the market" with the twenty year bonds, selling them to the extent of its necessities at the best rate they would bring, "entirely disregarding the great sacrifice" at which they must be sold "and also disregarding the great injury such course would inflict upon the takers" of bonds already acquired; or it "must issue demand notes, making them a legal tender." For, Stevens continued, "unless made a legal tender, any reliance would prove unfounded that the banks will or can take these notes to any considerable extent after the payment by them to the government of the remaining two instalments of the loan" still to be made. "For the notes, being in excess of any demand for circulation, would depreciate and be rejected." As to the alternative he preferred, Stevens said that no one was "a more decided advocate of maintaining the stability and soundness of all paper currency" and its "convertibility into coin at all times than I am and always have been, or more dreads the evils of irredeemable paper money." He "would be greatly relieved and gratified if any feasible plan" could be devised which did "not involve the use of demand notes as a legal tender." But after long consideration, he said, "I have been able to find none."[41]

A week later, in a letter dated New York, 29 January, Stevens commended Spaulding's account of the government's finances. He wrote the latter that there were but the alternatives Spaulding had said, which were those he himself had stated to Chase in his letter of the 21st. One was "to flood the market with the long stocks, submit to the very great depression in the price, and abide the consequences; a great augmentation of the public debt and ruin to many of the warmest supporters of the government [who would be the early purchasers of the government's obligations and losers from the fall in their market value]." The other alternative was, "for the present to issue demand notes, making them a legal tender. . . . I have," wrote Stevens, "long entertained and freely expressed these views, here and in Washington."[42]

198

The testimony of these letters of John Stevens is corroborated in one written seven years later by Henry F. Vail, the cashier of the Bank of Commerce, of which Stevens was president. In retrospect Vail wrote that "the officers and a majority if not all of the directors" of the bank had not agreed with "Mr. Gallatin and associates who visited Washington in January 1862." He himself, he said, and some of his bank's directors, had gone to Washington as members of a committee opposing the Gallatin delegation. At Chase's invitation, one of the directors of the Commerce, C. H. Russell, and perhaps others, had attended the meeting at the Treasury with Gallatin and his associates, Saturday afternoon, 11 January, "but totally dissenting from the propositions then made took no part in the proceedings. . . ." Mr. Russell, however, went before the Committee of Ways and Means and frequently was with the members of that committee and of the Senate Finance Committee, to whom he expressed his opposition to legal tender issues in any circumstances except those that had arisen. Mr. Vail said that he was again in Washington when the legal tender bill was pending in the Senate and appeared before the Finance Committee, to whom he explained "the workings of the bank settlements through the Clearing House and the impossibility of forcing a circulating medium of the demand notes issued by the Treasury unless they were made a legal tender. . . ."[43]

Spaulding records numerous other letters commending the legal tender proposal and condemning the countermeasures agreed to by Chase and the Gallatin committee. A banker associated with him in Buffalo wrote him, 13 January, to "send home the bank committee; their proposition is *awful*," and "let the demand notes assume the place of specie in every particular." The same day a Wall Street banking and brokerage firm, Thomas Denny and Company, wrote Spaulding their approval of his plan to make demand notes "a legal tender in all transactions" and urged taxes as well. John E. Williams, president of the Metropolitan Bank, New York, wrote Spaulding, 20 January, to congratulate him on the projected legal tender notes. Williams wished there were "a man of ability" at the head of the Treasury even though he lacked the "creative genius of a Hamilton" or the "general attainments of Albert Gallatin." He made Spaulding a number of practical suggestions on details of the legal tender issue. M. H. Grinnell, one of New York's wealthiest and most influential business men, wrote Spaulding, 30 January, to thank him for his speech on the 28th and to say that "nine out of twelve persons" in the city of New York agreed with him. "As for G——— and a few egotistical gentlemen that act with him, they should be driven out of Washington, as they only embarrass the government; and it seems to me that their policy, if adopted, would soon ruin the government credit and break down the country. Go a direct tax for one hundred and fifty or two hundred millions and then issue one hundred and fifty millions Treasury notes *legal tender*, . . . and the government credit will be saved from disgrace. There are not eight bank presidents that side with G———. He is an odd fish—has very little influence here." Whom Grinnell meant by "G———" is indicated by the context and by the circumstance that James Gallatin was at the moment the most conspicuous opponent of the legal tender proposal outside Congress. He was also the only member of the delegation and the only bank officer in New York, contemporarily listed, whose name began with G.[44]

George Opdyke, manufacturer, merchant, mayor of New York, and later banker, had called on Chase 22 January and told him he "favored a legal tender law." The 28th he wrote Chase from New York stating his reasons at length. Unless the government's "heavy floating debt shall be paid with reasonable promptitude and its accruing liabilities provided for, it will soon find difficulty in obtaining supplies for the army at any price." Delay in payments had already "depressed its certificates of indebtedness eight or ten per cent." The three alternatives were taxation, the sale of government bonds to the highest bidders, and payment of public creditors in government obligations bearing inter-

200

est. Taxes though necessary could not be collected in time "to meet the present emergency." The sale of bonds at the market would entail heavy loss and impairment of credit. "The floating debt is supposed to be upwards of fifty millions already, and it will doubtless reach one hundred millions before means of payment can be provided by any of the methods proposed. The public creditors are clamorous for their pay and are suffering serious inconvenience and loss for want of it. . . . To throw upon the market one hundred millions of government securities to be sold to the highest bidders in the present condition of things, with the credit of government weakened by the magnitude of its wants, the market already overstocked with its securities, and the capital available for permanent investments almost exhausted, could scarcely fail to reduce the price of six per cent [securities] to seventy cents or less on the dollar." The third alternative, "payment of public creditors in interest-bearing government securities, would be still worse." For "the same depression of price would ensue" and the loss of thirty cents on the dollar would be borne by the government suppliers. But beyond what necessity required, Opdyke believed the advantages of a national currency of uniform value throughout the land warranted the issue of legal tender notes.[45]

Secretary Chase wrote William Cullen Bryant of the *New York Post*, 4 February 1862, explaining his acquiescence in making government notes legal tender. He wrote that "a considerable number, though a small minority, of the business men and people are indisposed to sustain the United States notes by receiving and paying them as money. This minority, in the absence of any legal tender claims, may control the majority to all practical intents. . . . To prevent this, . . . I yield. . . ." He continued: "It is only, however, on condition that a tax adequate to interest, reduction of debt, and ordinary expenditures be provided, and that a uniform banking system be authorized, . . . securing at once a uniform and convertible currency . . . and creating a demand for national securities which will sustain

201

their market value and facilitate loans; it is only on this condition, I say, that I consent to the expedient of United States notes in limited amounts being made a legal tender."[46]

In this statement, after dragging his feet a year, Chase completed his acquiescence in the three-fold financial program—legal tender notes for the immediate emergency, taxes, and a uniform national banking system—propounded 23 January by John B. Alley and restated by Samuel Hooper.

IV

Meanwhile the newspapers were reporting much more support in the business world for a legal tender issue than opposition to it. The *Independent*, a religious weekly which seasoned its concern for the spiritual with lively concern for the material, had stated 26 December: "We firmly believe that our government . . . should not . . . borrow another dollar but should immediately issue demand notes for every expenditure, pledging the whole resources of the nation for their final redemption. These notes by a special act of Congress, *should be made a legal tender*." If necessary, it said, "change the Constitution." These, one may suppose, were the sentiments of the Reverend Henry Ward Beecher, who had become the *Independent's* editor just a week before. But the *Independent* had advocated a national currency all autumn, and it had wanted the banks to accept demand notes. In its issue of 5 December it claimed to have been the first to advocate demand notes and announced advocacy of a national currency, redeemable in specie, which should take the place of bank notes. A week later it had acclaimed Secretary Chase's report, whose "leading point is a recommendation of the issue of Treasury notes . . . to provide the country with a uniform currency." The *Independent's* confusion about means was not peculiar; it went well with a confirmed nationalism, both of which were typical of current popular opinion.[47]

As the foregoing indicates, dissatisfaction with the uncertain value of bank notes and desire for a uniform currency were much more earnest and widespread than understanding and agreement about the form, source, and nature of such currency. During the autumn of 1861 "national currency" had usually meant Treasury notes supplanting state bank notes and redeemable in coin. After Chase's December recommendation "national currency" might mean notes secured by federal bonds, issued by banks with national charters, and redeemable in specie, or it might mean Treasury notes made legal tender whether or not redeemable in coin. The former was preferred officially, but the latter became more popular.

The *New York Times*, 23 September, had ridiculed James Gallatin's criticism of the Treasury demand notes. A week later it had hoped the notes would make bullion transfers unnecessary. It had reported that the Secretary "believed—and in this he will no doubt have the concurrence of nine-tenths of the public—that with the introduction of United States notes payable on demand fairly established, as it soon will be, . . . the use and unvarying credit of this common medium in the ordinary receipts and disbursements of the government as well as in settlement with the banks will save the unnecessary and frequent transfer of large amounts of bullion." The *Times* had observed, 2 December, as an historical fact, that coin had been "almost entirely superseded by the use of more convenient and economical agencies—bills of exchange, bank notes, and checks." Hence, a fortnight later, it could "readily imagine much greater evils than the temporary suspension of payments in specie by the government or the banks or both together"; and three days later still it could find fault with the banks for not suspending and could call their stubborn continuance of specie payments "rather productive of mischief than otherwise" and a "game of mutual self-deception." On Saturday 28 December the *Times* had said editorially that "the public appears to be unanimous in the opinion that both the government and banks should suspend specie payments—that their vast operations, with those of the public, can not be carried on upon a hard-money basis." On Monday the 30th, again editorially, it had commented on the bankers' having "met on Saturday evening and after a prolonged sitting determined to suspend specie payments, to take effect to-day." The *Times* was gratified. In its opinion "the step now taken was inevitable." It had not been taken earlier, the *Times* supposed, because "it could hardly have been justified to the public till a serious inroad had been made upon the specie reserves held by the banks. Up to the present time the money with which the war has been carried on has been furnished by the cities of New York, Boston, and Philadelphia. . . . A suspension was inevitable because the flow of money was all in one direction—from the cities to the country. . . ." The *Times* the next day had approved the purpose of the Spaulding bill, just introduced, to make demand notes a legal tender, holding that it "would be a legitimate exercise of the highest sovereign or constitutional authority of the government. . . ."[48]

From then on the *Times*—hitherto uncommitted—vigorously supported the legal tender bill. It supported the bill not merely as a financial measure incidental to the federal government's need of funds but as a political assertion and exercise of sovereign power possessed under the Constitution and requiring to be affirmed in clarification of principles for which the Union had gone to war. All persons, the *Times* said, 6 January, "who regard the government as anything more than a confederation of states to be broken or weakened at will by secession or rebellion—all who believe the federal authority a power for the general good of the whole people as well as the symbol of sovereignty and allegiance—will welcome this resumption of one of its most important rights and duties. . . ."[49]

The *Tribune* could not make up its mind. It reported, 24 December, without criticism and apparently with sympathy, that among bankers advising the Secretary most were recommending an irredeemable government currency to be made legal tender; and it had published, a week later, the first draft of the legal tender bill. When the Gallatin delegation was in Washington, 11 January, the *Tribune* in its financial column had called the legal tender proposal "wise and equitable," but in an editorial it had said "we ponder and hesitate." It continued doing so.[50]

The *New York Herald* also supported the legal tender proposal. Back in August, along with the *Times*, it had advocated the use of Treasury notes, but with no consideration of their being legal tender. "It would be the greatest boon imaginable," it had said 12 August, "if the government could distribute one hundred millions of these Treasury notes through the country and so drive out of circulation the uncertain and various bank notes which are not used in trade." In October it had spoken of Treasury notes as preferable to depreciated bank notes; they "are a new national currency." The North would welcome a currency better than "worthless bank paper." Being "redeemable on demand at the sub-Treasuries," it had said overenthusiastically (for they were *not* redeemed if the Treasury could help it), the notes "continue to be received with favor, though, as was to be expected, persons not engaged in financial pursuits are slow to understand their character. Laborers and others employed by government . . . generally present them for redemption at the sub-Treasury and the cashier is thus kept unnecessarily busy. By and by it will be discovered that these notes are in fact as in name actual money." But "by and by" had proved to be slow in coming, for the *Herald*, 2 December, had to report persisting discrimination against the demand notes by the unsophisticated. "Laboring men have not yet learned that they are in effect money, and as fast as the laborers at the forts in New York harbor and the troops in Virginia are paid in these notes, they come back to the sub-Treasury for redemption in specie."[51]

This, of course, was a guiding reason why it was thought necessary to make the notes legal tender, and three days later, 5 December, the *Herald* had reported that in the Street

205

everyone was discussing the relative merits of a national bank, a large issue of irredeemable government paper, and further issues of Treasury notes bearing interest. The next day it reported that "Mr John A. Stevens, president of the Bank of Commerce, is in Washington in consultation with the Secretary of the Treasury," and that, as already mentioned, "Mr Stevens is popularly supposed to be in favor of a national bank of issue, whose notes shall be a legal tender." The important part of the statement is its evidence of recognition that whatever the nature and source of the currency that was needed, it must be a legal tender. The *Herald* spoke on Christmas day of the demand by the president of a leading bank for the issue by the government "of inconvertible paper money." By 4 January the legal tender bill had been published and the *Herald* declared it had been obvious for six weeks that the government would be compelled to pay its way with notes made legal tender and secured by "sweeping and heavy" taxes. Neither bankers nor anyone else could refuse "the new notes as money when they are made legal tender."[52]

The *Journal of Commerce*, of course, sang a different tune from that of the *Independent*, the *Times*, the *Tribune*, and the *Herald*. It had condemned abandonment of the sub-Treasury and the issue of demand notes, and as early as 10 August it had mentioned with disapproval the project of several New York "bankers to establish a paper money system." It excepted president George S. Coe of the American Exchange Bank from condemnation, because, though "a strong Republican," he had "objected positively to any issue of demand notes by the government. . . . But his arguments against the paper money system and its attendant measures," the *Journal* lamented, "seemed to fall upon unwilling ears." Coe, very likely, was less opposed to the legal tender notes, which his bank needed as much as others did, than exasperated with Chase for making them necessary. Strictly speaking, the term "paper money" bore the implication of its being not merely legal but a "legal tender." The term "legal tender," however, seems not to have become explicit and frequent in press reports till December. It must have been used in discussions by the more sophisticated long before it appeared commonly, for the one thing needful was a currency that would satisfy all legal requirements, which so far only silver and gold coin could do. The *Journal of Commerce*, 31 December, when the step to make demand notes a legal tender was explicitly taken, naturally blanketed the proposal under its consistent disapproval of "paper money."[53]

ADOPTION OF THE LEGAL
TENDER ACT

I

AFTER NINE days of stubborn debate, the legal tender bill had passed the House Thursday, 6 February 1862, by a vote of 93 to 59.

In the Senate the next day, Senator Fessenden, chairman of the Finance Committee, interrupted discussion of civil appropriations to ask that a bill authorizing the issue of ten million dollars of demand notes be acted upon at once. The ten millions were in addition to the fifty millions authorized the previous summer. The senator read aloud a brief letter just received from Secretary Chase with the draft of an even briefer bill that would authorize the issue that was requested. "The condition of the Treasury," the Secretary wrote, "requires immediate legislative provision. What you said this morning leads me to think that the bill which passed the House yesterday will hardly be acted upon this week." The Secretary could not wait, he said; he asked for immediate attention to his need.[1]

The Treasury had been hanging on the brink for weeks in a position which had held, precarious as it was, because the government's creditors had no alternative to waiting. Everyone knew that the question of money was before Congress and that Congress must act. The supply of equipment and materials to the armed forces and the payment of the men was being slowed down, and it must be so till Congress acted. The Secretary was unable to obtain more money on the terms set by Congress in July, which did not permit the government's bonds or notes to be sold at less than par. The market would not take them at par. At the moment bonds were at eighty-eight or so, and Treasury notes were worth but half of their face value in parts of the country. New issues could not be sold for more, if as much. The emergency, Fessenden told the Senate, was known to all, and he presumed there would be no objection to passing the Secretary's bill at once—which was done. The

211

bill went directly to the House, where Thaddeus Stevens brought it up at the opening of the next session, Monday, 10 February, and got it through, as in the Senate, without discussion.[2]

Two days later, the legal tender bill was presented by Fessenden with amendments which the Finance Committee proposed. The senator's address on the measure was painfully frustrate and indecisive. He could not suppress his abhorrence of what was purposed nor could he refuse to explain the purpose. He could offer nothing more satisfying than the implication that a pass had been reached where making government paper a legal tender had become unavoidable. The consideration that came nearest necessity, in his judgment, was that unless the notes were made legal tender, the banks either could not or would not accept them. The trouble, he understood, was most acute at the clearing houses, where inter-bank balances were settled. The banks were as implacable there as dogs over a bone, and something indefeasibly legal was needed to insure tolerance and peace. This reality Fessenden could not disregard. In his dilemma between conscience and necessity, he spoke one moment as a majority leader responsible for a measure already approved by the House and grasped desperately by a Treasury head who suffered the same compunctions as himself. He spoke the next moment as a legislator disciplined by a tradition considered for generations scarcely less sacred than any of the Ten Commandments and indeed rooted in one of them.* He acknowledged that in the light of what had come about, the first steps taken in the current financing now seemed to him to have been wrong. The government by its initial action the past summer and autumn had crippled the banks—then its first support—and now, he said, "we are driven to the point" where their power to help was become exhausted. "The government has no reason to suppose, unless it can offer much better security, that it should get money at a better rate than anybody else." But he seemed also to find

* The seventh for Roman Catholics, the eighth for Protestants.

some comfort in the general understanding that the measure about to be taken was temporary and that by bravely permitting the Secretary of the Treasury to sell bonds at the market price, Congress would be giving confidence to the country and especially to the purchasers of bonds. "We have abandoned," the senator said, ". . . the notion of putting our paper in the market at par when it is not entitled to command it." And this concession to reality had gone some way to reconcile the Finance Committee, including himself, to the bill as a whole. The Secretary would be empowered to sell the government's obligations, up to the amount of five hundred millions, "at any time at the market price"—the Secretary, he repeated, might "sell any amount, at any time that it may be necessary, for what he can get." This, in the senator's words, was "a bold, strong measure"; it would undo some of the errors of the past six months that had made the pending measure unavoidable.[3]

Reverting to the main question of the bill—on making government paper lawful money and a legal tender—Fessenden explained that his committee made "no recommendation," though they did report the bill back with the legal tender clause and from their doing so "an inference might be drawn" that they were definitely in favor of it. This they were not: "The committee, as a whole, had no opinion upon the subject, their opinions being so divided."[4]

Fessenden himself did not intend to speak in opposition to the legal tender clause "except incidentally." He intended rather to state the arguments "on both sides" as he understood them. But since personally he deplored making government paper a legal tender, since he thought it might have been avoided, and since he acquiesced in it because he had no alternative to offer but was obliged to get some decision made, his statement of the arguments was a model of ingenious ambiguity. The bill, he said, proposed "something utterly unknown in this government from its foundation."* It was something "of doubtful constitutionality, to

* The senator chose, evidently, to distinguish the present federal government, founded in 1789, from the organizations preceding it.

say the least," something that "has always been denounced as ruinous to the credit of any government which has recourse to it." No one, he said, "can deny it is bad faith." It "encourages bad morality both in public and in private" and "must inflict a stain upon the national honor." It would change the value of all property, induce inflation, and entail losses which must "fall most heavily upon the poor."[5]

Senator Fessenden's doubts about the bill distressed him. The legal tender clause, he wrote privately, violated all his views of right and expediency. "It shocks all my notions of political moral, and national honor. I am beset with letters and telegrams, and told on every hand . . . that without it we shall be utterly bankrupt and can not carry on the war. I do not believe it, and yet ought I to set up my own judgment as a standard of action? This thing has tormented me day and night for weeks; the thing is wrong in itself, but to leave the government without resources at such a crisis is not to be thought of." He told the Senate that he had been strongly advised against the legal tender bill by a leading financial man who "exclaimed against it with all the bitterness in the world." The same day he had received a letter from another leading financial man telling him that the country could not get along without the legal tenders. The two advisers were friends, and the senator said that he showed the letter to his caller, who read it and "expressed his utter surprise." But the senator received a telegram from this man the next day saying he had changed his mind and now thought the legal tenders "absolutely necessary." The same day, the senator said, he received a second letter from the other adviser, who had changed his mind too, and now opposed what he had previously recommended. James G. Blaine, who was at the time closely associated with Fessenden and later succeeded him as senator, wrote in 1884 that the two "authors of

---

It is true that the existing federal government had had no experience with paper made a legal tender, but the people themselves, in earlier generations, had had such experiences, by no means so bad and unwarranted as usually said, under their preceding forms of government.

these grotesque contradictions were Mr James Gallatin and Mr Morris Ketchum," both prominent New York bankers. But later correspondence of Ketchum's with Spaulding indicates that he became again reconciled to the legal tender notes, after his lapse into opposition. That Gallatin changed his mind is indicated also by the apparent end of his voluble opposition and by his moving, a few weeks later, that the Clearing House use the legal tender notes in its clearings. But Gallatin apparently did not become reconciled for long if at all to the Hooper-Alley-Stevens program, for in 1864 when the new national bank act was pending he was still making trouble for its sponsors.[6]

Fessenden was followed in debate by Senator Collamer, Republican of Vermont, who attacked the bill on constitutional grounds in sledgehammer style. "Let the necessity be what it may," he said, "I can not disregard my oath to support the Constitution," which was "an oath registered in Heaven as well as upon earth." The measure was also in his judgment, impractical, dishonest, demoralizing, and ruinous. It impaired contracts. It favored debtors, though the senator failed to realize that the debtors most concerned were the banks. He would authorize more notes for the Treasury but delete the language making them legal tender. Ensuing debate was largely upon his motion to that effect. Collamer's action was the same as that taken in the House by Justin Morrill, a fellow Vermont Republican.[7]

The next senator to speak at length was Timothy Howe, radical Republican of Ohio, who would have it demonstrated that the federal government had "resources equal to its utmost needs," whether they were all tagged in the Constitution or not. Congress, he said, was "clothed with unrestricted power to *'raise* and *support'* armies, to *'provide* and *maintain'* navies." It could not do this with coin. "Whatever our wishes may be, it is impossible to command the revenues for this war in coin." The banks had lent their coin to the government and were now "forced to suspend the payment of specie upon their own notes." Howe saw more at stake than the immediate war-time interest of the government. It could not and should not depend further on the banks, for "the banks have other work to do." Business needed more money, he said, and furnishing it was a responsibility of the banks that the government should not interfere with. "The truth is, the circulation of the country is not yet what the business of the country in its normal state demands"; it demands an increase of circulation rather than a decrease. Altogether, nothing more practicable than the pending bill's objective had been proposed. Neither borrowing nor taxes could be effectual in the country's predicament. "We must rely mainly upon a paper circulation," the senator asserted, and the paper *"must be* irredeemable."[8]

The following day, 13 February, another radical Republican, Henry Wilson of Massachusetts, who had been a shoe manufacturer before he became a politician, advocated the legal tender bill with the fervor of Senator Howe and of John Bingham in the House. "The entire business community with hardly a solitary exception," Wilson said, "men who have trusted out in the country in commercial transactions their tens and hundreds of millions, are for the bill with this legal tender clause." Without it the recipients of the government's notes—"our soldiers in the field, our sailors upon the decks of our vessels, the persons who have furnished millions and tens of millions of unpaid goods for the use of our army and navy, will be compelled to go into the market and submit to be shaved by the brokers and money lenders of the country." Senator Wilson had received letters from constituents, including "several large commercial houses representing millions of capital," who, they said, "do not know a merchant in the city of Boston engaged in active business who is not for this legal tender." He also reminded his fellow senators of "the families of your soldiers," in whose interest the Treasury notes should be made legal tender "so that when that little pittance comes from the field to them, to support them at home, they can use it to pay their necessary debts and support themselves without having to go through the process of broker shav-

216

ings." The issue, indeed, was "between brokers and jobbers and money changers on the one side and the people of the United States on the other."[9]

After Wilson, John Sherman, Republican of Ohio, made a less emotional argument for the legal tender bill. He contended that pressing necessity required that the government's notes be made a legal tender if the evils of a depreciated paper currency were to be avoided. Every organ of financial opinion agreed in this, he said. The Secretary of the Treasury, in official communications and in personal converse, had declared, according to Sherman, that making the notes legal tender was "indispensably necessary" to their security and negotiability. And the Secretary, said the senator—"a statesman of admitted ability and distinguished in his high position"—was known from his antecedents and opinions to be "probably the last man among the leading politicians of our country to yield to the necessity of substituting paper money for coin." Associations and groups of business men—"nearly all of whom are good financiers . . . agree fully in the same opinion." They had declared "in the most solemn form that this measure was indispensably necessary to maintain the credit of the government and to keep these notes anywhere near par."[10]

Either Sherman's quotation or the business men's reasoning seems at fault here, for the legal tender quality to be given the Treasury notes was less necessary to the credit of the government than to business men as debtors in need of a lawful substitute for gold which exacting creditors must accept. Much nearer the mark was the report from New York, quoted by Sherman, that a majority of bankers, though "opposed in theory to the use" of demand notes in large amounts, nevertheless thought it "the least of several evils which threaten," and agreed they "must have the benefit of a provision" that the notes "shall be a legal tender in payment of debts." The chambers of commerce of New York, Boston, and Philadelphia concurred in the bankers' opinion. The banks of those cities had already tied up their entire capital in government bonds and could lend

217

no more. It was the very bankers whose funds had financed the war so far, he told Congress, "who now beg you for this measure of financial aid." Among others, the cashier of the Bank of Commerce, "the largest bank corporation in the United States and one that has done much to sustain the government, appeared before the Committee on Finance and stated explicitly that the Bank of Commerce as well as other banks of New York could not further aid the government unless [the] proposed currency was stamped by and invested with the legal form and authority of lawful money, which they could pay to others as well as receive themselves." The government's creditors could not use the existing notes to repay their bankers because the bankers could not accept the notes; and the bankers "can not take them simply because they can not use them." It was "not a question of willingness or desire to sustain the government." The banks simply could not discharge their own obligations to their depositors without a legal tender.[11]

Meanwhile the money needed by the Treasury could not be obtained from taxes for six months at least; the House Committee of Ways and Means "have already been two months in framing a tax bill, and it is not yet framed." Enactment could not be expected before June. Yet in less than five months three hundred and fifty million dollars had to be obtained by the Treasury and paid out. Already, Sherman told Congress, one hundred millions was "due and payable to your soldiers, to contractors, to the men who have furnished provisions and clothing for your army, to your officers, your judges, and your civil magistrates." Selling bonds on the market would produce "something like sixty cents on the dollar," and this "not because any one doubts that they will be paid eventually, but because there is no money with which to buy them." For "by the laws of the United States, the Secretary of the Treasury can receive nothing in payment for bonds but gold and silver coin." And "where," he asked, "will the purchaser of your bonds get the gold and silver coin?"[12]

Senator Doolittle, Republican of Wisconsin, speaking

218

for the legal tender clause, reminded his colleagues that "while in theory the only money of our people is gold and silver, the fact is otherwise." It was instead paper almost exclusively; and "at this moment it is the irredeemable paper of suspended bank corporations." It had long been paper, "issued under the sanction of state authorities in violation . . . of the spirit and intent of those who framed the Constitution." The banks chartered by the individual states, Doolittle said, "have practically displaced the currency of the Constitution by substituting in its stead their own paper money." It was the states themselves, with their "shifts and devices" that were "emitting bills of credit by millions upon millions" despite the Constitution.* "This government," Doolittle said, "must assert its constitutional authority over the currency of the country in some practicable way, and it seems to me that the mode proposed in this bill is the simplest and most direct in the present exigencies."[13]

Most discussion of the legal tender bill in the Senate, both for and against, was Republican, because the membership was mostly Republican. Of the few Democrats who spoke at any length on the subject, Senator McDougall of California gave the measure vigorous support. He had found, he said, that the paper which was being issued for purchases in the field by the government "through its proper officers could not be negotiated at fifty cents on the dollar." All the opinions he had been able to gather from men in private life "with reputations as financiers" were that the pending measure would be ineffectual if the notes were not made a legal tender. He had just heard the same opinion "pressed earnestly" that morning by Secretary

---

* Doolittle criticized the opinion of the Jacksonian Supreme Court in the *Briscoe* case, 1837. That opinion had in turn flouted the opinions of other more important constitutional authorities than those who in 1837 made up the Court's majority. These others included, from the past, Joseph Story, then the Court's dissenting minority of one, John Marshall, John C. Calhoun, and Daniel Webster; and from among Doolittle's contemporaries, Secretary Chase and Senator Sherman. (Warren, II, 250, 301ff; B. Hammond, 564-71; Dunne, 40-44.)

CHAPTER 7

Chase, in whose financial judgment he had the greatest confidence. He himself believed the legal tender proposal "constitutional, just, and necessary."[14]

Senator Sumner, Republican of Massachusetts, half-heartedly defending the constitutionality of the legal tenders the same day, followed Justice Story's conclusion that the clauses of the Constitution prohibiting the states' coining money, emitting bills of credit, and permitting the tender of anything but gold and silver in payments due were all directed toward exercise by the federal government of a uniform monetary authority. The power of Congress to issue bills of credit had long been conceded and exercised, for Treasury notes were bills of credit; and, said Sumner in a conclusion something less than cogent, "if you assume the power to issue bills of credit, I am at a loss to understand how you can deny the power to make them a legal tender."[15]

The interest of the banks in having the government's notes made legal tender, so that they could make others accept the notes they were themselves expected to take, was a matter the House had ignored; Thaddeus Stevens, indeed, liked to make it appear, probably for political effect, that the banks opposed the bill, as, to be sure, some did. But in the Senate Fessenden and Sherman were emphatic about the banks' interest. Both made it a prime consideration in favor of the bill. To Fessenden it was the one point in the bill's favor. Preston King of New York, however, a Republican but formerly a Jacksonian Democrat, saw advantages to the banks in legal tender paper that he deplored. He was reported to fear a legal tender issue so greatly that he doubted if even the preservation of the Union could justify it. James Doolittle, Republican of Wisconsin, advocated the legal tenders as necessary, but he also deplored their benefits to banks and men of wealth. For, he said fairly, the bankers would put the notes in their vaults, "like so much coin, as a basis for expanding their own currency"; for every five-dollar Treasury note they put away they will issue three five-dollar notes of their own,

220

"thus trebling our paper circulation"—as, of course, they did. Doolittle's statement was substantially correct, except that the demand would be more than treble and would be greater for deposit credit than for circulating notes. In the commercial centers deposits far outran note circulation and their expansion was potentially greater. Few members of Congress understood this or that the government's legal tender notes would be highly advantageous to the banks; the greenbackers later proclaimed the contrary, because the government's notes seemed obviously to conflict with the banks' issue of their own circulating notes, which to the ignorant always appeared to be the essential function of banks and the source of the malign power attributed to them.[16]

Following the example of Justin Morrill's effort in the House, Senator Collamer's motion to strike out the legal tender clause and leave simply an authorization of more Treasury demand notes lost by 22 nays to 17 yeas. The bill itself, with amendments which I have still to describe, then passed the Senate, 13 February, by a vote of 30 to 7. Republican senators who had voted in vain to strike out the legal tender clause seem to have felt impelled thereafter to vote for the bill. In the words of Senator Anthony of Rhode Island, having nothing of their own to propose, they shrank from voting against "the only measure" which the government proposed and which after passing the House had gained, it was clear, the sanction of a Senate majority. Fessenden, despite his aversion to the bill, voted for it. Collamer of Vermont, Cowan of Pennsylvania, Preston King of New York, all three Republicans, and Kennedy of Maryland, Unionist, voted against it. On the other hand, three Democrats, Latham and McDougall of California and Rice of Minnesota, voted with the Republican majority.[17]

II

Having been passed by the Senate, the legal tender bill was returned to the House with amendments which Thaddeus Stevens, reporting them back from the Ways and Means Committee 18 February, called very important and very pernicious. The next day Spaulding opened debate on them with a sharp attack, saying they made the bill inconsistent and unreasonable. He found fault especially with the changes which required that interest on federal bonds be paid in coin and authorized the Treasury, in order to obtain the coin, to sell bonds for what they would fetch in the market. Soldiers in the field would be paid in paper, and bond-holders, sitting comfortably at home would be paid in gold. Why this discrimination, Spaulding demanded, and why this costly sacrifice of the government's obligations required by it? Were bankers entitled to a preference over soldiers and army suppliers— to a preference, moreover, costly to the government? No class of men, Spaulding declared, asked for such unjust preference. The people asked for the legal tender notes "pure and simple." They wanted a "national currency which shall be of equal value in all parts of the country, . . . secured by adequate taxation upon the whole property of the country, which will pay the soldier, the farmer, the mechanic, and the banker alike for all debts due." The government must, "while the war lasts, incur all the debt necessary to crush out the rebellion"; Spaulding thought it much better for the government and for the people to have a uniform means of payment. "In every view," the Senate amendment seemed to him "unnecessary, injurious, partial, and unjust." He hoped the House would not concur in it.[18]

On the other side, Justin Morrill took occasion to renew his condemnation of the prospective legal tenders and called their authorization "a blot on our national history that can not be effaced." In his opinion, the difficulties the bill was in were owing to its "departure from sound principles." He thought it was made somewhat less objectionable by the Senate's amendments though it could not be made good; for it was a vile delusion that the government's credit was improved by the legislative lie that paper was as good as gold. He would have relied on the vast

wealth of the country and the good faith of the government. A nation, he said, "not yet taxed a single dollar for
the cost of this war"—now in its tenth month—should be
able to negotiate a loan and have no need whatever of
resort to the "desperate scheme" about to be undertaken.
He did not believe that conditions had got to the point
where quackery was excusable; he wished the House
would get over its panic. His words expressed moral convictions vigorously, but they told nothing about the in-
expediency, in an economy at war, of reliance upon a
medium of payment that any creditor could lawfully refuse,
demanding instead his pound of flesh.[19]

The next day, 20 February, Samuel Hooper restated his
objections to the Senate's obstructive amendments. He denounced the requirement that interest on the government's
obligations be paid in coin instead of legal tender notes,
"because," he said, "its effect will be to depreciate these
notes as compared with coin by declaring them in advance
to be so depreciated." Restating Spaulding's criticism,
Hooper said the legal tender notes' opponents had also
made an unfair distinction in favor of bond holders, who
were to be paid in coined money while all other creditors
of the government were to be paid in what the notes' opponents denounced "as the meanest paper trash."[20]

Thaddeus Stevens, in closing a sharp, repetitious debate was in much the same position with respect to the
Senate version of the bill that Fessenden had been in with
respect to the House version. The bill was still his, though
"disfigured and deformed," and as Ways and Means chairman he could not repudiate it. He approached the question,
he said, with more depression of spirits than he had ever
felt before. "No act of legislation of this government," he
ventured, "was ever hailed with as much delight throughout the whole length and breadth of this Union, by every
class of people without any exception, as the bill which
was passed and sent to the Senate. Congratulations from
all classes—merchants, traders, manufacturers, mechanics,
and laborers—poured in upon us from all quarters. The

boards of trade from Boston, New York, Philadelphia, Cincinnati, Louisville, St. Louis, Chicago, and Milwaukee approved its provisions and urged its passage as it was." But now, Stevens mourned, "the beauty of the original bill" was lost. In earlier debate he had been asked if it were the intention, after the first issue of legal tenders, to go on and issue more millions of them. His answer had then been "No." But now, if asked, he could not give that answer. He expected the Senate amendments to produce such depreciation that the amount of notes would be doubled before Congress adjourned and that the circulation, eventually, would become "frightfully inflated."[21]

The House was unconvinced by these misgivings and joined the Senate in its half-way, self-defeating effort to save some shred of specie payments. It rejected the principal recommendations of its Ways and Means Committee members. Its concurrence was major but not complete, however, and its action being reported to the Senate the day it was taken, 20 February, the Senate proposed conferences on the differences remaining. The House acceded, and four days later the conference report, which represented exhaustion as much as agreement, was brought up and accepted in both chambers—in the House 97 to 22, in the Senate by voice vote. Samuel Hooper, co-sponsor of the bill, and Justin Morrill, its enemy, voted, for conflicting reasons, against the compromise. In order to correct a parliamentary oversight, the bill was resubmitted, passed again by both chambers the 25th, and approved the same day by President Lincoln.[22]

The act included one change of importance which originated in conference. It was a requirement that duties on imported goods be paid in coin, which would be used to pay interest on government bonds. Its intent was to provide an alternative to the sale of government bonds at the market in order to obtain coin for the payment of interest. The provision was of some permanent practical consequence but neither conciliated Stevens, Spaulding, Hooper, Alley, and their associates nor stirred them to resist it.[23]

224

Beside the more controversial of the Senate amendments, there was one of greater practical importance which authorized the deposit of legal tender notes by individuals and corporations in the sub-Treasuries. The arrangement was of most concern to banks and arose from the consideration that the notes, like other forms of money, would tend to accumulate in the banks as they were deposited therein for credit; and that rather than be let lie idle as vault cash they could be redeposited in the sub-Treasuries for use by the government, which, if they were left for periods of one or more months, would pay interest at a rate of five per cent for them. This arrangement had been suggested to Secretary Chase by his resourceful Assistant Treasurer in New York, John C. Cisco, who had made public announcement of it, 8 February, as an offer by the Secretary of the Treasury to receive on deposit in the sub-Treasury United States notes as a short-term loan to the government. This was advantageous to the government because it availed the Treasury of funds at a low rate of interest and made the notes more acceptable; and it was advantageous to the banks, because it gave them interest on funds otherwise idle and also provided a convenient means of settling clearing house balances. Chase had been so well pleased with the immediate results that he sought to fortify the arrangement with legislative approval and drew up a provision "with his own hand" which the Senate Finance Committee included among its amendments to the House bill. The aggregate amount for which the Treasury could be indebted at any time was twenty-five millions, but three weeks later, 17 March, the limit was raised to fifty millions. In July Congress raised it to a hundred millions, and in June 1864 to a hundred and fifty millions.[24]

III

The main provisions of the act authorized the Secretary of the Treasury to issue, "on the credit of the United States, one hundred and fifty millions of dollars of United States notes, not bearing interest, payable to bearer. . . ." It provided that the notes "shall be receivable in payment of all taxes, internal duties, excises, debts, and demands of every kind due to the United States, except duties on imports, and of all claims and demands against the United States of every kind whatsoever, except for interest upon bonds and notes, which shall be paid in coin; and shall also be lawful money and a legal tender in payment of all debts, public and private, within the United States, except duties on imports and interest as aforesaid; . . . and such United States notes shall be received the same as coin, at their par value, in payment for any loans that may be hereafter sold or negotiated by the Secretary of the Treasury and may be re-issued from time to time as the exigencies of the public interest shall require."[25]

Though somewhat limited in scope and temporary in purpose, the act was revolutionary. It went counter to the principle of the tenth amendment that the federal government possessed only those powers specifically assigned to it by the Constitution. It was contrary to the understanding that the authors of the Constitution had intended the power of issuing paper money to be withheld from the federal government as well as forbidden the states. It was contrary to the popular belief, religious as well as economic, that there could be no money, real and legal, but silver and gold and that the Almighty, as professed three years later by a Secretary of the Treasury, Hugh McCulloch, had placed the precious metals in the earth for the specific purpose of providing mankind with a standard of value and medium of exchange. It was contrary to the monetary practice of the United States since its formation—a practice the government had never before departed from. It recovered from desuetude the responsibility of the federal government for the monetary system and established for the first time the power of the federal sovereignty to do what had hitherto been generally considered both unconstitutional and inexpedient. It established a national monetary medium which derived its value from the will of the government.

It overrode state laws. All this makes the authorization of the greenbacks, 25 February 1862, of greater significance in the evolution of federal powers than in monetary history and of greater importance to the student of government than to the economist. As money the greenbacks were another example of what had often been done before in falling back on governmental credit in the last resort. But as an exercise of sovereignty they advanced the national government's powers far beyond what had ever been ascribed to it before. They lifted federal powers not merely above those of the states, above the limitations set by the tenth amendment, and above the bold attributions of Hamilton and Marshall, to a mystical level where, contrary to the latter's dictum, the nature of a thing could be changed by giving it, through legislative enactment, a new name. With those words the federal government did not resort to a stealthy deceit, as sovereignties had often done, but performed a miracle. It openly did the impossible. In response to the question President Lincoln had asked in his message to Congress, 4 July 1861, it affirmed that the American government was not going to be too weak to maintain its own existence, whether or not it was to become too strong for the liberties of its people.[26]

Paper made a legal tender, in contrast to paper bearing but a promise, had the advantage that it gave payments by the banks and by the Treasury to their creditors the finality of law. This important advantage was ignored by the sound-money people both at the outset and later, and possibly exaggerated by the legal tender notes' advocates in 1862. If the Treasury had been left to pay expenses with notes that were not legal tender, as Senator Collamer urged, it seems hard to believe that the inflation would have been much greater than it was, though legal difficulties would have been greater. The government's promise might well have been better received than its fiat, because promises were traditional, familiar, and commonly kept. If that were so, the controversy at its beginning in 1862 was more turbulent and tense than the possibilities justified.

227

But no one could do better than guess what the results would be in either case. The knot a stunted government faced was a Gordian one and could only be slashed—for better or for worse. Its intractible nature was implicit in that the legal tender notes were both money and promises to pay money. And probably to most people who thought about it, the implication of fiat in the words "legal tender" —something not needed on coin—conflicted with the implication of a promise, as the pistol poked by a robber in one's ribs would belie any statement that he was requesting a loan.

Much more important than this redundancy was the inconsistent provision making the legal tender notes ineligible for payment of import duties and interest on the public debt. It deliberately limited their use and degraded them as money. This second inconsistency was the more serious, for, as the sponsors of the measure immediately recognized, it doomed their legal tender notes to depreciation. The sudden recognition of Thaddeus Stevens that now the first issue of the notes would not be the last was correct. Yet it was also naive—he should never have supposed anything else. The need of a legal tender was imperative, but its immediate and full acceptance in the form of paper could not, merely because of its necessity, be taken for granted. Inconvertible paper was bound to be less acceptable than gold to a population willing to do without gold only so long as they knew they could get gold and convinced that it was both inexpedient and immoral to make paper a lawful substitute for gold, as if theft or mayhem could be authorized by statute and cease to be a crime. Uneasiness about something that had always been supposed to bring disaster could not be overcome readily, even if, as Stevens affirmed, it had been hailed with a great show of enthusiasm. The enthusiasts would soon be complaining that devils had got to work and ruined a brave project. But there was more to the difficulty than that. The dilemma presented on one horn the need of a legal tender to take the place of gold and on the other the investors' want of enough confidence to buy bonds without the customary assurance about repayment of principal and interest. A statute could supply the legal tender, but it could not supply the confidence. The legal tender notes' sponsors— Spaulding, Hooper, Stevens, and Alley—hoped nevertheless that sufficient confidence would follow the statute to make their expedient succeed, which meant among other things that it must be temporary. They were disappointed in their hope, but considering the predicament Chase had got into, one may wonder what better effort could have been made. As for the disasters which their opponents foresaw and which their later critics—especially Henry Adams and Wesley Clair Mitchell—continued for years to see, they were no worse than those that have attended other wars, and may be blamed on what preceded the legal tender act rather than on the act itself. That measure was the bold effort of astute and experienced men to meet a desperate situation, and its success was as nearly complete as conditions permitted. That the measure later produced a long political controversy is no more the fault of those men than it is to their credit that it also produced in time the present currency resting simply upon the credit of the American government and the obsolescence of gold.

IV

The need of making government notes a legal tender had been mentioned now and then for weeks preceding the debate on it in Congress; and an influential part of the press had supported the measure while it was pending. The *New York Times*, with approval, had quoted John B. Alley's opening advocacy of it, 23 January, Elbridge Spaulding's opening of debate on it, 28 January, and Samuel Hooper's "eminently just and merchant-like exposition" of it, 3 February. The same views were held, the *Times* said, by John E. Williams, president of the Metropolitan Bank, John Stevens of the Commerce, Moses Taylor of the City, and others with whom it contrasted those who were "most illiberal and least public-spirited." Making the government's paper a legal tender, according to the *Times*, 13 January, was approved by most people, "who desire to see the sovereign power of their government asserted and exercised in every practical way." The *Times*, 18 January, thought it pusillanimous to approach legal tender paper merely as an unavoidable necessity—as the only recourse for the Treasury in a desperate dilemma. It would not have the action taken apologetically but with full assurance of its propriety and constitutionality. The *Times* had also expressed a low opinion of the six or eight bank gentlemen, whose leader, James Gallatin, was called "crotchety"; he had opposed the issue of legal tender, and it had even been said that he refused the Treasury's demand notes already in use. According to its Washington letter of 21 January, the legal tender measure would be enacted and Secretary Chase would use the authority it gave him. "The House committee have conferred freely with him on the subject, and the prospect of his cooperation in what they deem indispensable is highly gratifying." This, presumably, was written under the eye if not by the hand of J. W. Simonton, Washington representative of the *Times*, who was both informed and influential. In the letter of 24 January it was reported that "Secretary Chase assents to the financial measures of the Committee of Ways and Means, which are in fact very nearly the same proposed in his annual report"—a statement like Hooper's, already mentioned, which sought to coax Chase into acquiescence in something that he detested.[27]

Henry J. Raymond of the *Times*, 2 February, had explained the legal tender measure in the New York Assembly, of which he was a Republican member, commending the measure's purpose and the full program of which it was a part. He quoted a letter from Thomas W. Olcott, a banker and Democrat of Albany, who affirmed the "absolute and controlling necessity of having the proposed issue of Treasury notes made a legal tender." Olcott supported the statement with the sagacious and original observation that military expenditures would produce inflation even if made in coin.[28]

This was something few persons recognized. Instead it was assumed as a basic principle that inflation arose from the use of paper currency not convertible into gold and was to be avoided simply by the use of gold or of paper currency convertible into it. No previous war of comparable magnitude had ever been waged by a country so highly industrialized as the United States had become; and the effect on prices of throwing the government's military demands upon productive means adapted almost wholly to the civil demands of peace-time was not understood as twentieth-century experience with war has made it. The necessity of curbing civil demands to compensate for the effect upon prices of enlarged military demands was not seen. Instead the advance in prices deriving from intensified demand was considered simply a monetary problem— and less a problem of the amount of money than the kind of money. That there was already some diffused recognition of the nature of the mischief, however, is evident in current remarks of the *Times* about the interdependence of government and business which the war had produced. The *Times* had said, relevant to the legal tender bill, that the loans and discounts of banks were "directly or indirectly based upon contracts with or supplies to the government" and "upon the ability of the Treasury to pay off the public creditors." For at that time, in less complex relationships than have since come about, the government supplier discounted his note at his bank in order to obtain funds for the payment of his employees and the purchase of materials. His note was due customarily within two months, and if the government did not pay him promptly with something that was generally acceptable he could not repay his bank promptly, the bank could lend him no more, and the government ceased to receive supplies. Expenditures for the armed forces, the *Times* reported, comprised "nearly or quite one-half the active business of the seaboard cities and of the states west." (And nine-tenths of the government's monetary transactions passed through New York City, according to John C. Cisco, Assistant Treasurer there.)[29]

Turning from the pragmatic, the *Times* had found the current constitutional objections to the legal tenders incongruous. "Why," its editor said, "any portion of the people of the loyal North and West, who have never yielded to the pestilent theory of state rights, . . . should for a moment question the inherent principle in the General Government of self-preservation and the authority under the Constitution" over currency was hard to understand.[30]

When the Washington bureau of the *Times* reported 26 February that the legal tender act had been approved the day before by President Lincoln, it remarked in retrospect that the measure had been supported by a "powerful influence among the banks, private bankers, and great merchants of the country." And already, it said, banks were preparing to extend their credits on the basis of the legal tender notes they would hold as reserves. The *Times* also reported passage of an auxiliary bill, later approved 1 March, authorizing the Treasury to fund the floating debt by issuance of twelve-month certificates, bearing six per cent interest, to creditors of the government willing to accept them. "This," said the *Times*, "will give immediate relief to the public creditors whose claims have been in suspense without any compensating interest." The act would also afford time for the Treasury to prepare the new legal tender notes. That the immediate response of the money market was favorable to the new statutes is indicated by a prompt decline in the quotations on gold.[31]

Meanwhile the Democratic *New York Herald* had been as firm as the Republican *Times* in repeating that government notes must be made legal tender. Its tone was more independent, however. It reflected business sentiment more closely than the *Times*, perhaps, and official Washington less closely. It ridiculed the Gallatin delegation that had gone to Washington "urging propositions so preposterous." It averred that legal tender notes were necessary; if government suppliers had to accept payment in interest-bearing notes which the banks refused to accept as money, they would have to sell the notes at any price, and the discount might become as much as thirty or forty per cent. "Expenses of the war will be increased in proportion, the credit of the government will be irreparably damaged," and banks, with all their capital in government obligations will be ruined. The *Herald's* report of the first argument for the legal tender notes as part of a three-fold program—John B. Alley's—was detailed, and it kept Spaulding's presentations prominently before its readers.[32]

The *New York Tribune*, in whose issue of 31 December Spaulding's draft of the legal tender bill seems to have had its first publication, had continued thereafter a wavering, tearful support of the program. It reported, 21 January, that the legal tender proposal was "daily receiving the urgent approval of the most distinguished bankers and merchants in New York," and that public sentiment seemed almost unanimous for it. Yet on its editorial page, 25 January, it was said: "We do protest against legal tender —at least of notes prior to this law." On the 27th the *Tribune* predicted that the Treasury note bill would be promptly passed with the legal tender clause and that an adequate tax bill would follow. "Meanwhile the public creditors are suffering severely for want of money." The 31st the *Tribune* reported that Spaulding, after his introductory speech on the legal tender bill, had received letters from "the leading New York and Philadelphia bankers heartily commending his views as wise in themselves and inevitable from necessity." It also reported that Secretary Chase favored the legal tenders. Meanwhile, on its editorial page, the 29th, the *Tribune* had described Spaulding's arguments favorably. He advocates, it said with rather more naiveté than Spaulding himself, not only legal tender but also appropriate taxes, funding of the notes, "but above all an early and successful advance of our army and a really vigorous prosecution of the war. . . ."[33]

In an editorial, 1 February, the *Tribune* lamented that

the Treasury was "embarrassed just when it should not be, and our legislators are meditating the desperate resort of making irredeemable paper a legal tender. If that must be," the editor had sighed, "it must." He had admitted that there were worse things than a depreciated currency; yet he believed it might be avoided with a popular loan of some sort and "with an assurance that this should end the war." In an editorial on the 10th the *Tribune* had said tragically: "Congress *must* provide funds for the vigorous and immediate prosecution of the War for the Union, and it seems to have been settled that it shall take the short and easy method of making Treasury notes a legal tender. We utterly dissent from this conclusion; and yet there has been so much delay and hesitation and vacillation that it is possible that no other means of giving immediate relief to the Treasury now remains." On the 18th the Senate's amendment directing that interest be paid in coin had been praised and the legal tender clause deplored. "The Irredeemables," the editor had said, "lack magnanimity and the spirit of reasonable concession." But the next day the need again was stressed. "The Treasury has been virtually empty for a month; at least one hundred millions of dollars are this moment due to people who need their pay and ought to have it; among them are thousands of volunteers who have suffered and dared for thirteen dollars per month and whose families are suffering for the two, three, four, or even five months' pay which the country promised them and of which they have not yet received one cent." When the legal tender bill became law, the *Tribune* reported the fact with objective regret, hopeful but skeptical.[34]

The Democratic *Journal of Commerce* had expressed as much antipathy to the legal tender bill as the Republican *Tribune*, or more. But its copperhead reputation made it almost as reserved in its opposition as the *Tribune* was made by its loyalty. The government's notes, the *Journal* had said, 31 December, must depreciate whether a legal tender or not. The *Journal* had published, however, a full account of Alley's address and also the communications of a writer who differed with it but was "able and courteous" in his argument that the government's notes should be made legal tender. While the bill had been pending, the *Journal* reported on it but was reticent in expressing opinion. "As it is now settled," it said 11 February, "that we are to have a paper currency almost exclusively—and the fact would remain even if the notes were not made a legal tender —it is the duty of all good citizens to make the best of it while it lasts and not to aggravate its evils by a reckless indifference. We have noticed, within a few days, a tone of sadness in financial circles where sound principles are cherished, as if this single mistake in regard to the currency were certain to ruin the country and it were now useless to make any further effort to stay the progress of evil. Such despair is not only unmanly, but it is out of keeping with the hopeful energy peculiar to American character." The *Journal* was condoling with the sad minority. And then, in a minor key, it made the prophetic observation: "Inflation itself is not an unmitigated evil."[35]

Finally, there is the religious weekly, the *Independent*, which in its enthusiasm for the federal government urged that demand notes be issued for every expenditure, making these notes a legal tender, and if necessary changing the Constitution. "There is danger," it had said, 6 February, "that the country may be actually bankrupted in consequence of the boggling over this financial measure of a Congress full of men who mean well enough but do not seem to know even the importance of doing something if it is not the best possible thing."[36]

NORTH AND SOUTH

I

SPECIE PAYMENTS had stopped 30 December 1861; the Treasury's demand notes were not made legal tender till 25 February; and new notes were not engraved, printed, and ready to be paid the government's creditors till early in April. The sub-Treasury in New York received its first notes on Saturday the 5th. So for almost two months no lawful money was circulating, and for more than three there was none in use that was commonly recognized as legal tender. Then how, it may be asked, did people manage in that interval? How could the banks and the government continue as long as they did in an illegal situation which, as Congress had been told again and again, made legal tender notes "absolutely necessary"? For the intervening weeks had not been a season of ease but one full of crises and anxiety. During their course there had been the matter of replacing Cameron with Stanton as Secretary of War, President Lincoln had issued his order for a general offensive against the Confederate forces, General McClellan had disregarded the order and taken his own time on the way to Richmond, at Hampton Roads the *Monitor* and the *Merrimac* had fought their indecisive but revolutionary duel, and Congress had debated the legal tender bill amidst wrangling over loyalty, enfranchisement of slaves, confiscation of rebels' property, and the legal status of secession. If ever the heavens were to fall, this had been the time for it. Yet week after week business continued as active as usual, or more so; and week after week the war went on, in a fashion. Then how, I repeat, did people manage without money?

The beginning of the explanation is that informally and by makeshift there was money. The absence of it, though in a lawful sense a fact, was not absolute. Most persons, especially bankers and merchants, who usually kept cash on hand, had it somewhere still. Occasionally some of it passed from one owner's safe into another's. Thus there was some circulation of it, of a fugitive sort. But there were also bank checks and bank notes, which continued as customary to be used in most transactions. Though bank credit was technically in dishonor, because the banks had announced that they would not, as usual, pay their creditors in gold on demand, the demand was seldom made. People were willing to accept bank checks and notes so long as checks and notes were accepted by others. Accordingly, the suspension of specie payments let the bulk of monetary transactions remain about what they were normally but made gold hard to get for the unusual and objectionable purposes— hoarding and speculation—for which it mostly might be demanded. Bankers, however, could and would release gold to their customers when it was legitimately needed, as for the performance of a contract. The New York banks, according to the *Tribune*, were "going on much as before . . . and all of them pay specie in certain cases." They retired their own notes, paying out government notes instead, and their gold reserves kept increasing; for gold continued to arrive from California, the war and the tariff diminished purchases of foreign goods, and the demand of Europe for American food staples remained unbroken. There was consequently no commercial reason for gold to be exported. So in the business world, apart from transactions in military supplies and apart from a prevailing uneasiness, there was no serious impediment to the course of monetary payments *de facto*. Debtors and persons under contract might be sued but actually there seems to have been little or no recourse to the law. Either it was that suit seemed unpromising, or that gold or other acceptable property was usually obtainable somehow, or that Congress was known to be at work on a solution, or that there was no time for suits to brew between the end of December and the authorization of legal tender notes 25 February or their actual appearance early in April. Creditors, as Chase said later when he was Chief Justice, were inclined to accept what

was offered them so long "as they would lose less by acceptance than by suit."[1]

This was probably true of the banks' creditors especially.
The banks were the most important group of debtors and
in some ways the most vulnerable—it was for this reason
that they were the source of the demand for a substitute
tender to take legally the place of gold. A decisive deter-
rent in New York, the most important business center, was
the decision of a state court in 1837—*Livingston* v. *Bank of
New York*—denying on grounds of equity the suit of a bank's
creditor who had been refused coin for his bank notes during the general suspension of specie payments that year. And
besides that, the law in New York stipulated that before
the complaint of a note-holder be entertained, the bank be
given ten days in which to meet the note-holder's claim,
and then only on its refusal or failure to redeem its obligation could court action be undertaken to annul its charter.
This requirement, which obviously was not very encourag-
ing to claimants, reflected a growing understanding, in the
courts and out, that to satisfy aggressive, random, individual
claims was inequitable and offensive to the general interest.
The latter clearly outweighed the interest of litigious individuals. Banks had also protected themselves by a stipulation in pass books, then universally used, that deposits entered therein were "payable in the currency of this state."
This stipulation, though of doubtful legal force, probably
was of some practical effect in freeing the banks from the
obligation that deposits of checks, notes, and presumably
even of specie itself, be repaid in gold.[2]

The laws, accordingly, though without uniformity, were,
on the whole, to the banks' advantage. So were expectations that legislatures would validate the suspension, as
had been done generally in 1837 and again less generally in
1857. In New York such action was forbidden by the constitution of 1846, article 3, section 5, but this was not commonly understood apparently, for the *New York Herald*
said in its financial column early in January that the sus-

241

pension would no doubt be legalized by the legislature.*
The bankers knew this was impossible, but they also knew
that in other ways the law offered them pretty good protection. They had to worry less about the damage that
could be done them by their depositors and note-holders
than about that which could be done them by their competitors. They were afraid of one another, being divided
by jealousy, by varying standards of what was sound and
unsound, and by differing convictions about government
financing and their proper responsibilities toward it. In
1862 there were fifty-five commercial banks in New York
City, which then occupied the lower part of Manhattan
only—against less than half that number in greater New
York City a century later—and the primitive practice of
pouncing on any competitor that showed weakness had not
yet given way to more refined ways of keeping the community pure. The New York Clearing House had dissension among its members. One party—the solid and orthodox
—believed in purgation and was ready to seize the gold of
its competitors if it could get them in debt to it in the clearings; the other party believed in forbearance, deeming that
the general interest, including that of the banks themselves
and of the government, required a truce and reliance upon
the rational exercise of federal authority—of which the
legal tender notes were to be the instrument—rather than
the mechanical and inflexible transfers of title to gold.
Among the stalwarts, for example, the Chemical and the
American Exchange respected little but specie; but the
Commerce and the City Bank, among others, stood for a
liberalism that the more conservative deemed dangerous.
Among the lesser fry, there were banks that could hang on
only by the skin of their teeth.[3]

Throughout the country similar relationships were
marked by difference of strength and of opinion. The situation, partly because of war and partly because of diversi-

* In Pennsylvania, a stay law in the banks' favor was enacted 11
April, apparently as retroactive relief. (*Bankers' Magazine*, June 1862,
pp. 925-26, 969.)

ties in state laws, was one of dark incertitude. There was in particular the requirement of reserves, partly statutory, as in Massachusetts, partly contractual, as in New York, and partly practical, as it was everywhere. In the general confusion, the wonder is not that some bankers wanted a statutory substitute for gold but that some did not.

Yet the interest of the bankers in an alternative to gold was far less than that of the Treasury, where Secretary Chase was having to do what most men do when they owe money and have none. He was avoiding the payment of his bills. He was falling behind with the payments due to the government's suppliers, contractors, and armed forces and was making shift as he could with whatever he could get his creditors to accept. Since there was a war and since Congress was trying to agree on a means of paying them, contractors went ahead as best they could and soldiers refrained from returning home. Thus forces were somehow kept in the field and somehow supplied. But to say that so long as this was true, there was no "necessity" for the legal tender law is a gross misuse of words. And the assertion of Henry Adams eight years later, that the legal tender enactment was a "miscarriage the results of which have exceeded in importance any defeat of the national armies or the failure of any campaign" in the Civil War, was nonsense. The unhappy conjunction of Secretary Chase's inexperience and stubbornness with the primitive practices established by the independent Treasury act of 1846 in its attempt to divorce the business of the federal government from that of the economy had brought the financing of the Civil War to a crisis which made some such action as the issue of legal tender notes no less "necessary" than the replacement of Secretary Cameron, the demotion of General McClellan, and the advancement of General Grant. "Necessity" is usually a matter of judgment, seldom utterly absolute, as Henry Adams and later Wesley Clair Mitchell would have it.* The judgment in early 1862 that

---

* The contention that "necessity" is something absolute was already a metaphysical stand-by of the Constitution's strict-constructionist

legal tenders were "necessary" was a good judgment and not gainsaid by the fact that the necessity was fortunately eased by forbearance, by makeshifts, by the expense and uncertainty of suits at law, and by the known likelihood of relief from Congress. From the spring of 1861 to the spring of 1862, the war was kept going by improvisations of all sorts. Production of war supplies lived on patriotism, speculation, and promises. The army was maintained with funds withheld from the soldiers and suppliers and on gifts from individual states. Peter was robbed to pay Paul. Creditors, instead of demanding what they could not get, got on with what they could get. In these circumstances, once the legal tender notes were authorized, their benefits were availed of by everyone, whether advocates or opponents.[4]

II

Some fairly prompt relief—mostly from incertitude—seems to have been realized. But doubt and dissension remained about the fifty millions of demand notes, bearing no interest, which had been authorized in the original war loan act by the special session the preceding summer and about the ten millions for the payment long due soldiers authorized in a recent joint resolution by the current session. These two issues had not been designated a legal tender, and there was what the *New York Times* cautiously called some "technical uncertainty" about them. Assistant Treasurer Cisco, in New York, wrote Chase 6 March that he was being asked every hour of the day whether the demand notes already issued were or were not legal tender. Lawyers were generally declaring that they were not, he said, and a number of New York banks were being sued for refusing to redeem their own notes otherwise than in the demand notes. These "suits" were probably no

---

interpreters, with reference particularly to the grant of powers to the federal government in article 1, section 8. (See John Marshall on "necessity" in *McCulloch* v. *Maryland*, 4 Wheaton 316, 1819, pp. 425-26.)

more than threats, but the uncertainty was embarrassing, nevertheless, and Cisco asked that Congress pass a "declaratory act" clearing it up. This was done in an act of 17 March 1862, explicitly stating that the fifty millions of demand notes authorized 17 July 1861 and the ten millions authorized 12 February 1862, were "a legal tender in like manner and for the same purpose" as those authorized by the act of 25 February 1862. But it was not till Saturday 5 April, as already said, that New York received any notes bearing the explicit statement that they were a legal tender.[5]

Meanwhile, the New York Clearing House Association resolved, as early as 7 March, that "the legal tender United States Treasury notes be used hereafter as a medium of settlement at the Clearing House." The resolution was moved by James Gallatin, whose alleged conversion to the virtue of the notes coincident with Morris Ketchum's conversion to their evil has already been mentioned. "The United States notes of legal tender," the *New York Times* reported 14 April, were being accepted "with a degree of favor amounting to almost universal confidence." Within the country they were "esteemed as in all respects the equivalent of gold." In its *European Circular*, 15 April, quoted the day following by the *Times*, the firm of Thomas Hallett and Company discussed the current effect of the legal tender circulation, which, it said, had not "so far" produced the evil results predicted for it. The notes had "advanced the price of gold but not excessively." They had been sought with eagerness. For the first time in a generation—that is, since Andrew Jackson put an end to the federal Bank of the United States—the country had "a paper currency of equal value" everywhere in the Union. If the value of the legal tender notes "could be kept at par as well as limited in amount," Hallett's said, "they would prove a valuable addition to the machinery of business and, by the addition of what would serve as so much capital, afford perhaps a not unhealthy stimulus to enterprise." But things might, of course, take a different turn. The legal tender act prac-

245

tically legalized suspension, besides adding a hundred and fifty millions of lawful money to the stock of gold. It was especially important for the banks that the new notes, being a legal tender, "served the same purpose as would so much more gold." Instead of being curbed (as some people supposed later), the powers of the banks were augmented by the legal tender issues. As the issues increased, the deposits of the banks would increase. Following the increase, said Hallett's, the market value of merchandise and property would rise.[6]

A month later, 12 May 1862, the *New York Times* repeated with patriotic pride that the new legal tender notes were being accorded "universal currency"; they were "accepted as lawful money not only without loss or inconvenience but with a pleasure which is heightened by the complete triumph of this measure over the opposition and apprehension of an influential class of financial people. . . . The difference against these notes as compared with gold is about two per cent less than when the law making them a legal tender was passed in February." During March, April, May, and June the Treasury made the most of the ease provided by the legal tender act, and Secretary Chase reported that by 1 July, "not a single requisition from any department upon the Treasury remained unanswered. Every audited and settled claim on the government and every quartermaster's check for supplies furnished which had reached the Treasury had been met."[7]

During the spring the economy had been stimulated not only by the first issue of greenbacks, as the legal tender notes were soon called, but by several important military successes. It was these, perhaps, that Secretary Chase had looked for. They had occurred along the Atlantic and along the middle border but most notably on the lower Mississippi, where New Orleans had been taken by General Benjamin Butler in April. This reconquest was followed by a spirited advance in government securities. The fiscal condition of the government, said the firm of Thomas Hallett and Company, attended its military and political position.

Business letters from Europe expressed surprise at "the steady and comfortable condition of fiscal affairs" amongst the Americans, who had been expected to become "ruined with paper inflation." Instead the prosperity seemed substantial and far more than a mental state. Domestic business was thriving, canal and railway traffic was brisk, and exports of domestic produce—grain, flour, meats, and other produce—were the "largest ever known." But when the train of the Union's military successes ground to a standstill, the cheerful aspect of these magnitudes was darkened. The Army of the Potomac remained fixed before Richmond. For weeks the press correspondents had been standing on their tiptoes awaiting from moment to moment "the last great blow at the Rebellion" which was to end the war; and the public had been on tiptoe with them. Gold now rose to 110 and exchange on London to 120. The press urged confidence in General McClellan despite his "inexplicable delays." General Banks was driven by General "Stonewall" Jackson down the Shenandoah and across the Potomac into Maryland. Confederate raiders penetrated the outskirts of Washington. The British were reported to be selling out their American investments. President Lincoln called for three hundred thousand more soldiers. The long awaited attack on Richmond opened at length but turned through days of cruel fighting into a Union disaster. It was the Fourth of July, and that morning there was panic in Wall Street. A fortnight later, President Lincoln relieved General McClellan as general-in-chief.[8]

During the summer business was more active, feverish, and confused. Continuing its advance, gold having risen to 120, London exchange rose to 131. Simultaneously, the *Times* reported, 25 and 26 August, the "extraordinary export movement" of foodstuffs—"the largest ever known" —and bank deposits were the largest "ever reported." Back in May, the *Times* had mentioned a proposal to issue four hundred and fifty millions more of greenbacks but had called the proposal ridiculous. However, a month later, 7 June 1862, Secretary Chase asked for another hundred and fifty. In requesting this authorization the Secretary showed no alarm and none of the hesitancy and aversion he had expressed before, but made his recommendation in casual, routine fashion. Though he said the condition of the Treasury made "prompt action highly desirable," his tone was not that of frightened urgency. He seemed, indeed, less concerned about funds for the Treasury than in the provision of greenbacks in small denominations for the convenience of the public.[9]

The request for more legal tender notes by an official known to have resisted their original issue, and coming so soon after the solemn averments in January and February that there would be no more, produced some disappointment but little dismay. Opponents of the legal tenders had the satisfaction of seeing their predictions coming true and traders that of seeing market values in Wall Street rise.

Debate on the measure prompted by Chase was opened 17 June by Spaulding, who was reassuring. He said that the funds needed during the latter half of the year could only be obtained by continuance of the plan that had been working so well—beyond "the most sanguine expectations of its strongest advocates." The notes, he said, were "the people's loan to the government and the most popular mode of borrowing ever adopted by any government." It was also the cheapest, because it cost the government nothing in interest. Spaulding's confidence was borne out by the ease with which the measure got through both Houses. He himself seems to have been carried away by the success of the legal tender notes. So apparently were both their advocates and their opponents; for the latter, though voting no, attempted little resistance otherwise. The success of the greenbacks could not be denied or explained away. There were still doubts of their wisdom, but most people accepted with confidence the fact of their success. The bankers, possessing legal reserves of greenbacks and well within the law, were at ease. The government's creditors, including the soldiers, were being paid. The spirit of nationalism was gratified by a federal currency, of uniform value, accepted everywhere, without haggling over discounts. People found it a blessing. The rise in prices was sometimes agreeable, sometimes not, but it was a diffused, scarcely palpable process for most persons, and for only the rarely sophisticated were the two things—the rising prices and the new, abundant legal tender—clearly related. People could and did take satisfaction in the obvious advantage of a uniform currency which was much more general and obvious than the disadvantage of rising prices. Certainly the ringing prophecies of disaster had not come true. Owen Lovejoy of Illinois had said in February that there was no precipice, no chasm, no possible yawning bottomless gulf so terrible, so appalling, so ruinous as that with which the nation was threatened by the greenbacks; but here were the greenbacks, it was June, and no yawning, bottomless gulf was visible. On the contrary, though apprehensions persisted, civil prosperity prevailed. And Lovejoy himself voted for the new issue. He regretted doing so, for it still seemed a sin to deal with paper money. But if there must be paper money, it should be issued by the government, not the banks. It should be the government's "privilege, exclusively, of not paying its debts." So he would not persist "in any factious opposition to what is a foregone conclusion." Thus the second legal tender act was passed, and 11 July it was approved.[10]

By the end of July, the greenback dollar had become worth in gold only ninety-one cents. This depreciation had been ascribed patriotically by the *New York Times* not to "want of confidence in the currency" but to the "operations of shrewd bankers, who foresee that as paper increased gold will advance." It was part of the current development which the press regarded as prosperity. Military demand for men and commodities added to civilian demand was driving prices up both in gold and paper. The issue of legal tender notes had enlarged bank reserves, which had enlarged bank loans, which had enlarged bank deposits. Money was abundant. By August, New York City bank returns showed the largest deposits ever reported.

249

The summer before, 17 August 1861, the banks had had deposits of ninety-two millions and note circulation of eight; a year later, 23 August 1862, the deposits had mounted to a hundred and forty-three millions and the note circulation to nine. This was an aggregate increase in bank liabilities of more than half.[11]

One illustrative consequence of the course of things in the summer of 1862 was that Thomas Jefferson's grandson, a clever young merchant in Boston, was getting rich. The war and the issue of paper money, he later wrote, had made him expect rises in the value of everything in the nature of real property. "I therefore bought freely," he said, "anything that came under my hand—pepper, coffee, iron, etc.—and at the end of the first year found myself, owing to having followed general principles, the happy possessor of one hundred thousand dollars. The next year I did as well, and, as I was wise enough to stop when our currency began to improve, I found myself in '63 comfortably off."[12]

After this second legal tender act, 11 July 1862, authorizing the issue of a hundred and fifty millions more, the Treasury was again comfortable for a short time. Its position worsened during the autumn and in his annual report, 4 December 1862, Secretary Chase announced that more money must be provided. He thought that the easiest way to raise it would be by the issue of more United States notes, but that such an issue would be "a positive calamity" and "as injurious as it would be easy." The consequences would be "inflation of prices, increase of expenditures, augmentation of debt, and ultimately, disastrous defeat of the very purposes sought to be attained by it." So he opposed any rise in the authorized limit on note issue, though prepared to find it unavoidable as a temporary expedient, and returned to his pet idea that "the chief reliance and the safest must be upon loans." If no more notes were authorized, it seemed to the Secretary certain that all the Treasury needed for the current year could be borrowed readily at fair rates; and he hoped that realization of the country's resources and assurance of its restored territorial integrity would make the same thing certain for the year following.[13]

Though these inflationary results were such as the opponents of the legal tender notes had expected, they were such as the advocates also had expected unless the two compensatory measures in their program were also adopted. These were taxes and a new borrowing procedure, both of which are considered in later chapters. The tax measure, in the absence of any existing procedure for internal revenue, proved to be legislatively difficult to agree upon and administratively slow to organize. A government that had never depended on internal revenue nor more than casually thought of it now and then—that prided itself in fact on putting no burden on its people—could not devise a system of taxation, create the necessary administration, and collect the taxes in a matter of months. At least it did not, though the legal tender notes had been advocated and authorized on the presumption that federal taxes would be levied. There was the same presumption with respect to borrowing, which was to be effected on a new and better basis. But this too was something that required abandonment of limitations, long revered, on federal powers. Legal tender notes alone could not make a stunted government sovereign.

In this situation, the Secretary's recommendations offered no clear course of action for immediate relief, and while Congress made its stabs at the problem, it kept receiving accounts of the renewed distress of soldiers and their families for want of pay due from the government. These were in general confirmed by a brief, tart Treasury report, 18 December 1862, showing that pay for the troops was again overdue—for some as much as three months—that the resources of the Treasury were inadequate to meet all the current demands, that priority was being given the most urgent debts so far as possible, and that no one could feel a deeper regret than the Secretary of the Treasury himself so long as a single American soldier lacked a single dollar of his pay. But he had laid before Congress the measures

251

he thought would enable him to meet current needs, and he hoped that if he were fortunate enough to get the concurrence of Congress all grounds of complaint would soon be removed.[14]

It is hard to see how immediate relief could have been derived from concurrence in the Secretary's diffuse recommendations, and nearly a month passed, with passages between Treasury and Capitol of "I did" and "you didn't," before Congress cut the knot with a joint resolution, approved by President Lincoln 17 January 1863, authorizing a fresh issue of legal tender notes in the amount of one hundred millions as "immediate provision for the payment of the army and navy." The soldier's thirteen dollars a month was little enough, and being in depreciated notes it was less even than it looked to be.[15]

Meanwhile, a comprehensive bill had been pending which accorded with Mr Chase's disposition to borrow. As passed and approved, 3 March 1863, it authorized him to go into debt nine hundred millions more and to issue fifty millions of greenbacks in addition to the hundred millions authorized by the joint resolution. This was the last issue.*

Four hundred and fifty millions was the whole amount of legal tender notes authorized which served as currency. Additional interest bearing bonds that were also legal tender were issued, but they were not part of the circulation. The circulating legal tender notes were about one-sixth of the total federal debt of two and a half billions at the end of the war. They became depreciated as it had been foretold, but not to the extent of ruin. Had Secretary Chase in July 1861 not defied the warnings pressed upon him, had he not clung to the specie requirements of the independent Treasury act but consented to use bank credit instead, then the

---

* The aggregate of greenbacks authorized was as follows:

Act of 25 February 1862	$150,000,000
Act of 11 July 1862	$150,000,000
Joint resolution of 17 January 1863	$100,000,000
Act of 3 March 1863	$ 50,000,000
Total	$450,000,000

suspension of specie payment might perhaps have been avoided. Instead he made it certain.[16]

The conflict over greenbacks after the war was a wholly different affair from the war-time episode. The latter ended when John B. Alley, who in January 1862 had been the first in Congress to propound temporary recourse to legal tender notes, became also the first, the war being over, to move their extinction. He did this 18 December 1865 by introducing a resolution concurring in the recommendation of Secretary Hugh McCulloch that retirement of the legal tenders be undertaken as soon as the business interests of the country permitted. That was what Alley and his associates had always purposed. His resolution was adopted without debate by a vote of 144 to 6. But it came to naught, having to give way to a sudden, impatient, popular belief— quite opposite to the Jacksonian hard-money notions previously prevailing and to the intent of the war-time advocates of the notes—that an abundant currency based simply on federal credit and the country's worth was required for the general good. The greenback era had begun, inspired by an implicit popular conception of a peace-time, continuing, managed currency.[17]

This belief in turn betokened popular abandonment of the Jacksonian concept of a passive and unofficious federal government, servile toward states' rights, for a concept of the federal government as an active, beneficent sovereignty, taking over powers hitherto reserved to the states. The 37th Congress initiated this change with no resounding manifesto infused with omniscience; but by stumbling through act after act it built up federal powers needed to preserve the Union. The first of these, which was frustrated by Secretary Chase, was the intended suspension of the independent Treasury act of 1846, whose specie requirement was broken down by the suspension, by the legal tender act, and by the national bank act. These first measures were financial. What may in the future seem an epochal culmination of the course then begun—and may now be viewed teleo-

253

logically—was the act of 1946 which committed the United States to the obligations of a welfare state.

Defense of the federal Union rested on two emotional considerations. The more general was the conviction that the Union allowed more individual liberty than any other government and that its disruption would impair the American's freedom to do as he pleased. It was a *laisser faire* conviction incompatible with the course which its defense entailed, though this, of course, was not recognized. The second was a conviction which readily grew from the obvious expectation that if the federal government could free the slaves, it could also do something for the farmer and the laborer, who wanted more of the benefits of industrialization than they were getting and more than the states, severally, could give them.

III

While the Union of northern states was trying to find ways to pay for an expensive war, the Confederacy of southern states had been doing likewise. Both governments had been unprepared for armed conflict, both had expected the conflict to be short, and both were finding their financial difficulties grievously embarrassing. Both borrowed early and taxed late, not merely because taxes were disagreeable but also because, in the absence of experience with a system of federal revenue, their levy and collection would take more time and attention than could be spared. Each belligerent grossly underestimated the other's staying power. The North discovered that secession was not a brash conspiracy merely, forced by a few traitors on Southerners as a whole. The South discovered that the Yankee soldier, though a trader, could not be stopped by offers to buy his rifle or his sword. Each side resorted of necessity to quick measures. Each was prodigal of paper emissions, the South the more so; but the confederate Congress did not make its paper legal tender.

This and other divergencies in the fiscal and monetary

procedures of the two governments reflected both practical conditions and constitutional idiosyncrasies. The
South had not the material resources of the North, though
her war was no less ambitious and costly than the North's.
Agrarian and virtually colonial, she had achieved nothing
of the North's industrial balance and nearness to self-suffi-
ciency. She lived by cotton and could not free her fate from
it; cotton kept her in a golden cage. She also lacked from
the outset the cash which is indispensable to quick, efficient, and sustained economic achievement. The North's
embargo on her external trade sealed her off from the funds
and the materials requisite in peace and still more so in war.
All her banks together had much less specie than those in
New York City alone. They began suspending in the weeks
following Lincoln's election, being indebted heavily as
usual to the Northern banks on trade balance and proudly
undertaking to discharge the debt—to their own and their
government's disadvantage. In consequence of this and
other constraints, the South was forced into general suspension of specie payments months before the North.*[18]

The confederate Constitution departed from the 1789
original by omitting the language forbidding the individual
states to issue bills of credit, but it retained the prohibition
against their making anything but gold and silver a legal
tender. The omission vaguely enlarged the Confederate
states' constitutional powers but at least removed any doubt
which the *Briscoe* decision had left in Southern councils
regarding the legality of notes issued by banks under state
charter. The legal tender prohibition followed an agrarian
hard-money tradition that was perhaps even stronger in
the South than the legal tender debates in Washington
showed it to be in the North. The net difference between

* The *Boston Daily Advertiser*, 19 September 1861, had been surprised by suspension of the New Orleans banks. They were "among
the strongest in the country and have withstood every convulsion in
the money market hitherto." They had continued gold payments in
1857, when metropolitan banks in New York and throughout the rest
of the country suspended them. (*Boston Daily Advertiser*, 30 August
1861; B. Hammond, 616, 680.)

the federal and confederate Constitutions with regard to
the two central governments' respective monetary powers
remained the same literally but in practice diametrically
opposite. For in the North silence in the Constitution gave
consent, but in the South silence was inhibitory, because
the central government, by Jeffersonian and Jacksonian interpretation and the force of the tenth amendment—which
was retained by the confederate Constitution—possessed
only the powers specifically delegated to it by the states
and the latter as sovereign entities reserved all powers not
specifically delegated. So, in the South the central government could issue notes under the authorization to borrow,
and the states, as sovereigns, could do the same. But
neither could make the notes legal tender because the central government had not been given the power to do so, and
the states had been denied it.[19]

In this situation both the confederate government and
the constituent states issued circulating notes similar to the
Treasury demand notes in the North. Some bore interest
at a rate of a penny a day on each hundred dollar note,
half of Chase's seven and three-tenths per cent; some two
pennies, the same as Chase's; and some none. But contrary
to tradition and the confederate Constitution's specific ban,
a demand that the Treasury notes be made legal tender
arose in the South months before it did in the North. It
was apparently the fervid revolutionary spirit of the South
and its more primitive economic situation that led to this
demand, which was less warranted by tradition in the
agrarian South than in the entrepreneurial North. Despite
their Constitution's ban, the Southern legal tender advocates argued that making paper a legal tender was permitted by the Constitution's delegation of power to declare
war, raise and support armies, and enact laws necessary to
those ends. This was an argument used also in Washington. But despite the South's resourcelessness and the North's
subsequent example, the effort to make Treasury notes
legal tender never succeeded in the South. Several of the
individual confederate states, however, enacted laws giv-

ing the central government's notes some substance of legal tender within their several jurisdictions by making them acceptable at face value in payment of taxes.[20]

In both North and South a paper legal tender was advocated for expediency alone, the respective Constitutions coming into the argument only as permissive or inhibitory. But whereas in the North, advocacy was primarily in the interest of banks and other debtors peculiarly subject to legal requirements, in the South it was primarily in the interest of a government in even more desperate need of credit than that of the North. Moreover, the North's authorization of legal tender was a hold-fast measure preliminary to a program of taxation and of borrowing that was fruitful, that limited the issues of legal tender paper to but a fraction of the debt incurred, that avoided the ruin apprehended by opponents of the issues, and that would still have avoided it in all likelihood, had the North lost Antietam, Gettysburg, and the effort to prevent secession. So the North's resort to legal tender paper was, for reasons peculiar to its situation, useful. The South's resort to it would have been useless. The demand for a paper legal tender in the North was supported by the prospect of funds to be obtained by taxation and borrowing. The demand "at the South" was supported, as in the thirteen states during the Revolution, by the absence of any alternative. The whole Southern situation was so bad, once the potentialities of intrepidity and military skill were exhausted, that a general resignation to it took the place of the sanguine measures undertaken in the North—where moreover there were more financiers whose experience fitted the needs of an industrial war than there were in the South. In the North an industrial system gave assurance of the necessary production of supplies, and required mainly a reform of the system of payments. In the South, a reform of the system of payments would accomplish nothing, the means of production being at want. Consequently the Southern financial procedure was a series of desperate makeshifts; and though making the confederate paper a legal tender might seem to have been a makeshift also worth trial, it was not promising enough to override traditional, practical, and constitutional objections. And it was not proposed as the temporary element of a constructive program of taxation and borrowing like the North's but rather as a substitute for such a program.

Besides the notes put in circulation by banks and by the confederate Treasury and individual states there were also notes issued by municipalities, business firms, companies, and individuals, less with the purpose of providing a circulating medium than of "paying" (or putting off) their own debts; though it was tempting to such borrowers to pose as providers of "money" and benefactors of their cause. Another source of circulating notes in the Confederacy was the North, where the Southern authorities at first got their notes printed surreptitiously; but failing to get them through the lines they had finally to rely on their own inferior and inadequate means of engraving and printing. Southern currency continued to be counterfeited in the North, however. Advertisements in Northern newspapers offered, for example, twenty thousand dollars in confederate bills for five dollars in cash; Union soldiers might use the bills to their advantage if they found themselves in Southern territory as invaders or prisoners. But because the industrial North had better means of engraving and printing than the agrarian South, the North's counterfeits were usually superior to the South's originals in execution and hence might be the more readily detected. This, however, made them none the less contributory to the South's monetary chaos.[21]

The Secretary of the confederate Treasury, Christopher G. Memminger, had not the imposing personality that Salmon P. Chase possessed, nor the noble delusions; but being a lawyer who had specialized in banking and commercial practice and who followed business procedure readily, he stirred up less trouble than Chase did and made the best of a weak position while Chase was unconscionably abusing the North's great economic advantages. Memminger was subjected to continuous political attack, less it seems, because he was a poor financier than because he was a poor, orphaned, German immigrant who somehow got educated; he was without family, figuratively and literally, and not a real son of the South. He was unprofessionally absorbed to an eccentric degree in theology and religion, which as with Chase disposed him to a hard-money doctrine incompatible with the situation in the South; but to this situation Memminger nevertheless accommodated himself, whether with less courage than Chase displayed in much less difficult conditions, or with greater common sense. Unlike Chase, who refused to use bank notes or checks, preferring to issue Treasury notes till it took a thousand dollars to buy a breakfast, Memminger dealt with realities reasonably. His far abler cabinet colleague, Judah P. Benjamin, who shone among the most brilliant men on the continent, accomplished for the Confederacy, in the end, no more.[22]

Since the bonds and currency of the confederate government became worthless in the end, the Confederacy's part in the war was financed in reality by a gradual, indirect confiscation of the property of the Southern people and of the foreign investors who bought its bonds—besides, of course, such Northern chattels as the Southerners had been able to seize. With respect to the paper currency and the bonds, insofar as they changed hands, Benjamin Franklin's observations about the continental currency of the American Revolution applied: As the paper passed from one person to another, losing a little of its value in each transaction, and by so much imposing a little of the total loss on each person through whose hands it passed, it worked pretty much as a tax might—less scientifically, perhaps, but effectually nevertheless.[23]

Both the South and the North hoped to make their respective paper currencies more acceptable by providing for their conversion into interest-bearing bonds. Both deluded themselves with the notion that the bonds would not fall in value and that since this currency would buy bonds at par it could not itself fall in value. Similarly, one might suppose that two drunken men could walk more

259

steadily together than apart. Instead bonds and notes fell in unison. *The Economist* (London), 21 June 1862, in comparing Northern and Southern financing, remarked that both sides expected the convertibility of their notes into bonds to sustain the value of the notes, though in fact the one would be no better than the other. *The Economist* said, however, that it was "far from insinuating" that the financial procedure of the North was on the same footing as that of the South, for "the Confederates never had a legitimate shilling." Yet it found, 18 October 1862, that "as in the North, so in the South, this great struggle has been carried on a little by taxes, somewhat by loans, and mostly by an inconvertible currency." In October 1862 that was still true of both sides, but it continued to be true thereafter only of the South. The North, which had the possibility of pulling itself together, slowly and clumsily did so.[24]

THE REVENUE BILL, HR 312

I

READERS WILL recall that in the act of 5 August 1861, described in chapter 2, the special session of Congress had authorized increases in import duties, a tax on land and other property, and a tax on incomes. Only the import duties had been put into immediate effect; the tax on property was collected for the federal government by all the states not seceding, except Delaware; the tax on income had been deferred till 1862. So, altogether, what is to be said of taxes while Chase was at the Treasury is little and mostly negative.[1]

During the latter half of 1861, Secretary Chase had been depending almost wholly on the bankers for money. Otherwise he got revenue from the tariff only and got very little, imports having shrunk drastically. So had income from the sale of public lands and from other minor sources. As to the property taxes authorized by the special session, the Secretary said in his annual report, 9 December 1861, that since it was "highly desirable to avoid, as long as practicable, introduction into the states of federal agencies for the assessment and collection of taxes," he was "relying on assurances from governors of various states that the amounts apportioned to them respectively will be assumed, collected, and paid through existing state agencies." He had accordingly "refrained from advising the appointment of the officers necessary for direct assessment and collection" by the federal government itself. That is, the federal government, while taking up the sword to curb states' rights in the matter of secession, was deferring to those rights in the sovereign matter of the purse; and in the North, on the same terms as in the South, the "sovereign" states were maintaining an anomalous responsibility for the general government's revenue. In the South, however, the individual states mostly *borrowed* instead of collecting their shares of the levy.[2]

263

CHAPTER 9

In his December report, Chase had also asked Congress to consider if it were wise to levy the income tax, which he had done nothing about, though authorized to arrange for its collection. For, since the property tax was to be collected by the states, he doubted if the income tax should be collected by the federal government; taken alone it would yield too little to justify the cost. He advised a modest increase of the property tax, however; higher import duties on tea, coffee, and sugar; and excise taxes on stills, liquor, tobacco, bank notes, carriages, legacies, legal evidences of debt, deeds to property, etc. From these levies and the income tax he hoped to derive fifty millions of dollars. It would be inapt to say that Chase, since the war was already costing two millions a day by his own estimate, was depending on revenue for less than a month's fighting; for the war, in the views he derived from Albert Gallatin, was to be fought on borrowed money and revenue was to be relied on for the ordinary expenses of administration and maintenance of the public credit. It was obvious, he had said, that taxes would supply little of the sums required. "For the rest the reliance must be placed on loans."* The ironic fact is that the war *was* financed as Gallatin prescribed and Chase approved; taxes were laid, but their total yield was a fourth of what was borrowed. Their main contribution was to sustain the government's credit in the money market by keeping orthodox tradition alive and thereby helping Jay Cooke

* In re-statement of Albert Gallatin's views, already described in chapter 2, I quote the following written by him in 1808: "The geographical situation of the United States, their history since the revolution and, above all, present events remove every apprehension of frequent wars. It may therefore be confidently expected that a revenue derived solely from duties on importations, though necessarily impaired by war, will always be amply sufficient during long periods of peace not only to defray current expenses but also to reimburse the debt contracted during the few periods of war." Thus, he wrote three years later, "forty millions of debt contracted during five or six years of war may always, without any extraordinary exertions, be reimbursed in ten years of peace." What Gallatin counseled was not peculiar to America; European governments did the same. (ASP vi, Finance ii, 243, 309, 497.)

sell the bonds which provided the funds with which the Union pushed doggedly on to victory.[3]

However, Chase did not neglect pious clichés about the need of reducing expenditure, which in the existing circumstances, were like the permission given the girl to swim but not go near the water. "Retrenchment and reform are among the indispensable duties of the hour," the Secretary said. Although the army was still half-clothed and half-armed, although it offered little threat to the enemy, and although there was at the moment no certainty that war with Britain would be avoided, nevertheless the Secretary, reporting to Congress the failure of revenue and the lack of money, thought "the first great object of reflection and . . . endeavor should be the reduction of expenditure. . . . Contracts for supplies to the army and navy as well as for public work of all descriptions, should be subjected to strict supervision and the contractors to rigorous responsibility. All unnecessary offices should be abolished, and salaries and pay should be materially reduced." He also recommended again that the property of rebels be confiscated, though it was still in their possession.[4]

The Secretary's report, it will be recalled, came out while the public was in alarm over the *Trent* affair, and his acknowledgment of the Treasury's difficulties made things worse. On top of that his failure to propose adequate revenue alarmed the people who had the money to lend but looked for assurance that what they lent would be paid back to them. And bankers, on whom the Secretary relied for the initial advances he would need as well as for permanent investment in the government's bonds and whose loyalty he had already been abusing, were alarmed by his main proposal, which was that a new system of banks, under federal control, be authorized.

In all of Chase's lifetime and that of his contemporaries, the bulk of the Union's revenue had been derived from duties on imports, which were not only abundant but easy to collect and—as it seemed—spared the Americans wholly from what has since become the heaviest part of their tax burden. It was evidently hard for Chase to grasp the idea of internal revenue on any but a small scale. Internal taxes levied by the federal government had been unpopular in principle even before the Whiskey Rebellion of 1794, not only because they were taxes but also because they would be the means of aggrandizing federal powers and impairing local and regional freedom. Even those states which in 1861 held the Union to be indivisible and secession a crime were jealous of their individual "sovereignty" and resentful of raids by the federal government into the customary area of their reserved rights. Chase could advert with confidence, as he had done in his July report, to the "preference which has always been evinced by the people of the United States, as well as by their legislature and executive, for duties on imports as the chief source of national revenue." It was "only on occasions of special exigency" that resort had been had "to direct taxation or to internal duties or excises." The Secretary proposed, he said, "no departure . . . from the line of policy thus sanctioned." With these words, he had left to Congress all initiative in devising adequate revenue. What Congress achieved seems small beside the magnitudes reached a century later, but it may be more justly appraised in the light of a statement by Professor Frederic C. Howe, an authority on federal finance writing in 1896, who thought "the amount of money extracted from the pockets of the people in the form of loans and taxes" to carry on the war, then thirty-one years past, "almost incredible." The total taxes collected during the war were less than seven hundred millions, but to Professor Howe "the tax legislation, wholly experimental in form, was of such vast proportions and so far-reaching in its consequences that the nation stood astonished at its resources and alarmed for the consequences of its acts."[5]

A century later, the wonder is that a war of such magnitude (counting the North alone) in men, casualties, and material could have cost so little in money. The supposition is fallacious, and the wonder is wasted. It did not cost little; the unit of measurement—the dollar—has shrunk to a fraction of its former value.

II

As I have already recounted, the Secretary's December recommendations had been assigned to two sub-committees of Ways and Means. One was under the chairmanship of Elbridge G. Spaulding of Buffalo, New York, who had taken up the Secretary's proposals for a new banking system but, under pressure of the December crisis and the banks' suspension of specie payments, had turned his attention to getting legal tender notes authorized. The other sub-committee, assigned the question of revenue, was under the chairmanship of Justin S. Morrill of Vermont, a retired village storekeeper, self-educated, one of the oldest and most respected members of Congress, eventually one of its longest-lived, and distinguished through the latter half of the century as a foremost advocate of protective tariffs and as legislative sponsor of the land-grant colleges.

The first accomplishment of the Morrill sub-committee was to obtain enactment, 24 December, of a bill increasing the duties on imports of coffee, tea, and sugar, which the Secretary had recommended and which Justin Morrill said was expected to yield "between seven and eight million dollars." Morrill was himself still of the opinion that increased rates would produce but little increase in receipts, but he thought it would be "quite as beneficial" if the rates diminished consumption and kept money from going out of the country. This enactment was merely incidental, however; the real work of the sub-committee, as the House was told, was to revise the revenue act of 5 August, which had been adopted by the special session with no feeling that it was adequate or more than an earnest show of purpose. But action on further revenue legislation would necessarily be slow—particularly because the legal tender measure had got precedence—and there was agreement, the state of the public credit being low, that the government's intent to

267

enact adequate measures for revenue should be affirmed promptly. Accordingly Erastus Corning, Democrat and banker of Albany, New York, a member of the Ways and Means Committee, who opposed the legal tenders, had introduced the resolution, 15 January 1862, promising enactment of a tax bill that would provide at least a hundred and fifty millions of revenue yearly. This resolution, which tripled the amount proposed by Secretary Chase, had passed the lower House after a brief discussion by a vote of 134 to 5 and the Senate two days later by a vote of 39 to 1. It reflected the exhortations of the James Gallatin delegation then in Washington, but independently of that it had the support of both opponents and proponents of the legal tender notes—of the opponents because they hoped a stand for revenue would weaken the appeal of fiat money, and of the proponents, because they regarded the notes as but a stop-gap and ancillary to taxes.[6]

The passage of the resolution showed not only an independence of Secretary Chase's recommendations and fears, but a remarkable readiness to provide federal revenue, regardless of past practice and tradition. The unfamiliar direct tax on property was palliated by the arrangement that the individual states could collect it through their familiar agencies, but the even less familiar income tax also was accepted, with scarcely a question, though it was to be collected by the federal government directly. The proposed taxes had scarcely a breath of opposition in principle such as held up the legal tender proposal. The latter was of doubtful constitutionality and thoroughly repugnant to tradition. Direct taxes were specifically authorized by the Constitution, though in obscure terms, and local practice made them familiar. Income taxes had precedent in the "faculty" taxes levied in the colonies and continued in individual states on professions and trades and also in the income taxes levied in some states and well known to be levied in Britain. Although an income tax instituted by Congress thirty years later was invalidated in 1895 by the Supreme Court on the ground that it was "unapportioned" as required by the Constitution, this question did not arise in 1861 and 1862. The only impediments in the way of the new tax legislation were those of finding practicable and fair means of levy and collection. Every member of Congress had constituents whose peculiar situation made relevant provisions of the bill objectionable, and these had to be disputed, often at length. Accordingly it took Congress twice as long to enact the tax measure as it took to authorize the first issue of legal tender notes.[7]

III

Justin Morrill opened debate on the revenue bill (HR 312) Wednesday 12 March 1862, two months after the Corning resolution was adopted and a fortnight after passage of the legal tender bill. In a lively address of historical importance, he briefly stated the needs of the Treasury and told his countrymen that he and they, because of those needs, were presently to be "driven . . . like Milton's Adam, from our untaxed garden." The pending bill, he said, had "its fingers spread out in all directions, ready to clutch something to buoy up the sinking credit of a nation which has hitherto generally sheltered its capital and its labor from all tax gatherers, except through the indirect process of the custom house." The committee proposed to lay "duties upon a large number of objects rather than confine them to a narrow field"; and it proposed "a system by which all descriptions of duties could be assessed and collected" through one agency to be directed by "a commissioner of internal revenue." Morrill acknowledged the help of the individual states in collecting the direct tax authorized by the act of 5 August 1861, but he insisted that a single federal agency, as provided by the new bill, could do the work far less expensively than could the states, which retained fifteen per cent of what they took in.[8]

The government could "not afford to return to the pusillanimity of the old Confederation," request the states to help it, "and shiver in the wind if any should fail to do so." Con-

269

sidering the magnitude of the sacrifices imposed upon the country by the Southern insurrection, Mr. Morrill said that the federal government—"the most parental and benign of all earthly governments in its hour of need has the right to *demand* whatever may be the measure of its necessities." Direct federal taxes, he feared, "must for many years . . . be the rule and have a place in our statutes as a part of our ordinary legislation." He remarked that foreigners considered the obligations of the federal government of doubtful worth because of that government's "incapacity for taxation," and declared that in the measure he was introducing, admittedly novel and severe, "representative democracy is now on trial." If the members of Congress failed to provide an adequate revenue they would "deserve to be pickled in history as representative imbeciles." He said the committee sought to obtain adequate revenue as lightly and equitably as possible by taking careful account of the origins and uses of materials subject to tax and the effect of the tax upon consumption. The duty on whiskey and rum, he said, would "still leave it possible for any man or brute to get drunk" in America more cheaply than in any other country he knew of. "Persons who like good liquors," he said, "are patriotic on the subject of taxation and never quarrel about the price"; and those "who swallow that which is said to be 'sure to kill at forty rods' will have it at any hazard of life or purse." He described the importance of the new petroleum industry as a source of revenue, described the problem of taxing transportation, and took satisfaction, as an ardent protectionist, in the fact that manufacturers had now become "the strongest pillars of our support." For "a burden that would paralyze the agriculturists of the country will be taken on the backs of steam giants with alacrity and confidence." Advertising was also a new source of revenue.[9]

The income tax Morrill thought to be "one of the least defensible" that was being proposed. Nearly every one subject to it had already been taxed upon the sources of his income; "the dividends of banks, the interest on railroad

270

bonds, and United States official salaries" were already taxed. The income tax was "an inquisitorial one at best." But because of "the considerable class of state officers and the many thousands who are employed on a fixed salary, most of whom would not contribute a penny unless called upon through this tax," it has been thought best, he said, not to forego it.[10]

The new revenue bill, as these items show, reflected far more than the Union's need of money. It reflected the revolutionary expansion and proliferation of the North's economic activity, recent and swift, and it directed the sudden, bold penetration of the new economy by a federal authority which had long shrunk from interference in the interests of its people. But it was not this interference with personal rights that aroused most opposition. It was interference with states' rights. William H. Wadsworth of Kentucky, formerly a Whig but now a Democrat and enemy of the Lincoln administration, followed Justin Morrill directly with complaint against the revenue bill's revolutionary encroachment on "the reserved rights of the states." He said that the bill not merely imposed customary burdens but made novel pretensions to an unprecedented federal supremacy. He recalled how, in the long contest during his day "between the tendency toward *ultra* state rights and the effort of the federal government to preserve its just powers on a liberal construction of the Constitution," he had been in the minority resisting the tendency which now had culminated in secession. He had seen "the people of the states take away from the federal government . . . the powers to establish a national bank, to pass high protective tariffs, to make internal improvements, to legislate for the restriction of slavery in the territories." Those denials of federal authority, except the last, he had vainly opposed. But now the trend had changed and was sweeping to the opposite extreme; and he found himself resisting a "new and overshadowing danger" in "this tendency of the federal government to swallow up the powers reserved to the states and people respectively."[11]

Wadsworth's underlying objection to the revenue bill was that acceptance of it entailed acceptance of President Lincoln's policy and in particular acceptance of emancipation, in revulsion against which he delivered a fine encomium on the institution of slavery and the mutually advantageous concord it created between Anglo-Saxon and African. He would preserve the Union and he would also preserve slavery. "As the Anglo-Saxon race," Wadsworth said, "continues its grand march to the goal of civilization, lessening the distance between earth and Heaven, this inferior race will march with it and in the providence of God and by his means now undisclosed to man, perform, it may be, a more important part in the grand drama of life than it now does." For him the issue was particularly evil, because Kentucky, a slave state, was already threatened by the prospect of emancipation.[12]

But the same objection, incongruously, arose where emancipation was no problem; Roscoe Conkling of New York and Thomas D. Eliot of Massachusetts, both Northerners and Republicans, desired to restore the provision that any individual state, if it chose, might collect all the duties and taxes due within its borders and turn them over to the Treasury. The argument was that this would be cheaper and also that it would spare the people contact with federal tax collectors. For "no army that ever marched through the country," said Roscoe Conkling, was more hated than "that army" of tax-gatherers representing the federal government. Pendleton of Ohio agreed. The same effort had already been made with the Ways and Means Committee and had failed. Though this effort indicated the stubborn persistence of state loyalties in the North, it also stirred up a rejection of them by a majority whose loyalties were national. Yet the tenacity of states' rights was also indicated by the moderation of those who professed detachment from it. John Hutchins, of Ohio, thought the proposal presented "perhaps the most important question" to arise in discussion of the tax bill, but he also thought, temperately, that it was time to "get rid of the idea that there

272

is objection to the exercise of constitutional, legitimate authority" by the "general government in the states." Hutchins said that "we have been all carried away with the idea" of states' rights and "afraid of the concentration and consolidation" of governmental power; but he now advocated the active exercise of federal authority. Thomas N. Edwards of New Hampshire remarked that "every member here would seem to desire . . . to exclude as much as possible the action of the general government within the limits of any state"; but for himself he had "no great reluctance" to the exercise of all the federal government's "rightful powers . . . wherever it is expedient." In accord with this sentiment, the effort to keep federal tax gatherers out of the states was abandoned. Stiff and unprecedented taxes were accepted one after another, despite prolonged protests. There was renewed contention over the morality and constitutionality of a tax on slaves as property; abolitionists opposed the tax because it was abominable to class human beings as property, and the friends of slavery opposed it because it was burdensome. There was also considerable hesitancy about the terms of the income tax. William P. Sheffield of Rhode Island, a Republican, proposed a one per cent sales tax to which, however, Justin Morrill and others successfully objected.[13]

The bill came to a vote 8 April after a month of wearisome and contentious discussion which Thaddeus Stevens closed in a brief speech "listened to," the *New York Times* reported, "with deep attention by the House." More sanguine than he had been the previous summer after Bull Run, he thought that if the government used the means in its power the rebels could be so crippled within ninety days that five-sixths of the current expenses could be saved. "In that case," he said, "I feel no hesitancy in predicting that not another dollar of taxes need ever be imposed on the people to defray our whole debt." He expected an early victory and a Carthaginian peace. If then it were determined, "in accordance with the practice of nations, the dictates of wisdom and of justice, to make the property of

273

the rebels pay the expenses of the war which they have so wantonly caused, this tax need never be collected beyond the second year." Of the income tax he said that it had been "very difficult to adjust so as to escape double taxation . . . "; but "it would be manifestly unjust to allow the large money operators and wealthy merchants, whose incomes might reach hundreds of thousands of dollars, to escape from their due proportion of the burden. . . . While the rich and the thrifty will be obliged to contribute largely from the abundance of their means, . . . no burdens have been imposed on the industrious laborer and mechanic, . . . the food of the poor is untaxed; and . . . no one will be affected by the provisions of this bill whose living depends solely on his manual labor." At the close of Stevens' statement, the bill passed the House by a vote of 125 to 14.[14]

During the last two days of the bill's consideration in the House, there was fought at Shiloh and Pittsburg Landing what the *Herald* called "one of the greatest and bloodiest battles of modern days."[15]

IV

The bill (HR 312), when received in the Senate 10 April 1862, was referred to the Finance Committee, which considered it for a month. Then, 6 May, the committee's chairman, Senator Fessenden, reported it back with amendments. At the same time, Senator McDougall of California, a minority member of the committee, offered a substitute bill "which embodies," he said, "the views of the Board of Trade of Boston," and which had been endorsed by the Boards of Trade or Chambers of Commerce of New York, Philadelphia, Cincinnati, Chicago, and of every other city that had considered it. Its main purpose, while retaining an income tax, was to shift the burden from the manufacturer to the consumer by a sales tax of one per cent on the gross amount of all sales of merchandise, produce, live stock, etc., and on the gross receipts of railway and steam-

ship companies, hotels, restaurants, theatres, *et cetera.*
Senator Fessenden opposed Senator McDougall's substitute, it received desultory consideration, and it was dismissed by a vote of 33 to 3.[16]

Discussion of the House bill, as reported by Fessenden
with committee amendments, began 21 May and for the
most part continued daily, paragraph by paragraph. Senator after senator had some product or employment in his
state which, he argued, would be ruined by some levy or
other in the bill. "This bill," Senator Wilson of Massachusetts complained, "is and must be unequal and unjust towards my state and section of the country. It is one of the
most unequal tax bills ever proposed in any country or
any age." Ira Harris of New York described the small community of Gloversville, where the manufacture of gloves and
mittens of deer skin, goat skin, sheep skin, and elk furnished
employment to the women and children of the community.
The men hunted in the "great wilderness" on the borders
of which Gloverville was situated. About a million dollar's
worth of the gloves and mittens were sold yearly. But
the army quartermaster chose to buy knitted mittens and
gloves of yarn. The Gloverville people could not, in the face
of competition from yarn mittens and gloves, raise the price
of their leather mittens and gloves to cover the tax they
had to pay for skins. "They are charged two cents a pound
on these skins," Senator Harris said, and "then they are
charged three per cent *ad valorem* on their gloves; thus
making about six per cent tax." This would break up their
business, which had "greatly decreased" already. There
had been some hundred modest establishments engaged in
this work in 1856. Their number was "now reduced to about
twenty-five or thirty"; and unless Congress meant really to
"break down the business," the senator said, the imposition must be softened. It was not; but a change proposed
by the senator in favor of the manufacturers of draining
tile, who were few and "struggling for existence," was allowed, the tile being important to farming.[17]

Such detailed appeals for lightening the tax on every

conceivable product and activity, mostly peculiar to diverse regions and communities and unknown to others, were endless. City and country, East and West, jealously sought to shift the tax burden from one to the other. Senator Fessenden was worn out protesting against the whittling away at revenue desperately needed, at the loss of time spent in futile efforts to avoid disagreeable burdens, and at the brave assertions of patriotism offered in lieu of cash.

As in the House, differences arose over the propriety of laying a tax on slaves, to be paid of course by their masters; and again, as in the House, the enemies of slavery were divided. Some sought to penalize slave-owners as well as raise money, and others refused to touch money raised on an implication that men could be property. These differences extended to disagreement as to whether the proposed tax were a "direct" one and therefore in conflict with the requirement of the Constitution that "direct" taxes be apportioned according to population. Senator Sumner of Massachusetts, in proposing the tax, thought it clear that the tax could give no sanction to slavery. "The Constitution," he said, "knows nobody as a slave. All are 'persons.' But at the same time it does not assume to interfere with a well-known state institution by which 'persons' are degraded to be property. The condition of the slave is anomalous. He is property by the local law; he is a 'person' by the Constitution." Slavery, he said, was "a monstrous *fact*, beyond our reach in the states, except through the war power. . . . It is an intolerable nuisance intrenched in state lines; but we shall not treat it otherwise than as a nuisance when we tax it. In taxing it we do not assume its rightfulness."[18]

Senator Sherman of Ohio, who complained of "the long delay, the tedious discussion, the wearisome debate," prolonged it by calling the proposal both unconstitutional and impractical. "Will you treat the persons named in this amendment as chattels, slaves, property to be bought and sold? If so, the tax is proper. . . . If they are persons, recognized by the Constitution as persons," the tax proposed was unconstitutional, being a capitation tax, unless it applied to all persons and was duly apportioned according to population. But even if constitutional, he asked, would the tax be wise and expedient? It could be collected only from "the loyal men in the border states—from no one else."[19]

In the same way, taxes on liquor outraged both senators who liked to drink and those who did not. Timothy Howe of Wisconsin, radical Republican who favored both the tax on slaves and that on liquor, feared lest the ruin of the country "be effected by its morality." For, he said, here we are in a dire extremity to find the means of preserving the government; we offer to tax the vending of liquors; senators start back in affright: "it would not do; it was calculated to demoralize the nation; they could not afford it, and they would not vote for it." Then it is proposed, he said, to tax slavery. "We do not propose to authorize anybody to hold slaves or to work them; but if we find persons working them we propose to collect revenue from them, not to impose a tax which they can not afford to pay, nor to impose a tax which they ought not to pay, but a tax which they can afford to pay and which upon every principle of right and justice they ought to pay." Again senators drew back in affright; "we are told it is an immoral thing, a vicious thing, and that we can not afford to lend any sanction to it."[20]

With other opposition than the compunctions of half the abolitionists—especially with opposition from the loyal border states where slavery was still harbored—the effort to tax slaves as property failed in the Senate as in the House. But not without a stubborn struggle. Senator Sumner's proposal to tax slaves—which he asseverated it was not, since it metaphysically avoided recognizing the existence of "slaves" or use of the word—was brought up Wednesday, 28 May, and sharply debated. Debate was resumed the next day, again involving distinctions between "slaves" and "persons," between right and wrong, between a tax of two dollars a head and five dollars a head, and between different interpretations of the Constitution, of the debates in the constitutional convention, et cetera. Senator Sumner's proposal, amended in form, was voted down, 22 to 14. But a week later, 5 June, the senator brought up his proposal again, so worded as to tax persons "claiming" ownership of slaves and as to avoid both the constitutional question and the moral one of "recognizing" slavery. It was adopted without discussion by a vote of 19 to 16. But the next day, 6 June, a motion was made to reconsider the vote and, strange to say, after lively and lengthy debate it was adopted, 22 to 18. Then, at once, upon reconsideration Sumner's proposal was voted down, 23 to 17. It was a matter of moral and constitutional scruple, not at all of raising money.[21]

Thereupon, Senator Fessenden, in summing up the provisions of the bill, acknowledged its defects but held that defects were unavoidable in a matter so unfamiliar, dealt with under pressure. There had been, he said, no experience with federal taxation "for so long a period of years that we come to it a generation of men entirely unacquainted" with the subject and obliged to find a way in the dark. There was also difficulty because the country was "so peculiarly situated that we can not derive much benefit from the experience of others. . . . We are not a homogeneous people in any sense of the word. Our territory is very broad. The pursuits in which we are interested are exceedingly diverse. Population in some portions of the country is dense, while in others it is very sparse." In these circumstances differences of judgment were bound to be serious— as they still are. Should a farmer who incidentally dealt in horses be taxed as a farmer or as a horsedealer? Were insurance companies to be taxed on their premium receipts as income? Did the taxable income of banks include their deposits? Business and industry were still a financial mystery to a good part of Congress, whose task was "in its nature an experiment; . . . and it calls upon senators and representatives . . . to look with an eye single to the whole country, and to divest themselves so far as possible of local feelings and local interests." And, the senator said, nothing in the world was more difficult than this. The bill, he thought, was "in many particulars exceedingly imperfect." But it could not be otherwise. "We can only learn how to correct our errors by experience," and the senator believed it had been "well remarked that for an undertaking of this kind twenty years at least of practice is necessary to any reasonable degree of perfection." Meanwhile, they had not twenty years, but must do as soon as possible as well as possible.[22]

It was now 6 June and five months had elapsed since the joint resolution of January pledging the enactment of a measure promising no less than a hundred and fifty millions of revenue. Senator Fessenden expected no such sum for the current year and in general foresaw an appalling growth of public debt, which, however, only made prompt action imperative even if inadequate. In defense of the bill, he described the greater faults in the alternatives, including those in the bill as passed by the House. Whether Mr. Fessenden's account, gloomy and long, was nevertheless persuasive or whether some other discipline prevailed, the bill promptly passed the Senate, 37 to 1. The one vote against it was Lazarus Powell's of Kentucky, who held out as he had the previous summer against the war, against any supplies, against borrowing, and against taxes.[23]

The Senate, which had received the revenue bill (HR 312) 10 April, now returned it to the House, 6 June, with 312 amendments; it was reported by the *Times* that the House would scarcely recognize its bill. But the differences of moment were few and only one, over the property tax, raised difficulty; the Senate wanted to lay the tax for one year only, the House wanted it to be permanent. It was agreed instead to suspend it for two years afer the first year. The tax of seven and a half per cent on income exceeding fifty thousand dollars was stricken out, taxes of three per cent on income from six hundred to ten thousand and of five per cent on more than ten thousand were retained. The tax on musical instruments, watches, dolls, dogs, *et cetera*, was also stricken out and that on plate, carriages, yachts, and billiard tables was retained. And so on. The tax on whiskey aroused an unconscionable amount of insipid jocosity. The House accepted the compromises, 23 June, by a vote of 106 to 11; the Senate accepted them the same day with no nays; and President Lincoln approved the act 1 July.[24]

This revenue act of 1 July 1862, like the legal tender act of 25 February preceding, was a radical assertion of federal powers and an unrecognized commitment of them to new and increasing uses. Congress, like Secretary Chase, considered it a misfortune incident to war, certain to end therewith and lapse again into desuetude. That the act lay within the powers of the federal government was asserted with passion; that it might be followed by other war-time tax measures was realized; that it foreran a permanent system of internal taxes was neither asserted nor supposed. The income tax, authorized by Congress for the first time, was repealed in 1872. It was again authorized in 1894 and was declared unconstitutional by the Supreme Court in 1895. Not till 1913, after adoption of the 16th amendment, were the income taxes authorized that have since been paid by the Americans.[25]

V

The press found far more to report on currency and borrowings than on the revenue or "tax bill" as it was usually called. The reason for the difference may have been indirectly divulged by the *Times* in a report one day that the Senate had taken up the tax bill and that the galleries, which had been crowded with an audience expecting discussion of a bill to punish treason and rebellion, were soon empty. The willingness, even the eagerness, of the people to be taxed was often mentioned, but it usually turned out to be eagerness for a tax on some one else. When the revenue bill passed the House, 8 April, the *Journal of Commerce* complained of the bill's "great complexity," of its "evident unfairness," of the "horde of office-holders" which it would create, and of the "inquisitorial, summary, and oppressive character of its exactions." This was the complaint of people who opposed the federal government's assumption of effective powers. The *Herald* was inclined the same way but more mildly. In January it had been gratified by the Corning resolution to enact a revenue measure that would raise a hundred and fifty millions, and to see that Congress had "at last responded to what the public wanted"; but three months later when the bill left the House, the *Herald* complained that "in maturing the tax bill, the cost, convenience, and feasibility of collecting the revenue appears to have almost entirely escaped attention." One trouble was that while the tax bill loomed, the greenbacks were coming agreeably into use and performing a painless miracle. The *Herald*, after grumbling over the revenue bill, called the legal tender act "a perfect success," though when "first proposed in this journal, it was hailed with a perfect storm of denunciation." The *Herald* also approved of borrowing from banks, which it pointed out was standard European practice, and said with its tongue in its cheek that the national banking bill—"the last of the series of measures constituting the splendid financial system of the Secretary of the Treasury"—would be reported from committee the current week.[26]

Meanwhile the *Times* had conceded, when the revenue bill passed the House, in April, that it was imperfect and hoped the Senate would improve it. But it was "much to be doubted," the *Times* said in a bizarre figure of speech, "whether a system of taxation adapted to the wants of a people unaccustomed to taxation . . . can be generated at once *ab ovo* by any body of men, however patriotic and sagacious." And it reminded its readers editorially how Great Britain's tax system had been developed over a long period. The *Tribune*'s editor, also loyal but worried, said "we trust the Senate will be able considerably to simplify and improve the House bill, rendering it far less onerous without reducing its revenue-producing efficiency." A month later the *Tribune*, apparently reconciled to the bill's faults, praised Congress editorially: "We hold it one of the most laborious, earnest, painstaking bodies that ever devoted itself to legislation. It has not been so prompt and resolute as it ought in maturing and passing its loan and tax bills, but it may win a noble place in history by a few such days' work as that of yesterday, when the Senate passed the Free Homestead bill by the overwhelming majority of 33 yeas to 7 nays, every Republican present voting yea. . . ." The House at the same time passed the Pacific railway bill. "Two such measures," the *Tribune* said, "are not often so signally advanced in one day." Both, it might have remarked, were measures that broadened the exercise of federal sovereignty.[27]

Congress's accomplishment was praised by the *Times* with an editorial reminder to its readers, 23 June, that "for thirty years before this rebellion broke out, our national existence was a state of continual nightmare." Now it might be hoped the nightmare was ended. The federal government could rest directly upon taxes paid by the people. "The financial interests of the country will now feel relieved of any anxiety as to the revenue necessary to support the credit of the government." With satisfaction, like that expressed by the *Tribune*, the *Times* observed, 3 July, that President Lincoln had signed three notable pieces of legislation in one day: the revenue act, the Pacific railway act, and an act annulling statutes of the territory of Utah sanctioning polygamous marriage. Curious as the collocation of the third of these measures with the other two now seems, it was in 1862 significant evidence of sovereignty and federal responsibility. Thereafter the requirement that religious freedom be maintained and polygamy abandoned was persistently and pointedly enforced by Congress before and after Utah was granted statehood.[28]

WAYS AND MEANS VERSUS THE ADMINISTRATION

I

OF THE THREE elements constituting the financial program presented by John B. Alley a year before in his speech of 23 January 1862, the last to be taken up was the national currency scheme. The two other elements of Alley's program—the legal tender measure and the revenue measure —had got immediate attention from Congress and tardy enactment in spite of Secretary Chase's coldness toward them. While yielding to the legal tender and revenue measures forced on him by bankers and congressional leaders, Chase had stuck to his preference for the policy of wartime borrowing which he had taken over from Albert Gallatin, but in the form of his national currency plan—a plan which would provide loans to the government and a uniform national currency for the country. And—what was of peculiar importance to lawyer Chase—the plan would lodge with the federal government a major responsibility assigned to it by the Constitution but usurped by the states.

In that part of his annual report of 4 December 1862 dealing with the currency, the Secretary affirmed afresh his opinion "that a circulation furnished by the government but issued by banking associations organized under a general act of Congress" was preferable to any other. To most bankers, save some of the best who were indifferent to note circulation, his proposal was wholly unwelcome. They wished to be left alone, with greenbacks continued in use as a generous source of lawful reserves. They had on their side the politicians, who resisted abatement of all states' rights except those of secession from the Union and protection of slave-holding. His proposal was resisted as much in states that prohibited banking as in those that fostered it, for in either case states' rights would be flouted. The horrid proposal repugned Andrew Jackson's triumph over Nicholas Biddle and offered to renew federal entanglement with banking. When Chase first made his proposal, Decem-

285

ber 1861, it had been eclipsed by the *Trent* affair, the leading banks' loss of reserves, and the rising likelihood that
specie payments would have to stop. The suspension, when
it came, had concentrated attention to the conflict over legal
tender notes, and in the excitement, readers will recall, the
Secretary's proposal died a seeming death.[1]

Chase, however, had not abandoned his scheme, no matter how dead it appeared. In the midst of the conflict in
Congress just preceding the legal tender enactment, he
had written Senator Fessenden, 10 February 1862, that he
still thought the government's predicament required a bank
note currency secured by federal bonds. In succeeding
weeks, however, as he found the legal tender notes indispensable, his antipathy to them abated. During the spring,
with New Orleans taken, with General McClellan's pressure
on Richmond seeming to tighten, with the hundred and
fifty million dollars of legal tenders Congress had forced on
him, things looked easier. But by summer prospects darkened again. Early in June 1862 it was said he would have
to ask for another hundred and fifty millions of legal tender
notes. The rumor was disbelieved and then confirmed.
Prices rose, and by the middle of the month excitement in
the stock market was intense. The premium on gold and
European exchange advanced. In the press bad news and
cheerful reassurances jostled each other. The *New York
Times* in an editorial, 16 June, praised the first issue of legal
tender notes, which "has afforded the highest satisfaction
to the country," and praised the "wonderful financial success of the government" under the Treasury's "distinguished
head"; but it doubted the need of more legal tenders and
advised delay in acting on them. In an effort to be reassuring, however redundant and clumsy, the *Times* attributed
the rising price of gold and exchange not to want of confidence in the currency but to the operations of shrewd bankers who foresaw that as paper increased gold would advance.
It noted, 23 June, a heavy demand for gold at a premium
in excess of six per cent, opposed a new issue of legal tender notes, and exulted in the strength of the national

credit. The next day it reported a further rise in gold and spoke hopefully of McClellan before Richmond ready "to strike the last great blow at the Rebellion." On the 28th it reported that English investors were selling American securities, and on the 30th, that Treasury notes, made a legal tender, had given the country a uniform currency and "practically put an end to the suspension of the banks." But on 2 July it had to report a call for three hundred thousand more soldiers and as of 3 July that the "disastrous news from the army before Richmond . . . produced a very decided panic in Wall Street this forenoon." On the 8th the new legal tender measure was adopted and on the 10th shares were up and gold rose to 116, an advance of ten dollars in four weeks.[2]

Such premiums on gold and on London exchange were an uncanny accompaniment to the continued export of farm products in immense volume. Gold at a fraction less than 116, London exchange at 128, an "extraordinary export movement of grain and flour," and the persistent foreign demand for meat and other provisions, the "largest ever known," presented a solecism of considerable magnitude. The land was feeding Europe, being paid for it, and nevertheless gripping an empty purse. Coin had disappeared from circulation, and the use of postage stamps as a legal tender in amounts less than five dollars was authorized.[3]

On 2 July the internal revenue measure had become law. On the 11th Samuel Hooper again introduced the Administration's bill; it was referred to Ways and Means, where it lay till adjournment a few days later. Yet it appears that there had been some hope of opening the measure's path. For the *New York Herald*, 24 June, had reported that the sub-committee having it in charge would "be ready to report the bill this week." It was, the *Herald* said with the fantastic sort of inaccuracy that Chase seemed to inspire, "the last of the series of measures constituting the splendid financial system of the Secretary of the Treasury."[4]

About the middle of October, *The Economist*, London,

287

which had at first thought the South and its cause hopeless, now recognized that the "Slave States" had "for eighteen months met not only on equal but latterly on decidedly superior terms, an antagonist far richer, far more populous, far more abundantly supplied with all the material resources for a conflict than themselves" and had "inflicted on their adversary the most repeated, damaging, and sanguinary defeats." *The Economist* had, reluctantly, to agree with Mr Gladstone that Southern independence had become "as certain as any future event could be." That Mr Gladstone and *The Economist* were in the end mistaken, did not at the moment matter.[5]

Less than a fortnight earlier, in a letter of 7 October 1862, Secretary Chase had described the domestic monetary situation to John Bigelow, the American minister at Paris. Of the three hundred millions of legal tender notes authorized, he wrote, only a little more than half were in circulation, "i. e., in the vaults of banks and bankers and in the hands of the people. This circulation has not displaced that of the banks as yet; but on the contrary has actually caused its increase. It has, however, weakened it with the people, who are anxious for a national currency, uniform throughout the country, which no state bank can furnish." The Secretary was right about the popular desire for a national currency, especially in the West. But this national currency could be of two possible sorts: it could be the legal tender notes already in use, or it could be bank notes issued under federal authority and secured by federal bonds; and partisans of both were already mustering. Interest in a national currency was growing, but it was also splitting.

Chase also told Bigelow of his having recommended back in December "a general banking system for the United States, identical in its main features with the system organized in New York and adopted in Ohio." He said that in his judgment, "if the debt is kept within any reasonable limit by active prosecution of the war and tolerable economy in expenditure, the adoption of this system will furnish all the money that is needed, at reasonable rates, and insure an early return to specie payments. . . ." He not only expected his plan would "avert great disasters" but hoped through it "to be able to convert our financial troubles into permanent benefits to the country."[6]

About the same time that Chase wrote Bigelow in Paris, October 1862, he made an arrangement for the sale of bonds through Jay Cooke which resulted in fresh impetus for the national currency plan. Cooke had shown extraordinary ability and enterprise in selling bonds of the hundred and fifty million national loan of 1861 and had won Chase's confidence by his energy, resourcefulness, patriotism, and religiosity. He now became special agent of the Treasury for the sale of the five hundred million bond issue of 1862 known as the "five-twenties"—the bonds being callable in five years and maturing in twenty. Cooke had at first held back from the national currency scheme, not because he disapproved of it, but because he was unwilling "to make war upon the state banking system" and offend the bankers who were helping him sell federal bonds. But he joined in the growing nationalist feeling and came to believe that the benefits of Chase's plan, which the bankers themselves could share, warranted its adoption. Presently it would provide a currency uniform throughout the country and a large and permanent demand for government securities which, as the Treasury agent, he could supply.

So, about the time of Chase's second annual report, December 1862, Cooke resolved to combine his sale of bonds with support of the Secretary's recommendation. Since as government loan agent he was paying the newspapers large sums for advertising, he and his brother thought they had a right to space "in which to set forth the merits of the new national banking system." They suggested the substance of editorials, most of which they wrote themselves. These they "changed and freshened with new arguments almost daily," he said, "and for six weeks or more nearly all the newspapers in the country were filled with our editorials condemning the state bank system and explaining the great benefits to be derived from the national banking system now proposed." The Cookes appealed to members of Congress and every day laid on their desks the relevant copies of papers published in their districts.[7]

II

Chase's renewed national currency recommendation in his report of 4 December 1862 was more explicit than that of the year before. Still more explicit and well-reasoned was President Lincoln's vigorous support of it in his own message to Congress, 1 December. The President called the issue of legal tender notes "unavoidable," specie payments having been suspended; and yet, although the notes "satisfied, partially at least and for the time, the long felt want of an [sic] uniform circulating medium, saving thereby to the people immense sums in discounts and exchanges," he doubted very much if a circulation of legal tender notes, exchangeable for gold on demand and sufficiently ample in amount, could be "permanently, usefully, and safely maintained." He knew of no other mode by which "the great advantages of a safe and uniform currency" could be achieved so promisingly and unobjectionably as by "the organization of banking associations under a general act of Congress. . . ."* To these banks the government would furnish circulating notes of its own printing, uniform in appearance and secured by United States bonds purchased by the banks and deposited by them in the Treasury, where they would be held to insure conversion of the notes into coin. These notes, the President said, "would at once protect labor against the evils of a vicious currency and facilitate commerce by cheap and safe exchanges." At the same time the public credit would be greatly improved and the government's borrowings "greatly facilitated by the steady

---

* Banks incorporated under the free-banking laws of the states, on which the proposed federal law was patterned, were for obsolete reasons designated "associations." They still are, more than a century later, in both state and federal legislation. (B. Hammond, "Free Banks and Corporations," *JPE* xliv [April 1936], p. 184; B. Hammond, *Banks and Politics*, 580ff.)

market demand for government bonds" which the system would create. The plan would provide not only for new banks but for the transfer of existing banks from state to national charter and the substitution of federal bonds for state bonds to back their circulating notes.[8]

President Lincoln's account of the proposed system is clear except that it takes for granted a knowledge of the bank note currency to which the country had been condemned since Andrew Jackson's presidency. Some sixteen hundred banks in business under the authority of the individual states were providing notes for circulation in diverse denominations from a few cents up, without uniformity as to size, style, or kind of paper. Counterfeiting flourished. The notes of reputable banks were at a premium but those of most banks were at a discount. Nowadays the chance of one's receiving a note that is false is minute—most persons never have the misfortune—that of receiving one worth less than its face value is nil, and a note that is good is equally good everywhere. Many if not most banks that issued notes in 1812 sought to evade redeeming them by arrangements to put them in circulation far from home; the result was that the notes in use in one part of the country were obligations of unknown banks in some other part; they were not only of uncertain value but were filthy and ragged. Coin was practically unobtainable. Gold coins were hoarded, and silver, then worth less as money than as metal, had mostly been exported. Senator John Sherman, as well-informed as anyone, doubted if as many as one thousand silver dollars remained in the country. In these circumstances, President Lincoln in recommending a uniform national currency of equal value everywhere was recommending something of the utmost usefulness to both government and people. The only qualification to this, as already mentioned, is that the federal government's legal tender notes, in use now for the prior ten months or so, seemed to many persons a national, uniform currency preferable to notes issued by banks for their own profit.[9]

Following President Lincoln's recommendation had come

the longer-winded one from Secretary Chase. In more specific terms than the year before, he proposed a currency furnished by "banking associations organized under national legislation." In his 1861 report he had seemed to think his national currency plan would help finance a war that was to end within six months. Now in 1862 he expected "little direct aid" from it within two years. But still, in his opinion, "the chief reliance and the safest must be upon loans," and at the war's end a much larger investment market than ever before must be accessible to the Treasury. Independently of the war he also insisted again upon the necessity of reforming the currency and upon his preference for one that was national to that of the "variously organized and variously responsible banks now existing in the country." He acknowledged the help he had got from the banks in the autumn of 1861—"ventured largely and boldly and patriotically on the side of the Union and the constitutional supremacy of the nation over states and citizens"—but he also mentioned the "unexpected gains" the banks had made. The constitutional question he adverted to but briefly. "Statesmen who have agreed in little else," he said, "have concurred in the opinion that the power to regulate coin is in substance and effect a power to regulate currency and that the framers of the Constitution so intended." For the most part the Secretary's argument was more practical, clear, and assured than before, with, however, a proper but unlucky emphasis upon eventual rather than war-time benefits to be expected. "The central idea of the proposed measure," he said, "is the establishment of one sound, uniform circulation of equal value throughout the country upon the foundation [here he echoed Alexander Hamilton] of national credit combined with private capital." He complained of the current inflation, which he seemed inclined to blame on the legal tender notes, because the banks were holding them as reserves and letting their circulating notes increase in volume. Their deposits were increasing too, with greater inflationary effects, but that, of course, Chase and most of his contemporaries did not comprehend. This disenchantment with the legal tenders, which he had first abhorred and then embraced, was an early reversion to his original distrust of paper money and an early anticipation of his unhappy judgment against it years later, in the *Legal Tender Cases*, when he was Chief Justice of the Supreme Court.[10]

Though Chase had long been convinced that for both legal and practical reasons a national currency for which the federal government would be responsible was required, he seems at first to have sought no more than the issue of Treasury notes. It was in the furtherance of some such plan that he had got into trouble with the banks at the very start, September 1861, by impounding, as a reserve for the Treasury notes he issued, a good part of the coin delivered to him. Then he had made in his first annual report, December 1861, a proposal for a national currency of bank notes backed by federal instead of state bonds. Now, in his report, 4 December 1862, he said that "the Secretary [that is, he himself] still adheres to the opinion expressed in his last report that a circulation furnished by the government but issued by banking associations organized under a general act of Congress is to be preferred. . . ."[11]

While urging his national currency project officially, Chase was also drumming up support for it personally. He asked Assistant Treasurer Cisco in New York, 10 December, to obtain statements from bankers favorable to the Administration's plan. He wrote to newspaper editors, some of whom came to his help and some not. "Give us the plan," he wrote Joseph Medill of the *Chicago Tribune*, 13 December, "and I can borrow. Without it I can not borrow except at enormous sacrifices. Give me the plan and I can carry on the government to the close of the war, I hope, successfully. Without it there may be success, but I don't see it." He wrote Thaddeus Stevens, 23 December, that it was "next to impossible to collect the internal revenue in lawful money," and that he could see "no ground for belief that the funds necessary for the pay of the army and the prosecution of the war can be in any way provided without the

293

support to public credit expected" from the plan. Stevens was unmoved.[12]

But a fortnight after having restated his recommendation, 4 December 1862, Secretary Chase received impressive support from a prominent and influential predecessor of his, Robert J. Walker, a lawyer and politician who had been a Jacksonian Democrat distrusted by Jackson. Walker, born and reared in Pennsylvania and married to a great-granddaughter of Benjamin Franklin, had been a senator from Mississippi for ten years and a vigorous supporter of legislation authorizing the independent Treasury, which as a very able Secretary of the Treasury in President Polk's cabinet it was his fortune to organize. Since 1849, when Polk's term ended, Walker had lived on in Washington, practicing before the Supreme Court, active in speculative railway, mining, and other business enterprises, and, as a politician, writer, and public speaker, in the country's territorial expansion. In Natchez he had been a slave-owner and typical Southerner. But in Washington by 1862 he had become passionately opposed to slavery and secession, had freed his slaves, and, though still a Democrat, was Unionist. In 1857 he had been appointed governor of Kansas by President Buchanan but his free-soil efforts to kill the Lecompton constitution had been insolently and faithlessly frustrated. Altogether, he was a man of substantial influence, respected by all but copperheads. He was also an effective journalistic economist (not to be confused with his contemporary, Amasa Walker of Massachusetts) and had progressed not inconsistently from the narrow, binding, hard-money principles of his Jacksonian, independent Treasury days to a recognition of what federal sovereignty could do. He had "contended," he wrote, "during the last fourth of a century that all state bank currency is unconstitutional"; and in 1840, he had indeed justly condemned banks of circulation, justly approving the deposit and discount function as alone proper. The states should not interfere with the currency, the control of which "is one of the highest and most important attributes of sovereign power. . . ." He had commended, in the circumstances, the issue of legal tender notes but joined Chase in the complaint that they had been "diverted from their legitimate use as a currency and made the basis of bank circulation." Alarmed by the state of the federal finances, he prepared a prompt and spirited defense of the Administration's national currency plan, which was released 19 December 1862 from advance sheets of the February 1863 issue of his *Continental Monthly*. With unqualified support of the Administration he urged "resumption by the government of the great sovereign function of regulating the currency and giving to it uniformity and nationality." He approved the action of the man at present occupying the chair he once had occupied and who, he said, "after a year's experience and deliberation . . . reiterates his former recommendation with words of solemn import and arguments of great force. . . . The plan of the Secretary is clear, simple, comprehensive, practical, and effective." He denounced vigorously the states' resistance—New York's particularly—to the Administration's national currency proposal as a trespass on states' rights. "The rebellion is the child of state usurpation, state supremacy, state allegiance, and state secession," he said. "And now the government is paralyzed financially, in its efforts to suppress the rebellion, by a question as to state banks. . . ." Alluding evidently to the complaint of New York's Superintendant of Banks against the federal government's interference in his responsibilities and his state's sovereignty, Walker called the New York language "the very language of rebellion—the echo of South Carolina treason."*[13]

---

* One may be excused, I hope, for finding it difficult to cite Robert J. Walker, a man of extraordinary force in public life, without mention of his extraordinary physique, the two seeming strangely bonded together. He was a compound of energy, intelligence, and bodily diminution—weighing barely a hundred pounds, standing barely five feet high, and being the father of eight children. Secretary Chase sent Walker abroad, where he had great repute among British political leaders as an advocate of free trade; he seems also to have been very useful in cultivating a market for the North's securities and in spoiling that for the South's. (Shenton, 2-4, 190-200.)

III

Congress was in a bad state during December 1862, the 37th's first month of its third session. It was distrustful and tense with bitterness over military weaknesses. McClellan's prolonged attempt on Richmond had failed, Shiloh had been a massacre, Bull Run had again been a rout, Antietam a sanguinary draw, Fredericksburg slaughter. General had replaced general. The Union army's morale was low; soldiers had gone unpaid for months; recruitments lagged. There was dismay and suspicion of treachery in high places, a conviction of the Administration's weakness and of President Lincoln's personal incompetence. Abroad, the South was high in esteem. In Washington the radical Republicans had listened trustfully to Chase, who thought himself far abler than the President—as many others did—but when the Secretary failed them in the December Cabinet crisis following Fredericksburg, they were angered. Chase was so abashed by the collapse of his ambitious scheming, that he submitted his resignation, which, however, the President magnanimously induced him to withdraw. The radicals' reception of his national bank plan was for a while contemptuous, though in the end most of them voted for it. For like him they were nationalist.[14]

Proponents of the national plan at the outset seem to have been mostly minorities of various groupings: a minority of bankers, a minority of Republicans, a minority of Democrats. In less cohesive groupings than these—for example, the press, business enterprise, unreconstructed Whigs, the West, and the general public—loose majorities seem to have favored the plan simply because the existing chaos of the bank note currency was so bad and because nationalism was gaining in appeal. Among these proponents were nascent greenbackers, so far an inchoate force but presently to become a vociferous and powerful one.

The first formal action of the 37th Congress on Chase's national currency plan was taken 7 January 1863 when Samuel Hooper, as in the previous session, introduced the bill (HR 656) embodying the Administration's recommendations and the bill was referred to Ways and Means. The next day, 8 January, Thaddeus Stevens "made an adverse report" on it—"coldly dismissed" it, A. G. Riddle of Ohio, a fellow Republican, said afterwards. Later the same day, however, on Stevens' motion, Hooper's bill was put on the calendar for 16 January. But already, also on Stevens' motion, a finance bill of his committee's authorship (HR 659), "to provide ways and means to support the government" by borrowing and taxing, had been put on for the 12th. Stevens, in giving his committee's bill this priority, was in effect substituting it for that sought by the President and his finance minister.[15]

Meanwhile, in the Senate, John Sherman of Ohio, had done a strange thing. Early on Monday, 5 January, when Congress reconvened after its fortnight's holiday recess, he had introduced in the Senate a bill (S 445) that would authorize a federal tax on bank notes, meaning, of course, the notes of state banks, there being no others. His action preceded any in the House on the Administration's bill and had, as recorded in the *Congressional Globe*, no obvious tie with the latter (HR 656), which Samuel Hooper, as just said, introduced two days later, 7 January. Then, the day following that, 8 January, Senator Sherman, speaking in a characteristically direct and vigorous fashion for the bill he had introduced three days before, took a slashing offensive against the state banks. In a chapter of his *Recollections*, published in 1895, Sherman included an account of this attack entitled "Abolishment of the State Banks." This title I find inexplicable, for in 1895 when the chapter was written state banks were more numerous than national banks, they were becoming still more numerous, and they had never at any time been abolished. The purpose had been to abolish them, of course, and thirty years after the events he was recounting that nationalist purpose. It seems to have remained stuck in his mind more firmly than the failure to achieve it.[16]

Sherman's charge was that the state banks violated the

Constitution and provided on the whole a miserably poor currency, which he urged be gradually taxed out of existence. He was stating the matter, he said, simply as one of taxation. "But," he explained, "I should not be candid—I should not state my real purpose—if I did not say frankly that I have another and a much higher object than this to accomplish. The purpose of this bill is to induce the banks of the United States to withdraw their bank paper in order to substitute for it a national currency, or rather the national currency we have already adopted. This is not a new object. I might read to you from volumes of speeches of our greatest statesmen from the foundation of the government to show you that the establishment of a national currency, based upon the laws of Congress, either of gold or silver or some form of currency, has ever been regarded as indispensable to the prosperity of the country." He cited Alexander Hamilton, James Madison, George Dallas, Joseph Story, and Daniel Webster. Others he might have mentioned were John C. Calhoun, and John Catron, who was still, with his Jacksonian brother, Chief Justice Taney, a member of the Supreme Court. Having quoted Daniel Webster, "with this authority," he said, he was "willing to stand upon the affirmation, notwithstanding the long acquiescence of our people, that banks of circulation authorized by the states are unconstitutional and should be dispensed with."* What he proposed, he said, was what Thomas Jefferson had suggested a half-century before. "Put down the banks," Jefferson had written, and in place of their notes let Treasury notes be issued. "But," Jefferson had also said, "no remedy is ever to be expected while it

---

* So far it was only the issue of notes which threw doubt on the state banks' constitutionality, but that peculiarity of banking in the United States was so common that the question of constitutionality was raised against chartered banks *per se*, as if banking and note issue were synonymous. The Americans got this peculiar notion from the anomaly that the first American banks were corporate banks of issue with charters based on that of the Bank of England, which was not a typical bank but unique. Old world banking was typically private, not corporate, and a matter of deposit and discount, not circulation.

rests with the state legislatures." It must come from Congress, to which Jefferson hoped the states would yield their concern with banks. (Sherman did not bother to mention the feeble decision of the Jacksonian Supreme Court in *Briscoe* v. *Bank of Kentucky*, 1837, that state banks and their notes *were* constitutional.)[17]

In regard to expediency, Sherman made the necessary distinction between banking proper and the issue of bank notes. Banking proper, he explained, was the lending of money, the discounting of bills drawn against sales of commodities, and the maintenance of deposit balances transferable on order. That was what banking had been for centuries in the Old World. The issue of notes circulating as money among the Americans was a novel privilege accorded a certain class of corporations; it was not essential to banking, and it was more characteristic of bad banking than of good. The strongest banks, Sherman said, had the least note circulation and the weakest the most. Notes were a form of liability easily evaded; deposits were not.[18]

In this speech of 8 January Sherman said nothing about a new currency in the form of bank notes prepared under national authority and secured by federal bonds. He said nothing about a new bond market created by the new banks offering new notes constituting a new national currency; though to Secretary Chase this new currency and the new market for federal bonds were of the utmost immediate practical importance. Sherman seemed, 8 January, to prefer continued use of Treasury notes as a national currency—"the national currency we have already adopted"—at least while the war lasted, and a return eventually to coin, whether for actual circulation or as a reserve for redemption of greenbacks. "We ought as soon as possible," he said, "to go back to the basis of gold and silver coin"; but during the war this was impossible; paper money was a necessity. His stress on coin may have reflected simply an orthodox deference to an arbitrary metallic standard of value, resistant to manipulation, with use of Treasury notes as a means of payment convertible into coin, but

299

not a legal tender. The current combination of greenbacks and bank notes was especially inflationary, because, as already said, the greenbacks held by the banks constituted legal reserves and enabled the banks to increase their loans, their deposits, and their note circulation. Sherman might have said, if questioned, that as bank notes disappeared under his tax, resumption of specie payments and repeal of the clause making Treasury notes a legal tender would end the existing inflation.[19]

This speech of 8 January was obviously tangential to the recommendations of Chase and the President and to the bill of Hooper's (HR 656) embodying them. Sherman, as he made clear later, was certain of the evil these excited though undecided about its corrective. He mentioned Chase's recommendation approvingly in but brief and imprecise terms. What he stressed was that the issue of notes, besides being no essential function of banks, was, as carried on, unconstitutional, miserable, and condemned by the most venerable authorities. Yet he did not say that state bank notes should be replaced by national bank notes; he said they should be replaced by the Treasury notes "already adopted"—which would naturally mean greenbacks. Nor did he mention national banks as constituting a new market for government bonds. What he said sounded, by omission, by addition, and by emphasis, different, from what President Lincoln and Secretary Chase had been recommending. Yet in the main it came to the same thing: it took from the states and gave to the federal government. It was aggressively nationalist.

Chase and Hooper, however, had been monstrously polite to the state banks, speaking softly of the unconstitutional and unsatisfactory currency they furnished and coaxing them to be nice and exchange their affiliation from state to federal authority. Sherman, on the contrary, entered the controversy hammer and tongs as Robert Walker had done, with an unsparing attack on the currency of state bank notes and making the most of wretched evils familiar to every one. This was especially appealing to westerners, the principal victims and enemies of banks. Sherman was skilful with his telling quotations from Thomas Jefferson, a prophet whom western agrarians revered. Instead of Chase's leaden discursiveness on constitutionality and the importance of a new market for government bonds, Sherman hit the banks hard, in plain words emphasizing evils which were a daily and ubiquitous nuisance to everyone but the shady characters profiting by them.

Sherman closed his argument with an appeal obviously directed to present Democrats and to former Democrats now turned Republican, for more votes than those of former Whigs were needed. "I have shown you," he said, imputing to Jefferson and to the facts somewhat more than was strictly justified, "that under circumstances very similar to ours . . . Mr Jefferson . . . with great sagacity pointed out the very mode to which we must now resort if we would maintain a national currency. We have already our United States notes precisely of the character stated by him, based upon taxes, based upon the credit of the United States. . . . We have done just as he says we ought to have done. All that remains for us is by wise measures to induce the withdrawal of the local bank circulation of the country, not by an arbitrary edict striking them dead or deranging the currency of the country, but by a tax, reasonable and moderate in itself, to be increased if policy dictates. . . . This policy will confine the banks to that ordinary business of banking known among all the commercial nations of the world. If this is done by moderate and wise legislation, as Mr Jefferson truly says, we may maintain this war until our flag floats from Louisiana to Maine in every portion of our beloved country."[20]

What Sherman described in this address seems to me preferable to what, a month later, he helped Lincoln and Chase to get; but it was presumably more practical to join the President and Chase in what they presented in the mildest terms as a shift of existing arrangements from state to federal auspices.

The effectiveness of Sherman's appeal became apparent

presently in what Owen Lovejoy of Illinois said in the House a week later. Lovejoy, a preacher by profession, a Lincoln Republican, an abolitionist—his brother Elijah had been killed in his presence by a pro-slavery mob in Alton—expressed his agrarian views in a declaration that directly recalls what John Sherman had said in the Senate the week before. Lovejoy himself cited Justice Story, one of Sherman's authorities, in a picture of the federal government correcting an evil which the states had fostered and which Jefferson had declared that they could never be expected to remedy. "I hold," Lovejoy said, "that this whole theory of banking is vicious, fallacious, and deceptive; and I believe that these banks have had more to do with our ever-recurring commercial disasters and collapses than any other cause whatever." Seeing, as Jefferson had, that banks were an evil for which states' rights were responsible, he had become Hamiltonian in his conception of federal sovereignty. He followed Justice Story in the conviction "that where the federal government legislated at all, it was absolute and exhaustive and that the states had no business to legislate" in the same field. If the federal government decided to authorize a national currency, its right to do so, Lovejoy averred, was "exclusive" and "shuts out all the competing rights or supposed rights of a state" to parallel its action. "My conviction," he said, "is and has been that these bank issues have been always unconstitutional, have been always a curse to the country, and never have been an advantage at all." (It is important to bear in mind that what Sherman said explicitly and Lovejoy meant implicitly was that *the evil of banking lay in note issue.* Neither opposed deposit banking, though Lovejoy as an agrarian probably distrusted it.) So, adopting a course urged by Sherman, who wanted banks, and by Jefferson, who did not, Lovejoy voted in the end for national banks and federal sovereignty. Not to do so would simply entrench the powers of the states and the source of the present banking evil. He had come to a quite un-Jacksonian vision of the states as harborers of evil and of the federal government as the ruling and compassionate power that would curb the infamous "rights" under which slavery and banking had flourished.[21]

A fortnight before Lovejoy expressed his convictions about the scope and beneficence of federal powers, slaves in all areas that were in rebellion had been proclaimed by the federal Executive to be thenceforward and forever free.

IV

The same day, 8 January, that Sherman spoke in the Senate, and apparently about the same hour, Thaddeus Stevens in the House had brought up his committee's finance bill (HR 659) "to provide ways and means for the support of the government." He had had it made a special order for Monday, 12 January, and had made his "adverse report" on the national bank bill (HR 656), already introduced by Hooper the 7th and referred to Ways and Means. Stevens, when he made his adverse report, hadn't Hooper's bill with him, but later the same day he brought it up and got consideration of it "postponed" to Friday the 16th, four days *after* consideration of his committee's finance bill (HR 659). His action, which had all the appearance of intent to obstruct the Administration's measure, initiated a strange sequence.[22]

For when Spaulding of New York took up the committee's finance bill on the 12th as calendared, he used half his time or more to attack the Administration's bill, calendared for four days later, and to contradict Sherman's denunciation, in the Senate four days earlier, of the state banks, one of which, in Buffalo, was Spaulding's own. Spaulding contended, contrary to Sherman, that the state banks were both constitutional and expedient. He based their constitutionality on the Supreme Court's *Briscoe* decision of 1837, which Sherman had justifiedly ignored, and on general acquiescence, traditional, judicial, and practical, in the legality of their operations. He thought the national bank plan unfair to the state banks and incapable anyway of yielding the funds needed by the Union, either for the current year or the next one. "In these perilous times," Spaulding said, "state stocks are held in much higher estimation in many of the states than United States stocks. Banks will be loath to part with state securities. They will not throw their state bonds, which are worth a premium of eighteen per cent, upon the market and depress them to raise the price of United States stocks; and without doing this they have not the means of purchasing federal bonds. . . . It is plain that great injury must be encountered and large losses sustained if state bonds are forced on the market to make room for United States securities." Rather than experiment and threaten the existing banks Spaulding would authorize more legal tender notes. That would stimulate business; it would "make money plenty" and help people to pay taxes and buy bonds. To that extent he agreed with Sherman. And like Sherman, indeed, he quoted Jefferson in defense of paper issues by the government in time of war.[23]

The day following Spaulding's digression against the Administration's bill, 13 January 1863, Justin Morrill of Vermont, another Republican member of the Ways and Means majority, took over the attack. He condemned the Administration's proposal as a free banking scheme.* Free banking, he said, had been "partially successful in the rural districts of New York" but had "utterly failed almost everywhere else." Under free banking "men without means, skill, or character, if able to obtain a temporary loan so as to purchase the first batch of bonds, may establish a bank." The well-managed banks already in business

* "Free banking" laws were part of the Jacksonian heritage. Their purpose was to allow anyone to establish a bank and issue circulating notes without obtaining a special legislative charter. The term "free banking" was used for a while in a different sense years later, but in 1863 it had reference only to the substance of New York's free banking law of 1838, since then adopted in numerous other states and recommended as the substance of a national banking act. A free banking law had been enacted in the province of Upper Canada in 1850, but to little effect and in 1866 it was repealed. (B. Hammond, 666-67.)

under state charter would not make the change to national charter voluntarily, and it was both unfair and of no advantage to force them. Meanwhile the banks already had large holdings of government bonds, and the new plan, even if "fully executed," would give the Treasury very little help. "The purpose of this new national banking scheme," Morrill said, "is not to regulate the currency, as it must be confessed it was in the power of the old United States Bank to do, but to uproot all the state banks issuing currency . . . in order to make room for funding United States bonds. . . . Practically, the bill is shaped only to reach the country banks. . . . The city banks, having little or no circulation and relying upon large deposits as the basis of discounts, will be exempt from the crushing out process. . . ." Morrill showed that the note circulation of New York City banks was but five per cent of their deposits, and that the circulation of certain banks was negligible, if anything. Banks indifferent to circulation would be indifferent to a tax on circulation. The law could not make them take bonds in order to obtain the privilege of a circulation for which they had no use. "In any calculation that may be made as to the working of this new national banking scheme the Atlantic city banks may be left out." Morrill, much as he disliked legal tender notes, preferred them to the Administration's free-bank notes.[24]

These discussions began in a tense situation, centered on arrearages in soldiers' pay and the consequent distress of soldiers' families. Less than a week earler the *New York Times* had reported a conviction in Washington that a third issue of legal tender notes would be needed in a matter of months. The same day that Spaulding began the Republican attacks on the national bank bill, 12 January 1863, the *Times* had bad news of the New York markets. "The excitement through the last week," it said, "is without precedent in the magnitude of the speculation." In the past ten or twelve years there had been few parallels to the rapid advance in prices of shares, of commodities (now including gold), and of foreign exchanges. Of a visit by Secretary Chase to Wall Street, the *Times* said that "from what has since occurred between the Secretary and our principal bankers and private capitalists, we are led to suppose that one of his objects in visiting New York at the present moment—following the unanimous but respectful decision of the Committee of Ways and Means that they could not report his free banking scheme as part and parcel of the main Treasury bill of the session—was to attempt to enlist a further sentiment in its favor through the banking influence of this city as an alternative to the more direct issue of United States notes of lawful tender by the government."* The *Times* thought Chase was meeting "but little encouragement." The next day, 13 January, reporting a special dispatch from Washington, the *Times* said: "It is quite clear from Secretary Chase's known views and known firmness that he does not yield to the determination of the Committee of Ways and Means in regard to his measures but will make an effort to secure their adoption by Congress in full or in a modified form."[25]

Meanwhile, the excited advance in the price of gold and stocks continued. It was, of course, a fall in legal tender note values, the law being in conflict with fact, and was attributed in part to a discouraging report that an attempt on Vicksburg by Union forces had been abandoned. But the inflationary advance was also attributed by the *Times* to "the inconclusive meeting of our bankers with the Secretary of the Treasury on Saturday night." On Wednesday the 14th the Secretary returned to Washington.[26]

Also on the 14th (still January) Thaddeus Stevens introduced a joint resolution that would authorize the issue of another fifty millions of greenbacks for immediate payment of arrears to the armed forces. It was amended on Owen Lovejoy's motion to authorize a hundred millions

* Without Hooper's vote the committee's decision could not have been unanimous; the *Times* report, however, implies that the decision was not on the Administration's national bank plan *per se* but on some suggestion that Hooper's national currency bill (HR 656) be combined with the committee's finance bill (HR 659). Against that there may have been accord from both sides and hence unanimity.

and passed the House at once and the Senate the next day. A year before Lovejoy had seen the greenbacks only as ruin for the country; now he saw them as bad for the state banks and voted for them eagerly, much to the satisfaction of Samuel Hooper, who had reported Lovejoy's shift to Chase in June.[27]

President Lincoln approved the resolution the 17th. The *Times* was pleased; the "soldiers will get their greenbacks and their destitute families will be enabled to buy victuals and pay rents. . . ." Unfortunately, however, it already took one hundred and sixty-four dollars in greenbacks to get one hundred in gold. Prices of commodities had risen woefully, and the destitute families about to get the greenbacks promised them would probably find they could buy much less than was expected.[28]

V

In Congress, 15 January, the day following Chase's return from New York and adoption of the Stevens-Lovejoy resolution authorizing a new issue of greenbacks to pay the army and navy, Elijah Ward, a conservative New York lawyer and Democrat, made a still more searching attack on the national bank proposal (HR 656) than Spaulding's and Morrill's. Like them, he denounced it (HR 656) while speaking on the Ways and Means bill (HR 659). He deplored the issue of legal tender notes but thought no better of the new bank plan. He knew, he said, "of no greater trial for a statesman or legislator than this: to be compelled to choose between two measures when his judgment condemns them both." Ward, as Morrill had done, stressed the minor importance of bank notes beside that of bank deposits; he called attention sharply to Chase's "delusion"; he was harsh with the Secretary for making no proper use of the banks as they were and for insisting instead on the clumsy, unnecessary task of replacing them. No other speaker touched so accurately on the fuzziness of Chase's ideas. The Secretary, Ward said, "speaks of the insufficiency of the bank circulation to support the great activity in business resulting from enormous military and naval preparations and is apparently ignorant . . . of the power of the banks themselves, by means of bills of exchange, drafts, checks, and certificates of deposit, to transact any amount of business that the necessities of the nation" require without the handling of great amounts of coin. New York was the business center of the Union, and "nearly all our domestic and foreign exchanges meet in that commercial emporium." In that city alone, Ward said, banking facilities existed for the transaction, daily, of business in an amount "ten times the estimated daily expenses of the government. . . ." As a Democrat, of course, Ward had political objections to abandonment of state organizations for national; but what counted most were his practical objections to the discard of competent facilities already at hand for others still to be authorized and got going.[29]

Ward had more to say of the limited understanding which the Secretary disclosed in concluding, from a belief that the currency had undergone but a slight increase, that no inflation existed. That it did exist, Ward said, was "known not only to our financiers and merchants" but was "painfully felt in the home of the laborer and made palpable by practical facts and figures to every one who purchases the common articles necessary for daily food and clothing. . . ." Furthermore, he said, "dividend-paying stocks and securities and nearly all other forms of personal property have risen in nominal values to a greater extent than gold; and the general inflation has already seriously affected the price of real estate itself, which many cautious men are beginning to purchase as a secure investment. . . ." To Ward it was "vain to affirm that gold had risen but that paper money has not fallen." The Secretary, in a sinking boat, might equally well deny that it was going down and swear instead that the water under it was rising.[30]

Such resistance from the Democrats, though they as a party had but few votes, was serious when the Republicans were divided and important men among them were knifing a measure recommended by the President and his finance minister. Following Ward the same day, 15 January, Amasa Walker, Republican of Massachusetts, who was first a business man like Samuel Hooper, but became one of the country's foremost professional economists, commended the finance bill (HR 659) for its provision of taxing bank notes, which he wanted put out of existence, as Sherman did, and their "void . . . filled with federal notes." The state banks "never had any constitutional right to issue such a currency" as they did. Walker praised Chase, "in whose ability, integrity, and patriotism," he said, "we have the fullest confidence." Then four days later, 19 January, he tore to pieces the national bank plan which was the Secretary's choice. He declared, on the grounds taken by Elijah Ward, that the proposed banking and currency system— "a most pernicious system"—would attract "irresponsible persons" only. "The oldest and best banks," he believed, would not accept it at all. They would not be interested in buying bonds in order to issue notes; only "wild cats" were interested in that. The proposed plan would increase the number of weak banks and further depreciate the currency; it meant free banking, "one grand deception, one grand failure, one grand swindle." The Secretary himself expected a sale of no more than twenty-five million dollars a year. "How much of an object is it," Walker asked, "in this disturbed condition of public affairs, for us to establish a system which is not to produce more than twenty-five millions a year by the sale of bonds?" He was "astonished that so able a man in finance" as his Massachusetts colleague, Samuel Hooper, should be supporting a scheme that he himself found fraught with "immense injury." Walker had either changed his mind with a vengeance or else misunderstood Chase—as he might well have done—for following the Secretary's first proposal of a national bank note currency in December 1861, Walker had praised it warmly. "Your proposal for a uniform currency is most important," he had written Chase. It was "a noble and beneficent one," he said. "Business men of intelligence" approved it, but the banks did not, "especially the smaller and weaker ones, whose business is not and never was legitimate banking." (From Oberlin College, in Ohio, Walker had been able to observe the wild nature of much western banking.) But now, thirteen months after Chase's first proposal, Walker expressed himself very differently about it. He still favored the extinction of state bank notes by taxation but he would replace them with Treasury notes as John Sherman had urged in the Senate the previous week and Robert J. Walker the previous month.[31]

I have already mentioned the possibility that the nationalism in Owen Lovejoy's remarks of 15 January reflected the influence of Senator Sherman's attack on state bank circulation in his address of the 8th, and I now mention the possibility that Amasa Walker's remarks of the 15th also reflect that influence. Both Lovejoy and Amasa Walker, like Sherman, vigorously condemned the state bank circulation, wanting it extinguished and replaced with Treasury notes; but Lovejoy accepted the Administration's course, which was to substitute national charters for state charters and national bank notes for state bank notes, the ultimate replacement of the latter with Treasury notes being his determined end. Amasa Walker preferred the Ways and Means Committee's course, which was to extinguish state bank circulation by a progressive federal tax and replace it with Treasury notes, leaving the state banks to continue in business as banks of deposit—a consummation which Robert J. Walker had recommended and which Amasa Walker seems to have taken for granted, which Sherman at least implied, and which was much like what the country finally got years later. The difference was one of practical and political expedience, but participants in the decision were so passionate about the best way of getting out of the mess they were in, that deadlock was in the end barely avoided.

Following Amasa Walker's plea for the Ways and Means bill (HR 659) and his attack on the Administration bill

310

(HR 656) 15 January, another Republican, John A. Gurley of Ohio, denounced the latter with aggressive questioning of Secretary Chase's judgment in making so much of it. He quoted Chase's admission that "little direct aid" was to be expected from his plan "during the present, nor very much, perhaps, during the next year." This, Gurley thought, as had Elijah Ward and Amasa Walker, "a very remarkable statement." Little aid was to come "for a year or two from a plan brought forward here to instantly relieve" the government's need. It was "pressed upon the attention of Congress and insisted upon as the one thing needful to sustain the credit of the country. . . . We may well ask if the present unsettled period is the proper time to commence financial experiments for the benefit of coming years. . . . What the country now needs and expects is some sensible, practical plan whereby money will instantly flow into an empty Treasury to meet the demands of a mighty army and navy; and not the adoption of doubtful theories that can confessedly do nothing for the nation till long after it is either saved or lost. Its fate rests, in a measure, upon the means to purchase supplies this month, next month, and coming months. . . . The very admission that we shall derive little or no benefit from the plan for one or two years should secure its instant rejection. . . ."[32]

Gurley condemned the plan also for fostering only weak banks; he too observed that the better banks issued few notes or none, but did a deposit business; and he cited the statement of Francis Spinner—known as General Spinner, a former New York banker now an official of the Treasury Department—that a bank dependent for its success on the privilege of issuing notes for circulation was "no bank at all." Finally Gurley chided the Secretary for not using the authority already given him to raise money by the sale of bonds and for denying that the authority had been given. The matter was of special importance at the moment because of public concern over the unconscionable failure of the government to pay its armed forces. Four days later, 19 January, Gurley read again from the act granting the authority. There could be no difference of opinion, he thought, about its meaning. "It gives full and complete authority to the Secretary to sell the bonds, not at par value, not at any specified time or sum, but *'at any time, at the market value thereof.'* There has not been a business day or week since that time, when any of the many agents of the Secretary in New York could not have placed one million or several millions in the market and sold them at or somewhere near par." To bring the matter home, Gurley quoted the resolution passed by the House a week before by a vote of 122 to 3, calling on the Secretary to explain why he had not, "as authorized by law, provided the means necessary to pay the soldiers of the army" and "why the bonds, if necessary, have not been sold to meet the payments due the said soldiers." (The resolution, as first offered, had called the payments due the soldiers "unreasonably and unjustly delayed"—words that because of their implied reprimand were deleted from the resolution before it was adopted.) The answer received, Gurley said, rested not upon the common, accepted meaning of the phrase, "at the market," but upon the Secretary's private, unrealistic interpretation of it as meaning "at the daily quotations of sales in New York." In fact it meant, as "everybody knows," the price that offerings will bring "when placed upon the market" for sale, as at an auction. Gurley's sharp criticism of the distinguished fellow Republican and fellow Ohioan at the head of the Treasury aroused rebuke from Owen Lovejoy of Illinois, who was now committed to the Administration's national bank plan. "If I rightly apprehend the drift of the speech of the gentleman from Ohio," Lovejoy said, "it was simply an attack upon the Secretary of the Treasury, originating in what motives I know not. God alone searches the heart." (Both Gurley and Lovejoy were or had been preachers.)[33]

Meanwhile, 16 January, Roscoe Conkling, Republican of New York, asked if the Secretary approved the Ways and Means Committee's finance bill (HR 659). Conkling's question was but parliamentary. For obviously the Secretary could not like a rival measure that was rudely crowding his own off the calendar. If the Secretary approved the committee's finance bill, Conkling said adroitly, "that is a ground of encouragement. If on the contrary, the scheme is unsatisfactory to him, and he is of opinion that he cannot get along with it, that fact would be equally weighty against the bill."

Hooper answered at once, avoiding direct mention of the Secretary's disapproval but making it evident by a circumstantial statement of his having talked with Chase that morning. He said he believed that the finance bill favored by Ways and Means was not satisfactory to the Secretary. Parts of it, he said, seemed "to conflict with the recommendations of the Secretary" and threatened to make it difficult if not impossible for the Secretary to do what was needed.[34]

At the next sitting, Monday 19 January, Albert G. Riddle, Republican of Ohio, reverted to Conkling's question and Hooper's answer, which had indirectly confirmed the supposition that Chase was dissatisfied. It was Riddle's intention, with the information he had got, "to support the plan of the Secretary of the Treasury" or some plan based upon its principles; "and it is not the least merit with me," Riddle said loyally, "that it is the plan of the Secretary." Thereupon Hooper again addressed the House at length on the desirability of a system of national banks. Hooper began by reminding the House that twelve months before, when the first issue of greenbacks was being considered, a three-fold program had been presented (by the Massachusetts colleagues, John B. Alley and Hooper himself), of which the issue of legal tender notes was the first and temporary part. The three measures "formed a comprehensive system" that was "necessary to the successful prosecution of this war." They were the issue of legal tender notes, the levy of taxes to raise a hundred and fifty millions of revenue, and "a national banking law." The first had proved itself "universally popular" and successful. The second, also successful, was providing more money than had been counted on. "The remaining one of the three measures to perfect this system" now awaited enactment. A nation, said Hooper, "which leaves the power to regulate its currency to the legislation of thirty-four different states abandons one of the most essential attributes of its sovereignty; and it is justly said by an eminent financial writer, who was once distinguished as the head of the Treasury Department, that this abdication by the government of its power to control the currency of the country has furnished one of the main supports of this rebellion." The allusion was, of course, to Robert J. Walker. Prompt enactment of this last of the three measures Alley had proposed twelve months before was important, Hooper said, even though its benefits might not be immediate. It would "create confidence" by providing at once a permanent system better than any the country had ever had. It would set up banks in which the interests of capital would be associated with the interests of the federal government. These banks would serve the Treasury as its fiscal agents. Hooper considered "these benefits of far more importance to the Treasury than the more direct benefit of creating a permanent demand for . . . government bonds." The proposed national banks were "the most important feature of the system of finance" undertaken a year before. Unless the program then recommended was carried through by enactment of the national bank measure, then the authorization of legal tender notes was truly, "as stated by those who opposed them, a departure from all the sound principles" of finance and an embarkation "upon the uncertain ocean of uncontrolled paper currency."[35]

VI

Following Hooper, Valentine B. Horton, Ohio Republican, complained that all this discussion of the national bank plan (HR 656) bore on a subject "not legitimately" before the House. The *actual* subject, he said, was the finance bill (HR 659) prepared by Ways and Means, but it was being "almost entirely ignored." The committee's finance bill, though calendared for discussion, was indeed being ignored, one speaker after another addressing himself to the Administration's bank bill instead, for or against it. The bank bill, though "coldly dismissed" by Thaddeus Stevens and his committee, dominated debate, neither its friends nor its enemies letting it be.[36]

This *impasse* was punctuated presently with the arrival and reading of a letter from President Lincoln, 19 January, in which he said that he had signed the joint resolution authorizing one hundred million dollars more in legal tender notes for immediate payment of the army and navy, though he regretted that so large an additional issue had been found necessary "when this circulation and that of the suspended banks together have become already so redundant as to increase prices beyond real values, thereby augmenting the cost of living to the injury of labor and the cost of supplies to the injury of the whole country." He deplored the tolerance of increasing inflation, thinking it plain that continued issues of greenbacks "without any check to the issues of suspended banks" and without adequate provision for borrowing "must soon produce disastrous consequences."

The President then recurred to the national bank legislation, which he had recommended already in his message to Congress when it convened the month before. It was clearly necessary, he said, to give every possible support to the public credit; and "to that end a uniform currency in which taxes, subscriptions to loans, and all other" public and private dues might be paid, was practically indispensable. Such a currency, he said, could be furnished by banks organized under national law, and "the securing of this circulation by the pledge of United States bonds . . . would still further facilitate loans" by increasing the demand for government bonds. He would not be performing his duty, he said, by simply approving what Congress had already done. "In view of the actual financial embarrassments of the government and of the greater embarrassments sure

315

to come if the necessary means of relief be not afforded," he must urge early sanction by Congress of what had been recommended but not yet done.[37]

The President was not merely supporting his finance minister but expressing his own Whig convictions. Twenty-three years before, he had opposed establishment of the sub-Treasury, had defended the United States Bank, and had favored its restoration. He had said that no duty of the federal government was more imperative "than the duty it owes the people of furnishing them a sound and uniform currency." What he now joined Chase in recommending differed in form but not in objective from what, in my first chapter, I told of his having advocated in 1839.[38]

But his letter received no parliamentary attention. According to the *New York Times* it was "extraordinary," and by the President's friends in both Houses was considered "injudicious." There seemed to the *Times* to be "very little chance" that Congress would agree to the "national banking scheme." So far indeed it did seem that nothing had been gained. Sherman had said his say in the Senate, and silence had ensued. The subject was still discussed in the House, but off the calendar. The bill embodying it (HR 656) though repeatedly argued was never formally brought up, though the Ways and Means Committee, according to the *Times*, had agreed that it be given "a fair vote." First it had been calendared 8 January for discussion the 16th, and it was discussed then and at other times but only in digression from the finance bill (HR 659). On the 19th, late in the day, both chambers had heard the President's letter; and in both its reception had been barely short of contemptuous. In the Senate there was no response beyond a motion that the letter be referred to the Finance Committee and cries of "Oh, No," when the presiding officer asked if there were a motion to have it printed. Thereupon the Senate adjourned. The House did the same after refusing to give the letter any attention. The day following, Thaddeus Stevens, peevish during debate on the Ways and Means bill at a question regarding the Administration's bill, refused to answer. On the 23rd, the conflict between the Administration and the Committee was again reflected in a short colloquy between Stevens and Samuel Hooper, respecting a letter in which Chase had expressed dissatisfaction with the Ways and Means finance bill (HR 659) and commended the Administration's bank bill to the committee's "most favorable consideration." Stevens reminded Hooper that the committee had rejected the bill. On 3 February, the bank bill was "next in order" but consideration of it was postponed "one week." The week passed and the bill was let lie untouched.[39]

This, however, was not the end. The Ways and Means Committee's finance bill (HR 659), patched and repatched in House and Senate, became law early in March. But by that time, strange to say, the Administration's abused national bank bill, dead in the House but brought to life in the Senate, had passed both chambers and was law.

The Administration had won.

317

THE ADMINISTRATION
BILL ENACTED

I

THE MEANS BY which the national bank measure was suddenly raised again from the dead and made law are evident only in general. It seems that Secretary Chase and his friends bestirred themselves and managed, by making the most of every chance, to squeak through with the bill. According to Senator Sherman, while Congress was engaged with other matters, the proposal made by Chase in December 1861 had continued to be discussed "among those whose business made them conversant with finance and currency," and "though it ran counter to the local interests of those engaged in the business of banking, it . . . steadily gained in favor" with the public in general. The bill met frustration throughout the second session and at the outset of the third, but its final success, despite stubborn resistance to it among the divided Republicans, indicates that besides a determined and competent direction, it had the support of a surging nationalism, especially from the West.[1]

As already recounted, Sherman, 5 January 1863, had introduced a bill in the Senate to tax bank notes (S 445), which meant, in effect, those of state banks, there being no others. This was two days before Samuel Hooper, in the House, had introduced the national bank bill (HR 656), abandoned the past summer at the end of the second session. The two measures—Sherman's and Hooper's—seem to have had little obviously in common except incompatibility with the existing currency of state bank notes, abolition of which in favor of greenbacks seemed at the moment the whole object of Sherman's attack. On the 8th, the day that Thaddeus Stevens, in the House, made an adverse report from Ways and Means on Hooper's national bank bill, Sherman in the Senate explained his bill to tax bank notes (S 445). But then, less than three weeks later, 26 January, with this first bill of his silently pigeon-holed, he introduced a national bank bill (S 486), which was "a little different," he said, from the Hooper bill (HR 656) introduced in the House but buried in committee. This second bill of Sherman's, that is, was in substance the bill urged upon Congress by President Lincoln, 19 January, in identical letters to House and to Senate, and flippantly treated by both.[2]

The same day that this second bill—the Administration bill—was introduced by Sherman, 26 January, a long letter on the subject, dated in Washington, was addressed to the *New York Times*; and two days later, 28 January, the letter appeared opposite the *Times*'s editorial page under the heading "The Financial Problem." It was signed S and presented a vigorous argument for the Administration's measure. It was followed by a second letter to the *Times* signed S, dated Washington, 27 January, and printed on the paper's editorial page 31 January under the heading, "The National Banking Scheme." A third and fourth letter, dated Washington, 29 and 30 January, and signed S, appeared on the editorial page of the *Times*, 2 and 3 February, headed respectively "The National Banking Project" and "The National Free Banking System." Arguments, phraseology, and quotations used by Senator Sherman in his speech of 8 January for a tax on state bank notes and in a speech of his still to be made 10 February for the national bank bill are presented also in the letters, but in varying order and detail. All four letters have an authoritative tone in the direct, energetic style of Sherman. Whether or not written by Sherman himself, they anyway reflect things he said in his speech of 8 January incidental to a prohibitory tax on state bank notes, and in turn things said in the letters are reflected in what he was to say 9 and 10 February for the national bank bill introduced by him 26 January. Plain words of Jefferson's in 1814 urging that the banks be "put down" and their notes replaced with Treasury notes were used in the S letter of 27 January precisely as in Sherman's speech of 8 January. In his *Recollections*, however, published in 1895, he makes no mention of the four S letters.[3]

In the second S letter—the *Times* 31 January 1863—there was friendly mention of Robert J. Walker, whose advocacy of a national currency I described in the chapter preceding this; and in the *Times* of 2 February, directly following the third S letter, there was a long communication dated in Washington 31 January and signed W, which included a letter of the same date from Walker to Senator Sherman. In this letter Walker tells Sherman that "the great coincidence of our views on the financial and currency question has given me much pleasure and increased confidence." They "had never compared opinions on this subject" before, Walker said, but "your speech was delivered in the Senate on the same day that my pamphlet was printed in New-York and both appeared here simultaneously in the same morning paper." (Walker refers evidently to Sherman's speech of 8 January; that of 10 February had not been delivered.) The coincidence, Walker said, was remarkable. They evidently met soon and discussed the subject, for "in compliance with my promise," Walker says, he now suggested for consideration a number of amendments to the Sherman bill and discoursed on them at some length. In the closing paragraph of the S letter preceding communication of this letter of Walker's to Sherman, there is cordial approval of a contention "forcibly stated by Hon. R. J. Walker" that in consequence of the proposed national currency's adoption "the interest of labor and capital, of the banks, and the Government, and the people . . . would for the first time become inseparably united and consolidated. . . . While Congress abdicates its authority to regulate the currency, leaving to the states the power to provide the circulating medium, it . . . clothes them with a power to overthrow the government." The measure was less economic than political.

The second bill (S 486)—that is, the Administration bill authorizing national banks and introduced 26 January—was brought up by Sherman 9 February, explained by him, discussed, and amended. The next day, 10 February, he made a longer statement for it which was followed by active discussion. In his *Recollections* Sherman mentions his two bills of 8 and 26 January but without consideration of the differences between them, which were great. For in his earlier bill he had purposed no more than taxing bank notes prohibitively and replacing them with Treasury notes; he had not even mentioned the national banks and national bank notes Chase and Hooper had been urging on Congress. But eighteen days later he introduced a bill only "a little different," he said, from Hooper's in the House, and, remaining silent about the proposal he had first made, he vigorously supported the national bank measure. This shift was abrupt, but Sherman made no acknowledgment or explanation of it either in Congress or in his *Recollections*. However in Theodore Burton's biography of him, 1908, a letter is quoted in which Sherman told his wife, after the debates, of the difficulty he had had in making up his mind what to do and say about the Chase-Hooper bill. "Chase," Sherman wrote, "appealed to me through Cooke to remodel the bill to satisfy my views and take charge of it in the Senate. The appeal was of such a character that I could not resist, although I foresaw the difficulties and danger of defeat. When I made the speech on taxation of state bank bills, I had not determined what to do, but carefully avoided any reference to the National Bank Bill. That speech brought me into correspondence with bankers and others, and while giving me some reputation, compelled me to study the preference between government and bank currency and led me to the conviction that it was a public duty to risk a defeat on the Bank Bill. I thoroughly convinced myself, if I could not convince others, that it was indispensable to create a demand for our bonds, and the best way was to make them the basis of a banking system."[4]

Though in his addresses to the Senate and in his *Recollections* Sherman mentioned no shift of purpose and no such uncertainty about the course to take as he told his wife of, he seems to have recognized the need of reconciling his

original proposal that state bank notes be replaced by
Treasury notes and his proposal shortly thereafter that they
be replaced by national bank notes. For in his *Recollections*
he mentions his having himself in his address of 10 February "narrated the history of the bill, of its introduction
in December 1861, its urgent recommendation by the Secretary of the Treasury in two annual reports, and the conditions that then demanded immediate action upon it."
The "history" implies a single purpose, running through
Chase's first recommendation, Spaulding's draft embodying that recommendation, to Sherman's own conclusive
action, including the bills introduced by Hooper in January
and July 1862 and in January 1863 and his own current bill
(S 486). He was evidently tying his two efforts together
and uniting them also with what, since Chase's original
proposal in his report of December 1861, had been done
by Chase himself, by Spaulding, by Hooper, and by the
President, toward replacement of the existing state bank
currency by a currency which national banks would
furnish.[5]

So, in his *Recollections*, in what Sherman told the Senate,
and in what was said in the S letters on shift from replacement of state bank notes with Treasury notes to replacement of them with national bank notes is acknowledged.
Sherman, his problem having been solved and his presentation completed, gives his effort a continuity which in the
process of its development it lacked. Like a sensible husband, he confided his difficulties to his wife, but he was
no Rousseau boring the world with them. In fact the continuity was real, though overshadowed by difficulties
which almost overwhelmed the men engaged in finding
the means to save the Union and make its sovereignty real.
What they had not done in times of peace, when circumstances were favorable but they themselves were not, they
had to do when disaster had become imminent; and in
such conditions reform had to be accomplished in excitement and confusion over the means but nevertheless in
basic agreement as to the end and its importance.

Actually, though Sherman struggled with uncertainty and had to feel his way instead of having a clear course to follow, he probably could not have done better than he did. For he began his effort with emphasis upon the execrable currency with which the country was trying to get on and with which everyone was acquainted. He drove home without stint a need which Chase, Hooper, and the President had mentioned but evidently shrank from being offensive about. They had been too much impressed by the embarrassing fact that in the Eastern states conditions were relatively satisfactory and the intended reform was therefore relatively unattractive. Sherman, by an unmincing attack on state banks as such, appealed effectively to the Western states, where banking had been so profligate that several states had tried to prohibit it. And in a bold appeal to nationalist sentiment he associated the establishment of federal sovereignty over money with resistance to the pretensions of states' rights in respect to slavery and secession. He stressed the neglected evils of the state bank note currency; and then, countering ungloved against the argument that federal interference with state institutions would be unconstitutional, he declared that it was the states themselves whose action was unconstitutional.

What seems to me particularly effective was his use of Jefferson's words in denunciation of states' rights in respect to banks and currency and recourse to federal authority in that respect. Nationalization of the currency had been flouted at the Capitol for more than a year. Sherman presented it as Jeffersonian; at the same time he associated the existing currency with slavery and with "rebellion," for which states' rights—"the accursed heresy of State Sovereignty lying at the foundation of the slave-holders' rebellion"—were responsible; and he associated the proposed nationalization of the currency with emancipation and the Union. "The policy of this country," he said 10 February, "ought to be to make everything national as far as possible; to nationalize our country so that we shall love our country.... This doctrine of state rights ... has been the evil of the times...."[6]

The next day, 11 February, Senator Collamer, Vermont Republican, answered Sherman in a long, surly address that was clear only in its expression of a sentimental provincialism and jealous concern for the protection of states' rights from federal infringement. The senator doubtless had a clear idea of what banks looked like but no such understanding of what they did as any Vermonter would have had of what a team of oxen yoked to a stone-boat did. Collamer very reasonably dismissed the bill as a war measure, quoting Secretary Chase's own words as evidence that it was not one. But he was most moved by the threatened end to state banks—a "derangement," he said, "utterly destructive of the condition of society in which I live." The enemy was the federal government, respecting whose tendencies he cited "the principle, laid down by Montesquieu, that power is always at war with its own boundaries." Collamer was aware that he was citing the Montesquieu principle at a time when any sort of doubt about the beneficence of power "was received as somewhat dangerous doctrine." He meant federal power. There were many powers, he said, which the states have the right "to exercise utterly independent of the United States government." The right of a state to charter banks was "certainly independent of the consent of Congress. ... The United States has no more power to tax a state institution out of existence than a state has to tax a United States institution out of existence." Otherwise the federal government could tax schools in New England and education itself out of existence. Senator Collamer believed Vermont to be as loyal as any state in the Union, "but," he said, "our people can be unnecessarily distressed to an amount that they will not endure." He would not threaten resistance by revolution but warned that his constituents would "hardly admire an Administration" which threatened them with "such calamities" as he apprehended. Though a Republican, he was above such subserviency to the Administration

327

as the Senator from Ohio seemed to expect when, the day before, he told the Senate that the whole Cabinet was in favor of the national currency bill. For that affront to the Senate, the gentleman from Ohio should have been called to order.[7]

Sherman answered Collamer and Collamer replied at length. Chandler of Michigan, business man and radical Republican, spoke briefly and to the point for the bill. "This is a question," he said, in answer to Collamer's plea, "of whether you will legislate for a few petty banks in New England or . . . for the preservation of this great nation. . . . Sir, I will sacrifice banks and Negroes and everything to save this nation. . . . I trust this bill will pass; for . . . all there is in it, in my estimation, is good." Senator Doolittle of Wisconsin, Republican, but former Democrat, saying that for nearly twenty years of his life he fought against the United States Bank, now thought that the state banks if not unconstitutional were anyway unsatisfactory and the national system should be adopted. Consideration of the bill ended directly with adjournment, and the next day, 12 February, the final vote being taken with no further discussion, the bill passed the Senate, 23 to 21. This bare majority was given Secretary Chase as a mere courtesy according to the *New York Herald*, which reported it to be "well understood" that the bill would be killed in the House "without loss of time." More than a third of the twenty-one votes against the bill were Republican, including those of other important party members besides Collamer himself— Edgar Cowan of Pennsylvania, James Crimes of Iowa, Preston King of New York, and Lyman Trumbull of Illinois.[8]

II

The same day the bill was received in the House. Its enemies kept it lying on the table a week, but on the 19th its friends succeeded in getting it out on the floor. Spaulding of New York, the Buffalo banker, who had fought it five weeks before, now spoke in its favor with the conviction of a half-way nationalist. The bill, he said, had been changed in a way fair to the state banks. He thought state banks and national banks both constitutional, and the bill no longer being coercive against state banks he would vote for it. He looked for no considerable relief for the Treasury from it for two or three years—nor for any related decrease in the use of greenbacks—but he saw it as the commencement of a national currency of great benefit to the public and the federal government. In all its essential features, he said, the bill was like the free-banking law of New York, which had done well for twenty-five years. The currency provided by it would have not only the public credit behind it, as the legal tender notes had, but also private wealth. Both the President and the Secretary of the Treasury advocated it. Being a former Whig like the President himself, he regretted the absence of an institution such as the Bank of the United States had been. "If there had been established years ago a sound national bank of two hundred million dollars capital, which had been in full operation as the fiscal and financial agent of the government at the time of the breaking out of the present rebellion, what a mighty support it would have been in sustaining the government at the present time!" This was a risky argument to offer former Democrats now part of the Republican majority; and so was Spaulding's complaint that "the independent Treasury law unnecessarily isolated the government from all the capitalists and the accumulated capital of the country."[9]

"At the very outset of this rebellion," Spaulding reminded his hearers, "there was no money in the sub-Treasury, and, notwithstanding the hostility heretofore and now manifested toward state banks, the government was obliged to resort at once to the state banks in New York, Boston, and Philadelphia for money to prosecute the war. The states had fostered and built up strong state institutions while the general government had been vacillating and weakened by conflicting views and opinions as to the constitutionality and policy of a national bank. It is now most apparent that the policy advocated by Alexander Hamilton of a strong central government was the true policy. A strong consolidated government would most likely have been able to avert this rebellion; but if not able to prevent it entirely, it would have been much better prepared to have met and put down the traitorous advocates of secession and state rights, who have forced upon us this unnatural and bloody war. A sound national bank, upheld and supported by the combined credit of the government and rich men residing in all the states of the Union, would have been a strong bond of union before the rebellion broke out and a still stronger support to the government in maintaining the army and navy to put it down.

"It seems," Spaulding said, "that the present is a propitious time to enact this great measure as a permanent system and that the duty of the government in providing a national currency shall no longer be neglected. . . . The government of the United States ought not to depend on state institutions for the execution of its great powers." However he saw in the current "imperiled condition of the Union more distrust of the stability of the general government than there is of the state governments. Some doubt exists," he said, "owing to divisions at the North, as to our final success in crushing the rebellion. Could you make it certain that the Union will be preserved and the national jurisdiction maintained over all the thirty-four states and the sixteen billion dollars of taxable property therein which is liable for our public debt—excluding therefrom the debt of the rebel government, said to be nine hundred million—the six per cent bonds of the United States would not be five per cent below par, while the six per cent bonds of the state of New York are worth a premium of twenty-eight per cent." What were needed, of course, were some decisive military victories, and their absence was the burden of constant complaint by men wrestling with the Union's financial difficulties.[10]

So in Spaulding's judgment the Secretary of the Treasury must not place too much reliance upon the national bank plan. "It will not give much relief to the Treasury for one, two, or three years. . . . It will go into operation slowly. The government having heretofore failed to provide a national currency, the state banks in the older states have been organized, become deeply rooted, and firmly established. It will take a long time to supplant these banks. . . . It will be towards the close of the war, when the government is firmly established and its authority respected in all the states, that it will be most valuable in providing a way for funding the public debt and establishing a permanent system of national currency. . . . It is more for the benefits to be realized in the future than during the pending war that I am induced to give it my support."[11]

In the strategy of the bill's advocates Spaulding's help was probably expected to be most influential, and it may well have been so. For he was the author of the greenbacks, with which the majority of the House, originally full of cold revulsion, had now fallen in love. He was also an upstate banker, in behalf of whose fellows the loudest complaints against Chase's national bank scheme were uttered. Moreover he was a prominent member of the Ways and Means Committee, and as such, only a few weeks before, he had been outspoken against the scheme. Finally, he was a representative of New York, the state still most powerfully opposed to it. If he could be brought around, it was evidence not only of the Administration's strength, as shown already in the Senate, but of some merit in the scheme itself. Spaulding was followed by another New York Republican, Reuben E. Fenton, who also had changed his mind. To the extent that speeches are influential, such witnesses as Spaulding and Fenton far outweighed Samuel Hooper, who was merely the bill's sponsor and despite his understanding and experience could say nothing for it that the House had not heard before.[12]

The next day, 20 February, discussion continued, though there was doubtless general agreement with Warren P. Noble, Democrat of Ohio, who said, in speaking against the bill, that "from the great and untiring efforts that are being made by the Secretary of the Treasury in its favor," its passage was "a foregone conclusion." The last speech was that of John B. Alley, who said he regarded the pending measure "as one of greater importance than has ever been agitated in this hall." A sound and uniform national currency, he believed, "would confer upon this generation and our posterity for ages to come inestimable blessings scarcely less valuable than the preservation of the Union itself."[13]

Then, after all possible efforts to delay action, the final vote was taken and instead of being killed in the House, as had been expected when the bill passed the Senate, it was adopted by a vote of 78 to 64. Its passage followed almost fifteen months of legislative snubbing since Chase first proposed it and after a few final hours of discussion scattered through but three days in the Senate and two in the House. Thaddeus Stevens, somehow won over, voted for it. Owen Lovejoy, Illinois Republican, supporter of the Administration, an agrarian enemy of banks, and a convert to the greenbacks, voted for it. Justin Morrill, Vermont Republican, supporter of the Administration, retired from business and a friend of banks, a man who hated greenbacks, voted against it. The paradox was not rare. President Lincoln approved the bill 25 February 1863.[14]

Opposition to the act during debate—both Democratic and Republican—had comprised, confusedly, the friends of state banks and the enemies of all banks. The act's supporters were more homogeneous, being primarily nationalist, less numerous, and dependent for success on deserters from the opposition. A vote for the bill was a vote for the Administration, or for federal sovereignty, or against states' rights; a vote against the bill was a vote against the Administration, or against federal sovereignty, or for states' rights. In this situation Democratic votes were obviously decisive and for this aid the Administration owed much to Thomas Jefferson's words as presented by Senator Sherman and to the vigorous arguments of the veteran Jacksonian, Robert J. Walker.

Though the Administration had won a victory, it was a far less important one in its effects than was thought—being important as an assertion of federal sovereignty, and as such leading to eventual achievement of great moment but not supplanting the existing currency nor ending the inflation which the Administration's supporters deplored. The emotion on both sides had been excited less by difference of opinion about the currency than by concern over the revolutionary change to be effected in the relative powers of the states and the federal government. These powers had been less obviously in conflict during debate on the original authorization of greenbacks a year before and still less obviously in conflict during debate on the revenue act six months before; for though both the legal tender and revenue measures enlarged the exercise of federal powers, they took nothing directly from the states except a traditional freedom from invasion by federal tax-gatherers. But the national bank measure, in offering a change of monetary authority threatened to deprive the states of a power they had exercised for eighty years—a power they had strengthened, with President Jackson's powerful help, by their victory over the Bank of the United States thirty years before, and with the Supreme Court's help under Chief Justice Taney. The bill's opponents were in reality resisting, but on a minor scale, the encroachments on states' rights which the South was resisting, on a major scale, with arms.

Sherman's two speeches, 8 January and 10 February, 1863—and his four S letters, if, as I believe, they were his—express a spirit of nationalism peculiar to the time of their utterance. The banks and the currency would be uniform throughout the country. They would unite the national credit with private credit and associate federal powers rather than state powers with private interest. The passage of the bill would, he said, promote a sentiment of nationality. "The policy of this country ought to be to make everything national as far as possible; to nationalize our country so that we shall love our country. If we are dependent

333

on the United States for a currency and a medium of exchange, we shall have a broader and more generous nationality. The want of such nationality, I believe, is one of the great evils of the times. . . . It has been that principle of state rights, that bad sentiment that has elevated state authority above the great national authority, that has been the main instrument by which our government is sought to be overthrown."[15]

This nationalist declaration, 10 February, echoed the sentence of the fourth S letter in which the notion that state corporations had any rights impregnable to federal authority was denounced, as, "in new form, the accursed heresy of State Sovereignty lying at the foundation of the slaveholders' rebellion." But Sherman's nationalism was not a wartime ardor merely; for though he believed the proposed national banks could not become adequate sources of funds for the federal government while the war lasted, they would serve, afterwards, its permanently augmented responsibilities and needs. After this war is over, he said, "this government must undertake responsibilities and incur debts and liabilities of which we have had no example in our previous history." The statement, prescient and in accord with the radical Republicans' course, is in clear contrast with notions, now familiar, about returning to a happy past.[16]

III

However, it was primarily sentiment and not fiscal expertise that occupied congressional debate on the national bank bill and governed the final vote. The winning side had little to say about the measure's efficacy in financing, and towards the end admitted that it would produce little or nothing to fill the federal purse. Instead, the measure's advocates were carried away by antipathy to states' rights and a mystical nationalist enthusiasm such as had authorized legal tender notes twelve months before. States' rights were associated by the majority with slavery and secession

—nationalist enthusiasm with emancipation and a benevolent central authority. Thus for Senator Sherman it was no expectation of financial success from constitutional reform that fired his efforts on behalf of the bill. It was instead his nationalist ardor, communicated with energy and directness, and his identification of the states' monetary usurpations with the "accursed heresy of the slaveholders rebellion" that gave force to his arguments.

The opposition also was mainly sentimental and imbued with provincial preferences; few of the minority opposed Chase on the ground that his measure was impractical.

As for the Secretary himself, when he thought hard, he seems always to have thought as a constitutional lawyer and not as a financial minister. He admitted only toward the end that the benefits he expected would not be immediate but eventual. Yet it was immediate ones that were required, and it was that that should have impressed him. But in the sequel even his constitutional reform failed to be achieved. The states were not ousted from participation in the monetary function and never have been. Instead they have again and again staved off what from one point of view may be called implications of his constitutional reform and from another invasions of their vigorously defended rights. The issue of notes by institutions which they regulated was stopped but not their provision of deposit credit transferable by check, though this was the monetary function of far the greater volume and importance. The country did regain from Chase's measure a uniform currency such as it had been without ever since Andrew Jackson ended the regime of the federal Bank, but the recovery was of no importance till after the war ended and never adequate before the present century. The Secretary, whose victims seemed to be hypnotized by the sheer pressure of his presence and the influence of the buttons on his front, won by no great majority but with credit for his ability to win at all when his measure was generally deemed to be dead as a door nail. And his jejune triumph had to be shared with John Sherman. What was of substance and saved the Secretary's administration of the Treasury was his contract with Jay Cooke, who prayerfully, shrewdly, and energetically went out for the money and got it.

When President Lincoln sent Congress his letter of 19 January explicitly supporting Chase's measure, he must have recognized, as Senator Sherman did, the political difficulties the measure faced and the weak assurances it gave of providing money. The Republican majority in both chambers, including many of the ablest and most influential members were opposed to it. The President was certainly aware of this uncomfortable fact and perhaps uncomfortable himself about what to do. The situation was not one from which he could remain withdrawn, however, and he took his ground decisively with Chase. To have done otherwise would very likely have stirred Chase to submit his resignation again barely a month after the cabinet crisis and this time for good. By siding with Chase, the President not only avoided that awkwardness but returned the courtesy of the Secretary's withdrawal of his recent resignation. The President could side with Chase in sincerity, moreover, because he too approved the Secretary's constitutional reform. He stood where he had a quarter of a century before, when he himself held the un-Jacksonian conviction that monetary responsibility, in terms of the Constitution, was the federal government's and as exercised by the states was usurped by them. Like Chase, he was a lawyer and more competent in constitutional matters than financial. The reasons he gave for the proposed reform were, like Chase's own, the reasons of a lawyer, and though far less his responsibility than his finance minister's, they were sincere.*

The worst that can be said of Chase's measure is that it was, as the *New York Herald* reported, "delusive." It also

---

* In thinking the President felt obliged to Chase for having withdrawn his resignation following the cabinet crisis and let his feeling be known when he had occasion, I follow Mr Allan Nevins. Two years later the President accepted Chase's resignation, but did so, ironically, when Chase was right and he himself was wrong—wrong at least as to management of the Treasury. (Nevins, II, 351ff.)

sacrificed official time, energy, and concord. But it was innocent compared to Chase's scuttling of the amendment, drafted during the special session eighteen months earlier which was to suspend the specie requirement of the independent Treasury act, an inexcusable misdeed blackened by breach of trust. As recounted in an earlier chapter, which dealt with the special session in the summer of 1861, an amendment had been drafted suspending the requirement of the act that what the banks lent the Treasury be delivered to it in gold. Chase had been fully aware that men more knowing and experienced than he himself were sure that what the act required was fatal, but when their draft adapting the act to unprecedented needs was submitted to him, he quietly undid their work under cover of mere elucidation, burying the force of the amendment deep in verbiage, and returning it to Congress with no intimation of the twisting he had given it. Only after the altered amendment became law did he assure its bewildered authors and advocates that it had not the meaning they intended it to have. Nor did he explain why it had not, but stifled their incredulity under irrelevant threats to inflate the currency till it took a thousand dollars to buy a breakfast.

Following this sly, disingenuous, rude, and ignorant behavior during the special session, Chase in his report of December 1861 to the second session of the 37th Congress proposed in very general terms the national currency plan that fourteen months later, February 1863, was enacted. As I have said earlier, his undoing of the amendment designed to suspend the specie requirement of the independent Treasury act may be evidence that so early as July 1861 he had thought of proposing a national currency and apprehended that suspension of the specie requirement would throw him onto the bankers' books and into their arms, with the result of compromising him and obstructing the contemplated proposal. This, if a fact, might explain why he refused as he did what, in the absence of some better alternative, was obviously advantageous to a borrower

337

whose needs were great and whose credit was something less.

Imaginably, with steady continuance of unfailingly favorable conditions, an unbroken flow of coin from lenders to the Treasury, from the Treasury to the government's suppliers and personnel, from these back into the banks as deposit might be maintained, and the banks enabled to deliver gold to the Treasury as fast as it returned to them. On the one hand, the food shortages in Europe and the active production of gold in California had made gold and consequently the reserves superabundant, while trade, except for the movement of foodstuffs to the seaboard, had subsided in a paralysis of uncertainty from the fear of what the South would do and with no demand for credit except from the Treasury. But on the other hand, the South's intrepidity, the fear and uncertainty paralyzing trade was sure, if prolonged, to foster the hoarding of gold, whereupon its return to the banks' vaults and its repeated delivery to the Treasury would be interrupted. To Chase's embarrassment, as he had been warned repeatedly in letters from his Ohio friend, Judge Nash, and as the bankers angrily feared, the gold did leak away into hoards, the banks were forced to stop delivering it, and the government had to fall back on IOU's in the form of legal tender notes.

Meanwhile in December, five months after his first refusal to employ bank credit in normal fashion, Chase had again turned from the banks as they were—damaged by him but still operable—and proposed that a new class of banks under federal control be authorized and set up. This would take time, of course, but his needs were still immediate. On that ground alone his proposal was obviously one of doubtful wisdom. Besides that, it was offensive to the bankers, on whom he was depending and who were being offered more uncertainties by him, and to the states, which already had their hands full helping the federal government preserve the Union and did not agree with him that what they had been doing since the Revolution was unconstitutional. Despite all these unpromising conditions, and thanks to the unconscionable respect in which he continued to be held, he had stubbornly stood fast for his constitutional reform. There were also the two great advantages in his favor that the currency issued by the state banks was not provided exclusively by the good ones but also by wild-cats and counterfeiters with the result that only the relatively few experts who dealt in bank notes for profit knew what was good, what was not good, and if good how good.

But, at the moment, what the government needed was means of preserving the Union, not rectification of a long familiar usurpation by the states of a federal responsibility nor for perfection of a long-endured currency. The banks which Chase was dealing with were on the whole sound, well-managed, possessed of abundant reserves, and eager to make the advances the Treasury needed. Instead of frustrating the amendment, Chase should have insisted upon its rescission. Had he done so—had he accepted the services of the banks the way they were—as was done with other instrumentalities—using them as the public did, accepting his funds in deposit credit, and making his disbursements by check, like a Christian, as an editorial in the *New York Tribune* had suggested a year before—he then could have sold his bonds more promptly, and by having the banks retain their reserves have smoothed his own path and perhaps made suspension avoidable or at least less demoralizing than it was.[17]

The currency, it is true, was abominably bad as well as unconstitutional, but it was not provided in great part by the metropolitan banks with which Chase was dealing, nor was it—whether good or bad—of major importance to the Treasury. By January and February 1863, when the conflict over his national bank bill was in its last and tensest stage, the Treasury had become so far committed to reliance on greenbacks and on Jay Cooke's successful sale of government bonds that passage of the bill was of no help to the financing of the war. It was a superfluous triumph of nationalist emotion, of Chase's pertinacity, and of John Sherman's spokesmanship.

IV

During the weeks in January and February that the Administration's bill was being wrangled over at the Capitol and the press in general had been making news out of guesses, Charles F. Dunbar's *Boston Daily Advertiser* had maintained an odd silence on the subject. The *Advertiser* did tell its readers that a million one dollar Treasury notes would weigh more than a ton and make a stack as high as the Washington monument. It did mention reports that the printers of the government's paper money were much belated—perhaps criminally so—and that the Treasury was preparing to do the printing itself. It did go so far as to quote President Lincoln's letter of 19 January urging enactment of the bill; but it made no comment thereon. It also mentioned "the firmness with which the several loyal states of the Union maintain themselves under the financial burdens thrown upon them by the war," but there was no similar mention of the burden thrown by it upon the federal government.[18]

This silence of the *Advertiser* on a controversial subject respecting which the gentleman who was its editor and co-proprietor was exceptionally well-informed and astute in judgment might be partially explained by the current pressure of other important matters—the fleetingly successful effort of Napoleon III to make Maximilian of Austria the Emperor of Mexico and the December crisis in President Lincoln's cabinet entailing the resignations submitted by Seward and Chase and then withdrawn by them. In an editorial full of uneasiness Dunbar thought "there is a very general concurrence of opinion throughout the country that Mr Chase could not be spared" from the cabinet.*

* The *Boston Daily Advertiser*'s editorials at this time were being "written without exception" by Mr Dunbar, according to Professor F. W. Taussig, whose authority I accept. Mr Dunbar was a part owner of the paper as well as its editor. (Dunbar, vii-viii.)

340

But not till 23 February, three days after the bank bill had passed both Houses and gone to the President, did Dunbar discuss the measure. He did this in a long and pondering editorial in which it was acknowledged that the *Advertiser* had doubted the wisdom of the Administration's measure from the first but had taken "little part" in the discussion—"no part at all" would have been closer to the bald truth—while the bill had been pending, though "we can scarcely say that we have been content" to be silent. The *Advertiser* had been silent, Dunbar said, in observance of "the duty of not opposing, except in cases of imperative necessity, measures which are put forward as needful . . . by those charged with the public defense." He conceded that there were "merits" in the statute but found it "a matter of some difficulty to determine" why it had been presented "as a war measure." Senator Collamer was quoted as unqualifiedly rejecting it as such and Congressman Spaulding as accepting it but qualifiedly. Yet Secretary Chase was reported to have "declared his inability to carry on the finances of the government without this measure." Whether that report were true or not, the *Advertiser* said, "it is certain that on the 19th of January the President took the unusual step of urging the passage of a measure similar to the present as 'almost if not quite indispensable' for the support of the public credit, for checking local issues, and for facilitating loans" required by the government for prosecution of the war.[19]

The *Advertiser* observed also that Samuel Hooper, "whose relations with the government are known to be most confidential, declared in the House that the new banking system was 'so necessarily connected' with the new loan as to make the two inseparable. Doubtless," the *Advertiser* said, "many both in Congress and out of it who claim no merit of original friendship for the system have felt some difficulty in opposing" it. The *Advertiser* quoted Hooper "with the fervent hope that his sanguine prophecies may be fully and speedily realized."[20]

The loyal but discerning criticism expressed by the

341

Advertiser's editor and by staunch Republicans in Congress indicates the weakness of Chase's argument, indulgently supported by President Lincoln and, perhaps with like indulgence, by Samuel Hooper and John Sherman, that the new measure was required by both war and postwar needs. It fell short of being a war measure because it neither required nor invited the action it authorized. It merely permitted the banks to do something they did not care to do and that states' interests hindered their doing. It assured no immediate action essential in a "war measure." It had diverted parliamentary time and attention from immediate needs and must similarly divert the Administration's time and attention from them. These strictures seem to me sound.

The day President Lincoln approved the bill, 25 February, the *Boston Advertiser* quoted what H. H. Van Dyck, the Superintendent of New York Banks, had said in his latest annual report in response to Secretary Chase's renewed proposal, in December, of the measure now made law. Van Dyck again doubted the practicability of the national scheme, as he had done a year earlier, but would not discuss it. "A far more important consideration," he now insisted, with italics, "is found in the utter lack of *constitutional power on the part of Congress to create corporations within the states without the assent of the state legislatures.*" Under the New York statutes, he went on warningly, "no association or person can issue, within this state, notes to circulate as money without depositing the required securities in this department. Without legislative instructions to the contrary, it will be my duty, during my continuance in office, to enforce this provision against all associations or individuals claiming authority from any other source. . . . I shall not hesitate," he said, to go to court in order "that we may learn authoritatively what powers over local institutions are still left to the states." The *Advertiser's* editor, doubtful himself, said temperately that he saw some advantage in getting settled "disputed points as to the powers of the general and state governments in the matter of the currency."[21]

Dunbar's editorials in the *Daily Boston Advertiser*, which present an exceptionally careful and intelligent judgment in the matter, seem to have been troubled by two dominant uncertainties. One concerned the lodgment of constitutional authority over banks and their obligations, in respect to which the more ignorant a man was of constitutional and monetary history, the easier it was for him to come down flatly for federal authority and not state, or for state and not federal. And such a man's decision was apt to be influenced by the part of the country in which he lived. In the East, where success and conservatism had come to prevail under state authority, that authority was preferred, not so much because it was legal as because it had been successful. In the West, where innocence and rascality had had more sweep, the preference was for greater federal authority. Dunbar belonged to the East. The second uncertainty concerned the Administration's undertaking an extension of federal authority which the war did not require and which bred increased faction. Dunbar, like Elijah Ward, the Democratic congressman from New York, was aware that the banks *as they were* could amply support the Treasury if not abused by it as they had been—deprived of their abundant reserves and forced into suspension in conditions otherwise exceptionally propitious. But Dunbar was troubled respecting his duty, as men of intelligence and conscience often are, when their government errs, as governments often do. And in respect to others like himself, whose opinions he must weigh professionally whether he agrees with them or not—notably Amasa Walker and Samuel Hooper of his own community, John Sherman of Ohio, and Robert J. Walker of Washington—in respect to them his editorial task must have been difficult. And the more so because judgments that had to be technically correct were also subject to the influence of conflicting political and legal judgments regarding sovereignty.

During debate, the bill was not an Administration measure in a 20th-century sense. At the time, however, it was generally thought to be one. The author of the S letter printed in the *New York Times* 28 January 1863 said that President Lincoln "in a recent message to Congress had practically announced the national banking scheme as an Administration measure. . . . *The Administration is and has been an entire unit upon this question.* The President and his constitutional advisers all agree that the proposed banking scheme is indispensable to the maintenance of the government." In the S letter printed by the *Times* 31 January, it was said that Secretary Chase's national bank plan was "emphatically endorsed by the President and all his associates in the cabinet." However, Gideon Welles, Secretary of the Navy, whose dislike and distrust of Chase was deep, recorded in his diary not only his own disapproval of the national bank scheme but another cabinet member's; and these two out of seven may not have been the only dissidents. Welles said characteristically that when Chase reported to the Cabinet on return from his visit to New York and Philadelphia the middle of January, the members listened without response, "not prepared" to have him be their authority or spokesman.[22]

The *New York Herald*, which opposed the bill, reported that about the time it passed the Senate, the Republicans were constantly in caucus. Mr Chase was with the Finance Committee "and no effort has been omitted by the government to secure strength" for this bill. At one period it seemed lost, "but by the exertions of several of the leading senators two votes were changed which secured its passage." The next day, after the bill passed the Senate by a vote of 23 to 21, the *Herald* reported that a majority of the Senate had been opposed to it; "but three or four senators from personal regard for Mr Chase changed their votes from no to aye in order that the Secretary might get the bill before the House, it being well understood that it will be killed there without loss of time"—just as the Hooper bill had been. The House was "wedded to legal tender." In the

Herald's opinion it would be fine to have a uniform national currency "instead of the heterogeneous and variable assemblage of bank notes which now circulate as money," but it was not "wise or fair," when the banks had all their capital in government bonds, "to choose this moment to make war upon them." Nor was it "politic, in the present delicate condition of the relations between the state and general governments, to provoke a conflict between the two jurisdictions on the subject of banking." In other words, conflict over secession and slavery was enough, without dragging in the banks. Besides decrying an attempt "to override and annul the banking laws of New York, Massachusetts, New Jersey, and Ohio," which were not the only states jealous of their powers, the *Herald* reminded its readers that in business circles the idea of making the new banking system finance the war and render greenbacks unnecessary was considered "a monstrous delusion."[23]

It was that. A few national banks were set up, notably by Jay Cooke, John Thompson, and other business men who were friends of Chase, but most state banks were not interested in the new system except as its ill-wishers. At the close of the year there were but sixty-six national banks against about fifteen hundred state banks.[24]

Part of this record was due to some characteristically stubborn notions clung to by Chase, who for a man of intelligence was capable of acting with incredible contrariety. Thus he required that existing banks give up their original names and be designated by numbers, as if bankers long and successfully in business were without sentiment and would as soon bear a number as an old and honored name, in several cases older than the federal government itself. When Chase relented, there was a brief rush for federal charters, and at the end of March 1864, thirteen months after the new system was authorized, there were four hundred and sixty-nine national banks with less than ten millions of notes in circulation, and little more than fifty millions of deposits. *Merchants' Magazine* was contemptuous of them. "The new banks are now of no probable use," it said in August 1864, "either to the government or to the public. They only continually inflate the currency with notes, which if ever uttered at all, should have been put out by the Treasury direct."[25]

But any expectation that the banks in the new system would go out of business soon, an attitude typical in the East, pretty quickly evaporated. Hugh McCulloch, former president of the State Bank of Indiana, was the supervisor of the new system, and as Comptroller of the Currency, sought the conversion of state banks to national charter rather than the chartering of new banks. He beat down Chase's more inexcusable notions and recommended changes embodied in the amending act of 30 January 1864. "The idea has at last become quite general, . . ." McCulloch said, "that the whole system of state banking, as far as circulation is regarded, is unfitted for a commercial country like ours. The United States is a nation as well as a union of states." The following year McCulloch was able to welcome legislative acts in several states facilitating the shift from state to national charter—action which indicated not so much an invasion of the states by federal powers as a domestication within the states of nationalism itself. At the same time, Chase's successor, William P. Fessenden, said in his first report as Secretary of the Treasury, 6 December 1864, that he had not been among the first to approve the national bank plan but was now convinced that its principles were sound and that the national authority should replace the states'. To this end he suggested that legislation be enacted as soon as possible which would "induce the withdrawal of all other circulation than that issued under national authority." At the same time Comptroller McCulloch thought that Congress should "prohibit the further issue of bank notes not authorized by itself and compel, by taxation, . . . the withdrawal of those which have been already issued." Four months later Congress took the action recommended, imposing a tax of ten per cent on state bank notes and thereby stopping their issue. "The national banks," John Sherman told the Senate 27 February 1865, "were intended to supersede the state banks. Both can not exist together." Yet they could and did. For while national banks were being established, he said, "the issues of state banks have not materially decreased. . . . If the state banks have power enough in Congress to prolong their existence beyond the present year, we had better suspend the organization of national banks." The tax was approved by President Lincoln at the end of his first term, 3 March 1865. There was still resistance, but in *Veazie Bank v. Fenno*, 1869, the Supreme Court upheld the tax as constitutional. Salmon P. Chase, now become Chief Justice, delivered the Court's opinion. Congress, he said, had undertaken "in the exercise of undisputed constitutional powers . . . to provide a currency for the whole country." These powers, until recently, had been "only partially and occasionally exercised." Lately, however, they had been called "into full activity," and Congress could do what was necessary to give its purposes effect. Two justices dissented— Samuel Nelson, a New York Democrat, and David Davis, an Illinois Republican.[26]

Had the tax been levied on checks as well as notes, it would have been effective, but as it was, never less than two or three hundred banks continued in business under state charter, finding neither note issue nor national charter necessary to their success. Only till 1892 were state banks less numerous than national or less important. And only in average size have state banks been less important. On the whole, the grip of the states on a power meant to be exclusively federal has been tenacious and successful. The larger state banks, to which note issue was negligible, were less affected by the tax than by a provision of the law that national banks could count as legal reserves (aside from coin and greenbacks in their own vaults) those funds deposited by them in other national banks but not those deposited in state banks. The effect of this restriction is illustrated in an entry made by the vice president of an Albany bank in his diary 11 May 1865: he said that he and two other officers of his bank had again discussed that day, as several times before, the advisability of surrendering their state charter for a national one. The writer was John V. L. Pruyn, long a member of Congress, and the bank's president was his father-in-law, Erastus Corning, also a member of Congress and as a member of the Ways and Means Committee in 1861 the first to resist Secretary Chase's national bank scheme. Both Corning and he, Pruyn wrote, "are very reluctant to give up our state organization, but it seems to be almost unavoidable. The turning point is that national banks (and most banks are becoming such) must keep their reserve fund on deposit with a national bank. If therefore we do not change, we shall lose our country bank accounts." They did change the same year, 1865.[27]

The consequence of Secretary Chase's effort to shift monetary authority from the individual states to the federal Union which the states comprised was not at all a clear concentration of that authority but a division of it between the states on the one hand and the federal government on the other. Though this consequence owed much to limited understanding, one may not doubt that something ranging between instinct and reasoned choice led developments away from concentration and toward a division and weakening of governmental power which promised— or seemed to promise—greater freedom to economic enterprise.

Had Chase been a competent financier instead of constitutional lawyer, he would not have impeded his immediate and proper task—financing—with an attempt at reform which aroused in his own party, to say nothing of the other, more opposition than any other Administration measure had to face during Lincoln's presidency. He would then have understood the extraordinary good fortune wasted on him by two years of crop failure abroad and the unprecedented flood of gold they produced at the one moment in the federal Union's history when it was needed most. He might then have dealt with the banks as a borrower and not as a dictator and have respected the bankers' knowledge of their own business instead of flouting it. He might then have obtained his money sooner, more cheaply, and more abundantly than he did. He might then have lessened the scandal of soldiers' going unpaid. He might then have lessened the difficulties of contractors who were supplying equipment, food, and clothing to the armed forces. He might conceivably have avoided suspension of specie payments instead of driving the banks and the Treasury into it as fast and hard as possible. These successes would have eased the difficulties of paying for the war and might have hastened its end in accord with a statement in the S letters that "success in crushing the rebellion and maintaining the Union is much more a financial than a military question." And they would have been achieved at the sacrifice of an attempt which did no more than complicate an often litigated problem of federal relationships that is now more than a century old, has survived a dozen or so of Supreme Court decisions,* and probably will survive still more.[28]

Had Chase fully succeeded in his effort the immediate effect upon the war would not have been very different from what it was, but the effect on governmental powers—with banking subject to federal regulation only—would have been considerable. Being considerable, it would not have been popular, and the dissatisfaction with such centralization as the Union now enjoys would be greater than it is. On the whole, it seems to me Chase's administration of the Treasury was a misfortune. But in an imperfect world one must put up with a great deal of imperfection. It fostered what is probably the greatest mass of redundant, otiose, and conflicting monetary legislation and the most complex structure of self-neutralizing regulatory powers enjoyed by any prominent country anywhere. It has put the federal government and the states in competition

---

* McCulloch v. Maryland, 1819; Osborn v. United States, 1824; Craig v. Missouri, 1830; Briscoe v. Bank of Kentucky, 1837; Veazie Bank v. Fenno, 1869; Legal Tender Cases, 1870; Juillard v. Greenman, 1884; Norman v. Bank of Ohio, 1935.

for the number and size of banks under their respective jurisdictions and has made insistence on proper practice most firmly exacting only when the authority concerned is embarrassed by institutions that it wishes would for God's sake creep into a rival jurisdiction to die.

As an alternative to the arrangement he recommended, Chase might have agreed with Spaulding and Morrill that a return to the simple and efficient regulatory action of the Bank of the United States was better; but perhaps he thought that federal adoption of a measure already familiar to most of the states and not reminiscent of a prolonged and bitter controversy would be more acceptable. Whether it would have been no one knows.

Since federal regulatory power is now mostly extended over corporations which are not chartered by the federal government itself but by individual states, it may also be thought that Chase should have proposed such an arrangement and not one concerned only with banks that obtained federal charters. Nothing of the sort seems to have occurred to him and his associates. They thought of money as comprising coin and circulating notes only—not checks against deposits at all. They were taking over a state law and followed its terms except where there was some obvious reason for doing otherwise. Moreover, though federal authority to regulate interstate commerce was clearly recognized and in a limited way exercised, banking was then considered in the courts and by legislators as related more closely to the federal government's monetary responsibilities under the Constitution than to its responsibilities with respect to interstate commerce, as the courts nowadays seem inclined to think. Being a federal concern, the monetary function of banks seemed to Secretary Chase and his congressional partners something whose alienation from federal control must be disciplined along with secession and slavery. Practically and morally, secession and slavery were far greater evils than neglect or misplacement of monetary control. And though it might be logical to undertake both reforms at the same time, it was not expedient. The monetary reform was not merely unnecessary but misguided and perturbing. It hindered preservation of the Union and suppression of slavery. But to the nationalist it was logical, and in his enthusiasm for federal sovereignty he persuaded himself that it was necessary. Had Charles Dunbar been in Washington he might perhaps have caught the fever and joined with Chase, with Hooper, with John Sherman, with Robert Walker, and with President Lincoln. Instead he was in an editor's chair in Boston, and despite his allegiance to the main objectives of the Administration, he did not overlook the fact that the North's existing financial apparatus was adequate and lay at hand, despite imperfection in its constitutional status. It needed only to be used sensibly, as it stood, without controversial overhauling and without untimely angry efforts to put the states where they belonged in relation to federal sovereignty. The immediate result of the program questioned by Dunbar was mischievous complication of the federal effort. Its lasting result is the stultifying bureaucratic complex of matchless redundancy with which the country is still blest.

CONCLUSION

I

THE FEDERAL program of war-time financing may be said to have ended formally with John B. Alley's resolution of 18 December 1865 concurring with the opinion of the Secretary of the Treasury, Hugh McCulloch, that the time had come for retirement of the greenbacks, issue of which Alley himself had been the first to recommend in Congress almost four years before. The resolution, eight months after Appomattox, expressed the opinion of Congress about "the necessity of a contraction of the currency with a view to as early a resumption of specie payments as the business interests of the country will permit" and pledged "cooperative action to this end as speedily as practicable." The resolution was adopted by a vote of 144 to 6, with 34 members not voting.[1]

In proposing this resolution Mr. Alley was consistent with his outline, 23 January 1862, of a program of recovery from the appalling situation into which a stunted federal government had been pitched by its unreadiness to do what it had committed itself to do, by the luckless incidents extending from Bull Run through Ball's Bluff to the *Trent* crisis, and by Secretary Chase's wayward performance at the Treasury. The program was to begin with monetization of the government's IOU's—a fiat giving legality to a situation lawless and chaotic. This legal tender act was prelusive in Alley's outline, as in reality, to a second act providing revenue, which so far had been growing less not more as need increased, and to a third act which would provide a uniform national currency. The first of these three, the legal tender act—which was probably suggested in discussions between metropolitan bankers and members of Ways and Means—was an orderly and realistic but disguised acknowledgment of bankruptcy. It protected both creditor and debtor from a further worsening of their situation. In no one's mind was it a means of getting something for

355

nothing. The alternative to it was federal acquiescence in the Southern states' secession and a mustering out of the Union's armed forces.*

Alley's resolution, adopted almost unanimously, came to naught. Contraction of the currency was feared, especially in the West, where agrarians inoculated a generation before with Jacksonian distrust of an aggrandized federal government and of paper money, emerged from the war years with enthusiastic faith both in such government and in such money. There followed the legal tender controversy, dominant in politics till the beginning of the next century and flaring up in its first three decades as late as Franklin D. Roosevelt's presidency. The men responsible for the original legal tender act of 25 February 1862 had no notion whatever of the eventual enthusiasm for greenbacks as a permanent currency and substitute for interest-bearing governmental debt. Their regret in recognizing the necessity was better disciplined than the blind opposition of those who refused to recognize that necessity; and the former's regret continued in opposition to perpetuation of the greenbacks, whereas many of the latter original opponents became ardent supporters of their perpetuation. The example of George Pendleton of Ohio, was notable; in February 1862 he gave Congress the best statement it heard against the legal tenders, on constitutional and material grounds, but six years later he became a leading greenbacker and had his proposal to pay the national debt in greenbacks accepted as a prominent tenet of the Democratic party.[2]

* It is remarkable how Henry Adams, by doctrinaire inattention to the facts, by picturesque language, and by regard only for a fixed notion of his own, should have riveted upon the minds of 19th-century historians and economists the credulous conviction that the resort to legal tender notes in 1862 was but an ignorant attempt by stupid men to finance the war without paying for it and that it was a disaster, wilful and unnecessary, of lasting magnitude, and worse for the Union than any military disaster. (Henry Adams, 279-86, 296, 300, 309-10; W. C. Mitchell, 49, 66-67, 275-76, 279, 419-20; B. Hammond, *AHR*, LXVII [October 1961], pp. 1-18.)

II

Of the eight presidential Administrations preceding Abraham Lincoln's, six were Democratic (though Andrew Jackson clung to his party's original name—"Republican") and only two were Whig. All six put first the principle of states' rights and confined the federal government strictly to those powers assigned to it by the Constitution, all else not specifically renounced by the states being left to them. Jackson and Van Buren had been voluble and active against the evil of centralization during their presidencies, and in 1840 the party drew up a statement of their principles stated succinctly in nine brief paragraphs. The federal government was pronounced to be "one of limited powers, derived solely from the Constitution," the provisions of which should be "strictly construed"; the federal government should abstain from "a general system of internal improvements"; and should not help the individual states engage in them or foster particular industries; it should practice the most rigid economy; it had no power to charter a national bank, or have anything to do with banks; it must refrain from interference in the institution of the states, the latter being "the sole and proper judges of everything appertaining to their own affairs"; it must not "interfere with questions of slavery" or "take incipient steps in relation thereto." These negations and restrictions on the federal government first adopted in 1840 were repeated verbatim in 1844, 1848, 1852, and 1856, and in 1860 were again affirmed in the belief "that Democratic principles are unchangeable" with respect to the matters mentioned. Meanwhile the Whigs and the new Republican parties in their "platforms" had never rebutted what the Democrats averred; they had given instead the impression of merely being less concerned and vehement about the matter. This, presumably, was because Southern Democrats, angered and alarmed by the intensification of Northern hostility

357

toward their "peculiar institution," kept pushing the party into more truculent attitudes. It was only in respect to slavery that the North repugned states' rights, and there the conflict had been confused in principle by outrage at the fugitive slave act. The act was federal, though the interest behind it was that of the slave states, which used both the principle of states' sovereignty and also the force of federal law in defending the rights of slave-holders and frustrating the efforts of slaves to flee and of Northern sympathizers to protect them. Simultaneously, such interests as the North otherwise had in national sovereignty were compromised by Northern efforts to frustrate the fugitive slave act itself. People who were clearly decided against slavery, morally and economically, fumbled in confusion over the choice of means—federal or state—to employ against it.[3]

This complication repeated a similar one in 1819 and 1824 when Maryland and Ohio, in the forefront of those states exacerbated by the presence in their sovereign borders of an alien, federal Bank of the United States, sought by taxation and withdrawal of police and court protection to impede the work of the Bank. Not only was the conflict of states and federal sovereignty the same as before; the terms of state law intended to frustrate the fugitive slave act were based on those of the earlier state laws intended to frustrate the federal Bank decades earlier. As became obvious when the 37th Congress wrestled about financial measures in support of the Union which met resistance from Republicans as well as Democrats, the Northern states were as jealous as the Southern concerning their rights under that reading of the Constitution which, with the influence of Jefferson, Jackson, and Van Buren had prevailed since the century began. It was first in respect to slavery and in recoil from the fugitive slave act, the Dred Scott decision, and bloody murder in Kansas, that there developed in the North the positive nationalist sentiment which displaced the equally positive and intransigent states' rights sentiment which in the South led into secession.

The South's rebellion was an extreme version of what New England had been tempted to do in 1812 about the second war with Great Britain; of what Maryland, Ohio, Kentucky tried to do in 1818-1825 about the federal Bank of the United States; and of what Ohio, Massachusetts, and Wisconsin did with the fugitive slave act between 1850 and 1859. All were results of the tensions to which federal forms of union are liable. The American Union had been an object of professed sentiment, trusted with little power. The Americans themselves, yearning for wealth, magnitude, and limitless freedom, had been like men in skiffs rowing with all their might toward destinations which, facing backwards, they could not see. But Southern secession, though in principle another instance of a minority's dissatisfaction, was far more bitter than any preceding it. So, threatened with disunion as never before, a far more intense nationalist reaction arose. It was both emotional and practical. It accepted the horrid necessity, if the Union were to be preserved, of arming it with powers which appalled its members and impaired the powers traditionally their own. It was in recognition of such a necessity that John Sherman denounced in the Senate the spirit of states' rights as "the evil of the times, that principle of state rights, that bad sentiment that has elevated state authority above the great national authority," and "the main instrument" by which the national government was "sought to be overthrown"—words which echoed those of the S letter written in Washington a fortnight before denouncing the opposition to the national bank measure for its assertion, "in new form," of "the accursed heresy of State Sovereignty lying at the foundation of the slave-holders' rebellion."[4]

III

The legal tender and revenue acts of February and June 1862, and the national currency act of February 1863, had already pushed the exercise of federal power beyond precedent in any field. In these acts the 37th Congress had advanced federal power over the Northern states no less than over the Southern; though this was not so apparent as it has subsequently become. The general impression then was that the North was asserting its will against the South, as indeed it had been doing. But fundamentally the federal government had asserted its will over any and all states. As between North and South, the Constitution took no cognizance. And now, a century later, disaffection with aggrandized federal power is mainly topical; it is regional only incidentally.

The measures dealt with in the preceding chapters directly concerned the purse, which, with the sword, is one of the two basic supports of sovereignty. But other measures of the 37th Congress which impinged similarly on federal and state powers and prestige were the Morrill land grant act for colleges, the act incorporating the Pacific railway, the homestead act, and the national bankruptcy act. In these measures, basic and lasting federal powers were realized. Though war-time enactments they were permanent measures whose purposes and powers were undiminished by peace. "We the People of the United States, in Order to form a more perfect Union, establish Justice, insure domestic Tranquillity, provide for the common defense, promote the general Welfare, and secure the Blessings of Liberty," were putting upon the federal government tangible duties read into the language of 1789 but never before recognized or exercised as in 1861 they began to be. Contemporary executive action, as in the suspension of *habeas corpus* writs in 1861 and the emancipation of slaves in 1863, paralleled legislative action.

Following the war and "reconstruction" of the South, other enactments eventually brought a lengthening train of new responsibilities to the federal government, in respect to interstate commerce, transportation, trade, police powers, education, social security, *et cetera*. The trend reached a new plane of ecumenical sweep in the Employment Act of 1946, in which it was declared to be "the continuing policy and responsibility of the federal government" to foster and promote "the general welfare . . . maximum employment, production, and purchasing power."*

This development begun a century ago has been attended by court decisions sometimes restraining but more often supporting and instigating it, as in *Veazie Bank* v. *Fenno* immediately after the War and in the recent school segregation and "one man, one vote" cases. In the period before Roger Taney's Chief Justiceship, the Supreme Court under John Marshall had upheld federal powers again and again. But it had merely held the fort, so to speak; it had turned no tide. The later legislative and court efforts of Northern states to frustrate the fugitive slave act of 1850, a federal statute, had been based pertinaciously on the earlier efforts of several states to frustrate the federal statute of 1816 chartering the Bank of the United States and the Supreme Court's decisions in 1819 and 1824 upholding it.[5]

As this is being written the highest court in the state of New York has ruled that national banks are in no real sense instrumentalities of the federal government and exempt from taxation by the states. This is an extraordinary affirmation of states' rights, defying the federal decision in *McCulloch* v. *Maryland*, 1819, forbidding state interference with federal legislation and giving tit for tat to the *Veazie Bank* v. *Fenno* decision, 1869, which upheld the fed-

* The Employment Act of 1946 begins with the following "Declaration of Policy," in quoting which I have taken the liberty of stressing certain passages:

"The Congress hereby declares that it is the *continuing policy and responsibility of the Federal Government* to use all practicable means consistent with its needs and obligations and other essential considerations of national policy, with the assistance and cooperation of industry, agriculture, labor, and state and local governments, to *coordinate and utilize all its plans, functions, and resources for the purpose of creating and maintaining, in a manner calculated to foster and promote free competitive enterprise and the general welfare*, conditions under which there will be afforded useful employment opportunities, including self-employment, for those able, willing, and seeking to work, and *to promote maximum employment, production, and purchasing power*." To what extent this language may put at odds the will of the people and the effective powers of the government I do not enquire.

eral power to tax state banks to death. For if the New York decision stands, the states have the same power to frustrate federal legislation that the national government has to frustrate state legislation. Such a situation, in which state powers and national powers can be used to achieve mutual nullification, is absurd; and the Supreme Court may be expected to avoid the absurdity by reversing the New York decision and maintaining the force of *McCulloch* v. *Maryland* and *Veazie Bank* v. *Fenno.*

Returning to the theme interrupted by the foregoing digression, I venture to observe that the aggrandizement of federal powers has not been brought about by any deliberate purpose pursued by the personnel of the federal government. It is due to the incompetence of the states and municipalities to perform piecemeal the responsibilities required to be performed in an immense homogeneous society. There is nothing near equality in the means of the various states and municipalities; and their populations are too prone to do what every one else is doing, as advertised by the press, the cinema, radio, and television, and made familiar by travel. Resumption of the virtues of provincialism has little chance. Regional responsibility for essential governmental functions will be adequate only when states become assembled in fairly comparable administrative groups numbering but a fraction of the fifty "sovereignties" now ranging fantastically in resources and population. People like to believe that the needs of every community are unique, that each can manage its affairs best, and that the inadequacy of its means is irrelevant.

Meanwhile until some catastrophe changes things, what the Americans have is a government with Hamiltonian powers following Jeffersonian ends, a collocation which would doubtless confound the two geniuses whose principles it reconciles. Neither Hamilton nor Jefferson conceived of power being put to such use. Their respective aims, which seemed to them and to their contemporaries quite disparate and conflicting, continued to seem so till 1861-1862, when a capital decision respecting disunion and slavery had to be made. That decision required a revolutionary change in the nature of the federal government and its relation to the states. The decision, first manifested in the effort to hold Fort Sumter and made effective by subsequent action of the 37th Congress, required abandonment of Jeffersonian and Jacksonian notions of a federal "sovereignty" benignly limited and its replacement in Hamiltonian form by one benignly empowered. The change could not be made without relinquishing convictions which had been long and stoutly held. But it was made.

Thereafter, the new federal sovereignty, having freed the slaves, began to be looked to by others as a savior. The farmers ceased to fear it, as they had been taught by Jefferson and Jackson to do, and instead besought its aid against the railways, the banks, and the "trusts." Labor turned to it for aid against the employer. The growth of population and the fruits of technical skill moulded the nation into greater homogeneity. The parcelling of authority among an increasing number of "sovereign" states varying in population and resources had to give way, irregularly, confusedly, and haltingly, to centralization. For the Civil War had fixed no sharp line dividing authority but had left a recondite, meandering watershed marked by ambiguities at every step. Following such demarcations in an expanding, proliferating economy, the federal government, a human institution, interposes from time to time its more or less uniform authority.

Under the umbrella of democracy, consequently, a peculiar response to authority has arisen—one of less than abject obedience, one of impatience and questioning. All men in the far past accepted taboo as a matter of course, and most in the present still do so. Men once found feudal and ecclesiastical authority congenial, for it gave every one his proper place in an order at once immediate and sublime —an order which men were often dissatisfied with but were slow in becoming disloyal to. *"E'n la sua voluntade è nostra pace"*—in this life as in the next. Men feel little of such spir-

363

itual repose now; and much as they dislike authority they cannot dispense with it.

So long as population continues its unruly, suicidal growth, the need of policing will grow too. And so long as the mania for interference with the natural environment continues to hold the nose of man to the grindstone of technology, only sovereignty can meet the cost. The course that is being run seems ineluctable. One can describe it and deplore it, but any hope of diverting it seems vain, like the fantasies of an old man regretting his loss of the vigor and hopefulness of youth.

NOTES

CHAPTER 1

[1] Acton, *Essays on Freedom and Power*, Ch. VII, 196, 199, 203-12, 240-44, 247-50. *Historical Essays and Studies*, Ch. IV.

[2] *Economist*, 8 Dec 1860, p. 1358; 12 Jan 1861, p. 31; 26 Jan, p. 87; 27 April, p. 450; 4 May, pp. 478-79; 18 May, p. 534. Bagehot, 348, 349ff.

[3] Canadian National Archives, *Baring Papers*, John A. Stevens to Baring Brothers, 15 June 1861. Historical Society of Pennsylvania, *Chase Papers*, John A. Stevens to Baring Brothers, 15 June 1861 (copy). New-York Historical Society, *John A. Stevens Papers* (Manuscript Volume 37), S. P. Chase to J. A. Stevens, 15 June 1861; Baring Brothers to J. A. Stevens, 6 July 1861. (Quoted through the courtesy of the Canadian National Archives, the Historical Society of Pennsylvania, and the New-York Historical Society.)

[4] *Cong Docs*, Serial 1117, 37th Cong 2d Sess, Sen Ex Doc 1, Message of the President, 3 Dec 1862, pp. 90-96.

[5] *Cong Globe*, 37th Cong 2d Sess, 3 Feb 1862, p. 617.

[6] *Economist*, 4 May 1861, p. 479. Trollope, 199.

[7] L. White, 437, 458.

[8] Nevins I, 228-29. Canadian National Archives, *Baring Papers*, John A. Stevens to Baring Brothers, 26 April 1861; to Joshua Bates, 9 Feb 1863.

[9] Richardson III, 298-99.

[10] Wiltse, 69-70. *NY Times*, 26 Feb 1861. *Cong Globe*, 37th Cong 1st Sess, 19, 22 July 1861, pp. 209, 222. B. Hammond, 149-58, 329ff, 429ff.

[11] Benton I, 158.

[12] Jackson v, 503-04. Congress, *Register of Debates*, 23d Cong 1st Sess, 20 June 1834, pp. 4640-41. B. Hammond, 491-92.

[13] 9 *US Statutes* 59, Act, 6 Aug 1846, secs 18, 19. *Cong Docs*, Serial 451, 28th Cong 2d Sess, Sen Ex Doc 88, Secty of Trsy Report, 10 Feb 1845, pp. 1-4. Studenski and Krooss, 119-20.

[14] 9 *US Statutes* 59, Act, 6 Aug 1846, sec 21. *Cong Docs*, Serial 918, 35th Cong 1st Sess, Sen Ex Doc 1, Secty of Trsy Report, 8 Dec 1857, pp. 78-82.

[15] *Ibid.*, Serial 749, 33d Cong 2d Sess, Sen Ex Doc 2, Secty of Trsy Report, 4 Dec 1854, pp. 14-17, 255-75. 9 *US Statutes* 59, Act, 6 Aug 1846, sec 16. 11 *US Statutes* 249, Act, 3 March 1857, sec 2.

[16] *Cong Docs*, Serial 749, 33d Cong 2d Sess, Sen Ex Doc 2, Secty of Trsy Report, 4 Dec 1854, pp. 14-17, 255ff, 271, 275; Serial 1093, 36th Cong 2d Sess, HR Ex Doc 2, Secty of Trsy Report, 4 Dec 1860, p. 10. Porter and Johnson, 2-30.

[17] *Cong Docs*, Serial 487, 29th Cong 1st Sess, HR Ex Doc 226, Secty of Trsy Letter, 7 Aug 1846, p. 15.

[18] Myers I, 174ff. Taus, 268. J. Hammond II, 350-51, 469, 478. Knox, *History of Banking*, 86-87. Kinley, 53ff.

[19] Lincoln I, 164, 209-10, 226.

[20] *Cong Docs*, Serial 1112, 37th Cong 1st Sess, Sen Ex Doc 1, Message of the President, 4 July 1861, p. 14.
[21] Dunbar, 294, 298-301. *Cong Docs*, Serial 1093, 36th Cong 2d Sess, HR Ex Doc 2, Secty of Trsy Report, 4 Dec 1860, pp. 7-8.
[22] McCulloch, 138-39.
[23] Dunbar, 303-07. *Economist*, 8 Dec 1860, pp. 1357-59.
[24] J. Davis I, 320-21. Rhodes III, 118, 126, 198, 234-35. *War of the Rebellion* I, 110. *Cong Globe*, 36th Cong 2d Sess, 24 Dec 1860, p. 190.
[25] J. Davis I, 209-13. *War of the Rebellion* I, 111, 115-18, 120-25; Rhodes III, 215, 222-25.
[26] Bayley, 75-76. Studenski and Krooss, 138.
[27] *NY Herald*, 14 Feb 1861. *NY Times*, 13, 14 Feb 1861. *Cong Globe*, 36th Cong 2d Sess, 12 Feb 1861, pp. 871-72; 13 Feb,

p. 893. Sherman I, 252-53. Bolles, 4-5. Bayley, 76.
[28] *Cong Docs*, Serial 1093, 36th Cong 2d Sess, HR Ex Doc 2, Secty of Trsy Report, 4 Dec 1860, pp. 7-9; Serial 1103, 36th Cong 2d Sess, HR Misc Doc 20, Secty of Trsy Letter, 18 Jan 1861, p. 5; Serial 1100, 36th Cong 2d Sess, HR Ex Doc 72, Secty of Trsy Letter, 21 Feb 1861, pp. 1-3, 23-26. Knox, *US Notes*, 76-78.
[29] *Cong Docs*, Serial 1103, 36th Cong 2d Sess, HR Misc Doc 20, Secty of Trsy Letter, Jan 1861, pp. 6-7. Bayley, 76. *NY Times*, 2, 3 March 1861.
[30] *Cong Docs*, Serial 1100, 36th Cong 2d Sess, HR Ex Doc 72, Secty of Trsy Letter, 21 Feb 1861, pp. 23-24. *NY Herald*, 4, 5 Feb 1861. Dix I, 370-73.
[31] Schuckers, 207-08. Donald, 1.

CHAPTER 2

[1] Richardson VI, 13-19, 24-26. Nevins I, 91. Ropes I, 111-12.
[2] *Cong Docs*, Serial 1112, 37th Cong 1st Sess, Sen Ex Doc 1, Message of the President, 4 July 1861, pp. 7, 10.
[3] *Ibid.*, Secty of War Report, 1 July 1861, p. 20; Secty of Navy Report, 4 July, p. 93; Sen Ex Doc 2, Secty of Trsy Report, 4 July, p. 6.
[4] *Economist*, 8 Dec 1860, p. 1357.
[5] ASP VI, Finance II, pp. 248, 309, 374, 497, 524-25.
[6] *Cong Docs*, Serial 1112, 37th Cong 1st Sess, Sen Ex Doc 2, Secty of Trsy Report, 4 July 1861, pp. 6-8.

[7] *Ibid.*, pp. 8-10.
[8] *Ibid.*, pp. 11-13.
[9] *Ibid.*, pp. 12-13.
[10] *Ibid.*, pp. 12-14.
[11] LC, *Chase Papers*, George, D. Lyman to Chase, 20 June 1861; Charles A. Davis to Chase, 28 June.
[12] *NY Times*, 8 July 1861. *NY Herald*, 7 July. *NY Tribune*, 7, 8 July. *Independent*, 11 July.
[13] *NY Times*, 2, 8, 9, 10, 11 July 1861. *NY Herald*, 13 July.
[14] *NY Times*, 12 July 1861. *Cong Globe*, 37th Cong 1st Sess, 10 July 1861, p. 61.
[15] *NY Times*, 13 July 1861. 12 *US Statutes* 259, Act, 17 July 1861.

16 *Cong Docs*, Serial 1121, 37th Cong 2d Sess, Sen Ex Doc 2, Secty of Trsy Report, 9 Dec 1861, pp. 7-8.

17 *NY Times*, 22 July 1861. *NY Herald*, 24 July.

18 12 *US Statutes* 292, Act, 5 Aug 1861; 432, Act, 1 July 1862.

19 *Cong Docs*, Serial 8573, 69th Cong 1st Sess, House Doc 398, *Formation of the Union*, pp. 363-64, 580. Hamilton (Lodge) VIII, 381. Dunbar, 94-115. *Cong Globe*, 37th Cong 1st Sess, 24 July 1861, pp. 248-50, 273; 29 July, p. 330. 3 Dallas (US) 171; 157 US 429; 158 US 601. Story I, 668-74. Seligman, Chs. IV, V, *passim*.

20 *Cong Docs*, Serial 1112, 37th Cong 1st Sess, Sen Ex Doc 2, Secty of Trsy Report, 4 July 1861, pp. 6, 9.

21 Taussig, 158-59. Dewey, 300. *Cong Globe*, 37th Cong 1st Sess, 17, 18 July 1861, pp. 171, 174-76, 202-05.

22 1 *US Statutes* 580, Act, 9 July 1798; 597, Act, 14 July. 3 *US Statutes* 22, Act, 22 July 1813; 53, Act, 2 Aug; 164, Act, 9 Jan 1815; 255, Act, 5 March 1816. 12 *US Statutes* 294, sec 6. *Cong Globe*, 37th Cong 1st Sess, 24 July 1861, pp. 246-52; 25 July, pp. 269-74; 26 July, pp. 280-87; 27 July, pp. 299-308; 29 July, pp. 323-31. Dunbar, 98-101. Studenski and Krooss, 75-78. Balinky, 167.

23 *Cong Globe*, 37th Cong 1st Sess, 24 July 1861, pp. 249-52; 25 July, p. 268. *Ibid.*, 2nd Sess, 13 March 1862, pp. 1226-27.

24 *Ibid.*, 1st Sess, 25 July 1861, pp. 269-74; 27 July, pp. 299-308; 29 July, pp. 323-31; 30 July, p. 354. Ratner, 54-56.

25 *Cong Globe*, 37th Cong 1st Sess, 19 July 1861, p. 208; 24 July, p. 244; 25 July, pp. 253-55; 26 July, pp. 278-79; 27 July, p. 297; 29 July, pp. 313-23; 30 July, pp. 335-36, 354.

26 *Ibid.*, 2 Aug 1861, pp. 395-96, 415.

27 *Ibid.*, pp. 395-400, 415-16.

28 *Ibid.*, 10 July 1861, pp. 57-58; 2 Aug, pp. 396, 399, 400.

29 *Ibid.*, 24 July 1861, p. 251.

30 *NY Times*, 22, 23, 24, 27, 29, 30 July 1861.

31 LC, *Chase Papers*, Simeon Nash to Chase, 18 July 1861.

32 *Ibid.*, Nash to Chase, 18 July 1861, 27 Aug, 17 Sept, 11 Nov; Davis B. Lawler to Chase, 17 Sept; Enoch T. Carson to Chase, 19 Sept; Joshua Hanna to Chase, 28 Sept.

33 US National Archives, Trsy Records, Corr with Committees, Vol. V, 1860-64, p. 201, Chase to Fessenden, 26 July 1861.

34 Spaulding, Introduction, 1-2; Appendix, 51-52.

35 *Ibid.*

36 *Cong Globe*, 37th Cong 1st Sess, 1 Aug 1861, p. 383.

37 *Ibid.*, pp. 373-74, 383; 2 Aug, pp. 396-97.

38 12 *US Statutes* 313-14 Ch. XLVI.

39 *NY Times*, 2, 3, 4, 5 Aug 1861.

40 *Ibid.*, 3, 5 Aug 1861. *NY Tribune*, 5 Aug.

41 *NY Herald*, 3, 5, 8, 9 Aug 1861.

42 *Journal of Commerce*, 2, 5, 13 Aug 1861.

43 *Ibid.*, 15 Aug 1861. *Independent*, 8 Aug.

44 *Boston Daily Advertiser*, 2, 5, 8, 15, 21 Aug 1861. Dunbar, vii-ix.

CHAPTER 3

[1] *Cong Docs*, Serial 1121, 37th Cong 2d Sess, Sen Ex Doc 2, Secty of Trsy Report, 9 Dec 1861, p. 8.
[2] Bolles, 20. Spaulding, Appendix, 89-91.
[3] *NY Times*, 24, 25 June 1861; 2 July; 13, 17, 19, 20 Aug. *NY Herald*, 1, 7, 9, 15 July; 14 Aug. *Journal of Commerce*, 18 Sept. *Bankers' Mag*, July 1861, pp. 78-79.
[4] *NY Times*, 20 Aug 1861. Appleton's *Cyclopedia* 1861, p. 63. *Bankers' Mag*, Oct 1861, p. 318; May 1863, p. 900. *Merchants' Mag*, March 1862, p. 277. *Cong Docs*, Serial 1149, 37th Cong 3d Sess, Sen Ex Doc 1, Secty of Trsy Report, 4 Dec 1862, p. 227.
[5] *NY Times*, 22 July 1861; 10 Aug. *NY Herald*, 12, 13, 14 Aug. *Independent*, 8, 22 Aug.
[6] Gibbons, 60. B. Hammond, 699-700.
[7] Spaulding, Appendix, 89-90. *Bankers' Mag*, Aug 1862, p. 136. Nevins i, Ch. 16.
[8] Spaulding, Appendix, 91. *Journal of Commerce*, 15 Aug 1861. *Lippincott's* xxxviii, Aug 1886, pp. 200-06.
[9] Spaulding, Appendix, 85, 91. *Boston Daily Advertiser*, 2, 5, 15 Aug 1861.
[10] LC, *Chase Papers*, Simeon Nash to Chase, 17 Sept 1861. Schuckers, 277-78. *Cong Docs*, Serial 1149, 37th Cong 3d Sess, Sen Ex Doc 1, Secty of Trsy Report, 4 Dec 1862, p. 14. *Cong Globe*, 37th Cong 2d Sess, 20 Feb 1862, p. 899; *Ibid.*, 3d Sess, Appendix, 8 Jan 1863, p. 48. Sherman i, 254, 269.
[11] *Boston Daily Advertiser*, 15 Aug 1861. *Journal of Commerce*, 15 Aug.
[12] Spaulding, Appendix, 97.
[13] Warden, 387-88.
[14] *Ibid.*, 386-87.
[15] Spaulding, Appendix, 97. Mitchell, 25-28. McCulloch, 135. *Bankers' Mag*, Feb. 1862, pp. 626, 632; Aug, pp. 135ff.
[16] *NY Times*, 5, 14 Aug 1861. *NY Herald*, 23 Sept.
[17] Spaulding, Appendix, 90. *NY Herald*, 14 Aug 1861; 3 Oct. *Boston Daily Advertiser*, 13, 15, 19, 20, 21, 23 Aug. *Bankers' Mag*, Sept 1861, pp. 161ff. Appleton's *Cyclopedia* 1861, pp. 295ff.
[18] *NY Times*, 16, 17, 19 Aug 1861. *Bankers' Mag*, Sept 1861, pp. 161ff; Feb 1862, p. 626.
[19] *NY Times*, 16 17, 19 Aug 1861. *Independent*, 22 Aug. *Bankers' Mag*, Aug 1862, pp. 135ff. *Cong Docs*, Serial 1121, 37th Cong 2d Sess, Sen Ex Doc 2, Secty of Trsy Report, 9 Dec 1861, pp. 8-9. Bolles, 24, 31-33.
[20] *Cong Docs*, Serial 1161, 37th Cong 3d Sess, HR Ex Doc 25, Condition of Banks Report, 31 Dec 1862, p. 134 (NY Loan Committee). *Bankers' Mag*, Aug 1862, pp. 135, 146.
[21] State of Ohio, Ex Docs, vol 20, part i, Public Doc 4, *Inaugural Address of Salmon P. Chase*, 14 Jan 1856, p. 39. Schuckers, 278-79. *Cong Docs*, Serial 1121, 37th Cong 2d Sess, Sen Ex Doc 2, Secty of Trsy Report, 9 Dec 1861, p. 17.
[22] Hamilton (Lodge) i, 307. LC, *James K. Polk Papers*, John Catron to Polk, 11 Sept 1837, 2 Jan 1842. Sellers, 321.
[23] *Cong Docs*, Serial 1121, 37th Cong 2d Sess, Sen Ex Doc 2, Secty of Trsy Report, 9 Dec 1861, p. 18.
[24] *NY Herald*, 5, 15 Oct 1861. *Journal of Commerce*, 12, 13, 16,

17 Aug. *Independent*, 15 Aug. LC, *Chase Papers*, S. A. Mercer to Chase, 23 Sept 1861. Spaulding, Appendix, 92. Bolles, 27-31.
[25] *NY Herald*, 9, 12, 15 Aug 1861; 1, 4, 5, 16 Oct. *NY Tribune*, 6 Aug.
[26] *NY Times*, 19 Aug 1861; 30 Sept.
[27] *NY Tribune*, 25 Jan 1862.
[28] *Bankers' Mag*, Oct 1861, pp. 311-13.
[29] Spaulding, Introduction, 2-3; Appendix, 51-52, 91-92.
[30] *Ibid. Boston Daily Advertiser*, 15 Aug 1861. *Independent*, Aug.
[31] Spaulding, Introduction, 2.
[32] *Cong Globe*, 37th Cong 2d

Sess, 20 Feb 1862, p. 899; *Ibid.*, 3d Sess, Appendix, 8 Jan 1863, p. 48; 10 Feb, p. 841. Sherman I, 254-55, 269.
[33] Bolles, 25-29.
[34] H. White (1st ed., 1896), 150-51; (4th ed., 1911), 107-08.
[35] Sherman I, 269.
[36] Sumner, 450-60.
[37] Knox, *History of Banking*, 135.
[38] Dewey, 279, 282-83.
[39] Mitchell, 25-26, 35-37. *JPE* VII, (June 1899), pp. 309ff.
[40] Hepburn, *History of Coinage and Currency*, 181-82; *History of Currency*, 183-84.
[41] Redlich, Part II, 92-93.

CHAPTER 4

[1] *Cong Docs*, Serial 1121, 37th Cong 2d Sess, Sen Ex Doc 2, Secty of Trsy Report, 9 December 1861, p. 9. *Bankers' Mag*, Sept 1861, pp. 161-70; Aug 1862, pp. 135-50.
[2] *Ibid.*, Oct 1861, pp. 290-92; Aug 1862, pp. 138-39. *Boston Daily Advertiser*, 11, 25, 26 Sept 1861. *Journal of Commerce*, 17 Aug 1861.
[3] LC, *Chase Papers*, Simeon Nash to Chase, 17 Sept 1861; 11 Nov.
[4] *Ibid.*, David B. Lawler to Chase, 17 Sept 1861; Enoch T. Carson to Chase, 19 Sept; Joshua Hanna to Chase, 28 Sept.
[5] *Ibid.*, James Gordon Bennett to Chase, 9 Sept 1861.
[6] *NY Herald*, 30 Sept 1861. *Independent*, 3 Oct.
[7] *NY Herald*, 30 Sept 1861. *NY Times*, 30 Sept. *Journal of Commerce*, 1 Oct.
[8] Spaulding, Appendix, 97-99.

[9] *Ibid.*, 89-96. *Bankers' Mag*, Sept 1861, pp. 224-26; Aug 1862, pp. 138-39. *Cong Docs*, Serial 1121, 37th Cong 2d Sess, Sen Ex Doc 2, Secty of Trsy Report, 9 Dec 1861, pp. 9-10; Serial 1161, 37th Cong 3d Sess, HR Ex Doc 25, Condition of Banks Report, 31 Dec 1862, pp. 127, 130, 134-35 (NY Loan Committee); Serial 1193, 38th Cong 1st Sess, HR Ex Doc 66, Secty of Trsy Letter, 2 Apr 1864, pp. 1-2.
[10] *NY Herald*, 7, 10, 16, 17, 30 Sept 1861; 4, 5 Oct. *NY Times*, 4, 12, 17, 23, 30 Sept. *Boston Daily Advertiser*, 4 Sept; 4 Oct.
[11] Field, 255, 256.
[12] *NY Herald*, 2, 10, 17, 23, 30 Sept 1861; 3, 7, 15 Oct. *NY Times*, 12, 13, 14, 16, 30 Aug; 17, 23, 30 Sept.
[13] Appleton's *Cyclopedia* 1861, pp. 63-65. Rodkey, 375-82. 86 Massachusetts Reports (4 Allen)

1-16, *Commonwealth* v. *Bank of Mutual Redemption.*

[14] *Cong Docs,* Serial 1161, 37th Cong 3d Sess, HR Ex Doc 25, Condition of Banks Report, 31 Dec 1862, pp. 126ff (NY Loan Committee); pp. 48ff (Mass. Bank Commissioners). *Bankers' Mag,* Dec 1861, pp. 462-65; July 1862, pp. 135ff (NY Loan Committee Report). *NY Times,* 17 Sept 1861.

[15] *Cong Docs,* Serial 1328, 40th Cong 2d Sess, HR Ex Doc 2, Secty of Trsy Report, 30 Nov 1867, pp. 395-96.

[16] *NY Herald,* 1 July 1861. *Appleton's Cyclopedia* 1861, p. 304. *Cong Docs,* Serial 1149, 37th Cong 3d Sess, Sen Ex Doc 1, Secty of Trsy Report, 4 Dec 1862, p. 243.

[17] *NY Herald,* 22 July 1861; 9, 14, 21 Aug; 2, 3, 7, 10, 16, 17, 23, 30 Sept; 3, 7, 15, 22 Oct; 18, 19, 27 Nov.

[18] Nichols, 439-40. *Journal of Commerce,* 12, 15, 18, 20, 30 Sept 1861; 1, 15, 23 Oct.

[19] *NY Times,* 8 Oct 1861. *Boston Daily Advertiser,* 5, 9, 12, 24 Oct; 4, 6, 7, 8, 9, 11 Nov. *Bankers' Mag,* Oct 1861, p. 318.

[20] *Boston Daily Advertiser,* 24 Oct 1861; 4, 6, 7, 8, 11, 13, 20, 21 Nov.

[21] *NY Herald,* 18, 19, 21, 22, 26, 27, 28 Nov 1861. *Journal of Commerce,* 20, 21, 22, 23, 25, 26 Nov.

[22] *Boston Daily Advertiser,* 18 Nov 1861. *Journal of Commerce,* 18, 21, 23, 26, 30 Nov.

[23] *NY Herald,* 21, 22, 26, 28 Nov 1861. *NY Times,* 14 Dec. *Journal of Commerce,* 18, 20, 21, 23, 25, 26, 27, 30 Nov. *Independent,* 21 Nov. *Boston Daily Advertiser,* 19, 21 Nov; 4, 6, 7, 9, 11, 12 Dec.

[24] *NY Herald,* 4 Nov 1861. *Appleton's Cyclopedia* 1861, pp. 299, 304.

[25] Schuckers, 277-78, 430-31. Wolseley, 3, 34, 38.

[26] *NY Herald,* 30 Oct 1861.

[27] LC, *Chase Papers,* Governor E. D. Morgan to Chase, 28 Oct 1861.

[28] *Journal of Commerce,* 19, 22, 30 Nov 1861. *NY Herald,* 15 Nov. LC, *Chase Papers,* E. B. Washburne to Chase, 31 Oct 1861; E. W. Dunham to Chase, 21 Dec.

CHAPTER 5

[1] *Boston Daily Advertiser,* 16, 17 Dec 1861.

[2] *NY Herald,* 18, 19, 21 Nov 1861.

[3] *Ibid.,* 7, 10, 11, 12, 13 Dec 1861.

[4] *Boston Daily Advertiser,* 17, 18, 19 Dec 1861.

[5] *Ibid.,* 23, 25 Dec 1861.

[6] *Cong Docs,* Serial 1121, 37th Cong 2d Sess, Sen Ex Doc 2, Secty of Trsy Report, 9 Dec 1861, pp. 9-10.

[7] *Ibid.,* pp. 11, 14, 15.

[8] *Cong Docs,* Serial 1118, 37th Cong 2d Sess, Sen Ex Doc 1, Secty of War Report, 1 Dec 1861, pp. 5, 10; Serial 1121, 37th Cong 2d Sess, Sen Ex Doc 2, Secty of Trsy Report, 9 Dec 1861, pp. 11-12.

[9] *Cong Docs,* Serial 1112, 37th Cong 1st Sess, Sen Ex Doc 1,

Message of the President, 4 July 1861, pp. 10-11; Sen Ex Doc 2, Secty of Trsy Report, 4 July 1861, pp. 6-8; Serial 1121, 37th Cong 2d Sess, Sen Ex Doc 2, Secty of Trsy Report, 9 Dec 1861, pp. 9-10, 14.

[10] *Ibid.*, pp. 12-16, 18-20.

[11] *Ibid.*, pp. 19-20.

[12] *Ibid.*, pp. 17, 20. Sherman I, 298.

[13] *Cong Docs*, Serial 1121, 37th Cong 2d Sess, Sen Ex Doc 2, Secty of Trsy Report, 9 Dec 1861, pp. 18-20; Serial 1149, 37th Cong 3d Sess, Sen Ex Doc 1, Secty of Trsy Report, 4 Dec 1862, pp. 16-17.

[14] Spaulding, 11-13.

[15] *NY Times*, 24 June 1861; 12 July; 19 Aug. *NY Tribune*, 6 Aug. A. M. Davis, 44ff. Schuckers, 279. LC, *Chase Papers*, John W. Caldwell to Chase, 22 Oct 1861.

[16] *NY Herald*, 9, 10, 12 Aug 1861. *Journal of Commerce*, 12 Aug.

[17] *Bankers' Mag*, Dec 1861, p. 404.

[18] *Journal of Commerce*, 15 Nov 1861. *NY Times*, 2 Dec. *NY Herald*, 2, 5, 6, 7, 13, 16 Dec. *NY Tribune*, 7, 24, 25 Dec. *Economist*, 28 Dec 1861, p. 1430.

[19] *Boston Daily Advertiser*, 11, 12, 13 Dec 1861.

[20] *Cong Docs*, Serial 1161, 37th Cong 3d Sess, HR Ex Doc 25, Condition of Banks Report, 31 Dec 1862, pp. 93ff (State of NY Banks).

[21] *Ibid.*, pp. 94-96.

[22] *Ibid.*, pp. 97-98.

[23] *Ibid.*, p. 98.

[24] B. Hammond, Ch. 4.

[25] *Journal of Commerce*, 26 Nov 1861. *Bankers' Mag*, Feb. 1862, p. 576.

[26] *Economist*, 23 Nov 1861, p. 1294; 14 Dec, p. 1377; 28 Dec, pp. 1429, 1436.

[27] *NY Times*, 14, 16, 17 Dec 1861. *NY Tribune*, 18 Dec.

[28] *Merchants' Mag*, Jan 1862, pp. 101-02.

[29] *NY Times*, 19 Dec 1861. *NY Herald*, 19 Dec.

[30] *NY Times*, 20 Dec 1861. *NY Tribune*, 19, 20, 24 Dec. *Journal of Commerce*, 19, 20 Dec. *Cong Docs*, Serial 1121, 37th Cong 2d Sess, Sen Ex Doc 2, Secty of Trsy Report, 9 Dec 1861, p. 10. LC, *Chase Papers*, E. W. Dunham to Chase, 21 Dec 1861.

[31] Appleton's *Cyclopedia* 1861, pp. 63, 306. *NY Herald*, 19 Dec 1861. *NY Tribune*, 17, 18, 19 Dec. *NY Times*, 18, 19 Dec. *Bankers' Mag*, Feb 1862, pp. 628-29.

[32] *NY Herald*, 19, 20, 21, 23, 26, 29 Dec 1861.

[33] *Ibid.*, 30 Dec 1861. *NY Tribune*, 30 Dec. *NY Times*, 30 Dec. *Bankers' Mag*, Jan 1862, p. 491.

[34] Spaulding, Appendix, 93-94. Bolles, 36.

[35] *NY Times*, 30 Dec 1861. *NY Herald*, 30 Dec.

[36] *Bankers' Mag*, Jan 1862, pp. 509-10.

[37] *Ibid.*, p. 558.

[38] Spaulding, 7-8.

[39] *Ibid.*, 11-12.

[40] *Ibid.*, 13-14. *NY Tribune*, 31 Dec 1861. *Cong Globe*, 37th Cong 2d Sess, 30 Dec 1861, p. 181.

[41] *NY Herald*, 6, 25 Dec 1861. *NY Tribune*, 24, 25 Dec. 26 Barbour (NY) 304, *Livingston v. Bank of New York*. Schuckers, 243.

[42] *Cong Docs*, Serial 1149, 37th Cong 3d Sess, Sen Ex Doc 1, Secty of Trsy Report, 4 Dec 1862, p. 9.

CHAPTER 6

[1] Spaulding, 15-16.
[2] *Ibid.*, 16. B. Hammond, Ch. 4. *Cong Globe*, 37th Cong 2d Sess, 7 Jan 1862, p. 218.
[3] Spaulding, 18-22. Donald, 62-64. *NY Tribune*, 13 Jan 1862. *NY Herald*, 13, 14, 17 Jan. *NY Times*, 16, 17 Jan.
[4] *Ibid.*, 18 Jan 1862. Spaulding, 20-21.
[5] *Ibid.*, 21-22.
[6] *NY Tribune*, 13, 14, 21, 22 Jan 1862. *NY Times*, 13, 16, 17, 18 Jan. *Cong Globe*, 37th Cong 2d Sess, 15 Jan 1862, pp. 344-49; 17 Jan, pp. 376-77; 21 Jan Appendix, p. 419.
[7] *Ibid.*, 15 Jan 1862, pp. 344, 349.
[8] Spaulding, 26-27.
[9] *Ibid.*, 13-16, 92, 96, 148.
[10] *Ibid.*, 27. *Cong Globe*, 37th Cong 2d Sess, 22 Jan 1862, p. 435.
[11] *Ibid.*, 23 Jan 1862, p. 457. *AHR* LXVII (Oct 1961), pp. 8-9. Donald, 64.
[12] Spaulding, 28.
[13] *Cong Globe*, 37th Cong 2d Sess, 23 Jan 1862, pp. 457-59.
[14] *Ibid.*, pp. 458-59.
[15] *Ibid.*, 38th Cong 1st Sess, 24 March 1864, p. 1267; 6 April, pp. 1449-50.
[16] Spaulding, 22, 27, 45-46. *Cong Globe*, 37th Cong 2d Sess, 22 Jan 1862, pp. 435, 439.
[17] Spaulding, 28ff. *Cong Globe*, 37th Cong 2d Sess, 28 Jan 1862, pp. 523ff.
[18] *Ibid.*, pp. 523-24. Spaulding, 30-33.
[19] *Cong Globe*, 37th Cong 2d Sess, 28 Jan 1862, pp. 524, 526. Spaulding, 33, 37.
[20] *Cong Globe*, 37th Cong 2d Sess, 28 Jan 1862, pp. 524, 526. Spaulding, 35, 39.
[21] *Cong Globe*, 37th Cong 2d Sess, 29 Jan 1862, p. 549.
[22] *Ibid.*, pp. 549-50.
[23] *Ibid.*, pp. 550-51.
[24] *Ibid.*, p. 551.
[25] *Ibid.*, 28 Jan 1862, p. 523; 29 Jan, p. 549; 3 Feb, pp. 617-18. Spaulding, 26-27, 45, 57-60.
[26] *Cong Globe*, 37th Cong 2d Sess, 3 Feb 1862, p. 618. Spaulding, 58-59. Schuckers, 245.
[27] *Ibid.*, 243-45.
[28] Spaulding, 46.
[29] *Cong Globe*, 37th Cong 2d Sess, 4 Feb 1862, p. 634. Spaulding, 60.
[30] *Cong Globe*, 37th Cong 2d Sess, 3 Feb 1862, pp. 615-17, Appendix, 43. *NY Times*, 25 Jan 1862.
[31] *Cong Globe*, 37th Cong 2d Sess, 6 Feb 1862, p. 691.
[32] *Ibid.*, 4 Feb 1862, pp. 629-33.
[33] *Ibid.*, pp. 633-40.
[34] *Ibid.*, 6 Feb 1862, pp. 679-81.
[35] *Ibid.*, pp. 682-84, 691. Dartmouth College Archives, Thomas M. Edwards to Asa D. Smith, 10 Feb 1868.
[36] *Cong Globe*, 37th Cong 2d Sess, 22 Jan 1862, pp. 439, 440; 6 Feb, pp. 687-89. Spaulding, 85.
[37] *Cong Globe*, 37th Cong 2d Sess, 6 Feb 1862, pp. 691, 693.
[38] *Ibid.*, p. 695.
[39] *Ibid.*, pp. 686, 690.
[40] LC, *Chase Papers*, John B. Austin to Chase, 18 Jan 1862.
[41] Warden, 406-07, 409. Historical Society of Pennsylvania, *Chase Papers*, John A. Stevens to Chase, 21 Jan 1862.
[42] Spaulding, 47.
[43] *Ibid.*, Appendix, 57-58.
[44] *Ibid.*, 23, 24, 25. *Bankers' Mag*, Feb 1862, pp. 622-23.

[45] LC, *Chase Papers*, George Opdyke to Chase, 28 Jan 1862.
[46] Warden, 409.
[47] *Independent*, 5, 19, 26 Dec 1861; 30 Jan 1862; 6, 27 Feb.
[48] *NY Times*, 23, 30 Sept 1861; 2, 16, 19, 28, 30, 31 Dec.
[49] *Ibid.*, 6 Jan 1862.

[50] *NY Tribune*, 24, 31 Dec 1861; 11 Jan 1862.
[51] *NY Herald*, 12 Aug 1861; 4, 5, 7, 11, 15 Oct; 2 Dec.
[52] *Ibid.*, 5, 6, 7, 25 Dec 1861; 4 Jan 1862.
[53] *Journal of Commerce*, 2, 5, 10, 12, 13, 15, 16 Aug 1861; 31 Dec.

CHAPTER 7

[1] *Cong Globe*, 37th Cong 2d Sess, 7 Feb 1862, p. 705.
[2] *Ibid.*, 10 Feb 1862, p. 726.
[3] *Ibid.*, 12 Feb 1862, pp. 763ff, 766.
[4] *Ibid.*, p. 764.
[5] *Ibid.*, pp. 763-65.
[6] *Ibid.*, pp. 766, 804; *Ibid.*, 38th Cong 1st Sess, 24 March 1864, p. 1267; 6 April, p. 1449. Blaine I, 423. Fessenden I, 194, 301-02. Spaulding, 195.
[7] *Cong Globe*, 37th Cong 2d Sess, 12, 13 Feb 1862, pp. 767-71, 788.
[8] *Ibid.*, 12 Feb 1862, p. 772, Appendix, pp. 53-55.
[9] *Ibid.*, 13 Feb 1862, pp. 788-89.
[10] *Ibid.*, p. 789.
[11] *Ibid.*, pp. 789-91.
[12] *Ibid.*, pp. 789-90.
[13] *Ibid.*, Appendix, p. 57.
[14] *Ibid.*, Appendix, pp. 58-60.
[15] *Ibid.*, pp. 797-98; Story II, 227.
[16] *Cong Globe*, 37th Cong 2d Sess, 12 Feb 1862, p. 773; 13 Feb, p. 802, Appendix, p. 58.
[17] *Ibid.*, 13 Feb 1862, pp. 800, 804.
[18] *Ibid.*, 18 Feb 1862, p. 874; 19 Feb, pp. 881-83.
[19] *Ibid.*, pp. 886-87.
[20] *Ibid.*, 20 Feb 1862, p. 899.

[21] *Ibid.*, pp. 900-01. Spaulding, 125-32, 141-43.
[22] *Cong Globe*, 37th Cong 2d Sess, 20 Feb 1862, pp. 898-902, 909; 24 Feb. pp. 929, 938-40, 946-48, 953, 976, 994. Spaulding, 148.
[23] *Cong Globe*, 37th Cong 2d Sess, 24 Feb 1862, pp. 929, 938. Spaulding, 148.
[24] Schuckers, 269-70. Spaulding, 100. Appleton's *Cyclopedia* 1862, pp. 454-55. *Cong Globe*, 37th Cong 2d Sess, 13 Feb 1862, pp. 772-73, 802-03; 11 March 1862, pp. 1156, 1162-64. Bayley, 157-58.
[25] 12 US *Statutes* 345, Act, 25 Feb 1862.
[26] *Cong Docs*, Serial 1112, 37th Cong 1st Sess, Sen Ex Doc 1, Message of the President, 4 July 1861, p. 7. 29 US (4 Peters) 433.
[27] *NY Times*, 9, 11, 13, 16, 18, 22, 23, 24, 25, 27, 28, 29, 30 Jan 1862; 3, 5 Feb.
[28] *Ibid.*, 3 Feb 1862.
[29] *Ibid.*, 5, 6 Feb 1862. Gibbons, 60.
[30] *NY Times*, 10 Feb 1862.
[31] *Ibid.*, 27, 28 Feb 1862. *Cong Globe*, 37th Cong 2d Sess, 25 Feb 1862, pp. 945, 954-55. 12 US *Statutes* 352-53, sec xxxv, Act, 1 March 1862.

32 *NY Herald,* 4, 5, 6, 8, 13, 14, 17, 18, 20, 24, 30, 31 Jan 1862; Feb, *passim.*
33 Spaulding, 13. *NY Tribune,* 31 Dec 1861; 21, 25, 27, 29, 31 Jan 1862.

34 *Ibid.,* 1, 10, 18, 19, 26 Feb 1862.
35 *Journal of Commerce,* 31 Dec 1861; 11, 24, 25 Jan 1862; 11 Feb.
36 *Independent,* 19, 26 Dec 1861; 30 Jan 1862; 6, 27 Feb.

CHAPTER 8

1 *NY Times,* 31 Dec 1861. *NY Tribune,* 4 Jan 1862. *Merchants' Mag,* March 1862, p. 309. 79 US (12 Wallace) 577.
2 26 Barbour (NY) 304. *Bankers' Mag,* Nov 1857, pp. 416-17; Feb 1862, pp. 628-29; B. Hammond, 698-99.
3 *NY Herald,* 6 Jan 1862. *NY Times,* 30 Jan; 5 Feb.
4 H. Adams, 279-317. Mitchell, 51ff. *AHR,* LXVII (Oct 1961), p. 1.
5 12 US *Statutes* 259, 338, 370. US National Archives, Trsy Records, Asst Treasurer's Corr, John J. Cisco to Chase, 6 March 1862. *NY Times,* 31 March 1862; 7, 14, 18 April.
6 *Ibid.,* 31 March 1862; 7, 14, 16, 18 April. *Bankers' Mag,* April 1862, pp. 809-11; June, pp. 923-24, 971.
7 *NY Times,* 12 May 1862. *Cong Docs,* Serial 1149, 37th Cong 3d Sess, Sen Ex Doc 1, Secty of Trsy Report, 4 Dec 1862, p. 10.
8 *NY Times,* 21, 30 April 1862; 28, 30 June; 2, 19 July; 24, 25, 26 Aug.
9 *Cong Docs,* Serial 1141, 37th Cong 2d Sess, HR Misc Doc 81, Secty of Trsy Letter, 7 June 1862, pp. 2-4. *NY Times,* 7, 8 April 1862; 8 May; 16 June; 13, 18, 25, 26 Aug.

10 *Cong Globe,* 37th Cong 2d Sess, 17 June 1862, pp. 2766-68; 23 June, pp. 2884, 2885.
11 *NY Times,* 17, 28 June 1862.
12 Coolidge, 12.
13 *Cong Docs,* Serial 1149, 37th Cong 3d Sess, Sen Ex Doc 1, Secty of Trsy Report, 4 Dec 1862, pp. 12, 24.
14 *Ibid.,* Serial 1159, 37th Cong 3d Sess, HR Ex Doc 16, Secty of Trsy Letter, 18 Dec 1862.
15 Mitchell, 100-09. *Cong Globe,* 37th Cong 3d Sess, 12 Jan 1863, pp. 283-84; 15 Jan, p. 334.
16 *Ibid.,* 13 Feb 1863, pp. 925, 945; 3 March, p. 1524.
17 *Ibid.,* 39th Cong 1st Sess, 18 Dec 1865, p. 75.
18 *Economist,* 8 Dec 1860, pp. 1357-59; 26 Jan 1861, p. 85. Appleton's *Cyclopedia* 1861, pp. 62-63. Dunbar, 294-313. Schwab, 127. Capers, 429. Yearns, 184-217. B. Hammond, 718-19.
19 Lee, 185.
20 Schwab, 86-87, 90, 98-102, 149-60. Todd, 90-92, 107-08, 118-19. Southern Historical Society, Papers XLIV, pp. 169-71; XLV, pp. 104, 133; XLVI, pp. 65-67, 224. Yearns, 184-217. Coulter, 155-56. Lee, 185.
21 Todd, 98-102, 116-18. Schwab, 149-63. Capers, 314, 316-18, 335ff, 350-51. Southern

Historical Society, Papers XLV, p. 220; XLVI, pp. 2, 65-67, 81.
[22] Todd, 26-29, 76-77, 91-94. Hendrick, 188-93. Yearns, 229-30. Coulter, 149-54. Schwab, 69-70. Capers, 429-37. Lee, 24-25.
[23] Franklin IX, 231-234.

[24] *Economist*, 21 June 1862, p. 674; 18 Oct, p. 1154. Lerner, *JPE* LXII, Dec 1954, pp. 506ff; LXIII, Feb 1955, pp. 20ff. Dawson and Cooper, *Michigan Law Review* XXXIII, March 1935, pp. 706ff; April 1935, pp. 852ff.

CHAPTER 9

[1] Bolles, Chs. IX and X.
[2] Schwab, 287-90. *Cong Docs*, Serial 1121, 37th Cong 2d Sess, Sen Ex Doc 2, Secty of Trsy Report, 9 Dec 1861, pp. 11-16.
[3] Dewey, 299. *Cong Docs*, Serial 1121, 37th Cong 2d Sess, Sen Ex Doc 2, Secty of Trsy Report, 9 Dec 1861, pp. 14-16.
[4] *Ibid.*, p. 12.
[5] *Ibid.*, Serial 1112, 37th Cong 1st Sess, Sen Ex Doc 2, Secty of Trsy Report, 4 July 1861, p. 7. Howe, 52.
[6] *Cong Globe*, 37th Cong 2d Sess, 23 Dec 1861, pp. 169-70; 24 Dec, p. 174; 15 Jan 1862, pp. 344, 349, 376.
[7] 158 US 601.
[8] *Cong Globe*, 37th Cong 2d Sess, 12 March 1862, pp. 1194-95.
[9] *Ibid.*, pp. 1194-96.
[10] *Ibid.*, p. 1196.
[11] *Ibid.*, p. 1197.
[12] *Ibid.*, pp. 1199-1200.
[13] *Ibid.*, 13 March 1862, pp. 1219, 1224, 1225-27; 27 March, pp. 1403, 1406.
[14] *Ibid.*, 31 March 1862, pp. 1455ff; 3 April, pp. 1527ff; 4 April, pp. 1544ff; 8 April, p. 1576. *NY Times*, 9 April 1862.
[15] *NY Herald*, 10 April 1862. Nevins II, 85.
[16] *Cong Globe*, 37th Cong 2d Sess, 10 April 1862, p. 1603; 6

May, p. 1966; 21 May, pp. 2254ff; 5 June, pp. 2581-87; 6 June, pp. 2608ff. *Bankers' Mag*, June 1862, pp. 913ff.
[17] *Cong Globe*, 37th Cong 2d Sess, 21 May 1862, p. 2254; 28 May, pp. 2400-01; 4 June, p. 2541.
[18] *Ibid.*, 28 May 1862, pp. 2401-03.
[19] *Ibid.*, pp. 2401-02; 29 May 1862, pp. 2419, 2426, 2428, 2430, 2476.
[20] *Ibid.*, 27 May 1862, pp. 2376-78; 28 May, p. 2405.
[21] *Ibid.*, pp. 2401, 2403; 29 May, pp. 2419-30; 5 June, p. 2587; 6 June, pp. 2598-2606.
[22] *Ibid.*, p. 2606.
[23] *Ibid.*, pp. 2607, 2611.
[24] *NY Times*, 7 June 1862. *Cong Globe*, 37th Cong 2d Sess, 9 June 1862, p. 2620; 12 June, pp. 2680-82; 13 June, p. 2708; 23 June, pp. 2873-77, 2890-91. 12 *US Statutes* 432-89, Act, 1 July 1862.
[25] 158 US 601.
[26] *Journal of Commerce*, 9 April 1862. *NY Herald*, 17 Jan 1862; 13 April; 7 May; 24 June.
[27] *NY Times*, 9 April 1862. *NY Tribune*, 9 April; 7 May.
[28] *NY Times*, 23, 24, 25 June 1862; 3 July. *NY Tribune*, 3 July.

1 *Cong Docs*, Serial 1149, 37th Cong 3d Sess, Sen Ex Doc 1, Secty of Trsy Report, 4 Dec 1862, pp. 6-7, 16-20.

2 US National Archives, Trsy Dept Corr with Members of Congress, VIII, 213. *NY Times*, 7, 8, 9, 13, 16, 17, 23, 24, 28, 30 June 1862; 2, 4, 8, 10 July.

3 *Ibid.*, 25 Aug 1862. A. M. Davis, 65.

4 *Cong Globe*, 37th Cong 2d Sess, 11 July 1862, p. 3258; 12 July, p. 3293; 15 July, pp. 3362-63. *NY Herald*, 24 June.

5 *Economist*, 18 Oct 1862, p. 1149.

6 Warden, 502-03.

7 Oberholtzer I, 331-32. Larson, 137.

8 *Cong Docs*, Serial 1156, 37th Cong 3d Sess, HR Ex Doc 1, Message of the President, 1 Dec 1862, pp. 7-8.

9 A. M. Davis, 12. Sherman I, 254.

10 *Cong Docs*, Serial 1149, 37th Cong 3d Sess, Sen Ex Doc 1, Secty of Trsy Report, 4 Dec 1862, pp. 14, 16, 17, 19, 21, 24.

11 *Ibid.*, Serial 1121, 37th Cong 2d Sess, Sen Ex Doc 2, Secty of Trsy Report, 9 Dec 1861, pp. 18-21; Serial 1149, 37th Cong 3d Sess, Sen Ex Doc 1, Secty of Trsy Report, 4 Dec 1862, pp. 16ff.

12 A. M. Davis, 69-71. Schuckers, 382-83.

13 A. M. Davis, 70-71. Jackson VI, 405. *Cong Globe*, 26th Cong 1st Sess, 21 Jan 1840, Appendix, pp. 137-42. *Continental Monthly*, Feb 1863, pp. 129-44.

14 Nevins II, 350-65. Fessenden I, 231-53.

15 *Cong Globe*, 37th Cong 3d Sess, 7 Jan 1863, p. 226; 8 Jan, pp. 235-36, 237; 19 Jan, p. 383.

16 *Ibid.*, 5 Jan 1863, p. 185; 8

Jan, p. 227, Appendix, pp. 47ff. Sherman I, 284.

17 *Cong Globe*, 37th Cong 3d Sess, 8 Jan 1863, Appendix, pp. 49-52. Jefferson VI, 245, 498.

18 *Cong Globe*, 37th Cong 3d Sess, 8 Jan 1863, Appendix, pp. 47ff.

19 *Ibid.*, p. 47.

20 *Ibid.*, p. 52.

21 *Ibid.*, 15 Jan 1863, p. 345.

22 *Ibid.*, 8 Jan 1863, pp. 235-36, 237; 12 Jan, pp. 283-84.

23 *Ibid.*, pp. 284, 286-88.

24 *Ibid.*, 13 Jan 1863, pp. 294, 296-97.

25 *NY Times*, 7, 12, 13 Jan 1863.

26 *Ibid.*, 13, 15 Jan 1863.

27 *Cong Globe*, 37th Cong 3d Sess, 14 Jan 1863, p. 314; 15 Jan, p. 323. Historical Society of Pennsylvania, *Chase Papers*, Samuel Hooper to Chase, 24 June 1862.

28 *Cong Globe*, 37th Cong 3d Sess, 19 Jan 1863, p. 381. *NY Times*, 16 Jan 1863.

29 *Cong Globe*, 37th Cong 3d Sess, 15 Jan 1863, pp. 334-35.

30 *Ibid.*, pp. 335-37.

31 *Ibid.*, pp. 340-41; 19 Jan 1863, pp. 391-92. LC, *Chase Papers*, Amasa Walker to Chase, 16 Dec 1861.

32 *Cong Globe*, 37th Cong 3d Sess, 15 Jan 1863, p. 342.

33 *Ibid.*, pp. 343, 344; 8 Jan 1863, p. 237; 19 Jan, pp. 389-90.

34 *Ibid.*, 16 Jan 1863, pp. 365, 366.

35 *Ibid.*, 19 Jan 1863, pp. 382, 384-87.

36 *Ibid.*, pp. 387-88.

37 *Ibid.*, pp. 392-93.

38 Lincoln I, 164, 210, 226.

39 *NY Times*, 20 Jan 1863. *Cong Globe*, 37th Cong 3d Sess, 19 Jan 1863, pp. 381, 392-93; 20 Jan, p. 411; 23 Jan, p. 485; 3 Feb, p. 697.

CHAPTER 11

[1] *Cong Globe*, 37th Cong 3d Sess, 10 Feb 1863, p. 840.

[2] *Ibid.*, 5 Jan 1863, p. 185; 8 Jan, p. 227; Appendix, pp. 47ff; 26 Jan, p. 505.

[3] *NY Times*, 28, 31 Jan 1863 (S letters); 2, 3 Feb (S letters). Sherman I, 284-99.

[4] *NY Times*, 2 Feb 1863. *Cong Globe*, 37th Cong 3d Sess, 26 Jan 1863, p. 505; 4 Feb, p. 703; 9 Feb, pp. 820ff; 10 Feb, pp. 840ff. Burton, 135.

[5] *NY Times*, 2, 3 Feb 1863. Sherman I, 294. *Cong Globe*, 37th Cong 3d Sess, 26 Jan 1863, p. 505; 10 Feb, p. 840.

[6] *Ibid.*, pp. 840ff. *NY Times*, 3 Feb 1863.

[7] *Cong Globe*, 37th Cong 3d Sess, 11 Feb 1863, pp. 870, 874, 877.

[8] *Ibid.*, pp. 877, 882; 12 Feb, pp. 896-97. *NY Herald*, 14 Feb 1863.

[9] *Cong Globe*, 37th Cong 3d Sess, 12 Feb 1863, pp. 914, 916; 13 Feb, p. 947; 19 Feb, pp. 1113-15.

[10] *Ibid.*, p. 1115.

[11] *Ibid.*, p. 1116.

[12] *Ibid.*, p. 1117.

[13] *Ibid.*, 20 Feb 1863, pp. 1143, 1145-46.

[14] *Ibid.*, pp. 1147-49.

[15] *Ibid.*, 10 Feb 1863, p. 843.

[16] *Ibid.*, p. 841; *NY Times*, 3 Feb 1863.

[17] *NY Tribune*, 25 Jan 1862.

[18] *Boston Daily Advertiser*, 10, 19, 20, 21 Jan 1863.

[19] *Ibid.*, 23 Dec 1862; 23 Feb 1863.

[20] *Ibid.*, 23 Feb 1863.

[21] *Ibid.*, 25 Feb 1863. *Cong Docs*, Serial 1187, 38th Cong 1st Sess, HR Ex Doc 20, Condition of Banks Report, 22 Dec 1863, pp. 87, 88; *Ibid.*, Serial 1161, 37th Cong 3d Sess, HR Ex Doc 25, Condition of Banks Report, 31 Dec 1862, p. 93 (State of NY Banks).

[22] *NY Times*, 28, 31 Jan 1863. Welles I, 223-24, 237-38.

[23] *NY Herald*, 13, 14, 21 Feb 1863.

[24] Federal Reserve Board, *Banking Studies*, 418.

[25] McCulloch, 169. *Merchants' Mag* LI, Aug 1864, pp. 136-37.

[26] *Cong Docs*, Serial 1186, 38th Cong 1st Sess, HR Ex Doc 3, Secty of Trsy Report, 10 Dec 1863, pp. 56-57; *Ibid.*, Serial 1222, 38th Cong 2d Sess, HR Ex Doc 3, Secty of Trsy Report, 6 Dec 1864, pp. 24, 48, 54. *Cong Globe*, 38th Cong 2d Sess, 27 Feb 1865, p. 1139. 75 US (3 Wallace) 548-49.

[27] Federal Reserve Board, *Banking Studies*, 418. Neu, 111. Dillistin, 83.

[28] *NY Times*, 28, 31 Jan 1863.

CHAPTER 12

[1] *Cong Docs*, Serial 1254, 39th Cong 1st Sess, HR Ex Doc 3, Secty of Trsy Report, 4 Dec 1865, pp. 1-16. *Cong Globe*, 39th Cong 1st Sess, 18 Dec 1865, p. 75.

[2] Unger, 81ff.

[3] Porter and Johnson, 2-31.

[4] *Cong Globe*, 37th Cong 3d Sess, 10 Feb 1863, pp. 840, 843. *NY Times*, 3 Feb 1863 (S letter).

[5] Garraty, 45.

WORKS CITED

Acton, John Emerich Edward Dalberg, Lord. *Essays on Freedom and Power*. (Gertrude Himmelfarb, editor) Boston, 1948.

Acton, John Emerich Edward Dalberg, Lord. *Historical Essays and Studies*. (John Nevill Figgis and Reginald Vere Laurence, editors) London, 1907.

Adams, Ephraim Douglas. *Great Britain and the American Civil War*. London, New York, 1925.

Adams, Henry. *Historical Essays*. New York, 1891.

American Historical Review. New York, 1896–.

American State Papers; Finance. Washington, 1832.

Appleton's *American Annual Cyclopedia*. New York, 1861-1875.

Bagehot, Walter. *Bagehot's Historical Essays*. (Norman St. John-Stevas, editor) New York, 1966.

Balinky, Alexander. *Albert Gallatin*, New Brunswick, N.J., 1958.

Bankers' Magazine and Statistical Register. Cambridge, Mass., 1849-1894.

Baring Papers. (Baring Brothers). Canadian National Archives, Ottawa.

Bayley, Rafael. *The National Loans of the United States*. Washington, 1882.

Benton, Thomas Hart. *Thirty Years' View*. 2v. New York, 1854-1856.

Blaine, James G. *Twenty Years of Congress*. 2v. Norwich, Conn., 1884-1886.

Bolles, Albert Sidney. *The Financial History of the United States from 1861 to 1885*. New York, 1886.

Boston Daily Advertiser. Boston, 1846-1872.

Burton, Theodore Elijah. *John Sherman*. Boston and New York, 1908.

Capers, Henry Dickson. *The Life and Times of C. G. Memminger*. Richmond, 1893.

Chase, Salmon Portland. *Inaugural Address*, 14 January 1856. Ohio Executive Documents. Columbus, 1858.

Chase Papers. (Salmon P. Chase). Library of Congress.

Chase Papers. (Salmon P. Chase). National Archives, Treasury Records.

Chase Papers. (Salmon P. Chase). Historical Society of Pennsylvania, Philadelphia.

Congress, USA. *Biographical Directory of the American Congress, 1774-1927*. Washington, 1928.

Congress, USA. *Congressional Executive Documents.*

Congress, USA. *Register of Debates in Congress*. 14v. Washington, 1825-1837.

Congress, USA. *The Congressional Globe*. 46v. Washington, 1834-1873.

Continental Monthly. New York, 1862-1864.

Coolidge, Thomas Jefferson. *Autobiography*. Boston and New York, 1923.

Coulter, Ellis Merton. *The Confederate States of America, 1861-1865*. Baton Rouge, 1950.

Davis, Andrew McFarland. *The Origin of the National Banking System*. Washington, 1910-1911. (National Monetary Commission, *Publications*. Vol. v [No. 1].)

Davis, Jefferson. *The Rise and Fall of the Confederate Government*. New York, 1881.

Dawson, John P. and Cooper, Frank E. "The Effects of Inflation on Private Contracts: United States 1861-1879." *Michigan Law Review* (1935).

Dewey, Davis R. *Financial History of the United States*. New York, 1936.

Dillistin, William H. *Historical Directory of the Banks of the State of New York*. New York, 1946.

Dix, Morgan. *Memoirs of John Adams Dix*. New York, 1883.

Donald, David Herbert, editor. *Inside Lincoln's Cabinet*. (S. P. Chase Diaries) New York, 1954.

Dunbar, Charles Franklin. *Economic Essays*. New York, London, 1904.

Dunne, Gerald T. *Monetary Decisions of the Supreme Court.* New Brunswick, N.J., 1960.

Economist. London, 1861-1862.

Edwards, Thomas M. Manuscript Letter, 10 February 1868. Dartmouth College Archives.

Federal Reserve Board. *Banking Studies* (by members of the staff of the Board of Governors of the Federal Reserve System). Baltimore, 1941.

Fessenden, Francis. *Life and Public Services of William Pitt Fessenden.* 2v. Boston and New York, 1907.

Field, Maunsell Bradhurst. *Memoirs of Many Men and Some Women.* London, 1874.

Formation of the Union of the American States. (Charles Callan Tansill, editor) 69th Congress, 1st Session, House Document No. 398, Washington, 1927.

Franklin, Benjamin. *The Writings of Benjamin Franklin.* (Albert H. Smyth, editor) 10v. New York, 1905-1907.

Freeman, Edward Augustus. *History of Federal Government, from the Foundation of the Achaian League to the Disruption of the United States.* (1 v. published) London and Cambridge, 1863.

Freeman, Edward Augustus. *History of Federal Government in Greece and Italy.* (J. B. Berry, editor; reissue of above with additional material) London, 1893.

Garraty, John Arthur, editor. *Quarrels That Have Shaped the Constitution.* New York, 1964.

Gibbons, James Sloan. *The Banks of New York, their Dealers, the Clearing House, and the Panic of 1857.* New York, 1858.

Hamilton, Alexander. *The Works of Alexander Hamilton.* 12v. 2nd edition. (Henry Cabot Lodge, editor) New York and London, 1903.

Hammond, Bray. *Banks and Politics in America from the Revolution to the Civil War.* Princeton, 1957.

Hammond, Bray. "The North's Empty Purse." *American Historical Review* (1961).

Hammond, Bray. "Free Banks and Corporations." *Journal of Political Economy* (1936).

Hammond, Jabez Delano. *History of Political Parties in the State of New York.* 3v. Buffalo, 1850.

Hendrick, Burton Jesse. *Statesmen of the Lost Cause.* New York, 1939.

Hepburn, Alonzo Barton. *History of Coinage and Currency in the United States.* New York, 1903.

Hepburn, Alonzo Barton. *A History of Currency in the United States.* 2nd edition. New York, 1924.

Howe, Frederic Clemson. *Taxation and Taxes in the United States Under the Internal Revenue System, 1791-1895.* New York, 1896.

Independent. New York, 1860-1863.

Jackson, Andrew. *Correspondence.* (John Spencer Bassett, editor) Washington, 1926-1935.

Jefferson, Thomas. *Writings.* 9v. (Henry Augustine Washington, editor) New York, 1861.

Journal of Commerce. New York, 1860-1863.

Journal of Political Economy. Chicago, 1892–.

Kinley, David. *The Independent Treasury of the United States.* Washington, 1910. (National Monetary Commission, *Publications.* Vol. vii [No. 2].)

Knox, John Jay. *A History of Banking in the United States.* New York, 1900.

Knox, John Jay. *United States Notes.* New York, 1899.

Larson, Henrietta Melia. *Jay Cooke, Private Banker.* Cambridge, Mass., 1936.

Lee, Charles Robert. *The Confederate Constitutions.* Chapel Hill, 1963.

Lerner, Eugene M. "The Monetary and Fiscal Programs of the Confederate Government." *Journal of Political Economy* (1954).

Lerner, Eugene M. "Money, Prices and Wages in the Confederacy," *Journal of Political Economy* (1955).

Lincoln, Abraham. *Collected Works.* (Roy Prentice Basler, editor) New Brunswick, N.J., 1953-1955.

Lippincott's Monthly Magazine. Philadelphia, 1868-1915.

McCulloch, Hugh. *Men and Measures of Half a Century.* New York, 1888.

Massachusetts. Supreme Judicial Court. *Massachusetts Reports.* Boston, 1816–.

Merchants' Magazine and Commercial Review. New York, 1839-1870. (Caption title: *Hunt's Merchants' Magazine.*)

Mitchell, Wesley Clair. *A History of the Greenbacks.* Chicago, 1903.

Mitchell, Wesley Clair. "The Suspension of Specie Payments, December 1861." *Journal of Political Economy* (1899).

Myers, Margaret. *The New York Money Market.* 4v. New York, 1931-1932.

Neu, Irene D. *Erastus Corning, Merchant and Financier.* Ithaca, 1960.

Nevins, Allan. *The War for the Union.* New York, 1959-1960.

New York Herald. New York, 1860-1863.

New York (State) Supreme Court. *Reports of Cases Argued and Determined.* Albany, 1808–.

New York Times. New York, 1860-1863.

New York Tribune. New York, 1860-1863.

Nichols, Thomas Low. *Forty Years of American Life.* London, 1874.

Oberholtzer, Ellis Paxon. *Jay Cooke, Financier of the Civil War.* 2v. Philadelphia, 1907.

Polk Papers. (James K. Polk). Library of Congress.

Porter, Kirk Harold and Johnson, Donald Bruce. *National Party Platforms, 1840-1960.* Urbana, 1956.

Ratner, Sidney. *American Taxation.* New York, 1942.

Redlich, Fritz. *The Molding of American Banking.* New York, 1951. (Vol. 2 of his *History of American Business Leaders.* Ann Arbor, 1947-1951.)

Rhodes, James Ford. *History of the United States from the Compromise of 1850.* 9v. New York, 1893-1919.

Richardson, James Daniel, editor. *A Compilation of the Messages and Papers of the Presidents, 1789-1902.* New York, 1903.

Rodkey, Robert Gordon. *Legal Reserves in American Banking.* Ann Arbor, 1934.

Ropes, John Codman. *The Story of the Civil War.* 4v. New York and London, 1894-1913.

Schuckers, Jacob W. *The Life and Public Services of Salmon Portland Chase.* New York, 1874.

Schwab, John Christopher. *The Confederate States of America.* New York, 1901.

Seligman, Edwin Robert Anderson. *The Income Tax.* New York, 1911-1914.

Sellers, Charles Grier. *James K. Polk, Jacksonian, 1795-1843.* Princeton, 1957.

Shenton, James Patrick. *Robert John Walker, a Politician from Jackson to Lincoln.* New York, 1961.

Sherman, John. *John Sherman's Recollections of Forty Years in the House, Senate and Cabinet.* Chicago, New York, 1895.

Southern Historical Society. *Southern Historical Society Papers.* Richmond, 1876–.

Spaulding, Elbridge Gerry. *A Resource of War—The Credit of the Government Made Immediately Available. History of the Legal Tender; Paper Money Issued During the Great Rebellion.* 2nd edition. Buffalo, 1869 [Preface, 1875].

Stevens Papers. (John Austin Stevens). New-York Historical Society.

Story, Joseph. *Commentaries on the Constitution of the United States.* Boston, 1851.

Studenski, Paul and Krooss, Herman Edward. *Financial History of the United States.* New York, 1952.

Sumner, William Graham. *History of Banking in the United States.* New York, 1896.

Taus, Esther (Rogoff). *Central Banking Functions of the United States Treasury, 1789-1941.* New York, 1943.

Taussig, Frank William. *The Tariff History of the United States.* 8th edition, New York, 1931.

Todd, Richard Cecil. *Confederate Finance.* Athens, Ga., 1954.

Trollope, Anthony. *North America.* Philadelphia, 1863.

Unger, Irwin. *The Greenback Era; A Social and Political History of American Finance, 1865-1879.* Princeton, 1964.

United States National Archives. Treasury Records.

United States Laws, Statutes, Etc. *United States Statutes at Large.* Washington, 1789–.

United States Supreme Court. *United States Reports.* Washington, 1754–.

United States War Department. *The War of the Rebellion.* Washington, 1880-1901.

Warden, Robert Bruce. *An Account of the Private Life and Public Services of Salmon Portland Chase.* Cincinnati, 1874.

Warren, Charles. *The Supreme Court in United States History.* Boston, 1922.

Welles, Gideon. *Diary of Gideon Welles.* (Howard K. Beale, editor) New York, 1960.

White, Horace. *Money and Banking.* 1st and 4th editions. Boston, 1896, 1911.

White, Leonard Dupee. *The Jacksonians: A Study in Administration History, 1829-1861.* New York, 1954.

Wiltse, Charles Maurice, *John C. Calhoun, Nullifier, 1829-1839.* New York, 1949.

Wolseley, Garnet Joseph, Viscount. *The American Civil War.* (James A. Rawley, editor) Charlottesville. 1964.

Yearns, Wilfrid Buck. *The Confederate Congress.* Athens, Ga., 1960.

INDEX

Acton, Sir John, 3-4, 10
Adams, Charles Francis, 9
Adams, Henry, legal tender act
  criticized, 229, 243, 356n.
Alley, John B., 194-95, 202, 224,
  229, 233-34, 285, 313-14; on
  national bank bill, 332; resolution on retirement of greenbacks, 253, 355-56; speech on
  legal tender bill, 173-78, 187,
  189, 191
American Exchange Bank, 74, 78,
  124, 206, 242
Anthony, Senator, 221
Antietam, battle of, 257, 296
Appleton, William, 62, 159
armed forces: after fall of Fort
  Sumter, 37-38; federal and
  state responsibility for, 12-13;
  payment of expenses: delayed,
  125-27, 134-35, 243-44,
  251-52, 311-12; Stevens-
  Lovejoy resolution on,
  306-07;
  see also Civil War
Austin, John B., letter to Chase,
  196-97

Bagehot, Walter, 5
Ball's Bluff, battle of, 123, 127
bank notes: circulation and deposits, 97-98, 305; as currency,
  136-37, 140-47, 156, 240, 291;
  federal bonds as security, 88,
  136, 140-47; greenbacks and,
  299-300; in national loan, 81-
  82, 93; state, 188; tax on, 141,
  310, 346-47; Sherman bill
  (S 445), 297-300, 321, 324
Bank of Commerce, New York,
  30, 73-74, 96, 218, 242
Bank of England, 298n.
Bank of the United States, 15,
  19, 87, 138, 245, 333, 350;
  Lincoln on, 24-25, 316; states'
  rights and, 358-59; Supreme
  Court action on, 148, 361

Bankers' Magazine: on currency
  reform, 143-44; on suspension
  of specie payments, 158-59
Banks, Gen. Nathaniel, 247
banks: as associations, 290n.;
  charters, 141, 290-91, 298;
  Chase's loan negotiations,
  73-105; Chase's plan accepted,
  85-86; checks as substitute
  for currency, 240; currency
  reform, reaction to, 147-48;
  Democratic policy on, 21;
  deposits, legal tender notes
  and, 249-50; free banking,
  304n.; gold reserves, *see*
  gold reserves; government
  and, 20-24; government
  bonds and, 39, 43-44;
  government funds deposited
  in, 20-21, 23-24; Jackson's
  attitude toward, 19; after
  legal tender act, 239-43;
  legal tender bill and, 217-18,
  220-21, 225; Lincoln's election,
  effect of, 26-28; Lincoln's
  proposal on, 290-91;
  national: bill on, *see*
  national bank bill; and
  currency, 143; exempt
  from state taxes, 361-62;
  after national bank bill,
  345-47;
  national loan payments, 109,
  111-22; in national loan plan,
  60, 62, 64-65; Northern,
  26-28; Southern, 27, 255;
  special deposits, 154;
  state: after national bank bill,
  347-48; Sherman's attack on,
  297-301;
  states' rights and, 138-39,
  285, 302-03, 326-27;
  suspension of specie payments
  and, 241; Treasury and, 20-23,
  39; Treasury notes opposed
  by, 95-96; Whig policy on,
  21-22

387